D0051713

Resource and Environmental Management

PROPERTY OF
HARRY SPALING

Resource and Environmental Management

Bruce Mitchell
University of Waterloo
Waterloo, Ontario

LONGMAN

Addison Wesley Longman Limited
Edinburgh Gate, Harlow
Essex CM20 2JE
England

and Associated Companies throughout the World

© Addison Wesley Longman Limited 1997

The right of Bruce Mitchell to be identified as author of this Work has been asserted by him in accordance with the Copyright, Design and Patents Act 1988.

All rights reserved; no part of this publication may be reproduced, stored in any retrieval system, or transmitted in any form or by any means, electronic, mechanical, photocopying, recording, or otherwise without either the prior written permission of the Publishers or a licence permitting restricted copying in the United Kingdom issued by the Copyright Licensing Agency Ltd, 90 Tottenham Court Road, London W1P 9HE.

First published 1997

ISBN 0 582 23796 3

British Library Cataloguing-in-Publication Data
A catalogue record for this book is available from the British Library.

Library of Congress Cataloging-in-Publication Data
A catalog record for this title is available from the Library of Congress.

Set by 33 in Garamond
Produced through Longman Malaysia, PP

Contents

v

Contents

List of Figures

List of figures

List of Tables

Preface

This book has been written as a replacement for *Geography and Resource Analysis* (first edition, 1979; second edition, 1989). When Longman indicated in 1993 that it would like a third edition of *Geography and Resource Analysis*, an opportunity was created to think about the objectives, structure and content of that book. While the book seemed to have found a useful niche in the literature, and undergraduate and graduate students had indicated that it was helpful for them in their studies, I decided that the field of resource and environmental management had evolved enough that I could not capture it by simply preparing a third edition.

As a result, I explained to Longman that rather than preparing a third edition, a new book would be appropriate. However, because of other commitments, I also indicated that writing could not begin until late in 1995, with completion targeted for mid 1996. Longman accepted the concept of a new book, and the work schedule. This book is the result. Like its predecessor, this book is intended for senior undergraduate students interested in resource and environmental management. It assumes that they have already been exposed to ideas in physical and human geography.

In this Preface, it is appropriate to indicate some of the things that this book is, and what it is not. Reactions to *Geography and Resource Analysis* from students suggested that some key features of that book should be retained. First, providing an extensive list of references was viewed as a strength. As a result, this book also contains numerous references to a wide range of studies. Second, an emphasis on "ways of thinking" and "ways of analysis" was deemed to be useful, and such features are continued. One consequence of this decision is that in places the book is abstract and conceptual. However, my experience is that students appreciate and value these characteristics, as long as their course instructor provides examples or case studies to illustrate practical implications. On the other hand, students commented that *Geography and Resource Analysis* was sometimes "hard reading" because of the compact style and numerous references. A conscious effort has been made here to create a more "user friendly" book, especially for undergraduates.

I also believe it is important to indicate what this book is not, or what aspects have consciously not been covered. First, while *Geography and Resource Analysis* explicitly related work in resource management to enduring themes in geographical investigation, this book does not make such connections.

Preface

Geography is a well-established discipline with strong traditions. It seems less necessary today to draw out directly the linkages between its traditions and themes, and a field of application such as resource management.

Second, considerable thought was given about whether to include Geographical Information Systems (GIS), and, if so, how best to do that. The challenge was viewed as multiple because: (1) GIS software is evolving quickly, as with most computer software, and therefore material quickly becomes dated, (2) considerable detail must be included if students are to obtain more than a superficial appreciation of GIS, and (3) many books specializing in GIS are available. The decision was to not include GIS in any substantive manner in this book. However, GIS is a very important tool for resource and environmental management, and students aspiring to work in this field should acquire at least a basic understanding of the technique.

The objectives, focus and content of this book have been influenced by many people, and I would like to acknowledge them. First, the opportunity to teach undergraduate and graduate students at the University of Waterloo and elsewhere since 1969 has provided many opportunities to observe the reactions of students to concepts and methods in resource and environmental management. Such reactions and comments from these students have strongly influenced the overall approach to this book. Comments from students who have used *Geography and Resource Analysis* also have been very helpful. Second, jointly teaching a graduate course at Waterloo for 27 years with George Priddle has provided a remarkable opportunity to share ideas and approaches. George's enthusiasm, and ability to identify the value of emerging concepts and approaches before they have become generally accepted, has made working with him a stimulating and enjoyable experience. Third, other colleagues with similar professional interests have provided a supportive atmosphere in which to teach and conduct research. The work and ideas of the following individuals at Waterloo have influenced my thinking, and therefore this book: Jim Bater, M. Chandrashekar, Terry Downey, Len Gertler, Bob Gibson, George Francis, Robbie Keith, Drew Knight, George Mulamoottil, Gordon Nelson, and Geoff Wall. Fourth, participation in a major group project in Indonesia, and another team project in Nigeria, exposed me to considerations, concepts and methods not represented in *Geography and Resource Analysis*, but included here. I express my appreciation to Canadian and overseas colleagues (especially Haryadi and Sugeng Martopo in Indonesia; and Peter Adeniyi and Lekan Oyebande in Nigeria) in those two projects for helping both to broaden and to sharpen my thinking.

Tracy Fehl, Gary Loftus and Dave Wood, graduate students at the University of Waterloo, provided research assistance while the book was being prepared, and their work was and is much appreciated. Others who provided information or suggestions were Jim Bauer, Aubrey Diem, Len Eckel, Pauline Peddle, and Lt. Colonel M. Pigeon. Joan Mitchell helped to arrange for permissions to use copyright material. At Addison Wesley Longman, I am particularly grateful for the interest and support of Sally Wilkinson, the editorial support of Tina Cadle and the external freelance copyediting skills of Patrick Bonham and external freelance proofreading skills of Dennis Hodgson.

The first and second editions of *Geography and Resource Analysis* were dedicated to my wife, Joan. It is with pleasure that I dedicate this new book to her. As stated in the second edition, she has always supported me in my different endeavours but also has helped to keep them in perspective.

Bruce Mitchell
Waterloo, Ontario
May 1996

Acknowledgements

We are grateful to the following for permission to reproduce copyright material:

Figure 1.1, 1.2, Table 1.1 and 1.2 from Canada National Defence report 1994: *Summary: EIS: Military Flight Training*, in public domain; Figure 1.3 from Environmental Change and Violent Conflict, *Scientific American*, p. 42, international edition (Thomas, H *et. al.*, Feb. 1993); Figures 1.4, 6.1 and Tables 8.1, 8.3, & 8.4 from *Resource Management in Developing Countries* (Omara-Ojungu, 1992) and *Geography and Resource Analysis* 2/e (Mitchell, 1989) Addison Wesley Longman Ltd.; Figure 1.5 and 1.6 from Coping with uncertainty in planning, reprinted by kind permission of the *Journal of the American Planning Association*, 51 (1): 63–73 (Christensen, 1985); Figure 2.1, 2.2 and Table 2.4 from *Bali: balancing environment, economy and culture*, Publication no. 44 (Martopo & Mitchell eds. 1995); Table 2.1 reprinted with courtesy of *Alternatives Journal: Environmental thought, policy and action*. Annual subscriptions C$24.00 (plus GST) from *Alternatives Journal*, Faculty of Environmental Studies, University of Waterloo, Waterloo, Ontario, N2L 3G1 *Alternatives*, 17 (2) 36–46 (Robinson *et. al.*, 1990); Table 2.2 from *Towards Institutional Change in the Manitoba Public Sector*, Sustainable Co-ordination Unit, p. 5 1992; Table 2.3 from *Canadian Water Management: Visions for sustainability* (Mitchell & Shrubsole, 1994), Canadian Water Resources Association, Ontario; Figure 3.1 and Table 3.1 reprinted from Agroecosystem analysis, *Agriculture Administration*, 20: 31–55 (Conway, 1985) with kind permission from Elsevier Science Ltd, The Boulevard, Langford Lane, Kidlington OX5 1GB; Figure 3.3 from Environmental Impact assessment in the Himalayas: an ecosystem approach, *Ambio*, 22 (1): 4 Royal Swedish Academy of Science (Ahmad, 1993); Figure 5.1 and Table 5.1 reprinted from Futures under glass: a recipe for people who hate to predict, *Futures*, 22 (8): 820–40 with kind permission from Elsevier Science Ltd, The Boulevard, Langford Lane, Kidlington OX5 1GB (Robinson, 1990); Figure 6.2 and 6.3 with kind permission Canadian Standards Association material is reproduced from the CSA Publication: PLUS 1107 (User's guide to Life Cycle Assessment: Conceptual LCA in Practise), which is copyrighted by CSA, 178 Rexdale Blvd., Etobioke, Ontario, M9W 1R3; Figure 7.1 from Drought and recovery: reproduced from the CSA Standard: Z760-94 (Life Cycle Assessment), and with kind permission of the Canadian Standards Association, material is reproduced livestock dynamics among the ngisonyoka turkana of Kenya in *Human Ecology*, 13 (4) p 371–389, Plenum Publishing Corporation (McCabe, 1987); Figure 7.2 and Table 7.1 from *Compass and Gyroscope, Integrating Science and Politics for the Environment*, Fig. 2–I p 18 and Table 3.5 p. 85 (Lee, 1993), Published by Island Press, Washington D.C. & Covelo California; Table 7.4 from Restoration under the Northwest Power Act, *Environmental Law*, 16 (3): 431–460 (Lee & Lawrence, 1986); Figure 8.1 from Ngamiland Western Communal Remote Zone Botswana *Splash* 10 (1) 1994, 8; Table 8.2 from Types of Strategic Alliances Table 1 in *Memorandum: MNR Guide to Resource Management Partnerships – Administrative Considerations*, Ministry of Natural Resources, Copyright 1995 Queen's Printer Ontario; Table 9.1 and 9.2 reprinted from The origins and practice of participatory rural appraisal, *World Development*, 22 (7): 953–969, with kind permission from Elsevier Science Ltd, The Boulevard, Langford Lane, Kidlington, OX5 1GB (Chambers, 1994).; Figure 12.1 from Implementation failure: a suitable case for review? p. 45 in *Achieving environmental goals: the concept and practice of environmental performance review*, E.Lykke ed. London, Belhaven Press 43–63 (Weale, 1992); Figure 13.1 and 13.2 from *Sustaining Canada's forests: timber harvesting*, SOE Bulletin No. 95–4, Summer 1995, p. 1 (bottom), p. 3 and p. 9, State of the Environmental Directorate, Canada; Figure 13.3 from *Water in Sustainable Development: Exploring Our Common Future in the Fraser River Basin*, Vancouver University of British Columbia, Westwater Research Centre (Dorcey & Griggs, 1991); Figure 13.4 from *Board Report card: Assessing Progress Towards Sustainability in the Fraser River Basin*, 1995, p 6, Fraser Management Program, Vancouver.

Whilst every effort has been made to trace the owners of copyright material, in a few cases this has proved impossible and we take this opportunity to offer our apologies to any copyright holders whose rights we may have unwittingly infringed.

Chapter 1

Change, Complexity, Uncertainty and Conflict

1.1 Introduction

Change, complexity, uncertainty and conflict are encountered in many aspects of life. They are often central in resource and environmental management. They can create opportunities as well as problems for analysts, planners, managers, decision makers and members of the public. One challenge is to recognize their importance, and to determine how to function in their presence. Another challenge is to know how to become an agent for positive change.

This chapter begins by outlining an experience that reflects all four of these elements. It also shows how they can affect individuals, and how such individuals are often connected, willingly or unwillingly, to a larger global system which has implications for their life styles and livelihood. The case study is followed by sections which in turn consider some key aspects of each element: change, complexity, uncertainty and conflict. The subsequent chapters focus on various concepts, strategies, methods and techniques which environmental and resource planners are using, or could use more effectively. The overriding purpose is to familiarize the reader with the strengths, weaknesses, opportunities and threats associated with alternative ways of addressing change, complexity, uncertainty and conflict.

1.2 Military low-level flights and indigenous people in Québec–Labrador, Canada

A military base was created at Happy Valley–Goose Bay in Labrador, Canada, during the 1940s, and military flight training started in the 1950s. Flight training, involving mainly low-level flying (under 300 m), has been conducted by the air forces of the United Kingdom, Germany and the Netherlands from the Canadian Forces base through an agreement originally signed in 1986 and renewed in 1996 with the Canadian Department of Defence. The agreement restricts low-level flights within a specified area covering 100,000 km^2 in the Québec–Labrador peninsula (Figure 1.1). The initial training agreement extended until 1996, and the European air forces wanted to renew the agreement. However, it was recognized that their interest in extending the agreement would be influenced by any new costs and restrictions resulting from an environmental review of the low-level flying (Canada National Defence,

?how applied to the cases

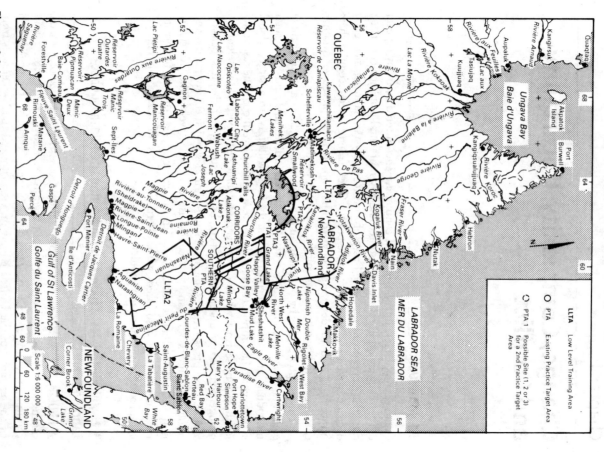

Figure 1.1 Key communities in the Québec–Labrador peninsula and low-level training areas (CEAA, 1995: 6)

1994). In early May 1995, the Defence Minister announced that the Canadian government had reviewed the environmental report, concurred with its recommendations, and would negotiate with NATO allies for a new agreement which would increase the flights to 15,000 to 18,000 per year, despite the protests of native people in the region. The government also indicated that it accepted a key recommendation to establish an independent institute for environmental monitoring and research to oversee environmental protection initiatives. After consulting with various groups, the government created this institute in December 1995.

The number of low-level training flights had ranged between 7,000 and 8,000 annually over a 30-week (mid March to mid October) training season, with the possibility for a maximum of 18,000 sorties annually. In designated areas, pilots were authorized to fly as low as 30 m above the tops of trees. The purpose of the flight training is to give the aircrew experience in avoiding detection by ground-based radar systems. Training flights average about 75 minutes, and on a typical mission, two or more aircraft fly together in formation. During these flights, the pilots improve skills related to navigation, manoeuvring, and release of non-explosive practice weapons within one specified practice target area.

The attractions of the Québec–Labrador peninsula for such low-level military training are numerous. Use of this area allows Canada to contribute to the readiness of North Atlantic Treaty Organization (NATO) air forces. This training venue is valued by European air forces because of the congested air spaces over their own countries. The infrastructure at Goose Bay provides necessary aircraft support facilities, crew accommodation, and access to retail, medical and recreation facilities.

Allied flight training has become the primary function of the Goose Bay base, and has created employment for a region in which alternative job opportunities are limited. In 1992, the Goose Bay base employed more than 1,600 people, over half being civilians, and expenditures at the base were almost $130 million. About 65% of the expenditures were paid directly by the Allied air forces. Without the Allied training program, Canadian Forces Base Goose Bay would likely be a relatively small regional airport, and the community of Happy Valley–Goose Bay would experience a marked reduction in economic activity.

No permanent aboriginal settlements are located in the training areas. Various mitigative measures have been taken to enhance positive impacts and to reduce negative ones. Following an environmental impact assessment in 1989, the Department of National Defence initiated an "Environmental Action Plan" designed to protect the natural environment. The following year, National Defence introduced a multi-component program to avoid low-level flights over sensitive wildlife species and resource users in the designated training areas.

Table 1.1 shows selected criteria developed for the wildlife species included in the avoidance monitoring program. The criteria were developed "with input from the scientific community and federal and provincial resource management agencies" (Canada National Defence, 1994: 5–8). Noticeably absent was input from local people who hunt, trap or fish in the training areas. Regardless of this shortcoming, National Defence monitors particular species and habitats, and if the pre-determined threshold for a species is reached then that area is closed to further low-level flights.

Table 1.1 Summary of wildlife avoidance criteria (Canada National Defence, 1994: Table 11)

Wildlife resource	Seasonal sensitivity		Occupancy sub-criteria	Closure sub-criteria	Altitude restrictions	Opening sub-criteria
George River herd of caribou	*High sensitivity periods*		Density of ≥5 caribou/km² within a grid cell, or	Closure of occupied grid cell(s) (484 km² each) and of a maximum of 8 × 484 km² buffer grids around the occupied grid cell	≥2,000 ft AGL	Until new data obtained, or Until end of critical period
	Pre-calving	1 May–5 June				
	Calving	6 June–30 June				
	Post-calving	1 July–10 Aug				
	Rut	16 Oct–15 Nov				
			Visual sighting of a single group of ≥500 animals (aggregation), or	Circular avoidance zone with radius of 36 km, centred on collar or group, *except*		
			Presence of ≥1 satellite or VHF collared caribou	During pre-calving, calving and post-calving, reduce buffer zone by 25% around outlying male collars only		
				During rut, reduce buffer zone by 25% around outlying female or male collars		
	Moderate sensitivity periods		As above	Reduce buffer zone by 25% around collar or group	≥1,000 ft AGL	As above
	August dispersal	11 Aug–30 Aug				
	Pre-rut	1 Sept–15 Oct				
	Late winter	1 Mar–30 April				
				Reduce buffer zone by 50% around outlying collar or group		

	Low sensitivity periods				
	Early winter 16 Nov–28 Feb	As above	Reduce buffer zone by 50% around collar or group. Eliminate buffer zone around outlying collar or group	≥1,000 ft AGL	As above
Red Wine herd of caribou	Calving 1 June–30 June	Density of ≥5 female caribou/100 km^2	Circular avoidance zone, with radius of 5 NM centred on the area containing the collar, group or density	≥1,000 ft AGL	Until new data obtained, or Until end of critical period
		Presence of ≥2 VHF or satellite signals within 5 NM × 5 NM area[1]			
	Post-calving 1 July–10 Aug Rut 1 Oct–1 Nov	Visual sighting of a group of ≥10 caribou	As above	As above	As above
	Calving (continued)	Presence of ≥2 VHF or satellite signals within 5 NM × 5 NM area			
	Other months	Visual sighting of a group of ≥10 caribou	As above	As above	As above
		Presence of ≥2 VHF or satellite signals within 5 NM × 5 NM area			
	Late winter 1 Mar–31 May	Visual sighting of a group of ≥25 caribou within designated winter range	Close designated winter range[2]	As above	As above
		Presence of ≥2 VHF or satellite signals within designated winter range			

Table 1.1 Continued

Wildlife resource	Seasonal sensitivity		Occupancy sub-criteria	Closure sub-criteria	Altitude restrictions	Opening sub-criteria
Other resident caribou	Any time		Visual sighting of a group of ≥10 caribou	Circular avoidance zone with radius of 3 NM, centred on group sighted	≥1,000 ft AGL	Until new data obtained
Moose	Late winter	1 Mar–15 May	Visual sighting of ≥0.5 moose/km^2 over a minimum area of 10 km^2 of habitat	Closure of 1 km buffer zone around sighted concentration	≥500 ft AGL	Until new data obtained, or Until end of critical period
Raptors: Gyrfalcon Golden eagle Peregrine falcon	Breeding period Breeding period	1 Apr–31 July 1 May–31 Aug	Active nest site or territorial pair present	Circular avoidance zone with radius of 2.5 NM around nest or pair sighting	≥1,000 ft AGL	Until new data obtained, or Until end of critical period
Bald eagle	As above		Confirmed active nest site	Circular avoidance zone with radius of 1 NM around nest site	As above	As above
Osprey concentration sites	As above		Designated concentration of active nest sites (currently only 2)	Closure of designated concentration areas	As above	As above
Osprey isolated nests	As above		Active nest site outside concentration areas	Circular avoidance zone with radius of 2.5 NM around nest site	As above	As above

Waterfowl[1]:

	Period	Dates	Threshold	Action	Altitude (AGL)	Duration
General	Breeding period	15 May–25 Aug	≥24 birds/km² in areas ≥25 km² / ≥23 birds/km² in areas 25–100 km² / ≥22.3 birds/km² in areas >100 km²	Closure of high-density area	≥700 ft AGL	Until new data obtained, or Until end of critical period
	Staging periods	15 Apr–31 May, 25 Aug–21 Oct	≥100 birds/km², or Visual sighting of a group of ≥500 birds	Closure of a buffer zone of 2.5 NM surrounding the habitat	≥1,000 ft AGL	As above
Black duck	Moulting period	1 July–21 Aug	Visual sighting of a group of ≥50 birds	Closure of buffer zone with 1 NM radius centred on sighted group	As above	As above
Harlequin duck Category I	Breeding period	15 May–31 Aug (south of 55°N) / 31 May–31 Aug (north of 55°N)	Category I: repetitive (≥2) sightings of harlequins in the same or subsequent years (i.e. occupancy verified)	Avoid area 1,000 ft to either side of sighting and 0.5 NM upstream and downstream of sighting	≥1,000 ft AGL along river valley, ≥500 ft AGL across river valley	As above
Harlequin duck Category II	As above		Category II: single sighting of harlequins in an area (i.e. occupancy not verified)	As above	≥500 ft AGL along or across river valley	As above

[1]NM = nautical miles.

[2]Designated late winter range refers to northeastern half of Red Wine Mountains, which receives concentrated use by caribou during the late winter period.

Some possible sources of impacts – jet exhaust, human-induced forest fires, contaminants from accidents – have been judged to be negligible, or in a few localized sites to be moderate. Primary concern has been with the impact of noise levels produced by fighter aircraft, flying at low altitudes, on wildlife, particularly during sensitive times such as pre-calving or calving for caribou. Military aircraft create noise levels that can exceed 125 dBA. The significance of that noise level can be judged against various noise-causing activities shown in Table 1.2. To interpret the information in Table 1.2, it is important to understand that the perceived noise level *doubles* with each 10 dBA increase.

The concern has been not just about the noise levels, but also with the suddenness of a "noise event". For example, a direct overflight at an altitude of 30 m occurs for only a few seconds from the time that the approaching aircraft is first heard until the time when it no longer can be heard. Thus, the exposure to the noise is brief, but the suddenness of the noise undoubtedly has a "startling effect" (Figure 1.2).

Environmental impact assessments have concluded that caribou herds are not affected by the low-level flying, but in recognition of the importance of caribou,

Table 1.2   Comparative noise levels (Canada National Defence, 1994: Table 2, p. S-10)

Type of environment	Noise level (dBA)	Specific noise sources
Pain threshold		
	130	50 kW siren (30 m)
	125	Pneumatic chipper
Jet airport/discotheque	120	Train whistle/chain saw
	110	Riding "older" snowmobile under maximum acceleration
Discomfort level		
	100	Beaver or Twin Otter aircraft taking off at 200 ft
	90	Diesel truck (8 m) or snowmobile accelerating (5 m)
Noisy urban area/building site	80	Alarm clock
Freeway	70	Sewing machine/vacuum cleaner
Annoyance level		
Noisy residential area	60	Conversation/air conditioner
	50	Washing machine
Quiet residential area	40	Refrigerator
Farm	30	Whisper/crickets
	20	Rustling leaves
Wilderness (no wind)	10	Human breathing

all overflights of calving areas are prohibited during calving periods. More generally, National Defence (1994: ES-3) has concluded that while jet noise can startle wildlife and people, "the noise does not appear to have a significant effect on moose, large carnivores, fur-bearing animals or waterfowl." It also concluded that mitigation initiatives for present and future flight training ensure that "associated economic and environmental interests are compatible and not mutually exclusive. Continued Allied training means maintaining both jobs for civilians and environmental protection measures, measures which include Allied and DND expenditures of $1.5 million for each year the Allies remain at Goose Bay" (Canada National Defence, 1994: ES-5).

A key outcome of the environmental assessment was the recommendation that the increased level of military low-level flying be conditional on the formation of a "Labrador Institute for Environmental Monitoring and Research", mentioned earlier. The task of this institute would be to provide advice about the low-level flying with particular attention to appropriate criteria for avoiding sensitive areas, mitigative measures, relevant research and effects monitoring, compliance auditing, boundaries for the low-level flying training area, and project-related land uses in the training area. Affected aboriginal groups in Labrador and Québec were to be equal partners in the institute. An Institute for Environmental Monitoring and Research was created by the federal government in December 1995, with the specific mandate to oversee environmental monitoring of Allied flight training at Goose Bay.

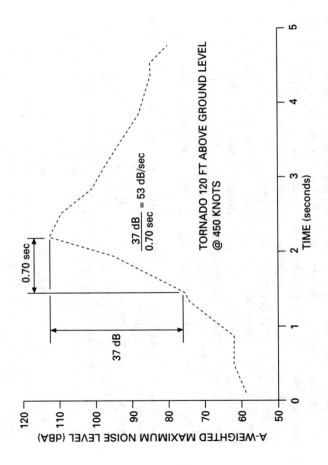

Figure 1.2 Graphic representation of an overflight (Canada National Defence, 1994: Figure 2, p. S-12)

The Institute was created as an advisory group which reports to the Ministers of the Environment and National Defence. A Board of Directors, with an independent Chair and strong aboriginal voting representation, governs the Institute. Funding will be provided from the Department of Defence, with a commitment to provide $2.5 million annually to support monitoring and mitigation measures. The Institute was expected to be fully functional by late 1996, and at that point would be responsible for the management of scientific investigations of the environmental effects of military training, with particular regard to effects research and monitoring. The potential role of the Institute could be considerable. If, as a result of work it initiates regarding cause and effects, findings emerge which show that significant environmental impacts are occurring and cannot be mitigated or justified, the Institute has the authority to recommend that appropriate action be taken to resolve the problem, including limiting or phasing out the military flying activity.

Other commentators, such as Barker and Soyez (1994), have not been so optimistic. They note that aboriginal people are the humans most affected by the overflights, especially Montagnais and Innu people in Québec and Labrador, respectively, Inuit living on the Labrador coast, and a small band of Naskapi near Schefferville. Each autumn, some 1,200 Montagnais, Innu and Naskapi harvest wildlife in the two designated training areas. The aboriginal people who travel into the training areas for seasonal subsistence hunting have been sceptical of the environmental impact assessment conclusions, have questioned the need for low-level flight training in a post Cold War world, and have questioned the effectiveness of the mitigation and avoidance program. Furthermore, the Innu and Montagnais have objected to what they view as "militarization" of their homeland.

Aboriginal people argue that they were not consulted when the Multinational Memorandum of Understanding was negotiated between Canada, the United Kingdom, Germany and the Netherlands. The Montagnais, Innu and Labrador Inuit also never signed treaties with Canada or the previous British colonial authorities, and are involved in protracted land-claim negotiations with the federal and provincial governments to clarify their homeland rights.

To promote their viewpoints, the First Nations people have developed a strategy which Barker and Soyez term "think globally, act globally", the reverse of the oft-repeated phrase "think globally, act locally" usually linked to sustainable development. To illustrate, through the Inuit Circumpolar Conference, a non-government organization for the Inuit people of Alaska, Canada and Greenland, a proposal was developed calling for the demilitarization of the north. In another initiative, members of the Labrador Innu, the Naskapi and the Montagnais from Québec toured Europe on several different occasions to lobby against military flight training over their homelands, as well as lobbied in United Nations forums. In October 1992, some Innu people blockaded a military base in the Netherlands to protest against

Box 1.1

Question: Now that the Cold War is over, why do we not stop this type of low-level flight training?

Answer: In fact, the requirement is perhaps even greater in today's world. Increasing regional tensions, geopolitical instability and illicit weapons markets all result in a rapidly changing defence environment. The 1990 Gulf War and recent events in the former Yugoslavia illustrate the continuing need for well-trained and capable air forces. Their speed, range, responsiveness and accuracy can be useful to a resolute world community as a strong military deterrent to aggression. In the event of unavoidable conflict, their availability may reduce the need for a much more dangerous commitment of ground troops. Also, combined training exercises improve the effectiveness of a common defence.

Low-level flying skills are not associated merely with weapons delivery; they are essential to the protection of crews when operating over hostile forces. Once those skills are developed, they must continue to be practised for reasons of safety and readiness.

Source: "Frequently asked questions: Allied low level training" from the Canadian Department of National Defence, 1996. Additional information on this subject is available on the Internet: http://www.capitalnet.com/~pmogb/

low-level flights by Dutch fighter aircraft in Canada, and in April 1995 a group of Innu demonstrated in Trafalgar Square in London. During the Trafalgar Square demonstration, the group Survival International climbed the 15-storey high Nelson's Column and hung a banner that stated: "Canada: Let the Innu Live". The aboriginal people also have called for independent commissions to conduct an assessment, as when the Québec Montagnais submitted a request to the International Human Rights Commission to investigate low-level flying. Civil disobedience has been used domestically, with the Innu people repeatedly occupying the Goose Bay airstrip to draw national and international attention to their concerns.

Those supporting the military flying program in Québec and Labrador also have sought international support. The Department of National Defence and its

Box 1.2

The federal Minister of Fisheries, also a Member of Parliament from Newfoundland and Labrador, was quoted as saying that the Innu opposition to training flights had to be viewed as part of a larger debate not only about the environment and traditional ways of life, but also about land claims. In his opinion, it was not possible to consider any one of those issues independently from the others.

supporters lobbied NATO partners in Brussels to gain support for a tactical training centre at Goose Bay. In addition, National Defence has organized tours for European journalists and elected officials to visit Goose Bay and other communities in Labrador. The Town Council of Happy Valley—Goose Bay also has hired public relations consultants to develop a strategy to support a training base, and to provide responses to criticisms.

The outcome, according to Barker and Soyez (1994), is that when interaction regarding resource use occurs among marginalized people in hinterland areas, domestic proponents in heartland areas, and users in foreign countries, the conflicts change from being national to transnational ones. The result is development of strategies on both sides to "think locally" but to "act globally", in order to enlist support for what is wanted. This pattern arises in various situations. Other examples have been the lobbying and debates in Europe regarding the seal hunt in the Gulf of St Lawrence and other coastal waters off Newfoundland and Labrador, and the "turbot war" between Canada and Spain in the winter of 1995. The broader implications are that decisions about environmental and resource systems increasingly are made not only on technical and scientific bases, and that planners and managers therefore must have the capability to see and deal with the "big picture".

Other implications can be identified regarding the following core themes in this book.

- **Change.** Planners and managers encounter changing conditions, needs and expectations. What might have been acceptable at one time period may not be accepted at a later time period.

- **Complexity.** The impacts of human activity on the natural environment and on cultures are often difficult to understand and predict. Cause-and-effect patterns are difficult to determine due to multiple variables and paths of interaction.

- **Uncertainty.** Planners and managers have to make decisions without complete information or understanding of the ecosystems for which their decisions can have consequences.

- **Conflict.** Different, and often conflicting, values and perspectives are usually involved in resource allocation and use decisions. Such differences frequently reflect different "world views", needs and expectations, creating major challenges for managers seeking to accommodate various legitimate points of view.

In the remainder of this chapter, some key ideas related to change, complexity, uncertainty and conflict will be introduced. The rest of the book will examine various ways for analysts, planners and managers to address these matters when dealing with environmental and resource management.

1.3 Change

As Baumann and Werick (1993: 3) noted, the opening scene of the Broadway play *Fiddler on the Roof* opens with Tevye, a peasant farmer, commenting about a fiddler who is on the roof of his home. Tevye poses a question for himself and the audience: "Why do we stay up there and how do we keep our balance? That, I can tell you in one word: Tradition." Tradition helps to provide stability,

Box 1.3

Often our society follows Tevye's lead and has as a justification for doing something only the fact that it has always been done that way. But society does not remain constant. Major and continued change is the social fact of our time. The costs of tradition, then, are enormous. It is crucial, therefore, to continuously reassess current and new policies, new technologies, and methods/ tools of analysis and evaluation. To survive in the global economy, we must embrace the concept of change and diminish the role of tradition.

Source: Baumann and Werick, 1993: 3.

continuity and respect. In that manner, maintaining traditional ways can offer many benefits. However, as the remarks in Box 1.3 reveal, tradition also can serve as an impediment when it hinders us from recognizing new situations, considering new opportunities, or thinking about new ways to achieve the same objectives. Also, there are times when traditional ways get overwhelmed by powerful forces for change, such as war, famine or disease, which affect both people and their environments. Several examples of change, with implications for environmental and resource management, are presented here to highlight the importance of being able to deal with changing needs, conditions and circumstances.

1.3.1 Environmental change and violent conflict

One implication of environmental change or resource scarcity is the increasing likelihood of conflict among people or nations. As explained by Homer-Dixon *et al.* (1993), human activity can contribute to environmental degradation or resource scarcity in three ways. First, human actions can result in a *decrease in the quality and/or quantity of resources* if they are used or harvested at a rate faster than they can be renewed. When this occurs, it is said that people are living off their natural capital, rather than from the interest off the natural capital. In some instances, such as use of non-renewable resources like petroleum, natural gas, zinc or silver, human use does deplete the capital, because such resources are renewable on a geologic rather than a human time scale. However, even renewable resources such as topsoil, forests or wildlife can be degraded if they are used at a rate faster than they can be replenished. A second source of degradation or scarcity is *population growth*. With population growth, a set amount of arable land or water must increasingly be shared among more people, resulting in a steadily reduced amount available per person. And third, *unequal access to resources or the environment* may cause problems. Unequal access is usually the result of laws or property rights which lead to or encourage the concentration of supply in the hands of a relatively small number of people, leaving others subject to scarcity. These three activities or factors can act alone or in combination.

Box 1.4 Conflict over water

Of 200 "first-order" river systems in the world, nearly 150 are shared by two nations, and more than 50 are shared by three to ten nations – and they support close to 40% of the population on the Earth. In the Middle East, water has been, and continues to be, a major factor for conflict, especially in the Jordan River valley. Other disputes have emerged between Pakistan and India regarding reduced flows in the Indus River, and between India and Bangladesh over flows in the Ganges River. Other disputes over allocation of shared waters have occurred in the river basins of the Nile, Euphrates–Tigris, Mekong and Rio de la Plata.

Source: after Myers, 1986: 252.

As Figure 1.3 shows, decreases in quality and quantity of resources, population growth and unequal access to resources contribute to scarcity or degradation, or both, which in turn becomes a trigger for many other second-order consequences. Thus, worsening environmental conditions may cause people to migrate or to be expelled from a region, giving rise to a phenomenon now referred to as "environmental refugees". It can lead to ethnic conflicts, when one group in a society perceives that another has achieved dispropor-tionate ownership or control of crucial resources. Thus, the process of change can have many phases or cycles, some of which may be far enough removed from the scarcity or degradation that most people do not recognize their fundamental causal role. Such a multi-layered process also contributes to significant

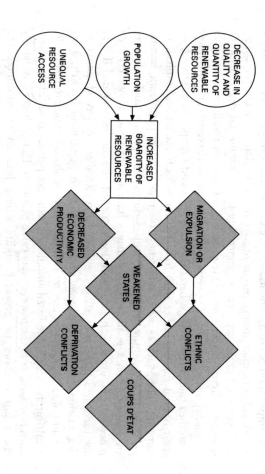

Figure 1.3 Some sources and consequences of renewable resource scarcity (Homer-Dixon *et al.*, 1993: 42)

Box 1.5

Population growth and unequal access to good land force huge numbers of people into cities or onto marginal lands. In the latter case, they cause environmental damage and become chronically poor. Eventually these people may become the source of persistent upheaval, or they may migrate yet again, stimulating ethnic conflicts or urban unrest elsewhere.

Source: Homer-Dixon *et al.*, 1993: 42.

complexity, making it difficult to know where to draw the boundaries around a resource or environmental "problem" or "issue".

1.3.2 Political ecology

The concept of "political ecology" has been developed to help in understanding the *political sources, conditions* and *ramifications* of environmental change, especially in the Third World (Bryant, 1992). Political ecology forces the analyst to go well beyond the attributes of only a biophysical or natural-system when seeking to understand cause-and-effect relationships, or when preparing strategies or plans. In Bryant's view, the three dimensions of political ecology direct attention to:

- **Political sources:** state policies, interstate relations and global capitalism, thereby highlighting the growing importance of national and transnational forces on the environment.

- **Conditions:** conflicts over access, with emphasis upon location-specific struggles. This dimension emphasizes that those with relatively little power can and will fight back to protect environmental conditions which are the basis for their livelihood. Understanding such conditions requires a historical and contemporary appreciation of the dynamics of any conflict.

- **Ramifications:** the political consequences of environmental change, with particular attention given to socio-economic impact and political process issues.

The issue of *state policies*, within the "political sources" dimension, illustrates how the political ecology framework extends an analyst's perspective regarding environmental changes. State policies have a potentially core role for inter-actions between people and their environment, as they help to establish priorities and practices for the state, as well as structure debate about environmental change. Thus, it is important to understand the origins, content, implementation and impact of such policies. Bryant further noted that policies are not developed in a vacuum. Instead, they emerge from interaction and struggle among competing interest groups which strive to influence the development and substance of policy. Furthermore, many policies have implications for the environment and natural resources, ensuring that the interests of many groups – government agencies, national and multinational companies, non-government organizations, multilateral agencies, donor organi-zations, and foreign governments – will end up overlapping with environmental and resource issues. For example, Black (1990) has outlined how a variety of different and conflicting pressures, some internal and some external, contributed to a major agricultural crisis in the Serra do Alvão in the interior of northern Portugal.

To be effective analysts, it is important to be able to identify and understand the differing and often conflicting pressures placed on policy makers, and the implications for the intent and output of policies. As an example, Bryant suggested that forest policies often attempt to reconcile interests in conservation with pressures from commercial and non-commercial users of forests. In turn, the forest policies which try to accommodate diverse interests are influenced by other considerations ranging from taxation to trade and industrial policies. As a result, the analyst often finds her or himself considering aspects which at first glance appear unconnected to environmental or resource issues.

Conflict regarding access within the "conditions" dimension further illustrates the need to take a broad political ecology perspective. More specifically, Bryant argued that the role of women in conflicts over access to resources in many developing countries is critically important, and yet has mostly been neglected, with a few notable exceptions such as the role of women in their struggle to retain access to common property land, water and forestry resources in India. Only recently have gender roles been examined systematically, a matter to be examined more thoroughly in Chapter 10.

A study of garden orchards in Gambia highlights the importance of considering the role of women in resource allocation conflicts (Schroeder, 1993). Two decades of drought through the 1970s and 1980s stimulated hundreds of women's groups to develop intensive and lucrative fruit and vegetable crops in low-lying communal market gardens. In a separate effort to use tree planting to achieve environmental stability, land developers encouraged male land holders to use female labour, which had been used primarily to irrigate garden plots, to plant orchard trees in the same locations.

One result was that the shade from the orchard trees eventually hindered the production in the garden plots, and led to men taking over control of the plots. The explanation for this shift in control is a gender division of labour for agriculture in the Gambian villages. In the Mandinka villages, men normally grow groundnuts (peanuts) and the coarse grains (millet, sorghum, maize) on higher ground during the rainy season. Groundnut production is the main source of foreign exchange for Gambia, so the male control of this crop gives them control over most of the cash income earned in agriculture. In contrast, women grow rice and vegetables in wet and low-lying areas, and their gardens represent the primary agricultural activity in the dry season. Most of the agricultural produce grown by women is used in home consumption.

The emergence of market-oriented vegetable gardens occurred due to a noticeable decrease in average precipitation. One response was for increased production in shorter-duration, drought-resistant or cash-earning crops. Rice and vegetables, grown in swampy and low-lying areas, were more capable of such production, and women became involved because such production involved crops and land for which they had traditionally provided the labour.

As the men looked for more drought-resistant crops from trees, they turned to mangoes, which grow well in wet, low-lying areas. However, mangoes are not compatible with an understorey vegetable or fruit crop. Thus, understanding of different gender roles becomes critical in designing policies to encourage tree planting to avoid environmental degradation.

1.4 Complexity

In considering the relationships among change and conflict, it is necessary to recognize that many other variables or factors besides environmental degradation and resource scarcity contribute to conflicts, as highlighted in the political ecology approach. Other variables include population growth, poverty, inequitable political systems and lack of economic opportunities (Figure 1.4). All of these in combination can contribute to instability within a society, can make it more vulnerable to environmental degradation, and can provide incentives to look outside its own borders for solutions.

Notwithstanding the above qualification about the relative significance of environmental degradation, the increasingly important role that environmental change can have in creating conditions which lead to conflict is being recognized. For example, Homer-Dixon *et al.* (1993: 38) concluded that "scarcities of renewable resources are already contributing to violent conflicts in many parts of the developing world. These conflicts may foreshadow a surge of similar violence in coming decades, particularly in poor countries where shortages of water, forests and, especially, fertile land, coupled with rapidly expanding populations, already cause great hardship." As a result, resource and environmental analysts need to be able to interrelate environmental changes to other variables which contribute to conflicts and disputes.

As Waldrop (1992: 12) noted, complexity creates major challenges for analysts, planners and decision makers. To illustrate, when dealing with global climate change, attention has to be given to issues as diverse as energy use, food production, forest harvest practices and transportation policies. In his view, complex systems are more spontaneous, more disorderly, and more subject to sudden and unpredictable change. Indeed, complexity is partially the reason why many systems seem chaotic, or discontinuous and erratic, and are best characterized by "jagged edges and sudden leaps" (Gleick, 1987: 5). Being aware of complexity does not make the resource and environmental planner's job easier, but it does prepare her or him for inevitable surprises, and to consider how to deal with the uncertainty that it generates (see Chapter 4).

1.5 Uncertainty

The complexity encountered in environmental and resource management contributes to situations in which decisions have to be taken in the face of considerable uncertainty. Our understanding of biophysical systems, of human societies, or of the interactions between natural and social systems is often incomplete and imperfect. Furthermore, we are aware that conditions and

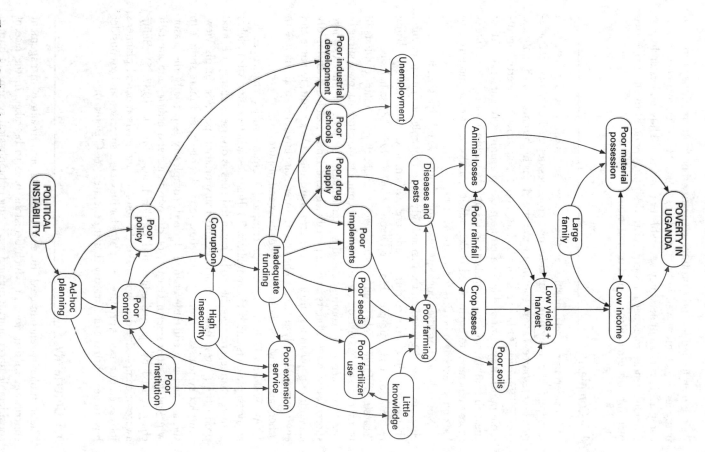

Figure 1.4 The relationship between political instability, economy and poverty (Omara-Ojungu, 1992: 60)

circumstances in the future could well change relative to what they are today. And, yet, decisions have to be made because it is not realistic to wait until analysts develop the depth of understanding that we would like to have before committing ourselves to a path of action. Given the reality of change, complexity and uncertainty, environmental and resource managers increasingly are examining approaches which allow for adaptation, and which accept that we should be able to learn from rather than be punished for mistakes. Some of the ideas and strategies for adaptiveness, flexibility and social learning will be examined in Chapters 4 and 7.

Given an uncertain future, it is helpful to be able to recognize different kinds of "uncertainty". Wynne (1992) has differentiated among four types of uncertainty, which are described in Box 1.6. By recognizing different kinds of uncertainty, we should be able to focus more readily on the kinds of issues that we should be considering.

Explicit recognition of uncertainty also helps us to identify the kinds of analysis or planning which may be most appropriate. As Christensen (1985) explained, problem-solving situations vary regarding the uncertainty about means and ends. She noted that when people are able to agree on what they want and how to achieve it, then certainty is high and planning can become the rational application of knowledge. When people agree on what they want but do not know how to achieve it, then planning becomes more of a learning process. If people cannot agree on what they want, but do know which alternative means are preferred, planning becomes a process of bargaining. And finally, if people cannot agree on either means or ends, then planning becomes a search for order in chaos. Figures 1.5 and 1.6 illustrate some of the characteristics of these four conditions, and their implications. The key message is that too often analysts or planners function as if they are always in cell A in Figures 1.5 and 1.6, whereas in reality the conditions are usually more similar to those in cell B, C or D. By recognizing different kinds of uncertainty, we should be able to diagnose more readily the types of conditions which characterize a problem, and thereby be able to handle it more effectively.

Box 1.6 Types of uncertainty

1. **Risk.** Know the odds.
2. **Uncertainty.** Do not know the odds. May know the key variables and their parameters.
3. **Ignorance.** Do not know what we should know. Do not even know what questions we should be posing.
4. **Indeterminacy.** Causal chains or networks are open. Understanding not possible.

Source: after Wynne, 1992: 114.

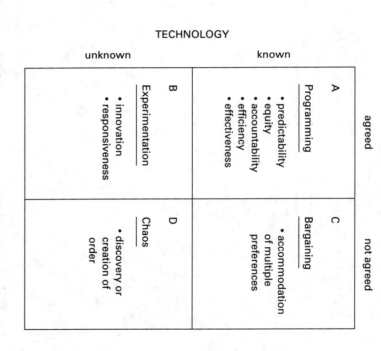

Figure 1.5 Expectations of planning organizations relative to prototype conditions of, and responses to, planning problems (Christensen, 1985: 66)

GOAL

	agreed	not agreed
TECHNOLOGY known	A Programming • predictability • equity • accountability • efficiency • effectiveness	C Bargaining • accommodation of multiple preferences
TECHNOLOGY unknown	B Experimentation • innovation • responsiveness	D Chaos • discovery or creation of order

1.6 Conflict

It is often suggested that the idea of "managing" the environment or natural resources is a misnomer, given rapidly changing conditions, immense complexity and high uncertainty. Instead, it is argued, what we should be focusing upon is managing human interaction with the environment and natural resources. If this latter position is accepted, then much of "environmental and resource management" becomes the management of conflict. This situation occurs because it is normal in a society to have individuals or groups with different values, interests, hopes, expectations and priorities. And often there is at least tension among these different characteristics, if not mutual incompatibility. In the extreme, as outlined above when discussing *environmental change and acute conflict*, different interests and expectations can lead to armed conflict within or between nations.

If a significant element of being an environmental or resource manager requires the ability to deal with conflict, a useful entry point is to be able to recognize some of the causes of conflict. While this and other aspects of conflict or dispute resolution will be addressed in Chapter 11, at this stage four basic

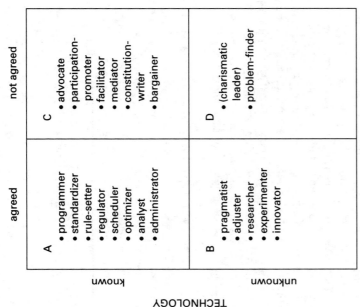

Figure 1.6 Planning roles categorized by planning conditions (Christensen, 1985: 69)

roots of conflict are identified, based on the work of Dorcey (1986). It should be noted that, in many situations, more than one of these causes may exist. First, different knowledge or understanding may lead to conflict. In other words, groups may be using different models, assumptions and information. Thus, one side in a dispute may believe that an aquifer is being overpumped, or that reserves of a mineral are sufficient for only seven to eight more years, whereas another may have concluded that the aquifer is not being overdrawn, or that the

Box 1.7 Basic causes of conflict

1. Differences in knowledge or understanding.
2. Differences in values.
3. Differences about distribution of benefits and costs.
4. Differences due to personalities and circumstances of interested parties.

Source: after Dorcey, 1986.

mineral reserves are sufficient for 30 years. With perspectives about the situation based on different evidence, or interpretations of it, the two sides then could be in conflict about whether a problem exists, and/or about appropriate solutions to deal with it.

Second, disputes may emerge because of *different values*. For example, there may be agreement about the nature of the problem, and the means to resolve it, but sharp divergence regarding the ultimate endpoint to be sought. For example, using the aquifer example, some may believe that as much water as possible should be extracted to support economic activities, whether agricultural or industrial. Others may believe that significant quantities of water should not be extracted for human use, in order to ensure that sufficient water can feed into streams and lakes and thereby support fish and other aquatic life, or to nourish wetlands dependent upon the ground water in the dry season.

Third, even if the various sides in a conflict accept the same evidence and diagnosis, and have similar values, conflict may emerge from *differences in interests*. In other words, conflict arises not because of different understanding (it is agreed that the aquifer is or is not being overpumped) or because of different values (economic development is necessary to provide employment), but because of differences regarding who will be the beneficiaries, and who will carry the burden of the costs. For example, one group may believe that the use of water from an aquifer for irrigation, financed through a subsidy from the government for the capital costs, is appropriate because it will lead to food self-sufficiency and the potential for export of food products, both of which could assist in reducing the national debt. Another group could believe that the country should not try to grow food that can be imported from other countries in which production costs are lower, and that water should be allocated only to those users, perhaps cities or industries, which can afford to pay a higher price for the water. For each of these groups, the provision of jobs and the support of economic development is important, but the difference is over the allocation of the benefits to rural and urban areas, and among agriculture, industry and service sectors.

Fourth, difficulties may arise because of *personality conflicts*, or *historical circumstances*. Thus, one group may be angry or bitter that at some previous time one of the other groups blocked its attempts to achieve something very important to it. As a result, regarding the current situation, there may be determination to use this occasion to "get even", or to "pay back" the other side. Or there may be the belief, based on perception or fact, that on a previous occasion another side was dishonest, or at least withheld some key information. Consequently, there may be unwillingness to trust or respect the other side, based on the earlier experience. On that basis, there will be reluctance to reach agreement for fear that yet again it will later turn out that the other side had not been open or honest.

To repeat an observation made near the beginning of this section, it is normal for more than one of these four causes to coexist in a dispute. Analysts should have the ability to identify which causes are present, and what their relative significance is. With such a diagnosis, it should be possible to begin to determine how they might be handled as part of the process of resolving or minimizing the conflict.

A final point should also be made. Conflicts or disputes are not necessarily bad or undesirable. They can help to identify when a process or procedure is not working effectively, and can remind analysts and managers that there are legitimately different values and views. The challenge is to try to ensure that conflicts become constructive rather than destructive factors in planning for, and making decisions about, the environment and resources.

1.7 Implications

The purpose of this chapter has been to indicate the pervasiveness of change, complexity, uncertainty and conflict for resource and environmental management. The conflict over the low-level military training flights in Québec and Labrador also illustrates that resource and environmental management often cannot be isolated from broader social, economic and political issues. As a result of connections to other considerations, the idea to "think globally, act locally" can be reversed to "think locally; act globally". The discussion of environmental change and violent conflict further highlights the important role that resource scarcity and environmental degradation can have as triggers for other conflicts, including warfare among nation states.

The concept of *political ecology* encourages us to take a broad perspective on resource issues, and to ensure that we understand their context before developing solutions. In that regard, resource and environmental management is not only a technical exercise. It requires people who can bridge scientific and civic concerns. Such a perspective also highlights the idea that who is an "expert" in resource and environmental management is not determined only by formal education. Experiential understanding can often be at least as significant as insight based on scientific theories and methods.

In the remaining chapters, the themes of change, complexity, uncertainty and conflict provide common threads. If we can improve our capacity to deal with these matters, the likelihood is great that we can improve our capacity for planning and management.

References and further reading

Ali A M S 1995 Population pressure, environmental constraints and agricultural change in Bangladesh: examples from three agroecosystems. *Agriculture, Ecosystems and Environment* 55(2): 95–109

Anderton D, A Anderson, J Oakes and M Fraser 1994 Environmental equity: the demographics of dumping. *Demography* 31(2): 229–35

Babu S C and R Hassan 1995 International migration and environmental degradation – the case of Mozambican refugees and forest resources in Malawi. *Journal of Environmental Management* 43(3): 233–47

Barker M L and D Soyez 1994 Think locally, act globally? The transnationalization of Canadian resource-use conflicts. *Environment*, 36(5): 12–20, 32–6

Baumann D D and W Werick 1993 Water management: why the resistance to change? *Water Resources Update* 90 (Winter): 3–9

Black R 1990 "Regional political ecology" in theory and practice: a case study from northern Portugal. *Transactions of the Institute of British Geographers*, New Series, 15(1): 35–47

Black R 1994 Forced migration and environmental change: the impact of refugees on host environments. *Journal of Environmental Management* 42(3): 261–77

Bowonder B 1987 Environmental changes in developing countries: a systems perspective. *Journal of Applied Systems Analysis* 14(April): 81–98

Bryant R L 1992 Political ecology: an emerging research agenda in Third World studies. *Political Geography* 11(1): 12–36

Canada National Defence 1994 *EIS: military flight training: an environmental impact statement on military flying activities in Labrador and Quebec: summary*. Ottawa, National Defence

Canadian Environmental Assessment Agency 1995 *Military flying activities in Labrador and Quebec: report of the Environmental Assessment Panel*. Ottawa, Minister of Supply and Services Canada, February

Christensen K S 1985 Coping with uncertainty in planning. *Journal of the American Planning Association* 51(1): 63–73

Cohen J and I Stewart 1994 *The collapse of chaos: discovering simplicity in a complex world*. New York, Penguin Books

Costanza R, W M Kemp and W R Boynton 1993 Predictability, scale, and biodiversity in coastal and estuarine ecosystems: implications for management. *Ambio* 22(2–3): 88–96

Döös B R 1994 Environmental degradation, global food production, and risk for large-scale migrations. *Ambio* 23(2): 124–30

Dorcey A H J 1986 *Bargaining in the governance of Pacific coastal resources: research and reform*. Vancouver, BC, University of British Columbia, Westwater Research Centre

Gleick J 1987 *Chaos: making a new science*. New York, Penguin Books

Gleick P 1990 Environment, resources and international security and politics. In E H Arnett (ed.) *Science and international security: responding to a changing world*. Washington, DC, American Association for the Advancement of Science, 501–23

Gleick P 1991 Environment and security: the clear connections. *Bulletin of the Atomic Scientists* 47(3): 17–21

Goldemberg J 1993 The geopolitics of environmental degradation. *Environmental Conservation* 20(3): 193–4

Harrington F H and A M Veitch 1991 Short-term impacts of low-level jet fighter training on caribou in Labrador. *Arctic* 44(4): 318–27

Higgins R 1993 Race and environmental equity: an overview of the environmental justice issue in the policy process. *Polity* 26(2): 281–300

Homer-Dixon T F 1991 On the threshold: environmental changes as causes of acute conflict. *International Security* 16(2): 76–116

Homer-Dixon T F 1994 Environmental scarcities and violent conflict: evidence from cases. *International Security* 19(1): 5–40

Homer-Dixon T F, J H Boutwell and G W Rathjens 1993 Environmental change and violent conflict. *Scientific American* 268(2): 38–45

Inman K 1993 Fueling expansion in the Third World: population, development, debt, and the global decline of forests. *Society and Natural Resources* 6(1): 17–39

International Geosphere–Biosphere Programme 1992 *Global change: reducing uncertainties*. Stockholm, The Royal Swedish Academy of Sciences

Johnston B R 1995 Human rights and the environment. *Human Ecology* 23(2): 111–23

Kendie S B 1995 The environmental dimensions of structural adjustment programmes: missing links to sustainable development. *Singapore Journal of Tropical Geography* 16(1): 42–57

Laituri M and A Kirby 1994 Finding fairness in America's cities? The search for environmental equity in everyday life. *Journal of Social Issues* 50(3): 121–39

Lonergan S C 1994 Impoverishment, population and environmental degradation: assessing the relationships. *Environmental Conservation* 20(4): 328–34

Lonergan S and B Kavanagh 1991 Climate change, water resources and security in the Middle East. *Global Environmental Change* 1(4): 272–90

Mabogunje A L 1995 The environmental challenges in Sub-Saharan Africa. *Environment* 37(4): 4–9, 31–5

Myers N 1986 The environmental dimension to security issues. *The Environmentalist* 6(4): 251–7

Myers N 1993 *Ultimate security: the environmental basis for political stability*. New York, W.W. Norton

Nelson J G, R Serafin 1996 Environmental and resource planning and decision making in Canada: a human ecological and a civics approach. In R Vogelsang (ed.) *Canada in transition: results of environmental and human geographical research*. Bochum, Germany, Universitätsverlag Dr. N. Brockmeyer: 1–25

Ojima D S, K A Galvin and B L Turner 1995 The global impact of land-use change. *BioScience* 44(5): 300–4

Omara-Ojungu P 1992 *Resource management in developing countries*. Harlow, Longman

Preston-White R 1995 The politics of ecology: dredge-mining in South Africa. *Environmental Conservation* 22(2): 151–6

Schroeder R A 1993 Shady practice: gender and political ecology of resource stabilization in Gambian garden/orchards. *Economic Geography* 69(4): 349–65

Shaw R P 1993 Warfare, national sovereignty and the environment. *Environmental Conservation* 20(2): 113–21

Suzuki D 1994 *Time to change: essays*. Toronto, Stoddart

Töpfer K 1994 Environmental policy as a factor in new security policy. *GeoJournal* 33(4): 349–54

Ullman R H 1983 Redefining security. *International Security* 8(1): 129–53

Waldrop M M 1992 *Complexity: the emerging science at the edge of order and chaos*. New York, Simon and Schuster

Westing A H 1989 The environmental component of comprehensive security. *Bulletin of Peace Proposals* 20(2): 129–34

Westing A H 1992 Environmental refugees: a growing category of displaced persons. *Environmental Conservation* 19(3): 105–16

Westing A H 1994 Population, desertification, and migration. *Environmental Conservation* 21(2): 110–14 and 119

Wynne B 1992 Uncertainty and environmental learning: reconceiving science and policy in the preventative paradigm. *Global Environmental Change* 2(2): 111–27

Chapter 2

Sustainable Development

2.1 Introduction

In Lewis Carroll's book, *Alice in Wonderland*, Alice comments that if you do not know where you want to go, any road will get you there. In contrast, Columbus knew where he wanted to go (the Orient) but ended up somewhere else (North America), because he did not know the route to take. The lesson is that it helps to know where you want to go, and also how to get there. Unfortunately, experience suggests that many resource and environmental planners too often are like Alice or Columbus.

Some believe that *sustainable development* is a good basis for such a vision or sense of direction. In this chapter, the nature of sustainable development, different views about the concept, the opportunities and problems created if it is used as a vision, and the implications of change, complexity, uncertainty and conflict for it, are considered.

2.2 Sustainable development

2.2.1 The concept

Sustainable development was popularized in the report *Our Common Future* prepared by the World Commission on Environment and Development (1987), also referred to as the Brundtland Commission, after its chair (Gro Harlem Brundtland), then the prime minister of Norway. Gro Brundtland explained in the Foreword to *Our Common Future* that she was invited in December 1983 by the Secretary General of the United Nations to conduct an inquiry and prepare a report to provide a global agenda for change. More specifically, the terms of reference from the General Assembly of the United Nations were (1) to propose long-term environmental strategies for achieving sustainable development by the year 2000 and beyond, and (2) to identify how relationships among people, resources, environment and development could be incorporated into national and international policies. The Commission included representatives from developed and developing countries, and held public meetings in various countries around the world.

In its report, the Commission was explicit that it had not developed a detailed blueprint for action, but rather a "pathway" through which people in

Box 2.1

Those who are poor and hungry will often destroy their immediate environment in order to survive: they will cut down forests; their livestock will overgraze grasslands; they will overuse marginal land; and in growing numbers they will crowd into congested cities.

Source: World Commission on Environment and Development, 1987: 28.

---

different countries could create appropriate policies and practices. Furthermore, the Commission members had quickly agreed that one issue was of primary significance: many development activities were leaving growing numbers of people poor and vulnerable, and at the same time were degrading the environment. This conclusion convinced the Commission members that a new path for development was needed, one that would sustain human progress not just in a few places for a few years, but for the entire planet into a more distant future. Thus, the planet's main environmental problem was judged also to be its main development problem.

The Commission focused on population, food security, loss of species and genetic resources, energy, industry, and human settlements. All of these were deemed to be interconnected and therefore could not be treated separately. Furthermore, the concept of sustainable development was judged to involve limits. Such limits were not "absolute", but were relative to the state of technology and social organizations, and to the capacity of the biosphere to absorb the effects of human activity.

Perhaps the most frequently quoted statement from the Brundtland Commission is that sustainable development is development that meets the needs of the present without compromising the ability of future generations to meet their own needs. However, less frequently noted has been its associated statement that sustainable development contains two key concepts. These are: (1) *needs*, especially the needs of the poor people in the world, to which overriding priority was essential, and (2) *limitations* created by technology and social organization regarding the capacity of the environment to satisfy both present and future needs. Thus, sustainable development, as interpreted by the Brundtland Commission, is an *anthropocentric* (human-centred) concept.

The Commission also offered some comments about *growth*. In its view, no set limits could be identified regarding levels of population or resource use beyond which ecological disaster would occur. Different limits existed for use of energy, water, land and materials. Notwithstanding this qualification, the Commission concluded that ultimate limits did exist. Sustainable development required that, well before such limits were reached, the world must have ensured equitable access to constrained resources, and have reoriented technology to relieve pressures. At the same time, it stipulated that every ecosystem in every place could not be preserved intact, because economic growth and development inevitably involved changes.

Having defined sustainable development, and explained what it implied, the

Box 2.2 Perspective on sustainability

Sustainability came into prominence with the publication in 1987 of *Our Common Future* by the World Commission on Environment and Development (Brundtland Commission). It introduced the creatively ambiguous phrase "sustainable development" as an idea to pursue. An intuitively attractive but slippery concept (rather like "democracy" and "justice"), it nevertheless served the intent of the Commission which was to further the debate about what should be the proper relationship between "environment" and "development". No society worth having should be unwittingly undermining the ecological basis of its own continuance, yet the constant litany of environmental problems caused by the degradative impacts of human activities signals that sustainability is indeed in doubt.

The discussion at this point often goes to questions about natural resources and, specifically, questions about how much should be sustained, at what level of quality, for how long a duration, and for whose benefit. This is guaranteed to run in circles. No resource systems, nor the institutions associated with them, can be sustained as is in perpetuity. Changes in both are inevitable. What *must* be sustained, however, is the capacity for renewal and evolution in ecosystems, and innovation and creativity in social systems. Sustainability is not some end state to be achieved, but a trajectory to be negotiated continuously and adjust learn to recognize the symptoms and evidence of non-sustainability and adjust accordingly. This is much easier said than done.

Source: Francis, 1995: 4.

Brundtland Commission then identified seven critical objectives for environment and development policies. These were:

- reviving growth
- changing the quality of growth (emphasizing development rather than growth)
- meeting essential needs for jobs, food, energy, water and sanitation
- ensuring a sustainable level of population
- conserving and enhancing the resource base
- reorienting technology and managing risk
- merging environment and economics in decision making.

Two key points deserve highlighting here. First, the Commission was explicit that while growth is essential to meet basic human needs, sustainable development involves more than growth. It necessitates a change in the nature of growth, to make it less material- and energy-intensive, and to make it more equitable in its impacts. Second, the Commission noted that a common theme in a strategy for sustainable development had to be the integration of economic and ecological considerations in decision making. For this to happen, the Commission concluded that there would have to be changes in attitudes and objectives, and in institutional arrangements and laws at every level. However, the Commission noted that changes in laws alone would not be sufficient to protect common interests. Such protection required community knowledge and support, which in turn necessitated more public participation in decisions about the environment and resources. These aspects are considered in more detail in Chapters 8 (Partnerships and Participation) and 9 (Local Knowledge Systems).

2.2.2 Principles for sustainable development

Following the publication of *Our Common Future*, considerable effort has been devoted to developing guidelines or principles for sustainable development. The rationale has been that without such guidelines or principles it is not possible to determine if a policy or practice is sustainable, or if initiatives are consistent with sustainable development. Creation of such principles has been a major challenge because, as the Commission recognized, economic and social systems and ecological conditions vary greatly among countries. The result was that no generic model or blueprint could be established, and each nation would have to work out what was appropriate for its context, needs, conditions and opportunities.

Notwithstanding these challenges in developing generic principles, it is helpful to identify general guidelines, which can then be modified for the conditions of a place and time. Table 2.1 provides one set of principles or guidelines. They represent one of the earlier systematic attempts to identify the characteristics of a sustainable society. If the principles are found to be inadequate or incomplete, they challenge the critic to make them more adequate or complete. In addition, for them to be operational or practical, a major task is to develop *indicators* for each principle. In other words, what information or evidence would be required for each principle to allow a decision to be made that a policy or an initiative was consistent with it? Are such data available from the information already being collected in countries as part of their censuses or other monitoring (see Chapter 13)? Or do new data collecting programs have to be established?

2.2.3 Perspectives on sustainable development

As a concept, sustainable development has attracted both criticism and support (Wood, 1993). Sustainable development has been criticized because some view the definitions or interpretations to be too vague or ambiguous, allowing it to be something for everyone, or allowing anyone to use it as a justification for actions, whether those be in the direction of economic growth or environmental protection. Others consider sustainable development to perpetuate the Western capitalist system, so reject it on ideological grounds.

The positive assessment in many ways is the mirror image of the criticisms. Thus, while some see vagueness and ambiguity as a problem, others believe these features provide flexibility and discretion necessary to custom design for the needs of specific places and times. While some view sustainable development as supporting traditional capitalistic systems, others believe its arguments for including real environmental costs and using environmental pricing, and valuing environmental attributes, are appropriate to modify traditional market thinking, which gives more weight to economic than environmental considerations.

While there will inevitably be supporters and detractors for a concept such as sustainable development, it is important to recognize that the concept does contain some paradoxes, tensions and conflicts. Dovers and Handmer (1992) identified what they viewed to be eight of the most obvious of these, each of which is considered below.

(1) Technology and culture: cause versus cure

The application of technology has allowed an improvement in the standard of living of many people around the world. It also has led to an increase in resource consumption and in production of wastes. Some societies have become very

Table 2.1 Principles of sustainability (adapted from Robinson et al., 1990: 44)

A. Environmental/ecological principles

1. Protect life support systems.
2. Protect and enhance biotic diversity.
3. Maintain or enhance integrity of ecosystems, and develop and implement rehabilitative measures for badly degraded ecosystems.
4. Develop and implement preventive and adaptive strategies to respond to the threat of global ecological change.

B. Socio-political principles

B1. *From environmental/ecological constraints*

1. Keep the physical scale of human activity below the total carrying capacity of the planetary biosphere.
2. Recognize the environmental costs of human activities; develop methods to minimize energy and material use per unit of economic activity; reduce noxious emissions; decontaminate and rehabilitate degraded ecosystems.
3. Ensure socio-political and economic equity in the transition to a more sustainable society.
4. Incorporate environmental concerns more directly and extensively into the political decision-making process.
5. Ensure increased public involvement in the development, interpretation and implementation of sustainable development concepts.
6. Link political activity more directly to actual environmental experience through reallocation of political power to more environmentally meaningful jurisdictions.

B2. *From socio-political criteria*

1. Establish an open, accessible political process that puts effective decision-making power at the level of the government closest to the situation and the lives of the people affected by a decision.
2. Ensure people are free from extreme want and from vulnerability to economic coercion.
3. Ensure people can participate creatively and self-directedly in the political and economic system.
4. Ensure a minimum level of equality and social justice, including equality to realize one's full human potential, recourse to an open and just legal system, freedom from political repression, access to high-quality education, effective access to information, and freedom of religion, speech and assembly.

dependent on technologies, which has been characterized as a "technico addiction".

In some cultures, there is virtually no questioning of the desirability of relying on technology. While some recognition is given to the environmental and social impacts associated with application of technology, there is rarely discussion regarding whether its application is the most appropriate response to a problem, particularly regarding the health of ecosystems. As a result, the mainstream view in many countries has been to apply technology to facilitate resource-intensive growth. Thus, technology has often been the solution to some problems and has created real opportunities, but at the same time has been part of the cause of environmental problems. Sustainable strategies for resource and environmental management will require a re-examination of the role of technology, which for some societies will require a re-examination of fundamental aspects of their culture.

(2) Humility versus arrogance

Consistent with the discussion of complexity and uncertainty in Chapter 1, Dovers and Handmer concluded that despite ever increasing quantities of information, our understanding of the global environment is characterized by increasing uncertainty. This is troubling for many Western cultures, which have a strong belief that the power of science and technology can allow societies to understand and control nature. Dovers and Handmer conclude that we must be humble, and be able to recognize that our knowledge at best is incomplete, and at worst may be wrong in almost every respect. On the other hand, they argue that we must be arrogant enough to make decisions in the face of inevitable ignorance. The worrisome concern, in their view, is that such humility seems to occur only with regard to the status quo, and arrogance emerges in our willingness to defend the status quo. This situation does not bode well for action required to move societies away from unsustainable activities. This tension will be explored more fully in Chapter 5.

(3) Intergenerational versus intragenerational equity

A key tenet of sustainable development is that meeting basic human needs today should not preclude future generations from being able to meet their needs, often characterized as accepting the desirability of achieving *intergenerational* equity. Some societies address this systematically. For example, Native Indian tribes in North America, such as the Algonquins, have traditionally included a person whose task is to represent the seventh generation in the future during any important group decisions. In the jargon of sustainable development, that person is responsible for thinking about intergenerational equity issues.

However, as Dovers and Handmer comment, if resources are to be preserved or held for future use, how does a society choose how much should be used today and how much should be set aside? This question is more challenging when there are many people today whose basic needs are not being met. And that is the situation in the world, when literally millions of people are unable to meet their basic human needs, let alone decide whether they "need" a second computer or VCR in their household.

At a simplistic level, the solution for today's problem is either to enlarge the resource supply, which may be achieved through the application of new technologies, or to redistribute the resource supply. The former is likely to pose problems related to environmental degradation, and the latter involves substantial challenges to the privileges and powers of elites in a society. Hence, sustainable development must be able to address both intergenerational and intragenerational equity issues. If the latter are not dealt with, it is unlikely that people who do not have enough to eat each day will be concerned about the needs of future generations.

(4) Growth versus limits

The joining together of "sustainable" and "development" produces a concept which for many people is an *oxymoron* (an expression in which words of opposite meaning are used together, such as "cruel kindness" or "make haste slowly"). From this critical oxymoron perspective, "sustainable" means some activity that can be continued over the long term. In contrast, "development" is interpreted as growth, which implies a primarily physical or material addition to production. The concept of endless and increasing growth is one of the characteristics of a cancerous cell, which, if left unchecked, often proves fatal. As a result, the idea of having endless growth raises the issue of whether there are ecological limits beyond which irreversible scarcity and/or degradation begin to occur.

The challenge about such limits, which also has been debated in the *carrying capacity* literature, is that limits are usually not fixed or absolute. Rather, they can be variable, and depend upon social values and technological capacity. Furthermore, depending upon social values and technological capacity, limits may be stretched or constricted. For example, Stone Age people did not have the technology to take advantage of bronze or other metals. Such "resources" were present, but they were not accessible to those people until technologies were developed that allowed them to transform what, until the arrival of such technology, had only been "neutral stuff".

The Brundtland Commission argued that growth was essential, if basic human needs were to be satisfied. However, the Commission also recognized the existence of constraints or limits. The dilemma is to determine what type of growth is needed to meet human needs, how to sustain such growth, and how

---

Box 2.3 The concept of limits

The concept of sustainable development does imply limits – not absolute limits but limitations imposed by the present state of technology and social organization on environmental resources and by the ability of the biosphere to absorb the effects of human activities.

Source: World Commission on Environment and Development, 1987: 8.

to ensure that growth does not unacceptably degrade the environment which provides part of the base for growth.

(5) Individual versus collective interests

The achievement of sustainable development requires some trade-offs between individual and collective interests. Many Western cultures have placed a premium on the primacy of individual rights and choice, as reflected in dependency on the private automobile, attitudes to property rights and land tenure, and preference for individual household units. Many have argued that a sustainable future will require much more use of public or mass transport, shifting of values from private land ownership to land stewardship, and acceptance of different sizes and types of housing.

Most environmental issues reflect *collective* problems emerging from many individual decisions which have *cumulative* negative consequences for the environment. Some individual sovereignty may therefore have to be constrained or forgone to achieve sustainable development. Such a move will generate tension within and among nations, as those required to forfeit some of their individual "rights" are among the most powerful and influential people in society, and may not forgo their "rights" (or privileges) with enthusiasm. Nation states also tend to be very protective of their sovereignty and rights. As a result, tension can be expected to occur in defining the appropriate balance between individual and collective rights.

(6) Democracy versus purpose

Sustainable development is often associated with an approach that seeks to empower local people, and to encourage their participation in development and environmental decisions. The rationale for this argument is that people living in an area will have to live with the impacts of development, and therefore are likely to be able to anticipate negative impacts. To achieve such empowerment, it is often argued, there needs to be both decentralization and deconcentration of decision making away from national to local governments.

There is much that is sensible about the arguments for greater local empowerment, including the improvement of ability to take advantage of local knowledge and understanding, as will be discussed in Chapter 9. However, as noted in the discussion about individual and collective interests, many environmental problems occur because of decisions taken by a variety of people in different places. If there is no capacity for overview or oversight, and no capacity for defining a general set of objectives or targets for something such as reducing emission of greenhouse gases, it is unlikely that local governments acting unilaterally will be able to make a significant contribution.

Thus, while there is a need to provide for more participation and local roles in environmental and resource management, there is also need for the creation of a common purpose or interest that people can work to achieve, even if decisions are being implemented at a local level. It is too simplistic to assume that if everything were delegated to the local level, all environmental problems would be resolved.

(7) Adaptability versus resistance

Most societies and their institutions resist change. This resistance can be beneficial through creating stability. However, such resistance also can create severe conservatism, and unwillingness to consider new visions, paths or actions. Indeed, often the "gatekeepers" who resist change are those who are best served by the status quo; they are not anxious to see their "comfort zone" affected.

A paradox exists because humans are among the most adaptable beings on the Earth. Again and again humankind has demonstrated creativity through technological innovations that have often allowed increased food production from farms, or more fish to be caught from the oceans. Nevertheless, these types of innovations have also contributed to pressure on the environment and resources. Once again, tension and conflict exist regarding the best way to institute change. For change is not always painless, and there will be some people who will gain more than others from any new arrangements.

(8) Optimization versus spare capacity

The concept of optimization is based on the idea that it is desirable to achieve the best possible use of resources or the environment. Such a perspective assumes that unused resources are "wasted". It is also a very anthropocentric viewpoint, by implying that unless resources are developed for human benefit, they are not being used optimally. This view does not recognize that other living things are dependent on the environment, and that human interventions sometimes have adverse consequences for them. On the other hand, with steady population growth and the need to satisfy basic human needs, the notion of optimization is very attractive to many people.

The challenge for sustainable development is to determine a credible way to give value to aspects not readily measurable in quantitative or monetary terms. A more basic issue, however, is that when we aspire to use resources and the environment to the fullest possible extent, there will be little or no spare capacity which would be extremely useful to have if and when a decision is made to change direction. If there is no spare capacity, then any change will have to come through redistribution of present use, which will mean that some people will be worse off than they were before the changes. Spare capacity provides the flexibility to consider some changes that could provide gains for some without taking away from others. However, once again it is difficult to defend the protection of spare capacity, when some people's basic needs are not being satisfied.

The eight contradictions presented by Dovers and Handmer (1992) deserve attention if sustainable development is to be transformed from a concept to action. In that regard, we should consider key issues, questions and opportunities associated with:

- the paradox of technology
- humility or arrogance in the face of uncertainty
- intergenerational and intragenerational equity
- economic growth versus ecological limits
- reconciliation of individual and collective interests
- balance between democracy and purposeful action
- different styles of resilience
- the role of optimization.

These eight issues provide the start of an agenda for anyone contemplating how to create a sustainable development strategy.

2.3 Sustainable development in developed and developing countries

The Brundtland Commission was emphatic that it did not have a blueprint for sustainable development, and argued that each country would have to develop its own approach. In that context, it is not surprising that there have been different interpretations and emphases in developed and developing countries. In developed countries, the primary interest regarding sustainable development has been to integrate environmental and economic considerations into decision making. Considerable attention also has been focused upon intergenerational equity issues. Furthermore, developed countries have been concerned that in incorporating environmental concerns they do not jeopardize their economic competitiveness, particularly given the low wage advantages of the developing countries. The developed countries have also argued that developing countries should modify their economic activities to avoid destruction of rain forests and other resources with global value.

In contrast, for developing countries the priority regarding sustainable development has been to meet basic human needs of its present citizens, and to ensure economic development. Thus, the focus has been more upon intra-generational than intergenerational issues. There has been understandable resentment from the developing countries when industrialized nations suggest that they should forgo development opportunities from harvesting rain forests in order to protect the global environment. The leaders of developing countries believe their citizens have the same right to have basic needs met, and that they should not be told not to do what all the developed countries did to achieve their high level of economic development. Indeed, at the Earth Summit in Rio de Janeiro during June 1992, many disagreements were based on the fundamentally different interpretation between developed and developing countries regarding what sustainable development should mean. In the following subsections, some examples are presented of approaches to sustainability in developed and developing countries.

2.3.1 Sustainable development in developed countries

Many cities, states, provinces and countries have developed *conservation strategies* or *sustainable development strategies* as one means to apply the ideas in the

Brundtland Report to their situation. In this section, the basic approach taken by the province of Manitoba in Canada is outlined.

The Manitoba Round Table on Environment and Economy (1992) explained that sustainable development was a general philosophy, ethic and approach to guide individual and collective behaviour with regard to the environment and the economy. More specifically, Manitoba defined sustainable development as *environmentally sound and sustainable economic development*, characterized by a vision as well as certain beliefs, principles and guidelines. Manitoba stated that its beliefs included the following.

- The province could not continue to develop economically unless the environment was protected.
- Continued economic development was required to pay for important environmental initiatives.
- The needs of the present had to be met without sacrificing the ability of future generations to meet their needs.
- Attention had to be given to long-term consequences of both environmental and economic decisions.

In addition to the beliefs noted above, the province accepted that there were limits on the capacity of the Earth to sustain and assimilate human development and activity. Respecting the ecological limits of the Earth required effort in a number of directions, including:

- generating more from less through more efficient and effective resource use
- reducing, reusing, recycling and recovering products and by-products from production and consumption
- ensuring environmentally sound value-added processing and manufacturing in secondary and tertiary sectors
- improving productivity through political, technological, scientific, institutional and social innovation
- reclaiming and rehabilitating degraded environments
- increasing the productive capacity and quality of natural resources
- conserving, and developing substitutes for, scarce resources.

To translate the vision and beliefs into action, Manitoba identified ten principles and six guidelines regarding sustainable development (Table 2.2). The government recognized that every principle and guideline might not apply to each initiative or activity. Nevertheless, it concluded that "sustainable

---

Box 2.4 Manitoba's vision for sustainable development

Our vision is one of a sound environment and sustainable economic growth. The environment will be clean, safe and healthy. Our economy will be sustainable and one in which quality growth is the norm. It will provide us with the ongoing wealth and ability to provide the goods and services for both present and future generations of Manitobans in an environmentally sound manner.

Source: Manitoba, 1992: 3.

Table 2.2   Principles and guidelines for sustainable development (Manitoba, 1992: 5)

Principles

1. **Integration of environmental and economic decisions:** requires that we ensure economic decisions adequately reflect environmental impacts including human health. Environmental initiatives shall adequately take into account economic consequences.

2. **Stewardship:** requires that we manage the environment and economy for the benefits of present and future generations. Stewardship requires the recognition that we are caretakers of the environment and economy for the benefit of present and future generations of Manitobans. A balance must be struck between today's decisions and tomorrow's impacts.

3. **Shared responsibility:** requires that all Manitobans acknowledge responsibility for sustaining the environment and economy, with each being accountable for decisions and actions, in a spirit of partnership and open cooperation.

4. **Prevention:** requires that we anticipate, prevent or mitigate significant adverse environmental (including human health) and economic impacts of policy, programs and decisions.

5. **Conservation:** requires that we maintain essential ecological processes, biological diversity and life-support systems of our environment; harvest reusable resources on a sustained yield basis; and make wise and efficient use of our renewable and non-renewable resources.

6. **Recycling:** requires that we endeavour to reduce, reuse, and recover the products of our society.

7. **Enhancement:** requires that we enhance the long-term productive capability, quality and capacity of our natural ecosystems.

8. **Rehabilitation and reclamation:** requires that we endeavour to restore damaged or degraded environments to beneficial uses. Rehabilitation and reclamation require ameliorating damage caused in the past. Future policies, programs and developments should take into consideration the need for rehabilitation and reclamation.

9. **Scientific and technological innovation:** requires that we research, develop, test and implement technologies essential to further environmental quality including human health and economic growth.

10. **Global responsibility:** requires that we think globally when we act locally. Global responsibility requires that we recognize there are no boundaries to our environment, and that there is ecological interdependence among provinces and nations. There is a need to work cooperatively within Canada, and internationally to accelerate the merger of environment and economics in decision making and to develop comprehensive and equitable solutions to problems.

Guidelines

1. **Efficient use of resources.** We shall encourage and support development and application of systems for proper resource pricing, demand management, and resource allocation together with incentives and disincentives to encourage efficient use of resources and full environmental costing of decisions and developments.

2. **Public participation.** We shall establish appropriate forums which encourage and provide opportunity for consultation and meaningful participation in decision making processes by all Manitobans. We shall endeavour to ensure due process, prior notification and appropriate and timely redress for those affected by policies, programs, decisions and developments.

Table 2.2   Continued

3.   **Understanding and respect.** We shall be aware that we share a common physical, social and economic environment in Manitoba. Understanding and respect for differing social and economic views, values, traditions and aspirations is necessary for equitable management of these common resources. Consideration must be given to the aspirations, needs and views of various regions and groups in Manitoba.

4.   **Access to adequate information.** We shall encourage and support the improvement and refinement of our environmental and economic information base and promotion of the opportunity for equal and timely access to information by all Manitobans.

5.   **Integrated decision making and planning.** We shall encourage and support decision making and planning processes that are open, cross-sectoral, incorporate time horizons relevant to long-term implications and are efficient and timely.

6.   **Substitution.** We shall encourage and promote the development and use of substitutes for scarce resources where they are both environmentally sound and economically viable.

development will not be achieved if they are disregarded" (Manitoba, 1992: 4). Having identified a vision, beliefs, principles and guidelines, the task for Manitoba became to prepare strategies for all major areas of human activity which impacted upon the environment and the economy. As a further illustration, Table 2.3 provides the sustainability principles for water management developed by the Canadian Water Resources Association. Could you develop a comparable set of principles for a major area of human activity, such as agriculture, forestry, energy, transportation or human settlement, in your country, state or municipality?

2.3.2 Sustainable development in developing countries

The Republic of Indonesia is the fourth largest country in the world in terms of population, and consists of more than 13,000 islands. Java, one of 27 provinces of Indonesia but only 5,600 square kilometres in area, is one of the best-known places in the country (Figure 2.1). Its image, enhanced by the movie *South Pacific*, is well established. Before examining some of the realities of the island, we remind ourselves of some of that popular image as captured by Bater (1995) in Box 2.5. The photographs in Figures 2.2, 2.3 and 2.4 highlight some of that image.

However, Bali faces many challenges as it tries to encourage vigorous economic development while respecting the integrity of the culture of its people and its physical landscape. The traditional economic base of Bali has been agriculture, reflected by 70% of its people living in rural areas and being farmers. However, since the early 1970s, international tourism has become a rapidly growing sector of the economy, a trend encouraged by the Indonesian central government as it strives to reduce the dependence of the national economy on petroleum-based exports. Promotion of tourism in Bali helps diversify the Indonesian national economy, but it could make the Balinese provincial economy too dependent on tourism. Possible negative impacts of that could be vulnerability of Bali to the decisions of tourists as to their choice of holiday destinations, to growing unwillingness of Balinese to continue working in the agricultural sector given the attraction of jobs in the tourism service sector, the competition for scarce water supplies between irrigation-based agriculture and five-star hotels, and the impact of foreign values and behaviour on Balinese culture. Thus, in seeking the "benefits" of modernization while maintaining the richness of traditional ways, the Balinese people need to reach decisions about appropriate trade-offs among economic, social and environmental goals. In brief, their choices will have to address many aspects associated with sustainable development.

The Balinese government uses five-year plans to guide development. In 1989, a collaborative initiative, called the Bali Sustainable Development Project (BSDP), was started. The BSDP involved joint work by people from

Table 2.3   CWRA sustainability principles for water management in Canada (Mitchell and Shrubsole, 1994: 5)

Sustainability ethic

Wise management of water resources must be achieved by genuine commitment to:

- ecological integrity and biological diversity to ensure a healthy environment;
- a dynamic economy;
- social equity for present and future generations.

Water management principles

Accepting this sustainability ethic, the CWRA will:

1. Practice integrated resource management by:
   - linking water quality, quantity and the management of other resources;
   - recognizing hydrological, ecological, social and institutional systems;
   - recognizing the importance of watershed and aquifer boundaries.

2. Encourage water conservation and the protection of water quality by:
   - recognizing the value and limits of water resources, and the cost of providing it in adequate quantity and quality;
   - acknowledging its consumptive and non-consumptive values to both humans and other species;
   - balancing education, market forces and regulatory systems to promote choice and recognition of the responsibility of beneficiaries to pay for the use of the resource.

3. Resolve water management issues by:
   - employing planning, monitoring and research;
   - providing multi-disciplinary information for decision making;
   - encouraging active consultation and participation among all members of the public;
   - using negotiation and mediation to seek consensus;
   - ensuring accountability through open communication, education and public access to information.

universities in Bali, Java and Canada, along with the provincial and central government in Indonesia, as well as some NGOs, to develop a sustainable development strategy which could be incorporated into the five-year plan for 1994 to 1999. This work was done at the invitation of the Balinese government, and with financial sponsorship of the Canadian International Development Agency.

Through a series of workshops, the BSDP decided that sustainable development had to be defined in a way which made sense relative to Balinese circumstances. The outcome was that sustainable development was defined to include:

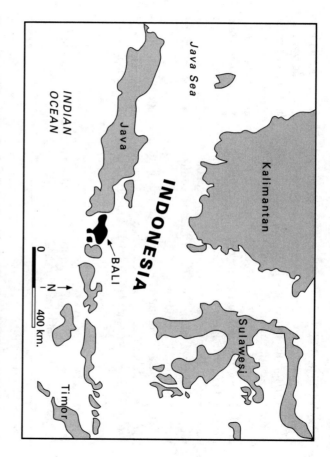

Figure 2.1 Bali, Indonesia (Martopo and Mitchell, 1995a: 4)

Box 2.5 Popular image of Bali

Bali. The name itself summons up a host of images. A tropical island – lush vegetation spilling down volcanic mountain sides, sand beaches, coral reefs and surf. A landscape sculpted by skilled hands over the centuries into a visually stunning hydraulic system of contoured terraced rice fields of every shape and size and all imaginable shades of green. Village tranquility, urban congestion. Friendly people, smiling faces, laughter. A crowded island where Hindu ceremony is articulated daily in ways which reflect a palpable, enduring culture. Paradise.

Source: Bater, 1995: 3.

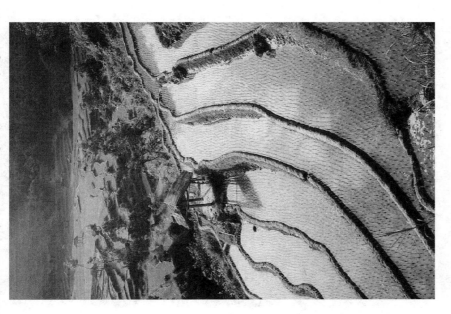

Figure 2.2 Bali: hydraulic landscape (Mitchell). The terraced rice or sawah fields in Bali not only allow intensive agricultural production, but also provide a strikingly attractive landscape.

- not only the continuity of natural resources (basic life supports), but also the continuity of cultural resources (from values and legends, to ceremonies and structures), and

- not only the continuity of production, but also the continuity of culture itself. However, continuity of culture does not preclude the possibility that aspects of culture might change over time since culture is dynamic rather than static.

It was also decided that sustainable development for Bali had to focus not only on the balance between the demand for and supply of resources, but also on the culturally based balances within the heritage of Bali. To simplify and streamline these ideas, the working definition for sustainable development focused on (1) the continuity of natural resources and production, (2) the continuity of culture and the balances within culture, and (3) development as a process to enhance quality of life (Martopo and Mitchell, 1995a: 20).

Figure 2.3 Bali: a vibrant culture (Mitchell). The impact of the Balinese culture is readily visible through offerings, temples and ceremonies. This is a small temple in the yard of a family. The offering of leaves, fruit and flowers is protected from sunlight by the umbrella. The black and white pattern on the cloth represents balance between the forces of good (white) and bad (black).

The BSDP used seven criteria to determine whether initiatives or activities were consistent with sustainable development (Figure 2.5; Table 2.4). The definition of sustainable development, and the criteria used to judge whether it was being achieved, anticipated many of the key principles contained in the Rio Declaration from the Earth Summit held during June 1992 (Table 2.5). These criteria can be contrasted with those used in Manitoba (Table 2.2).

The Bali sustainable development strategy was submitted to the provincial government in time for its recommendations to be considered during the development of the 1994 to 1999 five-year plan. Many of its recommendations were incorporated. In preparing the strategy, the project team was always conscious that much was still unknown and considerable uncertainty existed regarding the future. In that regard, the preparation of the sustainable

Figure 2.4 Bali: sun, sand and surf (Mitchell). Like many tropical island destinations, Bali offers sun, sand and surf for visitors. A challenge for a sustainable development strategy is to achieve harmony between the expectations, values and needs of foreign visitors, and those of the Balinese people.

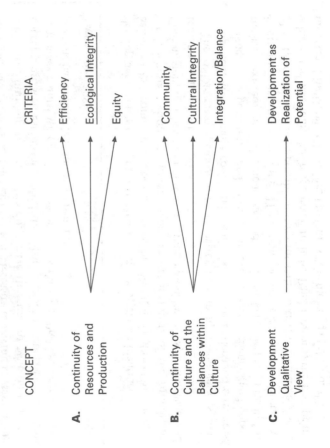

Figure 2.5 Sustainable development concepts and criteria for Bali (Martopo and Mitchell, 1995a: 20)

Table 2.4 Sustainable development criteria for Bali (Martopo and Mitchell, 1995a: 21)

1. **Ecological integrity:** to maintain life support systems, to preserve genetic diversity and to ensure the sustainable use of species and ecosystems.

2. **Efficiency:** to evaluate alternative paths or methods of development in terms of costs (money, time, personnel and public convenience).

3. **Equity:** to strive for equality of opportunity and recognition of needs amongst individuals and households, social groups, genders, generations and species.

4. **Cultural integrity:** to foster the preservation and renewal of life-enhancing/celebrating traditions of the Balinese culture as expressed in religion, art and institutions.

5. **Community:** to enhance local capabilities in participating in the development process and thus play a part in attaining other criteria, such as meeting basic needs, equity, ecological and cultural integrity.

6. **Integration/balance/harmony:** to achieve greater integration between certain key factors, such as economy and environment, and agriculture and tourism.

7. **Development as a realization of potential:** to enhance the capabilities at all levels; from the village, to the province, to the national, to address needs and improve the quality of life.

Box 2.6 An Indonesian perspective on sustainable development

As a developing country, Indonesia faces the necessity of having to start sailing while still building the ship. We don't have the time to wait until all the concepts are well established; until the theories are completed. The problems cannot wait until we can think the problems through. Problems come so fast that one has to find their solutions instantly.

Source: Salim, 1988: v.

---

development strategy had many similarities to the situation identified by Emil Salim's (1988) comments in Box 2.6, when he was Minister of the Environment for Indonesia. Salim also served as one of the members of the Brundtland Commission, and has been very active internationally in exploring ways and means to achieve sustainability.

The BSDP team decided that no matter how many investigations were completed, always more could and should be done to understand strengths, weaknesses, opportunities and threats. However, major challenges and opportunities existed, and decisions needed to be taken, despite incomplete information and understanding. The conclusion was that it was important to identify some alternative possible futures for Bali, so that it would be able to achieve and maintain the image given to it by Pandit Nehru, the first prime minister of India, when he referred to Bali as "the morning of the world".

Table 2.5   Selected sustainable development principles from the Rio Declaration (UNCED, 1992)

Principle 1: Human beings are at the centre of concerns for sustainable development. They are entitled to a healthy and productive life in harmony with nature.

Principle 2: States have, in accordance with the Charter of the United Nations and the principles of international law, the sovereign right to exploit their own resources pursuant to their own environmental and development policies. . . .

Principle 3: The right to development must be fulfilled so as to equitably meet development and environmental needs of present and future generations.

Principle 4: In order to achieve sustainable development, environmental protection shall constitute an integral part of the development process and cannot be considered in isolation from it.

Principle 5: All States and all people shall cooperate in the essential task of eradicating poverty as an indispensable requirement for sustainable development. . . .

Principle 8: To achieve sustainable development and a higher quality of life for all people, States should reduce and eliminate unsustainable patterns of production and consumption and promote appropriate demographic policies.

Principle 9: States should cooperate to strengthen endogenous capacity-building for sustainable development by improving scientific understanding through exchanges of scientific and technological knowledge, and by enhancing the development, adaptation, diffusion and transfer of technologies, including new and innovative technologies.

Principle 10: Environmental issues are best handled with the participation of all concerned citizens, at the relevant level. At the national level, each individual shall have appropriate access to information concerning the environment that is held by public authorities, including information on hazardous materials and activities in their communities, and the opportunity to participate in decision-making processes. States shall facilitate and encourage public awareness and participation by making information widely available.

Principle 15: In order to protect the environment, the precautionary approach shall be widely applied by States according to their capabilities. Where there are threats of serious or irreversible damage, lack of scientific certainty shall not be used as a reason for postponing cost-effective measures to prevent environmental degradation.

Principle 17: Environmental impact assessment, as a national instrument, shall be undertaken for proposed activities that are likely to have a significant adverse impact on the environment and are subject to a decision of a competent national authority.

Principle 20: Women have a vital role in environmental management and development. Their full participation is therefore essential to achieve sustainable development.

Principle 22: Indigenous people and their communities, and other local communities, have a vital role in environmental management and development because of their knowledge and traditional practices. States should recognize and duly support their identity, culture and interests and enable their effective participation in the achievement of sustainable development.

Source: The United Nations Conference on Environment and Development (1992) *The Rio Declaration on Environment and Development,* UNCED Secretariat, Geneva, Switzerland

2.4 Progress and implications

At the beginning of the chapter, the dilemmas of Alice in Wonderland and Columbus were noted. Alice did not know where she wanted to go; Columbus knew where he wanted to go, but not how to get there. It was suggested that resource and environmental managers need to know where they want to get to and what route to use to get there. However, even knowing both of those things can still lead to problems, as illustrated by Herman Melville's story in *Moby Dick*. Captain Ahab took his crew on the *Pequod* for a well-defined mission (catch and kill the white whale Moby Dick) and knew how he intended to do that. Notwithstanding clear ends and means, the outcome was a disaster for Ahab and the crew – Moby Dick got away, and Ahab and his crew, with the exception of Ishmael, drowned. Captain Ahab's experience is a reminder that a well-defined but poorly conceived objective pursued with tried and tested methods still can be shipwrecked.

Thus, while sustainable development does provide a vision for the future, there is not always a clear path to achieve it. Furthermore, even if the ends and means are identified, other events and decisions can create obstacles to its realization. For example, for several years the Indonesian government promoted 1991 as "Visit Indonesia Year" as a way to promote tourism, which would have created significant economic opportunities in Bali. However, the Gulf War in the winter of 1991 dramatically interrupted international travel patterns, especially by tourists in North America and Europe to Muslim countries. When I was working in Bali during March 1991, the occupancy rates in hotels had fallen dramatically from previous years and the beaches and other tourist sites were noticeably lacking in visitors, and this was in the year for which there had been heavy promotion. Thus, decisions taken on the other side of the world, and involving people and governments in numerous countries, had a direct impact on the province of Bali. This experience highlights the uncertainties and complexities that are encountered in trying to anticipate or effect change.

References and further reading

Bali Sustainable Development Project 1992 *Sustainable development strategy for Bali*. University Consortium on the Environment Research Paper #40, Yogyakarta, Java, Gadjah Mada University, and Waterloo, Ontario, in association with Udayana University, Bali

Barbier E B 1987 The concept of sustainable development. *Environmental Conservation* 14(2): 101–10

Bartelmus P 1994 *Environment, growth and development: the concepts and strategies of sustainability*. London, Routledge

Bater, J H 1995 Bali: place and people. In S Martopo and B Mitchell (eds) *Bali: balancing environment, economy and culture*. Department of Geography Publication Series No. 44, Waterloo, Ontario, University of Waterloo: 3–18

Bowen W M, M J Salling, K E Haynes and E J Cryan 1995 Toward environmental justice: spatial equity in Ohio and Cleveland. *Annals of the Association of American Geographers* 85(4): 641–63

Boyce J 1995 Equity and the environment: social justice today as a prerequisite for sustainability in the future. *Alternatives* 21(1): 12–24

Briggs J, G Dickinson, K Murphy, I Pulford, A E Belal, S Moalla, I Springuel, S J Ghabbour and A-M Mekki 1993 Sustainable development and resource management in marginal environments: natural resources and their use in the Wadi Allaqui region of Egypt. *Applied Geography* 13(3): 259–84

Cukier J and G Wall 1994 Informal tourism employment: vendors in Bali, Indonesia. *Tourism Management* 15(6): 464–7

Cutter S L 1995 Race, class and environmental justice. *Progress in Human Geography* 19(1): 111–22

Daly H E and J B Cobb (eds) 1989 *For the common good*. Boston, Beacon Press

Dias A K and M Begg 1994 Environmental policy for sustainable development of natural resources. Mechanisms for implementation and enforcement. *Natural Resources Forum* 18(4): 275–86

Dovers S R 1993 Contradictions in sustainability. *Environmental Conservation* 20(3): 217–22

Dovers S R and J W Handmer 1992 Uncertainty, sustainability and change. *Global Environmental Change* 2(4): 262–76

Ellery W N and T S McCarthy 1994 Principles for the sustainable utilization of the Okavango Delta ecosystem. *Biological Conservation* 70(2): 159–68

Francis G 1995 PI's perspective on sustainability. *Eco-Nexus* Eco-Research Project Newsletter, Waterloo, Ontario, University of Waterloo: 4

Franks T 1994 Managing sustainable development: Abdul Karim's dilemma. *Project Appraisal* 9(3): 205–10

Furuseth O and C Cocklin 1995a An institutional framework for sustainable resource management: the New Zealand model. *Natural Resources Journal* 35(2): 243–73

Furuseth O and C Cocklin 1995b Regional perspectives on resource policy: implementing sustainable development in New Zealand. *Journal of Environmental Planning and Management* 38(2): 181–200

Gagnon C 1992 Développement viable, politique québécoise, et industrie de l'aluminum. *Revue Canadienne des Sciences Régionales* 14(2): 233–56

Gertler L 1993 One country, two concepts: variations on sustainability. *Canadian Journal of Development Studies* special issue, 103–22

Goodland J A, H E Daly and S El Sarafy 1993 The urgent need for rapid transition to global environmental stability. *Environmental Conservation* 20(4): 297–309

Gow D D 1992 Poverty and natural resources: principles for environmental management and sustainable development. *Environmental Impact Assesment Review* 12(1/2): 49–65

Grubb M, M Koch, A Munson, F Sullivan and R Thomson 1993 *The Earth Summit agreements: a guide and assessment*. London, Earthscan

Grumbine R E 1994 Wildness, wise use and sustainable development. *Environmental Ethics* 16(3): 227–49

International Union for the Conservation of Nature, United Nations Environment Programme and World Wildlife Fund 1980 *World conservation strategy: living resource conservation for sustainable development*. Gland, Switzerland, IUCN

International Union for the Conservation of Nature, United Nations Environment Programme and World Wildlife Fund 1991 *Caring for the earth: a strategy for sustainable living*. Gland, Switzerland, IUCN, UNEP and WWF

Jones T 1996 Local authorities and sustainable development: turning policies into practical action through performance review – a case study of the London Borough of Hackney. *Local Environment* 1(1): 87–106

Karshenas M 1994 Environment, technology and employment: towards a new definition of sustainable development. *Development and Change* 25(4): 723–56

Kayastha S L 1993 Environment, development and quality of life. *Annals of the National*

Association of Geographers, India 13(2): 54–75

Kessler J J 1994 Usefulness of the human carrying capacity concept in assessing ecological sustainability of land-use in semi-arid regions. *Agriculture, Ecosystems and Environment* 48(3): 273–84

Kleinman P J A, D Pimentel and R B Bryant 1995 The ecological sustainability of slash-and-burn agriculture. *Agriculture, Ecosystems and Environment* 52(2–3): 235–49

Manitoba Round Table on Environment and Economy 1992 *Sustainable development: towards institutional change in the Manitoba public sector*. Winnipeg, Sustainable Development Coordination Unit

Manning E W 1990 Conservation strategies: providing the vision for sustainable development. *Alternatives* 16(4): 24–9

Maropo S and B Mitchell (eds) 1995a *Bali: balancing environment, economy and culture*. Department of Geography Publication Series No. 44, Waterloo, Ontario, University of Waterloo

Maropo S and B Mitchell 1995b The capacity for village sustainability in Bali. *Manusia dan Lingkungan* 2(5): 14–33

Mitchell B 1993 Sustainable development, uncertainty and the precautionary principle. *Indian Geographical Journal* 68(1): 1–5

Mitchell B 1994a Sustainable development at the village level in Bali, Indonesia. *Human Ecology* 22(2): 189–211

Mitchell B 1994b Institutional obstacles to sustainable development in Bali, Indonesia. *Singapore Journal of Tropical Geography* 15(2): 145–56

Mitchell B and D Shrubsole 1994 *Canadian water management: visions for sustainability*. Cambridge, Ontario, Canadian Water Resources Association

Nagpal T 1995 Voices from the developing world: progress toward sustainable development. *Environment* 37(8): 10–15, 30–5

Overton J 1993 Fiji: options for sustainable development. *Scottish Geographical Magazine* 109(3): 164–70

Pierce, J T 1992 Progress and the biosphere: the dialectics of sustainable development. *Canadian Geographer* 36(4): 306–20

Reed M G and O Slaymaker 1993 Ethics and sustainability: a preliminary perspective. *Environment and Planning A* 25(5): 723–39

Robertson W A 1993 New Zealand's new legislation for sustainable resource management: the Resource Management Act 1991. *Land Use Policy* 10(4): 303–11

Robinson J, G Francis, R Legge and S Lerner 1990 Defining a sustainable society: values, principles and definitions. *Alternatives* 17(2): 36–46

Salim E 1988 Foreword. In M Soerjani (ed.) *Enhancing the role of Environmental Study Centres for sustainable development*. Development of Environmental Studies Project, Jakarta, UNDP/World Bank/Government of Indonesia: v

Salim E 1991 Towards a sustainable future. *Development* 2: 61–3

Saskatchewan Round Table on Environment and Economy 1992 *Conservation strategy for sustainable development in Saskatchewan*. Regina, Saskatchewan Round Table on Environment and Economy

Serageldin I 1995 '*towards sustainable management of water resources*. Washington, DC, The World Bank

Tobin R J and A T White 1993 Coastal resources management and sustainable development: a Southeast Asian perspective. *International Environmental Affairs* 5(1): 50–65

United Nations Conference on Environment and Development 1992 *The Rio Declaration on Environment and Development*. Geneva, Switzerland, UNCED Secretariat

Voisey H, C Beuermann, L A Sverdrup and T O'Riordan 1996 The political significance of Local Agenda 21: the early stages of some European experience. *Local Environment* 1(1): 33–50

White R R 1992 The road to Rio or the global environmental crisis and the emergence of different agendas for rich and poor countries. *International Journal of Environmental Studies, A* 41(3/4): 187–201

Wood D M 1993 Sustainable development in the Third World: paradox or panacea? *Indian Geographical Journal* 68(1): 6–20

World Commission on Environment and Development 1987 *Our common future.* Oxford and New York, Oxford University Press

Young M D 1992 *Sustainable investment and resource use: equity, environmental integrity and economic efficiency.* Paris, UNESCO; and Carnforth, England and Park Ridge, NJ, Parthenon Publishing Group

Young M E 1993 *For our children's children: some practical implications of inter-generational equity and the precautionary principle.* Resource Assessment Commission Occasional Paper Number 6, Canberra, Australian Government Printing Service

Chapter 3

Ecosystem Approach

3.1 Introduction

In Chapter 2, attention focused on the concept of *sustainable development*, which is often held up as a vision or an end for resource and environmental management. The *ecosystem approach* can be viewed as one means to achieve sustainable development, and it is in that context that the ecosystem approach is considered in this chapter. The distinction between ends and means is important, as too often in resource and environmental management the ecosystem approach is treated as an end in itself, rather than as a means to an end. In the next section, various views regarding the ecosystem approach are considered. That will be followed by examination of comprehensive and integrated interpretations of the ecosystem approach, agroecosystem analysis, and some applications of the concept.

3.2 Nature of the ecosystem approach

As the comments in Boxes 3.1 and 3.2 highlight, there are many challenges to developing and implementing an ecosystem approach. The very complexity that the ecosystem attempts to capture can be overwhelming, and can leave the manager unsatisfied because answers are not forthcoming, or are provided after

Box 3.1 Complexity and ecosystems

Ecological systems have those features that now seem to frustrate both understanding and action in so many areas of man's [*sic*] interest. There is a bewildering, if fascinating diversity of species, interacting with physical and chemical variables. Even the most depauperate of forests has thousands of species of organisms. The variables are connected in a web of interrelations that are fundamentally nonlinear. Thresholds and limits, lags and discontinuities are all inherent to ecological reality. The organizational structure among the variables can seem indeterminate. The plankton community of a lake, for example, can be dominated by interrelations between one set of species in one year and a different set in another. And finally, ecosystems are open ones through which energy flows and within which material cycles.

Source: Holling, 1987: 139–40.

Box 3.2 Paradox and challenge

As environmental degradation and change continues, decision makers and managers feel significant pressure to rectify the situation. Scientists, in turn, find themselves under pressure to set out simple and clear rules for proper ecosystem management.

However, systems theory suggests that ecosystems are inherently complex, that there may be no simple answers, and that our traditional managerial approaches, which presume a world of simple rules, are wrong-headed and likely to be dangerous. In order for the scientific method to work, an artificial situation of consistent reproducibility must be created. This requires simplification of the situation to the point where it is controllable and predictable. But the very nature of this act removes the complexity that leads to emergence of the new phenomena which make complex systems interesting. If we are going to deal successfully with our biosphere, we are going to have to change how we do science and management. We will have to learn that we don't manage ecosystems, we manage our interaction with them. Furthermore, the search for simple rules of ecosystem behaviour is futile.

Take for example the diversity–stability hypothesis. This is a classic example of the kind of simple rule people are looking for.... [However,] ecosystems are dynamic and constantly changing. Stability gives way to the notion of a shifting steady mosaic. Thus, the diversity–stability hypothesis evaporates because the basic concepts of diversity and stability are just too simple to describe the complex reality of ecological phenomena.

Source: Kay and Schneider, 1994: 33–4.

too long a period of time. Advocates of an ecosystem approach need to be sensitive to the needs of managers, otherwise a concept which might be conceptually sound may not be accepted or used because it does not meet their practical needs. It is not enough to be convinced about the conceptual value of an ecosystem approach. We must also consider how it can be applied to solve real-world problems in a timely manner.

In this section, attention focuses upon the nature of an ecosystem approach, and on some of the ideas or guidelines associated with it. For those wanting to read in greater detail about ecology and the ecosystem approach, the following references should be helpful: Bocking (1994), McIntosh (1976), Norton and Walker (1982) and Walker and Norton (1982).

Bocking (1994: 12) has concluded that in the 1990s "generally, the [ecosystem] concept signifies the study of living species and their physical environment as an integrated whole. In environmental management, its significance is understood to lie in a comprehensive, holistic, integrated approach." This definition or interpretation captures the essence of what many people associate with an ecosystem approach – the concept of a system, as well as its component parts and the linkages between those parts. However, critics worry that if everything is connected to everything else, then the ecosystem approach can expand the scope of any problem to unmanageable proportions, and thus lead to analyses and planning processes becoming impractical.

Bocking's interpretation omits one feature, however, also usually associated with the ecosystem approach. This feature is that humans are part of, not separate from, the ecosystem. One implication is that analysts and planners should not be unduly *anthropocentric* (human-centred), but during management should include the needs of non-human species with which we share the planet.

3.2.1 Obstacles in developing ecological principles to use in an ecosystem approach

One of the challenges for ecologists and the ecosystem approach is to provide "sound principles" to guide resource and environmental management. However, Norton and Walker (1982) concluded that there are few unambiguous and relevant principles. Several reasons account for this situation. First, many of the principles are more "normative" than "positive" (scientific). For example, the idea that we should strive to avoid foreclosure of options is a normative rather than a scientific concept. Norton and Walker concluded that mixing normative and scientific issues raises questions about the credibility of ecological principles. Normative questions have to be addressed, but ecological principles usually cannot be expected to provide answers to value-based questions.

Second, positive or scientific "principles" occur at two extremes. At one end, general statements have been produced which are informative but not readily applicable. An example would be the idea that diversity leads to stability, and therefore that diversity is a desirable condition (see comments in Box 3.2). At the other end, "principles" related to *carrying capacity* have been developed for specific situations such as range, park or lake management. Such principles are helpful for those specific conditions, but are usually not transferable to other situations, and certainly do not and cannot provide answers to questions about the best use of a particular landscape.

Third, Norton and Walker argued that tight laws applicable in all conditions are unlikely to exist in ecology. As they noted, too many "ifs", "buts" and other qualifications exist to allow for definitive principles. This conclusion reflects the

Box 3.3 Problems of prediction

The structure and dynamics of all ecosystems are to a greater or lesser extent the result of stochastic processes. Indeed, most exhibit sharp shifts which are often crucial to their structure. These stochastic effects preclude deterministic management or planning policies which assume the possibility of perfect prediction. This principle emphasizes the need for ecosystem management and planning to be flexible and to make due allowance for unexpected events.

Source: Walker and Norton, 1982: 332.

considerable complexity and uncertainty associated with ecosystems, and our limited understanding of them.

3.2.2 Major themes in ecosystem management

Notwithstanding the very real obstacles to developing ecological principles to serve as the basis for ecosystem management, attempts have been made to identify dominant themes relevant to ecosystem management. For example, Grumbine (1994: 29–30) suggested that there are ten dominant themes.

(1) Hierarchical context

It is not sufficient to focus upon any *one* level (genes, species, populations, ecosystems, landscapes) of the biodiversity hierarchy. Attention must be given to connections between all levels. Such an approach is often characterized as a *systems* perspective.

(2) Ecological boundaries

Resource and environmental management requires attention to biophysical or ecological rather than administrative or political units. For example, migratory birds do not respect political or administrative boundaries, and any management plan for them must be based on boundaries that relate to their needs and activities. A difficulty, of course, is that an appropriate ecoregion for migratory birds may not be appropriate for managing water, and many overlapping ecosystem units could soon be in use.

(3) Ecological integrity

Much attention has been devoted to ecological integrity, which is usually interpreted to mean protecting total natural diversity (species, populations, ecosystems) along with the patterns and processes which maintain that diversity. The emphasis has normally been upon conserving viable populations of native species, maintaining natural disturbance regimes, reintroducing native, extirpated species, and achieving representation of ecosystems across natural ranges of variation. However, as the comments in Box 3.4 illustrate, many problems must be dealt with when deciding which conditions represent "integrity".

(4) Data collection

To manage ecosystems there has to be research and data collection, particularly regarding functional (what if?) rather than descriptive (what is?) questions. Data are required regarding habitat inventory and classification, baseline species, disturbance regime dynamics, and population assessment.

Box 3.4 What represents integrity?

In essence, ecosystem management aims to restore forests to some biological condition that reflects fewer human impacts, but just *what* condition is a matter of arbitrary selection.

In Europe, ... the distinction between forests before and after human settlement is virtually impossible to make, and, as a result, determining desired forest condition is more difficult. Should forests there be returned to their pre-Celtic condition before about 15000 BC, to their pre-Roman condition, to their condition in the Middle Ages, or what? This question inevitably raises more fundamental questions – namely, whether less human impact is always preferable to more human impact, and, if so, why. These questions do not have scientific answers.

Source: Sedjo, 1995: 10, 19.

(5) Monitoring

Managers must record the results from their decisions and actions, so that successes and failures can be measured and documented. Useful information and insight are generated by systematic monitoring. This aspect is addressed in more detail in Chapters 7 and 13.

(6) Adaptive management

As considered in Chapter 7, an adaptive approach assumes incomplete understanding of ecosystems, and expects both turbulence and surprise. Emphasis is placed on treating management as a learning experience, and encourages approaching management as a series of experiments from which new knowledge leads to continuous adjustments and modifications. Monitoring is a key activity in adaptive management.

(7) Inter-agency cooperation

Whether biophysical or political boundaries are used, there will have to be sharing and cooperation among municipal, state, national and international agencies, as well as the private sector and non-government organizations. Planners and managers will have to improve their capacity to deal with conflicting legal mandates and management objectives. For example, within one government, an agricultural agency may emphasize removal of wetlands to improve crop production, while a natural resource agency may emphasize protection or restoration of wetlands to improve wildlife habitat.

(8) Organizational change

To implement an ecosystem approach there must often be alterations in the structures and processes used by resource and environmental management agencies. Such changes can be relatively simple (creation of an inter-agency coordinating group) to fundamental (reallocating power and changing basic values or principles). The key point is that most agencies are not oriented or structured to use an ecosystem approach. An example of such a change is provided in Subsection 3.5.1.

(9) Humans embedded in nature

As already noted earlier in this chapter, an ecosystem approach requires people to be considered as part of, rather than as separate from, natural systems. People cannot be separated from nature. The comments in Box 3.5, referring to the United States, illustrate challenges which must be overcome in some societies.

(10) Values

An ecosystem approach must recognize that both scientific and traditional knowledge, and human values, will be involved. Indeed, human values will have the dominant role in setting of goals for ecosystem management. Thus, ecosystem management is not just a scientific endeavour. It must also incorporate human values.

Give the above ten themes, Grumbine (1994: 31) developed the following definition of ecosystem management: "Ecosystem management integrates scientific knowledge of ecological relationships within a complex sociopolitical and values framework toward the general goal of protecting native ecosystem integrity over the long term." If this definition is modified to include traditional as well as scientific knowledge (discussed more fully in Chapter 9), then this interpretation of ecosystem management is one that provides a good focus.

Box 3.5 Conflicting ideas about the role of humans and nature

An ecosystem approach to land policy encounters resistance to the degree that it is inconsistent with the values, assumptions, institutions, and practices that shape the prevailing social arrangement which affects the custody and care of the land.... Thus, the factors involved in banking, taxation, insurance, and property law, when woven into a non-ecological matrix of public land policy, afford a very resistant, inadvertent barrier to an ecosystems approach.

To conceive an ecosystem approach to public land policy, one must have first arrived at an ecological viewpoint toward the world of man and nature. But this is not the viewpoint from which pioneers, land speculators, farmers, miners, stockmen, lawyers, bankers or local government officials have commonly seen the land.... An ecosystems approach ... would impose constraints upon single purpose approaches to the environment and would arouse hostility among individuals whose single purpose pursuits would therefore be constrained.

Source: Caldwell, 1970: 204–5.

3.3 Distinction between comprehensive and integrated approaches

The ecosystem approach encourages analysts and planners to consider the "big picture" by emphasizing entire systems, their component parts, and the relationships between those parts. Such a perspective is important, as it reminds us that many water problems (pollution, flooding) cannot be resolved by focusing only on water. Many sources of pollution are from land-based activities, and flood damage potential is strongly influenced by land uses. Conversely, many land-based problems (dropping agricultural production, loss of biodiversity) occur from too much or too little water. Thus, it is important that we take the "big picture" into consideration, and not become unduly focused on one element or component of an ecosystem. However, as already noted, a danger arises in knowing how widely to cast the net, how large an ecosystem to consider, and how many components and relationships to address. If the "big picture" becomes too big, the planners and analysts may become so entangled in the complexities of multiple components and linkages that they are unable to complete their analysis in a reasonable period of time.

An ecosystem approach is synonymous with a *holistic* perspective. However, such a perspective can be interpreted in either a *comprehensive* or an *integrated* manner. It is argued here that too often analysts and planners have advocated an ecosystem or holistic approach without having clearly thought through what that implies. By default, a holistic and a comprehensive approach have been considered the same, and this has led to some problems.

By definition, *comprehensive* means all inclusive. As a result, a comprehensive interpretation of a holistic approach indicates that whatever system is defined, the analyst or planner should examine all the components and all the relationships. Such an interpretation has several implications. First, it creates expectations that if we work diligently and study everything, it will be possible to understand the ecosystem, and therefore be able to control or manage it. Second, it also almost guarantees that a significant amount of time will be required to complete the analysis and a plan. As a result, there is a high probability that "the plan" will be a historical rather than a strategic document, because by the time all the work is completed events may have swept past the plan.

In contrast, an *integrated* approach retains most of the core ideas of being holistic, but is more focused and therefore more practical. The key distinction is that an integrated approach does not seek to analyse all components and linkages, but concentrates upon what are judged to be key components and linkages. Eventually, if enough components and linkages are examined, the integrated approach would expand to become the same as a comprehensive approach.

The integrated interpretation results in a more limited focus being taken for a number of reasons. First, it accepts that we are unlikely to be able to understand all of the variation in a system. If analysts or planners could account for and understand the components that cause 75–80% of the variability in a system, they would usually be very satisfied. Second, it is usually the case that a relatively small number of variables cause a large proportion of variation. As a result, understanding their role is usually sufficient for developing effective management strategies. All the extra effort and time needed to identify and understand the components that account for the remaining 20–25% of the variability are often out of all proportion to the benefits in achieving such understanding. Third, even if most of the variables could be identified and understood, many of them cannot be readily modified or changed by managers, so the "value added" from such insight is not high. And fourth, an integrated approach is likely to keep expectations for a plan more realistic, and also allow plans to be completed in a more reasonable time frame.

Thus, it is argued here that it is very important for analysts and planners to have a clearly thought-out interpretation of what they mean by an ecosystem approach before they become advocates of it. The conceptual value of taking a big picture perspective by considering a system, its parts and their connections is very high. However, operationally, if an ecosystem which is too large or complex is defined, the product from analysis and planning is likely to have little value. If analysts and planners cannot create useful products (strategies, plans) that help to resolve environmental and resource problems, then the credibility of the ecosystem approach will be damaged, to the extent that managers may be reluctant to use it. They may become concerned that an ecosystem approach represents a "black hole" into which management exercises may literally disappear, not to emerge until much too late to be helpful.

In Chapter 4, alternative schools or models of planning are reviewed. It is suggested here that the comprehensive approach to ecosystem management is similar to the *synoptic* or *comprehensive rational model*. What is likely to be more useful is to maintain a comprehensive perspective to scan for a broad range of issues and opportunities within an ecosystem, but then to use an integrated approach to achieve more focus for problem solving. In that manner, a blend of comprehensive and integrated approaches can be similar to the *mixed scanning model* described in Chapter 4. In the next section, an approach which has become known as *agroecosystem analysis* will be outlined, as in many ways it is a practical version of an integrated approach.

3.4 Agroecosystem analysis

Conway (1985, 1987) has developed the concept of agroecosystem analysis, which reflects many of the attributes of an integrated interpretation of an ecosystem approach. The purpose here is to outline the basic idea of agroecosystem analysis. Conway explained that agroecosystems are ecological systems which have been modified by human activity in order to produce food, fibre or other agricultural outputs. Like ecological systems, they are structurally and dynamically complex.

Conway's motivation for developing agroecosystem analysis was to improve our capacity to address problems which emerged from the application of new technologies in agriculture. In particular, he was interested in the environmental consequences of the agricultural revolution that had occurred in developing countries from the creation of new seeds, which, when used in combination with irrigation and agrochemicals, allowed dramatic increases in food production. However, short- and medium-term problems accompanied application of Green Revolution practices, including increasing incidence of pest, disease and weed problems, and deterioration of soil structure and fertility, along with increased indebtedness and inequity.

As the environmental and socio-economic problems from Green Revolution technology were recognized, each was addressed individually. However, as the comments in Box 3.6 highlight, in most cases the problems were interrelated. The concept of agroecosystem analysis was developed to provide a multi-disciplinary and holistic approach to addressing such problems.

Conway explained that the departure point for his approach was the notion of *system*, and the related idea of *system hierarchy*. Regarding hierarchies, he noted that the natural world, or farming systems, can be conceived as a nested hierarchy of systems (such as organism–population–community–ecosystem–biome–bio-sphere, for natural systems; or plant–crop–field–cropping system–farming system–household–village–region–nation–world, for an agroecosystem). To understand the behaviour of any level in the hierarchy, it is not sufficient to consider only the levels below it. Each level has to be studied in its own right, and with regard to its connections to other systems. This approach is a strong reminder that when we are studying an ecosystem or agroecosystem, we need to give attention to the idea of layers or hierarchies of systems.

Four properties of agroecosystems were identified by Conway, which are also relevant to understanding other ecosystems. Illustrated in Figure 3.1, these are as follows.

- **Productivity.** The output or yield of, or net income from, a valued product per unit of resource input. Productivity is often measured in terms of yield or income per hectare, or total production of goods and services per household or nation. It also can be measured as kilograms of grain, tubers, fish or meat, or it can be converted into calories, protein, vitamins or monetary units. The basic resource inputs are land, labour and capital.

- **Stability.** The constancy of productivity relative to small disturbing forces occurring from normal fluctuations and cycles in the surrounding environment.

Box 3.6 Interconnections between Green Revolution problems

… there has been a growing realisation that many, if not all, of the problems are essentially systematic in nature. They are linked to each other, and to the performance of the system as a whole. As a consequence problems that were initially viewed as side-effects often, it turns out, threaten directly the main objectives of development. Moreover, even where agricultural production is increased, this success may be short lived if attention is not quickly diverted to side-effects which threaten other equally important development goals.

Source: Conway, 1985: 32.

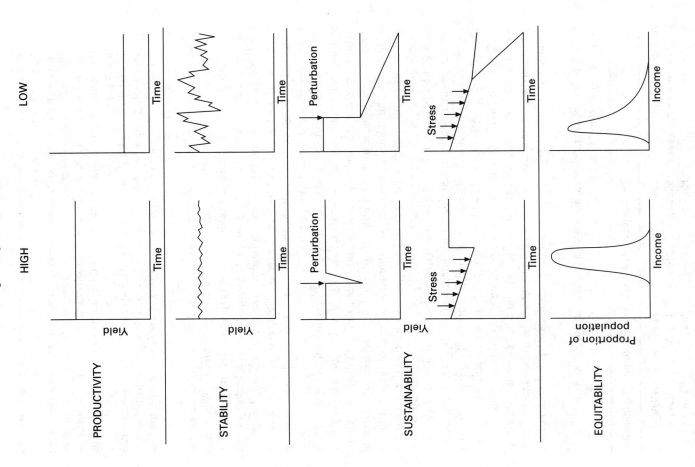

Figure 3.1 Four system properties of agroecosystems (Conway, 1985: 36)

Such fluctuations may be in climate or water available in rivers or aquifers, or in the market demand for crops.

- **Sustainability.** The capacity of an agroecosystem to maintain productivity when subjected to major disturbing forces. Such disturbing forces could range from regular but relatively modest disturbances, such as soil salinity or indebtedness, to less regular, unpredictable and much larger disturbances such as floods, droughts or new pests.

- **Equitability.** The (un)evenness of the distribution of the benefits among humans from productivity. Equitability is normally measured through the distribution of benefits and costs associated with the production of goods and services from an agroecosystem.

Conway explained that the four properties can be used either as *neutral descriptors* of the behaviour of a system, or as *performance indicators*. When used as indicators, they can highlight trade-offs that may occur. As an example, he indicated that a large-scale irrigation project might achieve higher overall productivity, but at the expense of equitability and sustainability. Efforts to achieve equitability could inhibit productivity. Thus, choices exist, and the thrust in management of ecosystems ultimately reflects choices between sometimes mutually exclusive properties.

To illustrate, Conway noted that traditional agricultural systems such as shifting cultivation (*swidden agriculture*) usually have low productivity and stability, but achieve high equitability and sustainability (Table 3.1). Traditional cropping systems score higher than swidden cultivation in terms of productivity and stability properties, yet retain a high level of sustainability as well as some equitability. When new technologies are introduced, productivity usually goes up, with other properties normally falling. The introduction of high-yield varieties of rice during the Green Revolution fits this pattern. Overall productivity increased, but yields fluctuated widely. One consequence was development of new seeds with combined properties of high productivity and stability, but they are still rated low with regard to sustainability.

This introduction to selected aspects of agroecosystem analysis illustrates several important considerations. First, what is judged to be *ecosystem integrity* is determined by the properties of an ecosystem judged to be important. Different weights can be given to productivity, stability, sustainability and equitability.

Table 3.1 Types of agricultural activity as a function of agroecosystem properties (Conway, 1985: 37)

	Productivity	Stability	Sustainability	Equitability
A. Swidden cultivation	Low	Low	High	High
B. Traditional cropping system	Medium	Medium	High	Medium
C. Improved	High	Low	Low	Low
D. Improved	High	High	Low	Medium
E. ?Ideal (best land)	High	Medium	High	High
F. ?Ideal (marginal land)	Medium	High	High	High

Box 3.7 Trade-offs between agroecosystem properties

The pursuit of high productivity in both the developed and less developed countries has brought with it declines in sustainability and equitability that increasingly are being regarded as undesirable. Our present priority is for policy research, practical analytical tools and development packages aimed at increasing agricultural sustainability and rectifying undesirable inequities.

Source: Conway, 1987: 111.

No mix is "right" or "correct". Choices are available, and normally would be made relative to needs and conditions for a place and a time. In that regard, this point confirms the argument of the Brundtland Commission, presented in Chapter 2, that there is no blueprint for sustainability. Custom-designed strategies must be developed. Second, the concept of *nested hierarchies* emphasizes that whatever ecosystem boundaries are chosen, there will always be other ecosystems whose properties and behaviour will be relevant to the one being examined. We must not lose sight of such connections, even though for pragmatic reasons we may choose not to examine them in the same detail as the linkages among components within the ecosystem being addressed. The examples presented in the following section show some of the opportunities, and problems, involved in transforming the ecosystem concept from idea to action.

3.5 Examples of ecosystem approaches

3.5.1 "Profound superficiality"

During the mid 1990s, the lead federal environmental agency (Environment Canada) in Canada was reoriented and restructured (Mitchell and Shrubsole, 1994). The purpose was to improve the capacity to achieve sustainable development through an ecosystem approach. One outcome was that the unit with federal responsibilities for water was eliminated. As part of an assessment of the reorientation and restructuring, Bruce and Mitchell (1995) concluded that this decision seemed to have created a paradox.

The paradox involved the following elements. On one hand, many people believed that water was a significant management concern for the country, and would become even more significant during the twenty-first century both in Canada and throughout the world. This view appeared to be confirmed by discussions at the Earth Summit during 1992 in Rio de Janeiro. So, at a time when more international recognition was being given to water, the paradox was why the federal government appeared to be withdrawing or moving out of water management. With no specific federal agency responsible for water, there was concern that it would be difficult to know who to contact in the federal government about a water problem.

The disappearance of the water agency reflected an attempt to implement an ecosystem approach and integrated resource management by Environment

Canada. The dismantling of the water agency was a conscious and deliberate attempt to break down what was viewed as an over-sectoral approach. Instead of having people concentrated in a water agency, the intent was to relocate water specialists into a variety of Environment Canada divisions and branches, to ensure that the connection of water to other environmental components was made. In this manner, the decision could be viewed as responding to the challenge issued by the Brundtland Commission's *Our Common Future*. The Commission had concluded that too many national and international organizations had been created on the basis of "narrow preoccupations and compartmentalized concerns". It challenged countries to move towards a more integrated approach to environmental and development problems. The Commission had argued that the real world of interconnected economic and ecological systems was unlikely to change, and therefore the policies and institutions would have to. In its words, such a modification was "one of the chief institutional challenges of the 1990s and beyond" (World Commission on Environment and Development, 1987: 10).

The downside of this initiative was that in-depth capacity regarding any component of the ecosystem, such as water, could be weakened significantly by dispersing people with expertise throughout an organization. If an integrated approach is to occur, there must be substantive knowledge and understanding to integrate. A major concern was that, regarding water, this substantive capability might not be maintained. It was this situation that led one commentator to conclude that what was occurring "smacks of profound superficiality". The restructuring was "profound" in that it recognized the need to create the capability to use an ecosystem approach in which the entire environmental system would be addressed. However, it had the danger of being "superficial" in that lack of attention to some of the basic components of the environment, such as water, could lead to poor science and analysis.

Two implications can be identified with this experience. First, every country and organization has the challenge in finding an appropriate balance between breadth (ecosystem approach) and depth (sectoral approach). Each offers advantages and disadvantages, and the task is to try to incorporate as many of the strengths from each approach as possible, while minimizing the disadvantages. Second, a distinction should be made between conceptual and operational decisions. In this example, while eliminating the water resources agency made conceptual sense, it created operational problems since a farmer or industrialist with a water problem would find it much easier to find a water agency than to find one that might be labelled as an "aquatic systems branch". Thus, while conceptually we need to strive to build an ecosystem approach more explicitly into planning and management, it may be that organizational structures should be maintained along sectoral lines, as those are the ones most easily recognized by the public.

3.5.2 The Baltic Sea ecosystem

The previous example from Canada illustrated some of the problems that can be encountered when applying the ecosystem approach. The problems increase when the ecosystem spans a number of countries, as is the case in the Baltic Sea, which is the largest brackish body of water in the world. As recently as 1950, the Baltic Sea was judged to be environmentally "healthy". However, by the 1980s it had severe water pollution and environmental degradation problems (Kindler and Lintner, 1993).

The catchment area for the Baltic Sea includes 14 countries and 80 million people (Figure 3.2). Nine countries share the coastline of the Baltic Sea: Sweden, Finland, Russia, Estonia, Latvia, Lithuania, Poland, Germany and Denmark. Portions of five other countries (Belarus, Norway, Ukraine, Slovak Republic, Czech Republic) are included in the catchment area because the headwaters of rivers which drain into the Baltic begin there. The Baltic Sea is significant for several reasons. The coastline has been a traditionally popular recreational area, leading to establishment of facilities catering to tourists. The coastal areas also provide spawning, nursery and feeding grounds for both freshwater and marine fish, and fishing is an important economic activity in the region.

With a total surface area of only 415,000 square kilometres, the Baltic Sea is vulnerable to pollution because of its confined nature and specific hydro-graphy. The Baltic Sea is connected to the North Sea by several narrow channels between Sweden and Denmark. The shallowest depth in these channels is only 18 metres. A consequence is that the Baltic Sea is primarily dominated by inputs of freshwater, and is not "flushed" by tides coming from the North Sea. Furthermore, the loss of wetlands in the nineteenth century to accommodate expansion of agriculture production, and more recently to support urban and industrial development, reduced the natural buffering capacity of the system. Pollution inputs come from various sources. Non-point sources include airborne emissions and agricultural runoff. Point sources include sewage treatment plants in cities, including untreated sewage from 30 million people, and industrial factories, especially pulp and paper mills. The importance of addressing the environmental degradation problems is highlighted by the fact that the principal sources of pollution – municipalities, industries, agriculture – are located not only on the coastline but also in the headwaters of the rivers draining into the Baltic Sea. As a result, resolving the water pollution and degradation problems will not be successful if attention focuses only on the sea itself. The entire ecosystem needs to be considered.

The role of agriculture as a source of water pollution illustrates the need to consider land-based activities. Significant agricultural areas are found in Russia, Estonia, Latvia, Lithuania and Poland, with Poland itself accounting for about 40% of the total arable land in the catchment. Agriculture is also important, and intensive, in Denmark and southern Sweden, with fertilizers being heavily used. For example, farming activity in the Danish portion of the Belt Sea catchment, a subsystem of the Baltic Sea, covers only some 12,400 square kilometres but discharges about 30,000 tons of nitrogen into the sea annually. In contrast, farming in the much larger Vistula River catchment, which covers 166,000 square kilometres and includes two-thirds of Poland and small parts of Belarus, the Slovak Republic and the Ukraine, annually discharges about 50,000 tons. The main discharges are nitrogen and

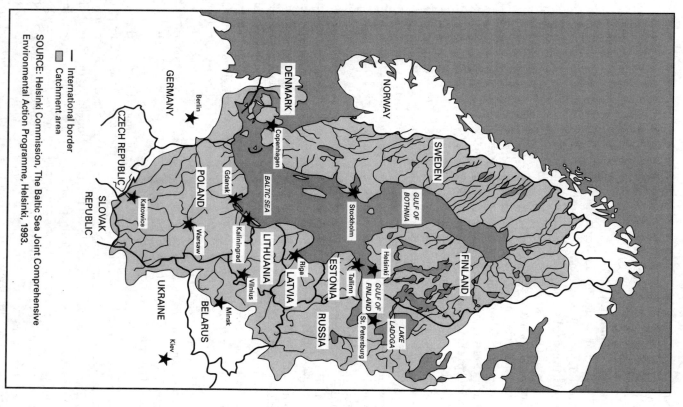

Figure 3.2 The Baltic Sea ecosystem (Kindler and Lintner, 1993: 9)

SOURCE: Helsinki Commission, The Baltic Sea Joint Comprehensive Environmental Action Programme, Helsinki, 1993.

— International border
▨ Catchment area

phosphorus from agrochemicals, and these contribute to the eutrophication of the Baltic Sea.

With 14 countries sharing the Baltic Sea ecoregion, unilateral action by any one country is unlikely to make a significant impact. The Baltic countries had recognized the problem for several decades, and in 1974 signed the Baltic Marine Environmental Protection Convention, known more popularly as the Helsinki Convention. The countries informally began to implement its provisions, and then in May 1980 its provisions formally went into effect. The Helsinki Commission (HELCOM) was established as the coordinating organization for the convention. However, until the end of the Cold War, efforts were concentrated on the open sea, with the coastal zone and inland areas being neglected.

As a result of changing political conditions, a meeting was held in Ronneby, Sweden, in September 1990. The outcome was the first Baltic Sea Declaration. The Declaration stated that the countries agreed to begin specific initiatives to achieve ecological restoration of the Baltic Sea, and to create the possibility of self-restoration of the marine environment as well as preservation of its ecological balance. The necessary activities are occurring through the Baltic Sea Joint Comprehensive Environmental Action Programme, a joint initiative of the Baltic Sea nations, inland countries contained within the Baltic Sea catchment, the Commission of the European Communities, and four international financial organizations. The Programme was formally approved in April 1992 in Helsinki by the Ministers of the Environment from the involved countries.

The strategy

Given experience in Canada, reported in Subsection 3.5.1 above, it is interesting to note that the main thrust of the Baltic Sea Joint Comprehensive Environmental Action Programme is to strengthen the ability of each participating country to implement an ecosystem approach. In the words of Kindler and Lintner (1993: 12), the emphasis is upon

... actions by each concerned government to carry out needed policy and regulatory reforms; to build capacity; and to invest in controlling pollution from point and nonpoint sources, safely disposing of or reducing the generation of waste, and conserving ecologically sensitive and economically valuable areas. To complement these activities, the program also includes elements to support applied research, environmental awareness, and environmental education.

The program

Six components have been designed to realize the overall ecological restoration of the Baltic Sea. The components are as follows.

- Policy, legal and regulatory changes to establish a long-term environmental management framework in each country.
- Institutional strengthening and human resource development to create the capacity

to plan, design and implement environmental management systems, to manage efficiently, and to enforce regulations.

- A program for infrastructure investment in specific activities to control point and non-point sources of pollution, and to minimize and dispose of wastes – with priority to municipalities, industries and agriculture.
- A program to help the management of coastal lagoons and wetlands.
- Support for applied research to create the knowledge base required to develop solutions, transfer technology, and widen appreciation about the critical problems.
- Improvements in public awareness and environmental education to develop a widely based and sustainable foundation of support for implementation of the other five components.

The strategy and program components illustrate that the Baltic Sea Joint Comprehensive Environmental Action Programme reflects the essential components of an ecosystem approach. It has defined a system, has identified key components of that system, and recognizes that linkages between the components must be considered. It also recognizes that people are part of the problem, and that therefore human resources have to be improved to facilitate effective management, and that education and information have to be provided if people are to understand the issues and support the implementation measures.

Such a program will not be inexpensive, nor will it be achieved in a few years. Kindler and Lintner (1993: 15) stated that the total cost of the 20-year program for all the countries included in the Baltic Sea catchment had been estimated to be about 18 billion ECU (European currency unit, or at an exchange rate of 1 ECU to US $1.20, about US $25.6 billion). To achieve documentable results, the program focuses on remedial action for 132 "hot spots", 98 of which are located in Russia, Estonia, Latvia, Lithuania, Belarus, Ukraine, Poland, the Czech Republic and the Slovak Republic.

Anticipated benefits

Numerous benefits are expected. The quality of water in the rivers draining into the Baltic Sea should improve notably. As these rivers are the principal sources of water supply for domestic needs of 80 million people as well as industry and agriculture, this improvement is expected to improve the health and well-being of the local people. Some of the fastest improvements are expected to occur in coastal waters. Such changes would allow several contaminated beaches to be reopened, which would contribute to re-establishment of tourism and local recreation. Reduction in nutrients should reduce algal blooms, lower eutrophication and improve oxygen levels, thereby having a positive impact on the fishery resource. It is expected that the open sea will improve at a slower rate, due to the difficulty for the Baltic Sea countries of controlling the impact of long-range atmospheric transportation of various pollutants from countries outside the basin. This issue is a reminder that no matter how broad the net is cast in defining the ecosystem, the ecosystem selected is usually a sub-component of some larger ecosystem which affects the unit chosen for analysis and action.

Box 3.8 Long-term perspective necessary

Given the current state of the Baltic Sea environment, however, the program cannot be expected to make any major impacts for about 20 years. But gradual and visible improvements, both environmental and economic, can be realized in the relatively near future.

Source: Kindler and Lintner, 1993: 31.

Finally, the Baltic Sea program is a reminder that an ecosystem approach normally has to be conceived and designed with the long term in mind (Box 3.8). This reality is often a challenge, as the time horizon of elected officials too often is only until the next election, which in most countries is four or five years. Nevertheless, initiatives such as the Baltic Sea program demonstrate that an ecosystem approach, even in the most complicated and challenging of situations, can be put in place.

3.5.3 The Himalayas

The Himalayan ecosystem in India involves two subsystems. The mountainous area covers 523,000 square kilometres, or 16% of the total area of the country. The lowland area, fed by Himalayan rivers, and including the Indo-Gangetic and Brahmaputran plains, includes 726,250 square kilometres. Combined, these two areas cover 38% of India, and are home to more than 300 million people (Figure 3.3). Forests cover about 35% of the total area. On the plains, altitudes begin at about 300 metres above sea level, with the highest mountain peaks reaching above 8,000 metres. Degradation of mountain ecosystems occurs around the world, but the Himalayan ecosystem is under the greatest stress.

Causes

Many causes contribute to the environmental degradation occurring in the Himalayas. Some key causes include: (1) unplanned land use, (2) cultivation on steep slopes, (3) overgrazing of naturally grassed areas, (4) major structural projects (roads, mines, dams, irrigation systems); (5) over-exploitation of village or community forests; (6) harvesting of broad-leaved plant species, and (7) shifting cultivation, especially in northeastern India (Ahmad, 1993).

Box 3.9 Mountain ecosystems

Mountain ecosystems are sensitive to quite small disturbances and the consequences of disturbance are often irreversible. This is especially true of tropical high mountains where relief and steep slopes are combined with huge contrasts in climate, soil and vegetation cover.

Source: Ahmad, 1993: 4.

Consequences

Degradation of the physical environment is reflected in many ways, such as through soil erosion and impoverishment, water impairment, atmospheric changes, avalanches, landslides, and land use practices. Soil erosion and impoverishment are one of the most serious problems, and illustrate the need for an ecosystem approach to deal with the issues.

Ahmad (1993: 5) suggested that about one-third of the total Himalayan land area has become "derelict" due to inappropriate land use, such as agricultural

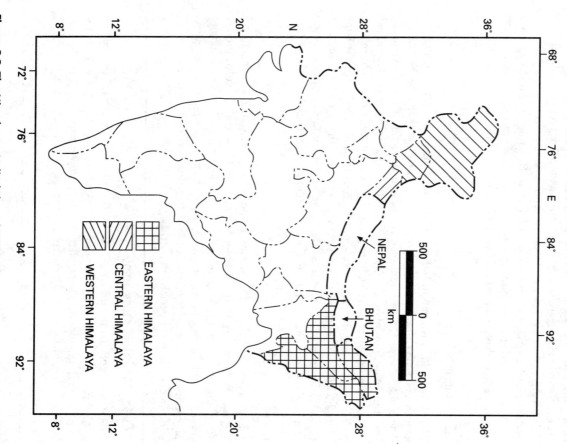

Figure 3.3 The Himalayas, India (Ahmad, 1993: 4)

production on very steep slopes without appropriate actions to counter erosion. Other contributing variables have been shifting cultivation based on short cycles, monoculture in mixed forests, destruction of native plant species and overgrazing. In his words, "soils are nutrient deficient and desertification is widespread".

The degradation of soil conditions has negative consequences for vegetation. Mountain ecosystems in general and the Himalayan system in particular normally have high biological diversity, but are fragile due to low resilience to changing conditions. Creation of large-scale plantations to grow chirpine (*Pinus roxburghii*) has changed physical and chemical properties of soils. Clear cutting and overgrazing have contributed to poor recycling of nutrients in deep soil horizons. A partial reason for clear cutting and overgrazing has been population growth, and the need to obtain fuelwood, fodder, construction timber and food. As a result, forest ecosystems have failed to recover and that has contributed to desertification.

Solutions

The solution to the multi-faceted causes and problems was viewed by Ahmad to involve two key aspects: (1) an ecosystem approach in which natural and cultural landscapes were viewed in an integrated manner, and (2) locally designed and appropriate strategies. Both aspects were to be used to achieve "ecologically sustainable development". A selection of the strategies is presented below, to illustrate the importance of dealing with various components of the Himalayan ecosystem, as well as the connections between them.

- **Watersheds and water resources.** Detailed understanding about soil characteristics and land use patterns is essential for development of watershed management programs. Initiatives to counter erosion should include both water- and land-based actions, including deep ploughing, mulching and maintenance of well-constructed terraces on steep slopes, as well as constructing check dams and subsurface drains. Agroforestry programs could stabilize soil conditions, and contribute food, fuel and fodder for the growing populations. A people's committee should be created from the villages in a watershed for which a program is to be developed, and in that way local knowledge could be drawn upon. The key point here is that many of the initiatives to deal with water resources involve land-based activities, which is consistent with an ecosystem approach.

- **Land.** The capability of the land should be determined through a classification and inventory system. Steeply sloping lands (45%) should not be used for agriculture, but should be used for revegetation. Lands with slopes of 30% could be used for agriculture, with appropriate actions to counter potential erosion. Numerous measures could be used, such as deep ploughing, contour cultivation, wing and strip cultivation, crop rotation, mulching, changes in the relief by contour farrows, ditches and dams, and well-prepared terraces.

- **Forests.** Large-scale afforestation and reforestation programs are needed. Marginal and common lands should be included in a plantation program, with priority given to broad-leaved tree species which provide good green cover. Villagers, including school children, should become involved in plantation activities, through contributing labour for planting. Villagers should have a right to use forest resources that grow as a result of their planting efforts to meet their needs for fodder, fuel and timber.

- **Wildlife.** Assessment of wildlife habitat is needed, especially regarding the carrying capacity. Exotic species (weeds and shrubs) should be controlled by the villagers. Alternative habitats should be created for rare and endangered species. Special consideration should be given to creating Biosphere Reserves or protected areas. Tribal cooperatives could be established to allow local people to make wildlife-based products through cottage industries.

- **Health.** Primary Health Centres should be established, and should provide basic health education, immunization programs and family-planning services. Local health guidance and pharmacies should be provided in each village, so that villagers do not have to make long treks to obtain basic medical advice or supplies.

- **Energy.** Large-scale hydroelectric projects should be replaced by small-scale projects. Wind and solar energy should be used, as well as wood from fast-growing and better coppicing tree species. These practices are suitable for both urban and rural areas. More biogas plants should be used to take advantage of cattle dung, instead of burning the dung in traditional stoves, which results in atmospheric pollution and health risks.

- **Women.** Women should be consulted in all planning and development decisions. Water supplies for both irrigation and domestic needs should be improved, along with supplies of fuelwood and fodder, to reduce the work load for women. Opportunities for alternative work should be provided, such as training for mushroom cultivation, handicrafts, bee keeping/honey, fruit preservation, cultivation of herbs, sericulture (silkworm breeding) and small animal (such as rabbit) breeding. See further discussion about the role of women in Chapter 10.

The examples noted above, for initiatives regarding water and watersheds, land, forests, wildlife, health, energy, and women, indicate that in an ecosystem approach it is necessary to consider a mix of activities, each of which addresses a number of components in the ecosystem. They also highlight that it is not sufficient to focus only on the biophysical or natural system. The initiatives planned regarding health and women indicate that people are part of the ecosystem, and thus can be part of both the problem and the solutions. And, as with the Baltic Sea program, the time horizon has to be a long one. Many of the necessary changes will take years, if not decades, to show results.

3.6 Implications

The experiences in Canada, the Baltic Sea countries and the Himalayas indicate that resource and environmental managers in many countries are explicitly using an ecosystem approach. This initiative is a positive one when it forces the attention of planners and managers to the interconnections between components of systems. However, it can also be problematic if the planners and managers seek to understand the totality of ecosystems. Our knowledge is usually not adequate for such detailed understanding. Furthermore, from a practical perspective, it is usually not necessary to understand the entire system. The key surely is to be able to understand those variables and their interactions that (1) cause the greatest variation in system behaviour, and (2) are amenable to modification through management intervention. For these reasons, an *integrated* approach appears to be the best interpretation regarding an ecosystem perspective. If an ecosystem approach does not produce insights and strategies that have practical value for managers, its credibility will be damaged and people may move away from it. As a result, resource and environmental managers have a responsibility to have a well thought-out interpretation of what they mean by an ecosystem approach, and how it can be applied to resolve real-world problems.

Ecosystem theory is still poorly developed, primarily because of the difficulty in general statements being applicable to conditions in a specific place and time. Ecosystem theory also is discredited when it becomes a mix of moral and scientifically oriented statements. Ecosystem understanding by itself cannot, and should not be expected to, provide anwers to moral questions. As a result, it appears that it will be some time before ecologists will be able to provide scientifically based guidelines to guide decisions. This situation should not be viewed as a fundamental weakness, however since most disciplines and professions experience this problem. Indeed, it is much more common for people, regardless of profession or discipline, to have to draw on experience and judgement in reaching decisions about what is the most appropriate decision or course of action.

References and further reading

Ahmad A 1993 Environmental impact assessment in the Himalayas: an ecosystem approach. *Ambio* 22(1): 4–9

Banks A 1994 Environmental cooperation in the Baltic Sea region. *GeoJournal* 33(4): 37–43

Barrett B 1994 Integrated environmental management. *Journal of Environmental Management* 40(1): 17–32

Bertram P E and T B Reynoldson 1992 Developing ecosystem objectives for the Great Lakes: policy, progress, and public participation. *Journal of Aquatic Ecosystem Health* 1: 89–95

Bocking S 1994 Visions of nature and society: a history of the ecosystem concept. *Alternatives* 20(3): 12–18

Born S M and W C Sonzogni 1995 Integrated environmental management: strengthening the conceptualization. *Environmental Management* 19(2): 167–81

Brink P, L M Nilsson and U Svedin 1988 Ecosystem redevelopment. *Ambio* 17(2): 84–9

Bruce J and B Mitchell 1995 *Broadening perspectives on water issues*. Canadian Global Change Program Incidental Report Series No. IR95-1, Ottawa, The Royal Society of Canada, August

Burke J J 1994 Approaches to integrated water resources development and management. The Kafue basin, Zambia. *Natural Resources Forum* 18(3): 181–92

Burroughs R H and T W Clark 1995 Ecosystem management: a comparison of Greater Yellowstone and Georges Bank. *Environmental Management* 19(5): 649–63

Cairns J 1994 Ecosystem health through ecological restoration: barriers and opportunities. *Journal of Aquatic Ecosystem Health* 3: 5–14

Cairns J and T V Crawford (eds) 1991 *Integrated Environmental Management*. Chelsea, Michigan, Lewis Publishers

Caldwell L K 1970 The ecosystem as criterion for public land policy. *Natural Resources Journal* 10(2): 203–21

Carroll J E 1982 *Acid rain: an issue in Canadian–American relations*. Toronto, C D Howe Institute, and Washington, DC, National Planning Association

Cawley R M and J Freemuth 1993 Tree farms, mother earth, and other dilemmas: the politics of ecosystem management in Greater Yellowstone. *Society and Natural Resources* 6(1): 41–53

Cocklin C and P Doorman 1994 Ecosystem protection and management in New Zealand: a private land perspective. *Applied Geography* 14(3): 264–81

Conway G R 1985 Agroecosystem analysis. *Agricultural Administration* 20: 31–55

Conway G R 1987 The properties of agroecosystems. *Agricultural Systems* 24: 95–117

Costanza R 1992 Toward an operational definition of ecosystem health. In R Costanza, B G Norton and B D Haskell (eds) *Ecosystem health: new goals for environmental management*. Washington, DC, Island Press

Dorney R S 1989 *The professional practice of environmental management*. New York, Springer-Verlag

Gilbertson M 1995 Complexity, causality, and the ecosystem approach. *Great Lakes Research Review* 1(2): 3–4

Goodman A S and K A Edwards 1992 Integrated water resources planning. *Natural Resources Forum* 17(1): 33–42

Grumbine R E 1994 What is ecosystem management? *Conservation Biology* 8(1): 27–38

Holling C S 1987 Simplifying the complex: the paradigms of ecological function and structure. *European Journal of Operational Research* 30(2): 139–46

Kay J J 1991 A nonequilibrium thermodynamic framework for discussing ecosystem integrity. *Environmental Management* 15(4): 483–95

Kay J J and E Schneider 1994 Embracing complexity: the challenge of the ecosystem approach. *Alternatives* 20(3): 32–9

Kindler J and S F Lintner 1993 An action plan to clean up the Baltic. *Environment* 35(8): 6–15; 28–31

Levins R 1995 Preparing for uncertainty. *Ecosystem Health* 1(1): 47–57

Low A R C 1994 Environmental and economical dilemmas for farm-households in Africa: when "low-input sustainable agriculture" translates to "high-cost unsustainable livelihoods". *Environmental Conservation* 21(3): 220–4

MacKenzie S H 1993 Ecosystem management in the Great Lakes: some observations from three RAP sites. *Journal of Great Lakes Research* 19(1): 136–44

Maitland A and D Aberley 1992 Watershed stewardship: the Village of Hazelton experience. In J Plant and C Plant (eds) *Putting power in its place*. Philadelphia, New Society Publishers, 91–9

Margerum R D and S M Born 1995 Integrated environmental management: moving from theory to practice. *Journal of Environmental Planning and Management* 38(3): 371–91

McIntosh R P 1976 Ecology since 1900. In B T Taylor and T J White (eds) *Issues and ideas in America*. Norman, Oklahoma, University of Oklahoma Press, 353–72

Mitchell B (ed.) 1990 *Integrated water management: international experiences and perspectives*, London, Belhaven Press

Mitchell B and D Shrubsole 1994 *Canadian water management: visions for sustainability*. Cambridge, Ontario, Canadian Water Resources Association

Newson M 1992 Land and water: convergence, divergence and progress in UK policy. *Land Use Policy* 9(2): 111–21

Norton G A and B H Walker 1982 Applied ecology: towards a positive approach I. The context of applied ecology. *Journal of Environmental Management* 14(4): 309–24

Rapport D J 1995 Ecosystem health: exploring the territory. *Ecosystem Health* 1(1): 1–13

Scudder T 1994 Recent experiences with river basin development in the tropics and subtropics. *Natural Resources Forum* 18(2): 101–13

Sedjo R A 1995 Ecosystem management: an uncharted path for public forests. *Resources* 121: 10, 18–21

Skjæreth J B 1993 The "effectiveness" of the Mediterranean Action Plan. *International Environmental Affairs* 5(4): 313–34

Slocombe D S 1993a Environmental planning, ecosystem science, and ecosystem approaches for integrating environment and development. *Environmental Management* 17(3): 289–303

Slocombe D S 1993b Implementing ecosystem-based management: development of theory, practice, and research for planning and managing a region. *BioScience* 43(9): 612–22

Walker B H and G A Norton 1982 Applied ecology: towards a positive approach. II. Applied ecological analysis. *Journal of Environmental Management* 14(4): 325–42

Wilson R R 1994 An integrated river management model: the Connecticut River Management Program. *Journal of Environmental Management* 41(4): 337–48

Wingfield M J and W J Swart 1994 Integrated management of forest tree diseases in South Africa. *Forest Ecology and Management* 65(1): 11–16

Woodley S and J J Kay and G Francis (eds) 1993 *Ecological integrity and the management of ecosystems*. Delray, Florida, St Lucie Press

World Commission on Environment and Development 1987 *Our common future*. Oxford and New York, Oxford University Press

Chapter 4

Complexity, Uncertainty and Turbulence

4.1 Introduction

In Chapter 1, an argument was made that many environmental and resource management situations are characterized by complexity and uncertainty. Indeed, many environmental and resource problems have been characterized as "wicked", "messes" or "metaproblems", to reflect the high degree of complexity involved. Furthermore, the presence of risk, uncertainty and ignorance ensures that solutions will usually be developed on the basis of incomplete knowledge and understanding of natural and social systems. And yet, life cannot stop until complete understanding is available. If decisions were to be made only after complete understanding was achieved, few decisions would ever be taken. We must be willing to take decisions, accepting that we will make errors. However, acknowledging the presence of complexity and uncertainty may allow us to approach decision making somewhat differently than in the past. It also may lead us to focus and structure our planning and decision-making organizations differently.

In this chapter, consideration is given to the importance of *turbulence* with regard to complexity and uncertainty. Consideration is also given to the concept of *chaos*. Attention is then given to the idea of the *precautionary principle*, as well as the concepts of *hedging* and *flexing*. Then, *alternative approaches to planning* are examined, with particular regard to their assumptions about the best way to address complexity and uncertainty.

4.2 Turbulence

Turbulent conditions seem to be more the norm than the exception. For example, at the beginning of the 1990s, who would have predicted that the Soviet Union would break up as a country? Who would have forecast that Nelson Mandela would become the leader of South Africa? While in hindsight such events can be understood, ahead of time or while they are unfolding they emerge as surprises to many people. They were not predicted much in advance. As a result, turbulence can create bewilderment, anxiety and even suspicion.

Turbulence occurs due to complexity and uncertainty, and due to rapidly changing conditions. In that context, Trist (1980) suggested that over time four different kinds of planning or decision-making situations can be identified. The

Box 4.1 Changing conditions

To be in the midst of change yet oblivious to it is characteristic of the human condition.

Source: Kates, 1995: 627.

importance of Trist's analysis is that it reminds us of the necessity to understand the circumstances which surround planning and management initiatives.

- **Type 1.** Type 1 is the simplest decision-making environment. It is one in which opportunities and problems are randomly distributed, and organization is simple. The best strategy involves each person doing as well as possible on a local scale. A market analogue would be a situation of "perfect competition", represented by a world of small factories, family farms and corner stores. The planning style can be characterized as *inactive*, or one in which the present is judged to be better than the past or the future. The conventional wisdom is captured by expressions such as it is better to wait and see, look before you leap, or let sleeping dogs lie. This is primarily a non-planning world.

- **Type 2.** In the second decision-making environment, conditions continue to be relatively stable or unchanging. However, opportunities and problems start to group or cluster. The best strategy is to find an optimal location to take advantage of the opportunities. While the market analogue for Type 1 was "perfect competition", for Type 2 it is "imperfect competition" with businesses becoming more specialized as they seek a comparative advantage. Here, the planning style is *reactive*, and the past is regarded as preferable to the present or the future. In this environment, folk wisdom stresses the good old days, or Paradise Lost. Planning is used here, as there is a best place to find.

- **Type 3.** At this stage, which Trist calls "disturbed reactive conditions", the environment is dynamic and changing. Other firms or competitors seek and attempt to get the same optimal locations. Firms are continually reacting to initiatives of other firms. The best strategy in this situation is to amass power, as competitive challenges can best be met through accumulated resources and abundant expertise under the firm's control. Bigger is better. The best market analogy here is "oligopoly", in which there are relatively few but large and specialized firms. This is the world of large industrial conglomerates or consortia, and of equally large government departments, in which emphasis is placed upon centralized control. In this situation, the future is viewed as better than either the past or the present. Consequently, emphasis is on improving the capacity to predict

Box 4.2 Future shock

... I coined the term "future shock" to describe the shattering stress and disorientation that we induce in individuals by subjecting them to too much change in too short a time.

Source: Toffler, 1971: 3.

Box 4.3 Interactive planning

It [interactive planning] requires the collaboration of interest groups . . .; the identification of shared values . . .; continuous learning . . .; and continuous evaluation and modification. . . . It is an open-ended unfolding process. [It has been called] adaptive planning.

Source: Trist, 1980: 119.

and to prepare. The art of the calculable becomes valued, with emphasis on econometric models, technical forecasts, operations research, and simulations. As in the second type, planning is important. Attention is given to judging where the best waves are going to come from, and then to ensuring that you ride the best one and keep others off it. The emphasis is upon technocratic planning.

- **Type 4.** Trist called the fourth type a "turbulent" environment or field. In this type, many large and competing organizations act independently and take actions in diverse directions. The outcome is unanticipated and discordant consequences shared by all. As Trist (1980: 117) remarked, "the result is contextual commotion – as if 'the ground' were moving as well as the organizations. This is what is meant by turbulence." No organization is so big that it can control things, or is able to do things on its own. A new value becomes collaboration, reflected through consortia-building, and sharing, all of which conflict with the basic values found in Type 3 approaches. For Type 4 there is no ready market analogy, other than the concept of *macroregulation*, or increasing involvement by the government in a collaborative manner with the private sector to try to achieve greater stability. The planning style is therefore best described as *interactive*. Neither the past, present nor future appears to be particularly attractive. Any desirable future will depend on people making it occur, thereby emphasizing the need to make choices between alternative futures. As a result, the interest is less upon forecasting most likely futures, but in creating most desirable futures (a distinction discussed more in Chapter 5). However, creating a desirable future cannot be done either alone, in isolation from, or in competition with, others. This is why an interactive and collaborative approach to planning and management is so necessary.

Having identified the four types of planning or management situations, Trist then examined the implications, which are several. First, the Type 4 situation requires a different approach to planning and problem solving. Trial and error approaches work well in Type 1 conditions. What might be called "craft knowledge" is appropriate in Type 2 situations, and the scientific method has most usually been applied in Type 3 circumstances. But the complex interdependencies of Type 4 situations are not usually amenable to a scientific approach, when that is interpreted as breaking a problem into its component parts. The complex "metaproblems" confronted require a systems approach in which attention is given to relating parts to the whole, and organizations to their larger environments. In the words of Trist (1980: 119), the systems approach is "synthetic, holistic, seeking to capture the gestalt of system connectedness."

Box 4.4 Institutional gaps

The objective of sustainable development and the integrated nature of the global environment/development challenges raise problems for institutions, national and international, that were established on the basis of narrow preoccupations and compartmentalized concerns. Governments' general response to the speed and scale of global changes has been a reluctance to recognize sufficiently the need to change themselves. The challenges are both interdependent and integrated, requiring comprehensive approaches and popular participation.

Yet most of the institutions facing those challenges tend to be independent, fragmented, working to relatively narrow mandates with closed decision processes. Those responsible for managing natural resources and protecting the environment are institutionally separated from those responsible for managing the economy. The real world of interlocked economic and ecological systems will not change; the policies and institutions concerned must.

Source: World Commission on Environment and Development, 1987: 9.

A second implication relates to the nature of public agencies, or the "bureaucracy". The dominant form of bureaucracy in most countries is one which is technocratic, singular (pursues only its own objectives), specialized, and centralized (see the comments from the Brundtland Commission in Box 4.4). This approach is best suited to deal with Type 3 conditions. However, as Trist observed, most environmental and resource problems involve Type 4 conditions. The outcome is that too often we rely upon a bureaucracy designed for conditions which no longer exist. And, as we know from military history, being prepared for conditions which no longer exist can be disastrous. For example, the French built the Maginot Line, an elaborate defensive system of trenches and bunkers, after World War I to protect themselves from the Germans. The Maginot Line was based on fighting styles in World War I, when armies occupied trenches opposite each other, and ground troops skirmished and attacked from the trenches. However, early in World War II, during 1939 and 1940, the Germans used the mobility of their Panzer tanks to sweep through Belgium and into France, and simply outflanked the Maginot Line, making it an anachronism. Resource and environmental management should not be like the Maginot Line – we should be preparing for conditions in the future, not those only from the past which may no longer be as relevant.

A third consequence of the Type 4 situation is that the style of comprehensive planning which involves creation of a master plan or blueprint, and which is often very useful in Type 3 situations, will be less appropriate, if appropriate at all. As Trist argued, the level of change created by an ever increasing rate of change is too great, and too often plans are dated before they can be implemented (see Chapter 12, which discusses implementation). Planning for Type 4 conditions requires continuous adaptive planning: *continuous* because frequent modifications will be essential; *participatory* because all stakeholders must have a role (see Chapter 8 about partnerships); *integrated* because various interests must be incorporated; and *coordinated* because the interdependence of issues and decisions must be recognized. A key lesson is that during planning there must be equal attention to the *process* as well as to the *product*. Another lesson is that ends need to be agreed upon before means are examined, one of the points highlighted in both Chapters 1 and 2.

4.3 Chaos

If turbulence contributes to complexity and uncertainty, the concept of chaos is even more unsettling. Chaos is order without predictability. In other words, some physical and social systems might be capable of being understood, in the sense that they can be described relative to a set of conditions or rules, but they remain fundamentally unpredictable.

Cartwright (1991) concluded that many of the problems that planners must handle – population growth, land use patterns – may well reflect chaos. In his view, while we may understand the "rules" that influence behaviour at the individual or "local" level, usually we cannot predict the outcomes or impacts at a global scale. The implications of such a conclusion are profound. As Cartwright (1991: 45) remarked, "No matter how much data we gather, no matter how global and complete our models, no matter how rigorously we test them, even so, according to chaos theory, prediction may in some cases be beyond our grasp."

As will be seen in the later section on planning models, planners have developed approaches that recognize situations in which there is incomplete understanding. However, these approaches have emerged for pragmatic reasons: there is not always sufficient time to get all the facts; it is often too costly to obtain all the facts; we lack the skill or means to obtain all the facts. In contrast, chaos theory indicates that trying to predict the future is not just impractical in some cases – rather, it is logically impossible.

More attention will be given to predictions or forecasting in Chapter 5. Nevertheless, three conclusions can be reached if it is accepted that chaotic systems are inherently unpredictable, and are not possible to understand fully

Box 4.5 Chaos

. . . chaos is not anarchy or randomness. Chaos is order, but it is order that is "invisible". Nor is chaos merely the result of "noise", or interference, or even insufficient knowledge. What chaos implies is a kind of inherent "uncertainty principle" – not just in how we perceive the world but in how the world actually works.

Source: Cartwright, 1991: 44–5.

Box 4.6

While the prediction of chaotic behavior may be impossible, understanding the order that gives rise to it may not be as difficult as we thought. Highly complex and unpredictable behavior, in other words, can be the product of quite simple and accessible rules.

Source: Cartwright, 1991: 45.

(Cartwright, 1991: 53–54). First, collecting more information and creating more sophisticated models for chaotic systems will probably have little value. Indeed, "research" might be unhelpful if it creates an unrealistic belief about the capability of planning. Planning strategies that assume the capacity for foresight will be inappropriate and can even be misleading at times.

Alternatively, planners must begin to work with not one or two forecasts about the future, but rather an ensemble or suite of forecasts. Planners normally test models or forecasts by using different assumptions about future conditions, and consider the consequences for the results. It is much less common for planners to begin or run their alternative models from different "starting points". It is normally assumed that we know what present conditions are, and do not consider alternative perspectives about them. Chaos theory challenges the notion that present conditions are known, and also the idea that even if different starting points were chosen it is unlikely that there would be major differences in outcomes. As a result, it becomes very important to be able and willing to explore which initial starting points have similar trajectories, and which do not. Rather than investing more time and effort in collecting more detailed data, or fine-tuning our models, we should look for patterns of behaviour, or points to which systems tend to return, even if we cannot readily predict them.

Second, the concept of chaos requires re-examination of some of our ideas regarding the virtues of order and predictability, and the messiness of chaos and disorder. It is possible that a chaotic environment could be at least as desirable as a neat or orderly one.

Third, we may need to accept that chaotic systems are predictable only at a local scale or on an incremental basis. At a global scale or on a comprehensive basis, chaotic systems are not predictable due to the cumulative effects of many different kinds of feedback within them. However, at a local or incremental level, the consequences of feedback over time may be identifiable. This conclusion becomes a strong argument for using planning strategies or models that are incremental rather than comprehensive, and that are based on a capacity to be adaptive rather than structured and "blueprintable". Thus, as the comments in Box 4.6 indicate, there are grounds to be optimistic and confident regarding handling chaotic systems.

4.4 The precautionary principle

In Germany, starting in the 1950s, there was discussion focused on the need for *vorsorge*, or foresight. Of particular interest was recognition of the need for caution, and to move away from always being reactive in planning and management. Various German governments formally incorporated the need for foresight into their procedures, and this later became known as the *precautionary principle*. This approach soon began to be included in international agreements, especially those regarding marine pollution. And, in 1992, Principle 15 of the Rio Declaration on Environment and Development from the Earth Summit endorsed the precautionary principle.

The precautionary principle reflects the old adage that an ounce of prevention is worth a pound of cure. It also stipulates that rather than waiting for complete understanding, or certainty, managers and decision makers should anticipate potential harmful environmental impacts from actions, and take decisions to avoid such harm. It also recognizes that uncertainty is reality, due to our lack of complete knowledge about ecosystem behaviour, faulty assumptions about ecosystem functions, inability to predict the size, needs and desires of future populations, and difficulty in forecasting future technical innovations. Given such uncertainties, the precautionary principle should be considered when making resource decisions in which (1) the range of possible impacts from one or more uses cannot be predicted, (2) one or more of the outcomes could have

---

Box 4.7 Statements of the precautionary principle

Bergen Declaration (ECE), 16 May 1990

In order to achieve sustainable development, policies must be based on the Precautionary Principle. Environmental measures must anticipate, prevent and attack the causes of environmental degradation. Where there are threats of serious or irreversible damage, lack of full scientific uncertainty should not be used as a reason for postponing measures to prevent environmental degradation.

"Maastricht Treaty", Treaty on European Union, February 1992, Article 130r, paragraph 2

Community policy on the environment shall . . . be based on the Precautionary Principle and on the principles that precautionary action should be taken, that environmental damage should as a priority be rectified at source and that the polluter should pay.

Rio Declaration, June 1992, Principle 15

In order to protect the environment, the precautionary approach shall be widely applied by States according to their capabilities. Where there are threats of serious or irreversible damage, lack of full scientific uncertainty shall not be used as a reason for postponing cost-effective measures to prevent environmental degradation.

extremely undesirable impacts for future people, and (3) substitutes are not available for the resource to be used.

Young (1993: 15–16) has suggested that three possible interpretations can be made of the precautionary principle when implementing it. These are:

- a conservative interpretation, in which use or activity is approved only if it poses no danger to an ecological system or does not reduce environmental quality, and is confined within boundaries that permit complete reversibility;

- a more liberal interpretation, in which uses or industries judged to be "risky" are required to use the best available technology, and in addition a precautionary safety margin is established which keeps ambient environmental concentrations well below a specified acceptable threshold; and

- a relatively weak interpretation, in which the requirement is the use of best available technology that does not involve undue expense.

These options illustrate that there is as yet no consensus regarding a definition of the precautionary principle. However, this situation is not necessarily bad, as it does provide scope to custom-design its application relative to local needs, conditions and circumstances. Young (1993: 14, 16) provided sensible advice regarding such questions. In his view, the principle should be used with actions involving adverse outcomes, particularly when such outcomes are suspected to be of a catastrophic kind. In this manner, its use should force debate about the types and magnitudes of human-induced change to the environment judged to be acceptable by a society. In addition, he commented that application of the principle should never mean that all developments with uncertain environmental impacts should be stopped. What it does mean, however, is that when a possibly irreversible action that could have unpredictable consequences in the future is being contemplated, all alternative options need to be considered before taking a final decision. He also concluded that such irreversible actions should be undertaken only when it is concluded that not doing so could impose significant social costs on the present generation.

Nevertheless, as Bodansky (1991: 43) cautioned, use of the precautionary principle does not provide a guarantee that serious environmental harm will never occur. Many contemporary environmental problems were not anticipated.

Box 4.8 Concerns

Although the precautionary principle provides a general approach to environmental issues, it is too vague to serve as a regulatory standard because it does not specify how much caution should be taken. In particular, it does not directly address two key questions: When is it appropriate to apply the precautionary principle? And what types of precautionary actions are warranted and at what price?

Source: Bodansky, 1991: 5.

In addition, even if regulators had opted for a cautious approach, many of the problems would probably not have been prevented. For example, CFCs (chlorofluorocarbons) and DDT were judged to be environmentally benign when they were first developed. Problems emerged later not because the regulators had approved their use in the context of uncertainties, but because scientists had not tested for the types of environmental impacts that later became a problem. Thus, extensive tests had been conducted on DDT regarding its acute toxicity, but no tests had been completed regarding its chronic effects — and it was the latter that caused problems for health. For CFCs, the properties (persistence and stability) that make it destructive to the ozone layer were judged initially to reduce the likelihood that they would cause negative environmental impacts.

While the precautionary principle is not and cannot be a panacea for complexity and uncertainty regarding environmental problems, it does provide a counterbalance to the "wait and see" attitude that often prevails. For, as Smith (1990: 112) has observed, "Scientific uncertainty is a difficult issue because uncertainty means that it is always possible to argue that better policies can be developed by waiting until a broader scientific consensus emerges."

4.5 Hedging and flexing

Hedging and flexing are strategies for decision making under conditions of uncertainty which are so severe that Collingridge (1983) characterized them as a state of "ignorance". Each is considered here.

4.5.1 Hedging

Hedging is one of the most frequently used strategies when having to make decisions under ignorance. Hedging involves a conscious choice to avoid the worst consequences by comparing all the options against the estimated worst case, and then selecting the alternative with the "least bad worst outcome". Hedging is consistent with the precautionary principle, in that it counsels caution and strives to minimize damage if the worst outcome occurs. However, Collingridge argued that while hedging is a reasonable strategy under extreme uncertainty, it is not the best strategy under conditions of ignorance. His position emphasizes the importance of being able to differentiate between conditions of risk, uncertainty and ignorance, as discussed in Chapter 1. Collingridge concluded that hedging is not a good approach when ignorance occurs because in such situations no decision can ever be known to be the correct one. Thus, there is always the likelihood that other options than the one taken might be better, if only the planner or decision maker were aware of them.

4.5.2 Flexing

Collingridge maintained that because any decision taken in ignorance may prove to be inappropriate, the decision maker should systematically look for error, or *monitor* any decision, by continuing to scan for other options after the decision has been taken. Furthermore, because there is little point in searching for error unless there is scope for making an adjustment, he recommended that decision makers should always favour flexible options, or ones that can be revised if they are found to be inappropriate. His conclusion was that decision makers should be prepared to take flexible decisions, to monitor them, and to modify them. The extreme caution stipulated by hedging becomes less important if there is the willingness and capacity to modify decisions in the light of new knowledge and understanding. In contrast to hedging, flexing involves seeking the best option, risking the worst outcome, but being ready to modify or reverse a decision if the worst outcome should occur.

4.5.3 Relative merits

The relative merits of hedging and flexing are as follows.

- Hedging is an appropriate strategy if it is unlikely that a decision or an action can be reversed or significantly modified. However, if decisions can be modified or reversed, then flexing is the more appropriate approach.

- Flexing is not a prescription for inaction. Flexing provides an opportunity to achieve the best possible outcome; it is not a prescription to do nothing and hope for the best. Hedging tends to lead to preservation of the status quo, or slight variations of it, or to premature adoption of new technologies since they are viewed as the way to resolve problems.

- Flexing increases flexibility by broadening the range of options considered, unlike hedging, which limits options.

- Hedging may contribute to the realization of the worst outcome because in situations of ignorance decision makers are often involved in competition with other decision makers, whose intents or activities are not easy to predict. For example, if one side develops a weapon system to protect itself from what it thinks the other side might do, the development of such a system might trigger the other side to take the action which was feared as it tries to create a hedge for itself. This pattern leads to the well-known phenomenon of self-fulfilling predictions.

- In many decision situations, the worst outcome may be ambiguous because a number of "worst" outcomes may be possible. In such situations it is difficult to know against which option to hedge.

- By seeking to avoid the worst outcome, hedging may also overlook real benefits that could be achieved by attaining some happier state. In contrast, flexing seeks out the best option, but recognizes that monitoring is needed so that if the worst does happen then changes can be made to limit damage.

Neither hedging nor flexing offers perfect solutions for making decisions in the face of complexity, uncertainty or ignorance. However, this brief review of them is intended to provide some context for the precautionary principle, and to encourage the reader to think about its strengths and weaknesses at both conceptual and operational levels. Most of the criticisms of the precautionary approach have emphasized operational issues. The above comments highlight that conceptual issues also exist, and require our careful attention.

Box 4.9 Approaches to decision making

Most principles of decision making under uncertainty are simple common sense. We must consider a variety of plausible hypotheses about the world; consider a variety of possible strategies; favor actions that are robust to uncertainties; hedge; favor actions that are informative; probe and experiment; monitor results; update assessments and modify policy accordingly; and favor actions that are reversible.

Source: Ludwig *et al.*, 1993: 36.

4.6 Planning models

Different schools or models of planning have been developed. Each reflects different values, assumptions and beliefs about the nature of the world for which planning is done, and about the role of the planner. Several of these models are considered below, with particular regard to the way in which they address complexity and uncertainty.

4.6.1 Synoptic planning

Synoptic planning, also referred to as *comprehensive rational planning*, is the dominant planning model. Most other models have been developed as a result of concern about, or criticisms of, the synoptic approach.

Synoptic planning has a number of well-established steps or phases, including (1) defining the problem, (2) establishing goals and objectives, (3) identifying alternative means of achieving the goals and objectives, (4) assessing

Box 4.10 Planning under uncertainty

Where planning for the future is *feasible* (based on good data and analytical skills, continuity in the trends being extrapolated, and effective means to control outcomes), then planning is unnecessary – it is simply redundant to what already goes on. Conversely, where planning is most *needed* (where there is absence of data and skills and controls in the presence of primitive or turbulent social conditions), planning is least feasible.

Source: Hudson, 1979: 393.

... planning processes can be understood as addressing different conditions of uncertainty. Thus planners must assess the actual conditions of uncertainty that characterize the particular problem they are confronting and then select a style of planning that suits those conditions.

Source: Christensen, 1985: 69.

the options against some explicit criteria, (5) choosing a preferred solution and implementing it, and (6) monitoring and evaluation. These phases are linked with feedback loops, creating the possibility of incorporating changes into planning as a result of findings or experience. The assessment of options is often completed by using methods such as benefit–cost analysis, operations research and forecasting. Quantitative analysis is often a central element of analysis.

The comprehensive rational planning model is based on the assumption that the people involved have the characteristics of Economic Man or Economic Person. This individual has the capacity to identify and rank goals, values and objectives, and can also choose consistently between them, having collected all the necessary data and having evaluated them systematically. This individual also judges alternatives against the criterion of economic efficiency, and seeks to optimize or maximize returns.

A further value associated with comprehensive rational planning is that if the planner or analyst collects enough information, completes enough analyses, and studies long enough, he or she will be able to understand the situation, and therefore to manage or control it. However, the reality is that in many situations the necessary data are not available. Even when such data can be collected, it is not always easy to analyse them due to the existence of intangible attributes. Furthermore, the assumption that the correct problem has been identified is not always verified.

As a result of the characteristics outlined above, and highlighted in Box 4.11,

Box 4.11 Problem solving

There are times, of course, when the models one has cannot accommodate the new information. One feels confused. Confusion is painful, and people strive ardently to quiet it, i.e., to make things understandable. Oftentimes, this striving manifests itself as a tenacious persistence to "get things straight". At other times, however, people jump to conclusions without adequately examining the problem. Their discomfort with the uncertainty is such that any solution will do. Moreover, if these efforts fail to bring cognitive closure, people typically respond emotionally with frustration, anger, helplessness, or apathy. Neither jumping to conclusions nor any of these affective states result in very effective problem solving. [A study] has provided a summary of problem-solving tendencies, which, even if exaggerated, suggests the real world implications and frustrations of an inadequate problem exploration. They claim that 90% of problem solving is spent:

- Solving the wrong problem
- Stating the problem so that it can be solved
- Solving a solution
- Stating a problem too generally
- Trying to get agreement on the solution before there is agreement on the problem.

Source: Bardwell, 1991: 605.

the synoptic or comprehensive rational planning model does not seem well suited to dealing with complexity and uncertainty. Its departure point is a belief that with enough effort and work it is possible to achieve understanding, and therefore to be able to manage or control systems. The comprehensive rational approach is unlikely to accept the concept of chaos. It also assumes a capability of participants (Economic Person) that can rarely be met. As a result, other planning models have emerged. The most frequently considered alternative is incremental planning.

4.6.2 Incremental planning

The incremental planning approach has also been referred to as *disjointed incrementalism* or as *muddling through*. Instead of accepting the idea of an Economic Person, this approach is based on the idea that people are "boundedly rational" and "satisfice" rather than maximize. In other words, while Economic Man is able to cope with the complexity of the real world, the boundedly rational person quickly simplifies the buzzing, booming confusion that characterizes the real world into a more simple model. Thus, in the incremental approach the planner is faced with, and being considered is "bounded" because not all the detail and complexity is considered. In addition, whereas the Economic Person strives to maximize, the boundedly rational person searches for a solution which is "good enough" or satisfactory – it does not have to be the optimum.

The incremental approach was developed to describe how things often happen in practice, but over time it has also been interpreted in a normative or prescriptive manner. That is, the model is offered as a preferred way of planning, because it captures much of the reality about the world in which planners function. Thus, in the incremental approach the planner is faced with, and recognizes, multiple problems, goals and values. She or he thus does not try to optimize, but rather to identify practically attainable goals that are generally satisfactory. Not all alternatives are known, and no attempt is made to consider a broad range of options. The cost in time, effort and money to obtain additional data and to identify a broader mix of alternatives is recognized to be high.

The incremental approach thus has a number of characteristics, including the following.

- The problem is not clearly defined. Often, the major task for the policy maker or planner is to determine the nature of the problem to be handled.
- Goals, values and objectives may conflict with one another.
- Only a limited number of options are considered, and those differ only incrementally from each other and from the existing policy or practice.
- For each option, only a restricted number of "significant" impacts are identified.
- The problem is redefined on a regular basis. Normally, it is thought that means are adjusted to ends. Under incrementalism, the reverse often happens. Ends are modified with regard to available means.
- No single correct solution exists. Indeed, the policy maker often does not know what is wanted, but does know what should be avoided. Policies move away from bad or undesirable things, without necessarily moving systematically towards good

or desirable outcomes. A satisfactory decision is one for which substantial agreement exists, even though not everyone may believe that the decision is the best relative to a given objective.

- The decision or policy process never ends. The process is viewed as a sequential chain, involving an ongoing series of incremental decisions.

With such attributes, the incremental approach concentrates attention upon familiar and better-known experiences, reduces the number of alternatives to be explored, and reduces the number and complexity of variables to be considered. The incremental planner may appear to be tentative, timid, indecisive, hesitant, cautious and narrow. At the same time, such a planner also may be viewed as realistic and pragmatic, and as a shrewd problem solver who is astute enough to recognize and accept the complexity and uncertainty surrounding environmental and resource issues. The incremental planner will deliberately choose a policy or option, knowing very well that it is not quite adequate, in order to leave open a range of other options. This path will be taken rather than selecting a policy that appears to be on target but would be difficult to modify. Attention will often be given to solving smaller problems (poor seed, for example) when it is recognized that the planner cannot solve a larger problem (low agricultural productivity). The incrementalist believes that policy making is serial or sequential, and as a result that continual nibbling is as good as taking one large bite. In this manner, the incrementalist approach is compatible with the ideas contained in the precautionary principle. As Lindblom (1974: II-34), the architect of the incremental approach, has remarked,

... most of us believe that because we became involved in our environmental difficulties piecemeal, we shall have to get out comprehensively.... Clearly the argument contains a fallacy. We did fall into our environmental problems through piecemeal gradualism. That still leaves open the possibility that the same route is the only route out of the problem.... Believing that everything is connected, we fall into the logical fallacy of believing the only way to improve those interconnections is to deal with them all at once.... But because everything *is* connected, it is beyond our capacity to manipulate variables comprehensively. Because everything is interconnected, the whole of the environmental problem is beyond our capacity to control in one unified policy. We have to find critical points of interventions....

As with all models, the incremental approach has weaknesses. A major criticism is that the incrementalist, in believing that an evolutionary approach is best, will not consider an abrupt or radical (or revolutionary) shift in policy or practice if conditions change markedly. Since the incrementalist only considers options which are marginally different from the status quo, such a planner is unlikely to consider innovative ways significantly different from current practice. There may be situations in which a sharp change in policy or practice is needed, and the incrementalist is unlikely to be prepared to consider a radical shift. As a result, incrementalists are often characterized as being reactive to existing conditions, rather than being proactive in trying to move towards an improved state of affairs.

4.6.3 Mixed scanning

Mixed scanning was developed to capture the strengths of both the synoptic and incremental approaches, but also to minimize their weaknesses. In particular, mixed scanning rejects the concept of Economic Person, and also rejects the aspect of incrementalism, which creates an inability or unwillingness to consider fundamental changes in policy or practice. A basic idea is that many incremental decisions can eventually lead to a fundamental shift, and that the cumulative effect of many incremental decisions is influenced by fundamental decisions.

The core ideas of mixed scanning are that (1) the decision maker relies heavily upon a continuous series of incremental decisions, but that (2) the decision maker is also steadily scanning a limited range of other alternatives, each of which represents a major departure from present practice. Thus, unlike the incrementalist, the mixed scanner looks for and considers options which are significantly different from the status quo. On the other hand, unlike the Economic Person, who uses synoptic planning, the mixed scanner restricts attention to a limited number of these markedly different options. As a result, the mixed scanning approach is less cautious than the incremental approach, but it remains pragmatic by recognizing the cost and effort required to examine a wide variety of options.

An analogy has been made with the way in which a captain functions on a large ship, especially as it enters a new port. The attention of the captain and others on the bridge is very focused while it approaches the harbour, watching for signs of shoals, small shipping and other obstacles to its successful entrance to the port. At the same time, the ship's radar is scanning 360 degrees, and provides information about possible storms or other inbound ships that the captain must consider in making decisions about the most suitable route to enter the port. Thus, the ship's captain is continuously scanning for distant but possibly significant aspects that need to be considered, while still keeping most attention focused on a smaller range of matters which require attention in the short-term future.

4.6.4 Transactive planning

The synoptic approach is often associated with the acceptance of expert input, and of a more centralized form of management or decision making. It usually assumes that the planners are in the best position to define the nature of the issues or problems that require attention, and to develop alternative solutions to them. In the *transactive approach*, the belief is that it is important to consider the experience of people who will be affected by the planning or decisions. Thus, planning is not a technocratic exercise conducted by experts, but rather should involve face-to-face contact between the planners and those most affected by their activity. In the transactive approach, the key characteristics are inter-personal dialogue and mutual learning.

Transactive planning therefore transforms the role of the planner from one of distant expert to one of facilitator and participant. The planner is not assumed to hold all of the necessary or useful knowledge and wisdom, but rather is one person of many with a constructive contribution to make. Transactive planning also seeks to achieve more decentralized decision making as a means to provide more control over planning by the local people. In this manner, the process is consistent with the ideas of social justice, equity and empowerment advocated by sustainable development (discussed in Chapter 2).

As Hudson (1979) has commented, in contrast to incremental planning, transactive planning gives higher priority to processes of personal and organizational development rather than to the realization of particular functional objectives. As a result, plans are assessed not only in terms of what they provide in effective delivery of goods and services, but also by the way in which they affect local people, especially their dignity, sense of effectiveness, values and behaviour, and capacity for growth through cooperation. Thus, transactive planning is an approach that places a high value on creation of partnerships (Chapter 8) and on incorporating local knowledge systems into planning (Chapter 9).

4.6.5 Perspective

No single planning approach or model is perfect. Each offers strengths and weaknesses. In addition, each makes different assumptions about the role of planners and analysts, and those for whom planning or analysis is being done. It is important to recognize the merits and shortcomings of various approaches, and not automatically to use a single approach. Depending upon circumstances and conditions, one approach may be more appropriate than another. We need to have a critical appreciation of the various approaches or models, so that we can consciously choose which one is likely to be most effective in a given problem-solving situation. It is also helpful to be able to recognize when viewpoints or comments reflect acceptance of one or another model, so that it is possible to identify why people are disagreeing about a process and to determine how to resolve such differences.

4.7 Implications

Complexity. Uncertainty. Turbulence. All of these conditions or characteristics appear to be more the norm than the exception in resource and environmental management. It appears that resource and environmental managers would be well advised to approach their task with the expectation that surprises will be usual, and change will be common. As a result, it is sensible to develop strategies and approaches that allow us to learn and adapt on the basis of experience.

The precautionary principle explicitly recognizes that our information and understanding may be inadequate, and yet that situation is not a reasonable excuse for not making decisions or taking action. In that context, when there is the possibility for reversibility of decisions, *flexing* appears to be a better approach than the more often used *hedging*. Furthermore, *mixed scanning* or *incremental* approaches to planning are more likely to be effective than a *comprehensive rational approach.* In the remaining chapters, attention will be given to various ways to deal with complexity and uncertainty, especially in situations characterized by rapid change and conflict. Interest will also centre on ways to move towards resource and environmental management that will be sustainable in the long term, and that will be consistent with an ecosystem approach.

References and further reading

Bardwell L V 1991 Problem-framing: a perspective on environmental problem solving. *Environmental Management* 15(5): 603–12

Blaikie P, T Cannon, I Davis and B Wisner 1994 *At risk: natural hazards, people's vulnerability and disasters*. London, Routledge

Bodansky D 1991 Scientific uncertainty and the precautionary principle. *Environment* 33(7): 4–5, 43–4

Bolton P A, E B Liebow and J L Olson 1993 Community context and uncertainty following a damaging earthquake: low-income Latinos in Los Angeles, California. *Environmental Professional* 15(3): 240–7

Briassoulis, H 1989 Theoretical orientations in environmental planning: an inquiry into alternative approaches. *Environmental Management* 13(4): 381–92

Burby R J 1991 *Sharing environmental risks: how to control governments' losses in natural disasters*. Boulder, Colorado, Westview Press

Burton I, R W Kates and G F White 1993 *The environment as hazard*. New York, Guildford Press, second edition

Cameron J 1994 The status of the precautionary principle in international environmental law. In T O'Riordan and J Cameron (eds) *Interpreting the accountancy principles*. London, Earthscan: 262–91

Cameron J and J Abouchar 1991 The precautionary principle: a fundamental principle of law and policy for the protection of the global environment. *Boston College International and Comparative Law Review* 14(1): 1–27

Cartwright T J 1991 Planning and chaos theory. *Journal of the American Planning Association* 57(1): 44–56

Christensen K S 1985 Coping with uncertainty in planning. *Journal of the American Planning Association* 51(1): 63–73

Cohen J and I Stewart 1994 *The collapse of chaos: discovering simplicity in a complex world*. New York: Penguin Books

Colglazier E W 1991 Scientific uncertainties, public policy, and global warming: how sure is sure enough? *Policy Studies Journal* 19(2): 61–72

Collingridge D 1983 Hedging and flexing: two ways of choosing under ignorance. *Technological Forecasting and Social Change* 23(2): 161–72

Costanza R and L Cornwell 1992 The 4P approach to dealing with scientific uncertainty. *Environment* 34(9): 12–20, 42

Cutter S L (ed.) 1994 *Environmental risk and hazards*. Englewood Cliffs, NJ, Prentice Hall

Dovers S R and J W Handmer 1995 Ignorance, the precautionary principle and sustainability. *Ambio* 24(2): 92–7

Friedmann J 1987 *Planning in the public domain: from knowledge to action*. Princeton, Princeton University Press

Funtowicz S O and J R Ravetz 1994 Uncertainty, complexity and post-normal science. *Environmental Toxicology and Chemistry* 13(12): 1881–5

References and further reading

Gleick J 1987 *Chaos: making a new science*. New York: Viking Penguin

Handmer, J and E Penning-Rowsell (eds) 1990 *Hazards and the communication of risk*. Brookfield, Vermont, Bower Technical

Hewitt, K (ed.) 1983 *Interpretations of Calamity*. Boston, Allen and Unwin

Hudson B 1979 Comparison of current planning theories: counterparts and contradictions. *Journal of the American Planning Association* 45(4): 387–98

Kates R W 1995 Labnotes from the Jeremiah experiment: hope for a sustainable transition. *Annals of the Association of American Geographers* 85(4): 623–40

Lindblom C 1974 Incrementalism and environmentalism. In *National conference on managing the environment: final report*. Washington, DC, Washington Environmental Research Centre, II: 32–4

Ludwig D R Hilborn and C Walters 1993 Uncertainty, resource exploitation, and conservation: lessons from history. *Science* 260(2 April): 17, 36

Morley D 1986 Approaches to planning in turbulent environments. In D Morley and A Shachar (eds) *Planning in turbulence*. Jerusalem, The Magnes Press: 3–23

Myers, N 1993 Biodiversity and the precautionary principle. *Ambio* 22(2–3): 74–9

O'Riordan T 1995 The application of the precautionary principle in the United Kingdom. *Environment and Planning A* 2(10): 1534–8

Palm R I 1990 *Natural hazards: an integrative framework for research and planning*. Baltimore, Johns Hopkins University Press

Pteak W J and A A Atkinson 1982 *Natural hazard risk assessment and public policy: anticipating the unexpected*. New York, Springer-Verlag

Reckhow K H 1994 Importance of scientific uncertainty in decision making. *Environmental Management* 18(2): 161–6

Shackley S and B Wynne 1995 Integrating knowledge for climate change: pyramids, nets and uncertainties. *Global Environmental Change* 5(2): 113–26

Smith D A 1990 The implementation of Canadian policies to protect the ozone layer. In G B Doern (ed.) *Getting it green: case studies in Canadian environmental regulation*. Policy Study 12, Toronto, C. D. Howe Institute: 111–28

Stebbing A R D 1992 Environmental capacity and the precautionary principle. *Marine Pollution Bulletin* 24(6): 287–95

Thapa G B and K E Weber 1995 Natural resource degradation in a small watershed in Nepal. Complex causes and remedial measures. *Natural Resources Forum* 19(4): 285–96

Toffler A 1971 *Future shock*. New York, Bantam Books

Trist E 1980 The environment and system-response capability. *Futures* 12(2): 113–27

Trist E 1983 Referent organizations and the development of inter-organizational domains. *Human Relations* 36(3): 269–84

Waldrop M M 1992 *Complexity: the emerging science at the edge of order and chaos*. New York: Simon and Schuster

White G F (ed.) 1974 *Natural hazards: local, national, global*. New York, Oxford University Press

Wiman B L B 1991 Implications of environmental complexity for science and policy. *Global Environmental Change* 1(3): 235–47

Woodward S 1982 The myth of turbulence. *Futures* 12(2): 266–79

World Commission on Environment and Development 1987 *Our common future*. Oxford and New York, Oxford University Press

Young M E 1993 *For our children's children: some practical implications of inter-generational equity and the precautionary principle*. Resource Assessment Commission Occasional Paper Number 6, Canberra, Australian Government Printing Service

Chapter 5

Forecasting and Backcasting

5.1 Forecasts: too often incorrect?

"Forecasting" is usually understood to mean the estimation of probable conditions or events in the future, based on present conditions and trends. For environmental and resource management, the emphasis has been upon forecasting the most likely or probable future related to the supply and demand of resources, given assumptions about population growth, changes in economies, technological innovations, consumption patterns, and evolving values. With the need to make numerous assumptions, it is not surprising that forecasts often turn out to be wrong.

Forecasts relevant to resource and environmental management have been made for a long time. For instance, in 1798, the Scottish clergyman Robert Malthus published his famous book, *An Essay on the Principle of Population*. Malthus's basic position was that the rate of population growth was much greater than the capacity of the Earth to support humans. This conclusion was based on the "facts" that in Britain, France and North America the population had been doubling every 25 years. It was not clear that food production would be able to increase at the same rate indefinitely. Malthus concluded that an inevitable outcome would be starvation and poverty, followed by widespread deaths due to famine and disease. In contemporary terms, such an outcome would occur because humans would exceed the "carrying capacity" of the Earth, and the rapidly growing populations would not be "sustainable".

However, as Kennedy (1993) explained, at least three developments allowed the British to avoid the abyss which Malthus thought was inevitable. First, people left Britain to seek better conditions elsewhere. Indeed, between 1815 and 1914, some 20 million people emigrated. Second, significant technological innovations, in what was later to be labelled the Agricultural Revolution, began about the time Malthus completed his analysis. One impact was a significant increase in food production. The third development was the Industrial Revolution, the early stages of which had started in the decade before Malthus presented his ideas. Industrial innovations substituted mechanical devices for human skill, and inanimate power (steam, then electricity) for animal and human strength. As Kennedy remarked, the response to the power of population came not from the capacity of the Earth, but from the power of technology, which pushed back limits and constraints. As a result, the "carrying capacity" or "sustainability thresholds" of the Earth were not set in absolute

04.

terms. Nevertheless, while Malthus' conclusions were not accurate for societies which could avoid the trap of food shortages, poverty and pestilence through migration, agricultural innovation and industrialization, for other societies without those options his forecast has been much closer to what has occurred.

Nearly 200 years later, in 1972, a book entitled *The Limits to Growth* was published. This book presented the results of a team led by D.H. and D.L. Meadows. This group developed a model to examine what were considered to be five major trends with global implications: (1) accelerating industrialization, (2) rapid population growth, (3) widespread malnutrition, (4) depletion of non-renewable resources, and (5) a deteriorating environment. The similarity to the concerns of Malthus are striking, although by this time "industrialization" was viewed as part of the problem rather than as part of the solution. The Meadows team emphasized that their model was imperfect, oversimplified and unfinished. Nevertheless, they reached the following conclusions:

- If growth trends in world population, industrialization, pollution, food production and resource depletion continued, the limits to growth on Earth would be reached sometime within the next 100 years. The most likely outcome would be a fairly sudden and uncontrollable decline in both population and industrial capacity.
- The forecast growth trends could be modified to create a condition of economic and ecological stability that would be sustainable far into the future. It was possible to ensure that the basic human needs of every person on the globe could be satisfied, and that each individual could reach his or her human potential.

The forecasts by the Meadows team later received sharp criticism. For example, Bailey (1993: 67) noted that their predictions for non-renewable resources "have been proven to be spectacularly wrong". He observed that *The Limits to Growth* had predicted in 1972 that due to exponential population growth rates, the world would run out of gold by 1981, mercury by 1985, tin by 1987, zinc by 1990, petroleum by 1992, and copper, lead and natural gas by 1993. In contrast to these figures, Bailey cited US Bureau of Mines calculations which showed that, at 1990 rates of production, world reserves of gold were adequate for 24 years, mercury 40 years, tin 28 years, zinc 40 years, copper 65 years, and lead 35 years. From this evidence, Bailey suggested that the forecasts in *The Limits to Growth* had little value and, in his opinion, were not useful because they were unnecessarily alarmist.

If people such as Bailey have been critical of environmentalists for being unduly pessimistic in their predictions or forecasts, there are also examples of

---

Box 5.1

I hold those environmental alarmists strictly accountable for their faulty analyses, their wildly inaccurate predictions, and their heedless politicization of science. . . .

Source: Bailey, 1993: xi.

people being remarkably optimistic. To illustrate, Easterbrook (1995) called for a new "eco-realism" which would reject much of the prevailing "environmental orthodoxy". He predicted that pollution in the industrialized West would end within our lifetimes and with little pain or disruption, and also that the anticipated environmental catastrophes from global warming were almost certain to be avoided. Indeed, he argued that adjustments to changing environmental and other circumstances occur virtually automatically through what he termed "organic self adjustment", as societies react to self-correct regarding resource imbalances. Thus, whether considering the prophecies of optimists or pessimists, the analyst should be able to identify the purposes and assumptions of the forecasts in order to judge what weight to give to them.

5.2 Forecasts: uses, assumptions and focus

Uses

Forecasts provide insight regarding what the future could be like if trends continue. Knowing what might be the most probable future allows resource and environmental managers to make choices to ensure that demand and supply are in balance, or to try to ensure that they are kept in balance. Forecasts can indicate where shortages may occur, and can help in making decisions regarding how best to deal with anticipated shortages. For example, in the early 1960s a forecast was conducted to determine if, for the balance of the twentieth century, enough natural resources were available to the United States to allow desired economic growth and development (Landsberg, 1964). Or, forecasts which identify resource shortages can be helpful in designing policies to change demand patterns, such as damping consumption and therefore extending the

---

Box 5.2

The obsessive concern of traditional resource policy with resource maintenance and development stems in turn from taking the assumption of a relatively fixed or limited resource base as an article of faith. Resource policy has, under the influence of this assumption, been dissuaded from investigating and acting on the most important and promising aspects of the supply–demand problem, namely how to lessen the dependence of the economy on a sustained (and more costly) or diminishing (and more costly) supply of natural resources. . . .

The assumption of a relatively fixed resource base merits scouting. Its meaning and its substantiation are pertinent to consider since the implications for resource policy goals, problems and methods which follow from the truth or falseness of the assumption are significant for resource policy with respect to the role of natural resources in furthering economic development.

Source: Miller, 1961: 79–80, 81.

useful life of existing resources until alternatives can be found or developed. As a result, there can be little doubt that forecasts can be valuable tools. However, there can also be little doubt that forecasts will often be incorrect.

Assumptions

Forecasts often turn out to be wrong because a mix of assumptions normally have to be made. If the assumptions are not met, forecasts cannot be correct. As an example, the forecasts regarding adequacy of natural resources and resource products in the United States during the early 1960s included estimates about the future population, labour force and gross national product, all of which were needed to forecast the size and shape of the national economy. To estimate future population levels, assumptions had to be made about birth, death and immigration rates. Once the national economy was predicted, then other estimates were made regarding basic human needs and wants: food, clothing, shelter, heat and power, transportation, durable goods – all of which in turn required assumptions. The estimates about requirements for end products (food, clothing) were translated into requirements for resource products, such as agricultural raw materials, steel, lumber and textile fibres. In turn, the implications of resource products for demands on land, water, fuels and other minerals were calculated. It is clear that any "forecast" regarding supplies of, or demands for, water, for instance, were built upon a wide array of other assumptions and estimates regarding the nature of the economy, technological change and the capacity for substitution.

The above example highlights that assumptions are a key ingredient in any forecast. To the extent that any of the assumptions turn out not to reflect reality, our understanding of what is the most probable or likely future may well be inaccurate.

Focus

Forecasts focus upon the most likely or probable future conditions. A reasonable question is whether such a focus is appropriate for environmental and resource management. As Bott *et al.* (1983: 11–12) observed, humans cannot know what *will* happen in the future. However, three basic questions can help us to cope with an uncertain future. These questions are:

Box 5.3

Three basic assumptions, built in from the start, were: continuing gains in technology, improvements in political and social arrangements, and a reasonably free flow of world trade. Two other assumptions on which the whole system of projections rests are that there will be neither a large-scale war nor a widespread economic depression like that of the early 1930s.

Source: Landsberg, 1964: 6.

- What *can* happen? (feasibility)
- What *ought* to happen? (desirability)
- What is *likely* to happen? (probability)

They concluded that too often forecasts focused on the questions of *probability*, and did not consider the questions of *feasibility* and *desirability*. Or, even worse, all three questions are treated as a single question.

In the view of Bort *et al.* (1983), recognizing the distinction between the above three questions is essential for dealing with the future. That is, we could spend a disproportionate amount of time and effort attempting to predict the most likely conditions and patterns for resource supply and demand. However, none of the most likely futures might be ones judged as desirable. As a result, they argued that it is important also to consider at least what are desirable futures. Humans have the option of making choices, and of intervening to create change. Thus, it seems logical to work on two parallel tracks. One would be to identify the kind of future we would like to have. The other would be to extrapolate from the present situation to estimate whether current trends and patterns are likely to lead to the desired future.

In dealing with an uncertain and complex future, the above perspective requires at least two considerations. Where would we like to be? And will the current path get us there? In that regard, we should do forecasting in the traditional way to estimate where the current path could take us. However, it is not sufficient to stop there. We must also consider where we would like to go, and what actions we need to take to reach the desired end point. At this stage of analysis, we also must consider the feasibility of the possible desired futures. Some may be more dreams or wishes than achievable futures. This "reality check" emphasizes that we should consider feasibility, desirability and probability together. In order to do that, we need ways to determine where we want to get to, and what needs to be done to make that possible.

Two important points should be highlighted at this stage. First, identifying a desirable future is challenging. For example, consider the debate about the nature of *sustainable development* or *sustainable societies*, discussed in Chapter 2. Many people advocate sustainable development as a desired future, and argue that many current policies and practices are unsustainable. However, many different interpretations have been developed for sustainable development, making it difficult to agree on just what this ideal future involves. Second, and following from the first point, most societies are not homogeneous. That is, different values and interests exist, reflecting differences by age, gender, race and status. At any given time, therefore, different groups may hold visions for the future which may conflict with one another. As a result, obtaining agreement on what constitutes a "common future" is often a formidable challenge.

Box 5.4 Paradoxes

A well-known set of paradoxes underlies futures studies. First, in the absence of time travel, the future is unknowable since it has not happened yet, though predictions can be made about the future with varying degrees of confidence. Second, the study of the future is really the study of data from the past and present, since that is the only data available. Third, what will occur in the future is to a large degree a function of choice and behavior in the present, both of which may be influenced one way or another by predictions and other thinking about the future. Fourth, despite the ostensibly scientific nature of future analysis, it is inherently value-laden, with forecasting models serving mainly to display the implications for the future of the assumptions embedded in the model inputs and structure.

Source: Robinson, 1988: 325.

5.3 Futuristic methods

Various methods have been developed to consider the nature of the future. Two of these are considered here: scenarios, and the Delphi method.

5.3.1 Scenarios

In a scenario, the analyst describes a logical sequence of events which follow from specified assumptions (Jantsch, 1967: 180–181). Scenarios are well suited to incorporating many aspects of a problem, and allow the analyst to gain a "feel" for likely future events as well as key decision points. The scenario focuses the investigator's attention on the dynamics and interaction of events. Frequently, several scenarios are prepared. While it is accepted that none will come true as outlined, the general patterns described are viewed as the most likely, if certain assumptions and decisions are made.

Scenarios have often been used to dramatize the nature of possible problems in the future. In *Silent Spring* (1962), Rachel Carson's first chapter was a scenario. Its purpose was to draw attention to the future consequences of indiscriminate use of chemicals to combat insects and weeds. The chapter describes a hypothetical town in the rural United States which at one time was a prosperous agricultural centre and enjoyed an abundance of wildlife, flowers and other vegetation. Carson then described how the situation changed. Livestock started to die for unexplained reasons. Adults and children became ill, with several sudden and unexplained deaths. The flocks of birds disappeared. Vegetation became withered and brown. Having caught the reader's attention, Carson then went on to explain what had silenced the voices of spring in many American towns – the overuse of biochemicals. She was not predicting that the voices of spring would be eliminated in all small rural towns in the future, but she was able to demonstrate that if current practices of using agrochemicals continued, there was a strong likelihood that there would be some negative impacts such as the ones outlined in her scenario.

5.3.2 Delphi method

The Delphi method is one of many "idea-generating strategies". Such strategies can be divided into two types: non-group and group. Non-group processes involve surveys in which participants do not interact with each other. In contrast, group processes incorporate workshops, nominal group techniques and Delphi surveys in which people do interact with one another. Evidence confirms that group processes are usually superior to non-group processes in that the former generate a greater number of higher-quality ideas.

Group processes can be developed in various ways. The usual brainstorming type involves creating a setting in which people engage in discussion with varying degrees of structure. Nominal group techniques (NGTs) involve people interacting in a very structured and controlled environment, such as when a facilitator for a group ensures that all people have an opportunity to comment. Through this approach, NGTs overcome some key problems associated with many group workshops or brainstorming sessions – a small number of people dominating the discussion, many people not contributing, and discussions getting "stuck" on particular topics. Nevertheless, NGTs still face the problems of needing to arrange for people to meet together at a common place and time, which can be both expensive and logistically difficult.

The Delphi method was designed to obtain the benefits of group brainstorming sessions, while avoiding or minimizing the problems noted above. The conventional Delphi involves multiple round surveys, usually with mailed questionnaires. Participants remain anonymous to one another, but through multiple rounds are exposed to the results of the group thinking. Thus, the Delphi method can be described as involving a series of iterative brainstorming rounds. The Delphi avoids the expense and logistical problems of bringing people to one place, eliminates the possibility of one or more articulate and aggressive people dominating the group, reduces pressure for respondents to conform to the views of influential senior participants, and allows respondents to have more time to reflect before expressing their views. Disadvantages are that each round of a Delphi questionnaire survey can be lengthy to complete, people drop out and stop participating as rounds continue, and the opportunity for the spontaneous discussion which occurs at face-to-face meetings is lost. Furthermore, the emphasis on reaching consensus can create its own pressure for conformity.

The conventional Delphi method was developed by the Rand Corporation during research whose objective was to identify the timing and significance of future developments regarding scientific breakthroughs, population growth, automation, space progress, future weapons systems, and probability and prevention of war. Rand proceeded in the following manner. Experts around the world were identified and invited to serve on a panel for one of the topics. For scientific breakthroughs, each panel member was invited to name inventions which were urgently needed and achievable in the next 50 years. Forty-nine items were identified. In a second round, panel members were given a list of the 49 items and asked to indicate the date on which there was a 50–50 probability of the breakthrough occurring. These estimates were combined and displayed as quartiles and medians, and returned to the participants by mail.

Reasonable consensus emerged for 10 items. In a third round, the consensus for the 10 items was presented, and dissenters were asked to elaborate upon why they disagreed. At the same time 17 items for which agreement had not previously been reached were presented. Panel members were invited to elaborate upon reasons for the timing they had identified. This exercise was repeated in a fourth round. At each stage, the number of items for which consensus was reached went up.

The conventional Delphi was designed to be a decision-helping tool, with the purpose of reaching consensus by experts regarding future activities or innovations. Thus, the Delphi has been used as input for forecasts for resource supplies or demands, in the belief that the findings from a Delphi are likely to be more accurate than the opinions of a single expert or a small group of experts. As de Loë (1995) has explained, the conventional Delphi has been used in the following ways related to resource and environmental management: (1) to predict occurrence of events or trends, (2) to rank alternative goals or objectives, (3) to create management strategies, and (4) to allocate scarce resources between competing options.

The output from a conventional Delphi, with its emphasis on consensus and convergence, can be very helpful for resource and environmental managers. However, de Loë (1995) has explained that a derivative, usually termed a *policy Delphi*, also can be useful. In a policy Delphi, the purpose is to generate the strongest and widest possible *different* views about alternative ways to resolve, or deal with, a policy issue. The departure point here is a belief that decision makers do not want analysts to make decisions for them. Instead, they want the analysts to identify all the options, along with supporting evidence. The process for the policy Delphi is the same as for the conventional Delphi. However, the ultimate purposes are quite different. The former emphasizes divergence; the latter, convergence.

Either the conventional or the policy Delphi can be used by resource and environmental managers as a technique to deal with an uncertain and complex future. In the next section, we will see how the Delphi might be incorporated into backcasting.

5.4 Backcasting

In the previous section, some characteristics of scenarios were outlined. Attention is given here to backcasting as one method to generate scenarios. In contrast to forecasts, which focus upon likely futures, backcasts focus upon identifying desirable and attainable futures. The general approach is to work backwards from a future end point judged to be desirable in order to determine the feasibility of achieving that end point, and to determine the specific actions required to achieve it. In some ways, backcasting is another name for "critical path analysis" or "programming, planning and budgeting", both of which have been used in business to plan for the future.

As noted earlier, the intent of backcasts is *not* to identify the most probable future. Instead, the interest is to identify relative feasibility and implications of alternative desirable policies. Thus, backcasting is designed to determine the consequences of different policies regarding the future, and those choices are not selected because of their likelihood of occurring through a continuation of present policies, but rather from creation of new policies. As Robinson (1990) has explained, while good forecasts are expected to *converge* on the most likely future, good backcasts are expected to *diverge* since their purpose is to identify the consequences of different choices.

Table 5.1 and Figure 5.1 outline the steps and characteristics of backcasting. The following discussion elaborates upon the points highlighted in the table and the figure.

5.4.1 Steps in the backcasting method

Step 1: Determine the objectives

Regarding the *purpose of the analysis*, it is essential to outline the kind of future that is to be explored. For example, if the interest were in a future in which climate change might occur, then the focus might be upon actions to be taken between now and some future end point to avoid, minimize or mitigate the impacts of climate change, or to identify what might be done to adapt to significantly different climatic conditions. As part of the statement about the purpose of analysis, attention should be given to the types of problems anticipated in the future that the backcasting is being designed to address.

Having explained the purpose of the analysis, the next sub-step is to explain the *temporal, spatial and substantive scope*. In the short to medium term, it may not be possible for substantive changes to be introduced and to have an effect. For this reason, a minimum of 25 to 50 years is suggested for backcasting, with even longer periods recommended. Time periods of between 50 and 100 years allow both life styles to be altered, and capital stocks to be turned over.

Box 5.5

In order to undertake a backcasting analysis, future goals and objectives need first to be defined, and then used to develop a future scenario. The scenario is then evaluated in terms of its physical, technological and socioeconomic feasibility and policy implications. Iteration of the scenario is usually required to resolve physical inconsistencies and to mitigate adverse economic, social and environmental impacts that are revealed in the course of the analysis.

Source: Robinson, 1990: 823.

Table 5.1 Outline of the backcasting method (Robinson, 1990: 824)

Step 1: Determine the objectives

1.1 Describe the purpose of the analysis
1.2 Determine the temporal, spatial and substantive scope of the analysis
1.3 Decide upon the number and type of scenarios

Step 2: Specify the goals, constraints and targets

2.1 Set goals, constraints and targets for the scenario analysis
2.2 Set goals, constraints and targets for the exogenous variables

Step 3: Describe the present system

3.1 Outline the physical consumption and production processes

Step 4: Specify the exogenous variables

4.1 Develop a description of the exogenous variables
4.2 Specify the external inputs to the scenario analysis

Step 5: Undertake the scenario analysis

5.1 Choose the scenario generation approach
5.2 Analyse future consumption and production processes at the end point and mid points
5.3 Develop the scenario(s)
5.4 Iterate as necessary to achieve internal consistency

Step 6: Undertake the impact analysis

6.1 Consolidate the scenario results
6.2 Analyse the social, economic and environmental impacts
6.3 Compare the results of Steps 6.1 and 6.2 with Step 2
6.4 Repeat the analysis (Steps 2, 4 and 5) as required to ensure consistency between goals and results

Clarification of the spatial scope is also essential, since political or administrative boundaries rarely coincide with ecosystem boundaries (see Chapter 3). Furthermore, some futures cannot be achieved by unilateral actions. For example, reduction of acid precipitation in the Scandinavian countries requires multilateral actions by those countries in cooperation with Germany, Britain and other European nations. Similarly, reduction of acid rain in Ontario and Québec requires bilateral action by Canada and the United States, since much of the acid rain which falls in Canada originates in the United States. It is usually recommended that political boundaries be used to define the spatial focus, since actions almost always have to address changes in human behaviour and policy that are rooted in politically defined regions. Finally, the substantive focus refers to the topics to be included or excluded from the analysis. To illustrate, a study of energy needs may accept existing forecasts of population growth, and concentrate upon identifying various responses to provide energy to the anticipated population. Alternatively, the study might not accept predicted population numbers, but instead might explore options (birth control, immigration policies) which could reduce population growth rates. At some stage, however, the analysts have to make clear which aspects are being

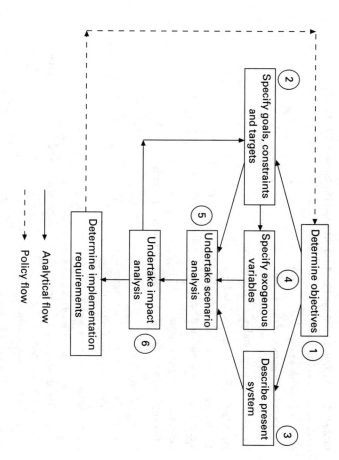

Figure 5.1 Outline of a generic backcasting method (Robinson, 1990: 824)

accepted as given, and which will be allowed to vary.

A final task is to decide upon the *number and type of scenarios*. Several decisions are needed. One is to decide whether a "base case" or "status quo" scenario will be established against which the outputs of backcast scenarios can be compared. The "base case" usually provides a conservative interpretation of the most likely future, and can provide a benchmark. The "base case" scenario may also help to highlight aspects unlikely to be sustainable in the longer term, and thereby help to draw attention to issues requiring attention. Another decision involves how many backcasting scenarios will be generated. Analysts usually have limited time and resources for their studies, so choices need to be made. The choices can range from exploring one scenario in detail, to identifying a broader range of scenarios with each being developed in less depth. As Robinson (1990: 827) cautioned, if the choice is taken to generate a number of scenarios, analysts must be careful since people tend to concentrate upon any "middle road" scenarios because they believe those to be the most likely or most reasonable view about the future. Although backcasts deliberately are not designed to be forecasts, people often interpret them as such, rather than as explorations of different possible futures. Robinson suggested that one way to counter the tendency to focus on the middle ground scenario is always to generate an even number of scenarios.

Step 2: Specify the goals, constraints and targets

Two aspects must be addressed. The first is to transform the objectives identified in Step 1 into more specific *goals, constraints and targets for the scenario analysis.* The prescriptive aspects can be specified in either positive terms (things to be achieved, such as a minimum standard of drinking water) or negative terms (things to be avoided, such as ensuring air pollution does not exceed certain standards).

Goals and constraints normally are expressed as quantitative targets whenever possible, to facilitate monitoring (see Chapter 13). However, quantification is not always easy for several reasons. First, some goals, such as "quality of life", do not readily lend themselves to being expressed only in quantitative terms. Second, even when goals can be stated quantitatively, it is not always easy or possible to collect appropriate data. For example, a goal might be to increase public participation in environmental and resource management. One quantitative measure could be the number of people from the general public attending open houses or public meetings to discuss environmental or resource issues. However, information only about number of people attending provides a very imperfect measure of public participation. As a result of this problem, most goals, constraints and targets are measured using both quantitative and qualitative terms.

A related task is to identify *goals, constraints and targets for exogenous variables,* or for those variables that provide the context for backcasting. Earlier in this chapter, the review of the work by Malthus and the Meadows highlighted the importance for environmental and resource management of population change, technological innovation, and economic development. Which aspects of these matters will be assumed as constant, and which aspects will be allowed to vary over the period of the backcast? Such variables can have significant impacts on rates of resource use or environmental degradation. The analyst has to be clear about their role during the period for which scenarios are to be developed.

Step 3: Describe the present system

Attention is usually given to describing basic physical processes and activities associated with the system being analysed, including exchanges to and from the natural environment. Two types of processes and activities need to be described. One relates to consumption of goods, products and services. The other focuses upon the production of such goods and services (recognizing that "production" can also involve consumption of goods and services).

When describing consumption or production processes, attention has focused upon the "end-use services" to be provided. For example, if the interest was on energy, then there are eventually two end-uses: to provide heat, or to complete work. Such end-uses can be disaggregated. Regarding provision of heat, for example, end-use categories for consumption could include home heating, air conditioning, water heating or drying. For completion of work, categories might include lighting, motive power or operating machinery. While an end-use approach theoretically allows for a complete description of human consumption processes, in practice there are many difficulties. No agreement exists about the definition and classification of end-uses. Data related to end-uses are often difficult or impossible to collect. As a result, if the end-use approach is to be used, important tasks include defining end-use categories for which data are available, or can be assembled.

Step 4: Specify the exogenous variables

In Step 2, exogenous variables were mentioned. The key task here is to take the goals, constraints and targets from Step 2 and transform them into quantitative descriptions of future values of such variables — whether population size, or nature of the economy. At this point, a dilemma is created. Exogenous variables, by definition, are outside the terms of reference of the backcasting scenarios. Yet, assumptions about them expose the scenarios to the same weaknesses associated with forecasts. That is, the scenarios will be valid only if the assumptions about exogenous variables turn out to reflect what actually happens. The usual way to handle this dilemma is to assume very conservative projections for the external variables, such as a high level of economic growth. The rationale is that if a sustainable scenario can be created under such conservative conditions, then it should be achievable under weaker economic growth.

Step 5: Undertake the scenario analysis

Developing scenarios requires establishing the assumptions which can be used to characterize the future state of the system of interest. Normally, at this stage, attention must be given to technological, economic, environmental and social considerations.

Regarding technological changes, the scenario builder has two options. One is to include only those technologies currently being used. The other is to include the introduction of new technologies which are judged likely to become available over the time frame being used. Since the time frame is normally relatively long, it is plausible to consider significant technological innovations. To identify such innovations, the Delphi procedure outlined earlier could be used. If the objective is to consider alternative futures in the long term, it is preferable to try to incorporate technological changes.

The same challenge arises for economic, environmental and social changes. For economic aspects, decisions must be made regarding changes of relative prices and costs, and about appropriate discount rates (Chapter 6). Environmental assumptions are also needed. For example, upper limits might be established for levels of waste generation, or for extraction rates for various kinds of resources. Such upper limits could be stated as targets to be met by a specified future date. The issue would then be to determine which actions were required to allow these targets to be met. Changes in social values would relate to new values (perhaps less materialism) which would make new policies feasible, which in turn could affect rates of resource use or environmental degradation.

Having established assumptions which characterize the desirable future state of affairs, the scenario builder can then translate those into end-use processes and activities regarding production and consumption, which in turn can be used to characterize the nature of the future society. At various points of time in the future scenario, attention is required to determine if the various components of the scenario are consistent with one another. If not, then adjustments have to be made until the scenario components are both plausible and consistent.

Step 6: Undertake the impact analysis

The final step should be to analyse the environmental, economic and social implications of scenarios. Such analysis requires the identification of explicit criteria against which the scenarios can be compared and assessed. For example, the criteria might reflect the attributes of a sustainable development, as outlined in Chapter 2. The key aspect is that the analyst should make clear and explicit the basis on which the alternative scenarios are being assessed. It is not normally a good idea to use "present conditions" as the baseline or criteria against which, the future will be different from the present situation. As a result, using the present situation is not likely to be informative or instructive for comparison. Another key aspect of impact analysis is to consider the feasibility of the scenarios. It is possible that some goals, constraints or targets developed in Step 2 are inconsistent or impossible to attain. For example, given certain environmental goals and targets, it may not be possible to achieve specified economic goals and targets. When that happens, the analyst must determine whether adjustments can be made to the scenario, or whether the scenario should be abandoned.

5.5 Analogies

Analogies can also be used to help understand unfamiliar or uncertain situations. Creating an analogy generally involves comparing two places or situations. Known information about one is used to make inferences about the yet to be observed, but anticipated, behaviour or structure in the other. The choice of places or experiences for comparison is a major challenge. Should we be more concerned with the *number* of similarities in structure and function, or with the *significance* of the similarities? While the former often seems to influence choices, many believe that signficance rather than frequency of similarities is most important.

Familiar analogies can be identified. The "greenhouse effect" has been used to characterize what is happening with regard to the process of climate change or global warming. This analogy has been effective because people know that greenhouses stimulate plant growth by containing warmth in an enclosed environment. The parallel between carbon dioxide, released from motor vehicles and factories, serving as a skin or barrier to trap heat escaping into the atmosphere, and the similar way in which the panes of glass keep heat in a

Box 5.6 Analogies and unfamiliar situations

When confronted by unknown situations, analogies can provide us with a feeling of understanding. They provide a first step toward knowing or, at least, considering the unknown.... In this regard, analogies are comforting because they provide a bridge between the past (the known) and the future (the unknown).

Source: Glantz, 1991: 14.

greenhouse, has helped people to visualize why global warming might occur. An analogy to another "Dust Bowl" in the American Midwest if temperatures increased and precipitation decreased has helped people to imagine what that region might be like if global warming were to occur. And, at the conclusion of the 1988 World Conference on the Changing Environment in Toronto, the official concluding statement compared the potential impacts of global warming with those that could be expected from nuclear war. As Glantz (1991: 14) explained, "this analogy was not made by 'idealistic, scientifically innocent environmentalists' but was used by the Toronto conference organizers to compare an unknown situation, the consequence of global warming, with a better-known, worst-case scenario, a nuclear holocaust, to capture the attention of policy makers, the public, and especially the media and to urge prompt policy action to address the global warming issue."

As Glantz has explained, analogies can be used for many purposes. They can be used for general education, to identify questions or hypotheses for further research, to forecast future states of systems, and to identify alternative policy options. The education function has already been noted above, when explaining how analogies to the greenhouse effect, Dust Bowl and nuclear war have been made to sensitize the public and policy makers about the processes and potential impacts of climate change. Comparisons have also been made between countries or regions to illustrate what future conditions could be like. Thus, under anticipated climate change scenarios it has been suggested that Iceland could have a climate similar to present-day Scotland. Such an analogy helps policy makers to visualize opportunities and problems that could be encountered regarding matters such as agricultural production, and what adaptations might be needed to cope with the new conditions.

The use of analogies for forecasting and generating policy options should, in the opinion of Glantz (1991), be treated with great caution. While analogies can be very useful in stimulating scientific questions or hypotheses about possible future conditions and their implications, or adjustments to them, they are less useful as forecasts to identify future states of a climate or society. In this manner, analogies have the same weaknesses as the forecasts discussed previously – they attempt to converge on the most likely conditions, rather than on the most desirable conditions. Also, there is always a danger that people who have particular interests or favour certain policies will put forward analogies

Box 5.7 Caution advised in using analogies

The plausibility of a physical or social analogy is not a sufficient reason for it to be used by policymakers because several plausible but contradictory policies could be formulated based on different analogs drawn from the same pool of objective scientific information. But, then, on which historical analog should a decision maker rely?

Source: Glantz, 1991: 13.

Box 5.8

Analogies can also provide clues, generate ideas, and spark reactions that lead to different searches for new analogies. Each analogy gives additional information about the target problem.... By providing useful insights, historical analogies may give societies the opportunity to capitalize on their strengths and to minimize their shortcomings.

Source: Glantz, 1991: 32–3.

which support their position, and ignore those which do not.

The above discussion indicates that, as with most things, analogies have strengths and weaknesses. Their careful use can help us to anticipate future conditions, even when we cannot predict exactly what will happen. They can be particularly helpful by providing a first cut at understanding the regional implications of some specified different conditions, such as altered climate. They also can help people in one region to benefit from the experience of people in another region, if there are reasons to believe that conditions in the first region could evolve to approximate those in the second region. Furthermore, analogies can stimulate thinking, as shown by the comments in Box 5.8.

5.6 Implications

People try to see into the future in many ways. Some read tea leaves. Others read palms. Others seek out gurus who are thought to have the ability to anticipate future events. Analysts construct sophisticated models to generate simulations based on different goals, values and assumptions. Whatever approach is used, the future remains uncertain and complex, and the likelihood of change is very high.

For resource and environmental managers, it is important to think about the future for various reasons. One, we want to anticipate possible undesirable conditions so that action can be initiated now to avoid or mitigate them. Two, we would like to act as agents of positive change in order to take decisions that will result in outcomes that will meet the needs and expectations of people in society, as well as consider the needs of non-human living things.

In this chapter, the key message is that there are at least three questions which deserve our attention regarding the future: (1) what is most likely? (2) what is most desirable? (3) what is most feasible? Too often, resource and environmental managers have focused primarily upon only the first question, and the preferred analytical method has been a *forecast*. And, since forecasts are based on a series of assumptions, it is not unusual for forecasts not to capture what actually happens. While forecasts have shortcomings, they are still needed, as they provide one way to estimate what pressures may be created relative to supplies of and demands for resources and the environment. To increase our effectiveness, however, it appears that we could improve our capacity to anticipate the future if we used *backcasts* in parallel with forecasts. In that manner we would simultaneously consider all three of the questions noted above.

Many methods or techniques are available for use in forecasting and backcasting. In this chapter, we reviewed the characteristics of scenarios, Delphi methods, and analogies. Each offers different strengths and weaknesses. It does appear that if we were to use these more systematically when looking into the future it is possible that we could more effectively anticipate what usually turn out to be rapidly changing conditions. Furthermore, as noted in Chapter 4, we should approach examination of possible future conditions with an attitude that surprises and turbulence are likely to be the norm. As a result, our scans into the future, and the strategies that we develop based on such scans, should be designed to allow the opportunity to learn from new experiences, adapt and move forward.

References and further reading

Bailey R 1993 *Eco-scam: the false prophets of ecological apocalypse*. New York, St Martin's Press

Barnett H J and C Morse 1963 *Scarcity and growth: the economics of natural resource availability*. Baltimore, Johns Hopkins University Press

Bott R, D Brooks and J Robinson 1983 *Life after oil: a renewable energy policy for Canada*. Edmonton, Hurtig Publishers

Carson R L 1962 *Silent Spring*. Boston, Houghton Mifflin

de Loë R 1995 Exploring complex policy questions using the policy Delphi. *Applied Geography* 15(1): 53–68

de Loë R and B Mitchell 1993 Policy implications of climate change for water management in the Grand River basin. In M Sanderson (ed.) *The impact of climate change on water in the Grand River basin, Ontario*. Department of Geography Publication Series No. 40, Waterloo, University of Waterloo: 189–217

Easterbrook G 1995 *A moment on the earth: the coming age of environmental optimism*. New York, Viking Penguin

Glantz M H 1991 The use of analogies in forecasting ecological and social responses to global warming. *Environment* 33(5): 10–15, 27–33

Jantsch, E 1967 *Technological forecasting in perspective*. Paris, Organisation for Economic Co-operation and Development

Kennedy P 1993 *Preparing for the twenty-first century*. Toronto, HarperCollins

Kuhn R G 1992 Canadian energy futures: policy scenarios and public preferences. *Canadian Geographer* 36(4): 350–65

Landsberg H H 1964 *Natural resources for US growth: a look ahead to the year 2000*. Baltimore, Johns Hopkins University Press

Lazarus M, S Diallo and Y Sokona 1994 Energy and environment scenarios for Senegal. *Natural Resources Forum* 18(1): 31–47

Mannormaa M 1991 In search of an evolutionary paradigm for futures research. *Futures* 23(4): 349–72

Meadows D H, D L Meadows, J Randers and W W Behrens III 1972 (second edition, 1974) *The limits to growth*. New York, New American Library

Miller M 1961 Resource policy and resource development. *Plan Canada* 2(2): 75–87

Naisbitt J 1984 *Megatrends*. New York, Warner Books

Needham R D and R de Loë 1990 The policy Delphi: purpose, structure, and application. *Canadian Geographer* 34(2): 133–42

Robinson J B 1982 Energy backcasting: a proposed method of policy analysis. *Energy Policy* 10(4): 337–44

Robinson J B 1988 Unlearning and backcasting: rethinking some of the questions we ask about the future. *Technological Forecasting and Social Change* 33(4): 325–38

Robinson J B 1990 Futures under glass: a recipe for people who hate to predict. *Futures* 22(8): 820–42

Sharma H D, A D Gupta and Shushil 1995 The objectives of waste management in India: a futures inquiry. *Technological Forecasting and Social Change* 48(3): 285–309

Toffler A 1970 *Future Shock*. New York, Random House

Chapter 6

Assessing Alternatives

6.1 Introduction

In previous chapters, attention focused upon change; sustainable development; ecosystem approach; uncertainty, complexity and conflict; and forecasting and backcasting. For all of these matters, alternatives exist and choices must be made. In resource and environmental management, people have relied heavily on *benefit–cost analysis* and *environmental impact assessment* as tools to help in assessing alternatives and in making choices. More recently, *life cycle analysis* has emerged as a third tool or method. In this chapter, each of these is examined. However, before doing that, the following section indicates the importance of being able to recognize different perspectives, and understanding that regardless of the assessment method applied, different conclusions can be drawn.

6.2 Differing perspectives can affect assessment

Various conditions, needs, values, assumptions and criteria can lead to different ideas about what alternatives are appropriate to consider, as well as which one should be preferred. In Chapter 2, we discovered that people from developed and developing countries have divergent interpretations about *sustainable development* due to their different needs, expectations and interests. We also know that if *efficiency* is the criterion for judging a policy, program or project, an assessment might be quite different than if the criterion were *equity* or *effectiveness*. We also appreciate that different evaluations are likely if priority is given to economic development over environmental protection (or vice versa). Furthermore, benefit–cost analysis may lead to different assessments from analysis based on environmental impact assessment. To emphasize the important role of different perspectives, this section summarizes an analysis by Russell (1994), a civil engineer, regarding the Three Gorges project in China.

The Three Gorges project, proposed for the Yangtze River in China, would be one of the largest water resource projects ever constructed in the world. The multi-billion-dollar project would involve a massive dam across the Yangtze River. Multiple benefits are anticipated by project designers, including downstream flood control, hydroelectricity generation and improved navigation. The impetus for the project is a desire to "control" or at least minimize devastating floods, which for centuries have caused loss of life and major economic disruption, and which today threaten about 10 million people.

Concerns about the Three Gorges project have focused on the need to relocate nearly one million people from the reservoir area, and the flooding of a gorge with high amenity value.

During the design of the project, a feasibility study by a consortium of engineering companies concluded that the project was viable, with a benefit–cost ratio of 1.5:1. In contrast, an environmental non-government organization noted many flaws in the design, and argued that the project could be disastrous for the Chinese people. Russell asked how two apparently well-qualified groups could have such different perspectives. His conclusion was that "it gradually became clear that they came from two quite different 'cultures': the large dam heavy civil engineering culture, and what might be called the new green culture" (Russell, 1994: 541).

With regard to the heavy engineering culture, Russell suggested that for civil engineers responsible for building large dams, one concern is dominant: the safety of the project. Such massive projects cannot be pretested, yet any failure could have catastrophic results. As a result, "it is not surprising that civil engineers are conservative and always think safety first" (Russell, 1994: 543). Furthermore, since there are never adequate resources for such projects, civil engineers establish priorities, and marginal or peripheral concerns are quickly set aside. Most attention is reserved for those aspects judged to be the most important. As the comment in Box 6.1 shows, environmental concerns often do not fall into the list of most important concerns.

Russell suggested that the *green culture* includes people who are usually well educated, articulate and well intentioned. Many are based in universities. They normally work as individuals or as part of loosely connected coalitions. Thus, they are relatively independent, and often do not have to accommodate interests other than the ones in which they believe. They have relatively few resources. Green culture people are often highly idealistic, such as when they suggested that China does not need additional power and should concentrate on achieving energy savings through more efficient industrial processes. In this regard, they argued for energy and environmental standards for a country in the early stages

---

Box 6.1 The large dam, civil engineering culture

Although engineers have an increasing sensitivity to environmental issues, such concern is not "built in" to the typical engineer to nearly the same extent, as is the case with safety issues. In summary, present-day civil engineers (the ones in control) have a deep personal and professional commitment to the safety of the projects for which they are responsible, a somewhat lesser commitment to economic viability of their projects (despite the old adage about engineers being able to do for $1, what anyone else can do for $2), and a still lesser commitment to the newer environmental issues.

Source: Russell, 1994: 544.

Box 6.2 Green culture

They do not have the same need to compromise as do team workers and, not being part of a professional group, can feel free to challenge any point, however important or inconsequential . . ., the writing is usually very good and very convincing and can raise important points that may not have been given due weight. But it can also lack balance and be quite unfair at times.

Source: Russell, 1994: 544.

of development which are often not met in much more developed and industrialized nations. At the same time, such observers often identify aspects that the more focused engineers overlook or consider to be of lower priority. Thus, Russell agreed that valid criticisms were made about underestimation of costs for the project, especially those linked to resettlement, insufficient consideration of many environmental problems, and use of too low interest rates in the benefit–cost analysis.

The existence of two "cultures" during the assessment of this project is a timely reminder that "truth" is rarely absolute, and can be influenced by the lenses through which the world is viewed. This point should be kept in mind when considering the following methods which are often used for assessing alternatives.

6.3 Benefit–cost analysis

6.3.1 Purpose and attributes

Benefit–cost analysis was developed to provide a systematic way to compare the economic benefits and costs of alternative projects. In its most basic form, benefit–cost analysis involves identifying all the benefits and the costs over the lifetime of a project, transforming the value of the benefits and costs at different time periods to a common time period, and calculating the ratio of benefits to costs. Normally, analysts or planners are interested only in alternatives with a benefit–cost ratio of greater than one. In other words, to be economically viable a project would be expected to return more than it costs.

Projects are then ranked relative to their benefit–cost ratios (B/C), and usually the project with the highest ratio is the preferred choice. However, analysts also often compare the difference between benefits and costs (B–C), and consider whether the project with the best B/C ratio could be redesigned to improve its net benefits (B–C).

Several matters should be highlighted regarding benefit–cost analysis. First, such analysis does not determine the *absolute* merits of alternative projects. It simply provides information about their *relative* merits, and those relative merits are based on comparisons of *economic efficiency*. Other criteria (equity, effectiveness) could be used to compare the relative merits of alternatives, and

┌───┐

Box 6.3 What does a benefit–cost ratio measure?

... it should be emphasized that these ratios are a measure of relative merit and not of absolute merit. If there are other ways of achieving the same purpose, the fact that a project has a benefit–cost ratio greater than 1 does not necessarily imply that it should be built.

Source: Sewell *et al.,* 1965: viii.

use of such criteria could lead to different conclusions. Second, benefit–cost analysis does not indicate whether the goals and objectives which alternative projects are designed to realize are necessarily the best ones for a society. Instead, the B/C analysis indicates the most economically efficient project to achieve already determined goals and objectives. Third, benefit–cost analysis assumes that it is possible to identify and quantify the benefits and costs of the project over its useful life span. Such estimates necessitate many assumptions, such as the cost of energy, labour and other inputs required to operate the project, perhaps for a 30 to 50-year period. As a result, B/C analysis has to address all of the problems that were discussed in Chapter 5 with regard to forecasting. Some specific matters that have to be handled in B/C analysis are discussed below.

6.3.2 Key issues

Discounting

In the introduction to B/C analysis, it was explained that analysts must identify all of the benefits and costs of alternative projects over their life span. However, a difficulty then arises. Is it reasonable to assume that $100,000 of benefits receivable in 10 years from the present has the same worth as $100,000 receivable in 20 years? Intuitively, most of us would rather have that money in 10 years than in 20, as it would be worth more to us. In B/C analysis, therefore, the procedure has been to *discount* both benefits and costs receivable in the future to their *present worth or present value.* That is accomplished by using the same kind of formula to calculate what the value of a sum of money would be in 10 or 20 years if it were invested today. A key decision, therefore, is the choice of *interest rate* used to do the discounting.

Discounting is necessary to transform the benefits and costs estimated for each year of a project, whose lifetime often extends over a period of 30 to 50 years for major projects, to some common base year (the present). However, the implications of discounting are profound, since the further into the future benefits are received the less is their present value. This consequence of discounting has drawn considerable criticism. Discounting the value of future benefits, it is argued, encourages a short-term perspective. In addition, discounting does not provide much incentive for analysts to consider issues of intergenerational equity, discussed in Chapter 2, if benefits in the future have a relatively low value. Alternatively, the consequences of discounting can lead designers or analysts "to be creative" in trying to ensure that most of the benefits occur as early as possible in the life-time of a project in order to increase the present value of present benefits. Thus, by changing the timing of when benefits emerge, it is possible to alter significantly a B/C ratio. As a result, the user of a benefit–cost analysis should not just read the final ratios, but also should take care to examine the manner in which benefits and costs were estimated and discounted.

Interest rates

If discounting is important in benefit–cost analysis to bring estimated benefits and costs in the future to a common denominator, then the selection of the interest rate to use in the discounting process becomes very important. Low interest rates increase the present value of future benefits, and proponents and developers are often criticized for using inappropriately low interest rates. As higher rates are applied, the present value of benefits becomes less.

The dilemma is that at any given time there is no one interest rate that prevails. The interest rate charged by a bank to a multinational corporation will normally be considerably lower than the rate an individual will be charged for a car loan or house mortgage. Governments, depending upon their credit rating, will be charged different interest rates by those lending money to them. As resource and environmental projects often involve multiple participants from both the public and private sectors, there is scope for legitimate differences of view regarding which interest rate should be used when discounting, particularly for *joint benefits*, which are those that cannot readily be assigned to any one participant.

Given the above, there is always potential for disagreement about what is an appropriate interest rate to use. The user of a benefit–cost analysis should always look to see what interest rate(s) was used, and consider the rationale used to justify the choice of interest rate. It is not unusual for benefit–cost analyses to be completed using several interest rates, so that the decision maker can then decide which one should be accepted.

Intangibles

If benefits and costs for the lifetime of a project are to be identified and summed so that a B/C ratio can be calculated, it simplifies matters if every benefit and cost can be quantified and expressed in monetary terms. The difficulty, of course, is that not all benefits and costs are amenable to quantification. The satisfaction and enjoyment that a society receives in knowing an area has been designated as a "natural area" to protect biodiversity is difficult to quantify. The benefits to health care from the discovery of new pharmaceutical products from rain forests, or the value of the traditional way of life of indigenous people living in the rain forest area, are difficult to quantify, compared with the market value of the timber from the trees, the minerals that might be mined, or the agricultural products that might be grown after the trees are cut down.

There are at least two approaches to deal with intangible aspects in benefit–cost analysis. One approach is to acknowledge that, for some aspects, quantification is difficult, and not to do it. While quantifiable aspects are given numbers and are used to calculate the ratio, non-quantifiable aspects are identified and discussed in an accompanying narrative. In this manner, decision makers are alerted about the existence of qualitative variables not included in the benefit–cost ratio, and can reach a judgement about their importance.

The other approach is to seek to quantify the intangible aspects. The position would be that if paintings and other forms of art can be given a value at art auctions, then it should be possible to develop quantitative estimates for most "unquantifiable" aspects. For example, if a benefit–cost analysis is needed to quantify the value of wildlife in an area under consideration for development, the analysts might add up the value of hunting licences for the animals, the estimated costs of those who travel to the area to hunt or observe the wildlife, and the fees paid to guides. Such an estimate is very "anthropocentric", in that it values non-human species with reference only to their value to humankind. Nevertheless, this type of quantification is done, and then the numbers are included in the calculation of the benefit–cost ratio.

The user of a benefit–cost study should take care to determine which approach, or combination of approaches, was used to deal with intangible matters.

Historic or sunk costs

Benefit–cost analysis is focused on the stream of benefits and costs predicted in the future from alternative projects. As a result, it is not appropriate to consider expenditures made prior to the time of the analysis. For example, if projects were being compared in two different areas, and significant investment already had been made in one of the areas, that previous expense should not be included in the analysis. Proponents often find it difficult to set aside such costs, and critics are even more quick to point out their omission, often arguing that if they were included the benefit–cost ratio would not have been so favourable. However, it is incorrect to include historic or sunk costs, and it is unfair criticism to claim they should have been included. Expenditures in the past have no bearing on the stream of benefits or costs in the future, even if emotionally it is difficult to set them aside.

General implications

The four matters (discounting, interest rates, intangibles, historic costs) emphasize that benefit–cost analysis does not establish the *absolute* merit of a project. Such analysis does indicate the *relative* merit with reference to the criterion of economic efficiency. The ratio (B/C) and net benefits (B–C) are helpful to the extent that it has been possible to estimate the stream of benefits and costs in the future, and that reasonable decisions have been made about various technical aspects of benefit–cost analysis.

6.4 Impact assessment

6.4.1 Origins, evolution and key attributes

Environmental impact assessment (EIA) was formally introduced through the National Environmental Policy Act of 1969 in the United States, which required federal agencies to consider explicitly the environmental implications of proposed development. Over time, other countries have incorporated impact assessment into resource and environmental management, through either a law or a policy decision. Initially, the focus in EIA studies was on the impacts on the biophysical environment. However, it was not long before criticism arose that the social impacts were being overlooked. Such criticism led to the development of what became known as social impact assessments (SIA). Today, assessments normally include both "environmental" and "social" dimensions, and hence the use of the abbreviated term, "impact assessment" (IA). It is usually assumed that economic dimensions are addressed through a parallel benefit–cost analysis.

As with sustainable development, many definitions and interpretations exist for impact assessment which focus on the environmental and social implications of development. However, most people would agree that an impact statement should: (1) identify the overall goals and objectives of the project, (2) describe alternative actions which could achieve the goals and objectives, (3) describe what environmental and social changes might occur without the development, (4) describe the nature, magnitude, and duration of impacts from alternative actions, (5) assess the significance of the impacts, (6) identify remedial action to mitigate or eliminate negative impacts, as well as actions to enhance positive impacts, (7) identify a preferred action, and (8) outline necessary action for monitoring.

In preparing impact statements, it is important for the analyst or planner to recognize that all impacts have a *temporal dimension* (Figure 6.1). In other words, direct impacts (1) occur from changes triggered by the project on initial conditions in the natural or social environment. However, it is not adequate only to examine direct impacts. Changed conditions lead to adjustment and adaptation (2) (discussed more in Chapter 7). Furthermore, during the planning or implementation phase, the development may be modified (3) in response to public reaction or experience. Any development also has a connection with earlier decisions and developments (4), and such "history" may condition willingness to accept a proposal or to consider various adaptation or mitigation measures. Finally, other factors external to the project (such as inflation, economic stagnation, taxation policies) may influence the project (5). Thus, we must be aware of the spatial and temporal boundaries which are important for examining the impacts of a proposed development.

6.4.2 Principles for impact assessment

Gibson (1993) has suggested that a set of principles can be identified for the design of impact assessments. While it is unlikely that any one design is perfect

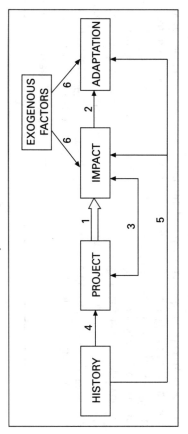

Figure 6.1 Temporal context for environmental impact assessment (Mitchell, 1989: 201)

for all circumstances, he believed that consideration of eight principles should help to improve designs. He stressed that the principles are interdependent and form a package. In his view, all have to be used together. The eight principles are considered below.

(1) An integrated approach By an integrated approach, Gibson meant that societies must consider the impacts of their activities at local, national and global scales, ensure that basic needs are met and poverty is alleviated, analyse patterns of consumption to determine implications from extraction of resources and from returning wastes to the environment, and focus not only on environmental implications but also on social, cultural and economic aspects and their interrelationships. It is also necessary to examine implications in the short, medium and long term. An integrated approach would also consider cumulative effects, which is best done by relating impact assessment to regional land use planning.

(2) All decision making should be environmentally responsible Impact assessment should apply as broadly as possible, including public and private sector initiatives for new projects or for expansion, modification, decommissioning or abandonment of existing ones. This principle also requires that proponents must know from the outset what their impact assessment obligations are. This principle means that policies and programs as well as projects should be subject to IAs.

(3) Impact assessment should focus on identifying best options rather than merely acceptable options This principle requires that the purpose and relative merits of alternative means are critically examined. This could result in questioning of the objectives, but more frequently would focus on the rationale for a preferred set of actions to realize objectives.

Box 6.4 Weaknesses in laws for IA

In practice . . . environmental assessment laws and processes have not been automatically effective. Their purpose is difficult and delicate. They are intended to force open and careful consideration of a new and generally ill-understood set of concerns, and they are directed at decision makers who are generally hostile to greater openness and to additional, imposed duties. Failure is easy. Moreover, laws and processes that are weak, unclear or simply difficult to administer with consistency and efficiency do not just fail to foster greater environmental sensitivity in planning and decision making; they tend also to undermine the general credibility of government efforts to encourage environmental responsibility.

Source: Gibson, 1993: 12.

(4) *Impact assessments should be based in law, and should be specific, mandatory and enforceable* This principle makes it clear that IA is an attack on the status quo, and is intended to lead to change in planning and decision making. Given the emphasis on change, voluntary adoption is inappropriate. The assessment expectations must be clearly understood, key tenets must be based in law, and compliance needs to be legally enforceable.

(5) *Assessment processes and related decision making must be open, participative and fair* This principle reflects the concepts of equity, empowerment and justice embodied in sustainable development (Chapter 2), and the concept of a participatory approach (Chapter 8). The rationale is that impact assessment is as much value-laden as scientific, and thus "broad participation and scrutiny is the best means of combatting narrow biases and encouraging careful attention to matters of public concern" (Gibson, 1993: 19). Openness and participation should also contribute to an even-handed approach to all parties and interests.

(6) *Terms and conditions of approval must be enforceable, and capacity must exist to monitor effects and to enforce compliance during implementation* Approval after a systematic review will have little value if there is not the capacity or commitment to track post-approval activity and effects, and to ensure compliance. While such provisions are common sense, many IA processes do not provide for what might be termed "enforceable approvals", or for monitoring. The role of *auditing* as a technique to facilitate compliance is considered in Chapter 13.

(7) *Efficient implementation should occur* While efficiency is hopefully a central concern in all regulatory processes, Gibson argued that it is particularly needed in environmental assessment because inefficiency will breed hostility and antagonism, which become a "formidable enemy". The long-term goal of IA is

to change proponents into people who automatically think, plan and act with regard to environmental and social consequences. Hostility and antagonism can become a major obstacle to achieving such a long-term goal.

(8) *Provision must be made to connect impact assessment to higher-level decision making* This final principle is tied closely to the first principle, which advocates an integrated approach. Thus, it is important that the results of IA be fed back into more general policy and program deliberations, and be used to help shape and develop criteria to be used for judging environmental significance.

Trade-offs to be considered

The eight criteria collectively set a high standard, and to a considerable extent reflect the *programmed approach* to be explained in Chapter 7. Thus, they minimize discretion, and seek to ensure that IA is automatically included as part of the process of approving development initiatives. After considering the arguments in Chapter 7 regarding *programmed* and *adaptive* approaches, you may wish to re-examine these criteria, to decide whether you believe any modifications should be made to them.

6.4.3 Strategic issues in impact assessment

Predicting effects

Given our imperfect understanding of ecological and social systems, it is often difficult to anticipate or predict what the effects of proposed development might be. In many instances, *baseline information* is either missing or incomplete. As a result, the state of the existing system is not well understood. It is for this reason that state of the environment and other types of monitoring are being advocated or initiated, as discussed in Chapter 13.

Our *theories* or *concepts* about ecological and human systems may also be incomplete, inconsistent or contradictory. For example, it is not universally accepted that diversity in a natural system always leads to stability. There is also questioning about whether "stability" is a state that should be expected or desired. Many argue that "resilience" is a more desirable end state for a system (see Chapter 4). Also, we often do not understand the conditions that may make a system "flip" or transform in some catastrophic manner. These aspects highlight the complexity and uncertainty with which analysts must deal, and our frequent ignorance or incomplete understanding.

Synergistic effects can also make predictions difficult. In other words, it may be possible to predict the outcome of a development on a particular component of a system if it is assumed that the component is isolated from all other components of that system. Rarely if ever is the assumption of "all other things being constant or equal" satisfied. When changes in one component of a system interact with changes in other components of that system, the final changes may be totally different from the changes that might be expected for any one component. It is this aspect which makes estimating *cumulative effects* so challenging, and this is discussed in more detail following the next subsection on intangible effects.

Intangible effects

Just as in benefit–cost analysis, impact assessment encounters problems in valuing environmental or social components which are not readily or easily measured in monetary terms. Biodiversity, ecological integrity, human health and cultural integrity are examples of aspects which are not easily quantified in monetary terms, or readily comparable. Yet one of the basic issues in impact assessment is determining the relative merits of alternative actions, just as the relative economic efficiency of alternatives is estimated in benefit–cost analysis. Ideally, having established the relative merits, the analyst or planner can then begin to explore trade-offs, to design a project that will enhance positive environmental and social impacts, and minimize negative ones. However, when it is difficult to measure some impacts, considering trade-offs becomes challenging.

Cumulative effects

In order to be practical, IA procedures usually have a cut-off threshold, determined by variables such as capital costs or number of employees, below which assessments will not be conducted. This practice has evolved to avoid unnecessary regulations or restrictions on relatively small and innocuous activities. The danger, of course, is that the total sum of many small developments may be greater than the sum of the individual parts. This dilemma is characterized as one of *cumulative effects*.

Cumulative effects can occur for many reasons. The most obvious is the *additive effect* of many small activities. One home owner burning coal to heat a house may not create a serious air pollution problem. But if every house in a major metropolitan area is burning coal, then smog can become a serious problem. *Time crowding* can create cumulative effects, such as the congestion experienced on major highways in cities during rush hour. For most of the day, the capacity of the highways and roads is adequate, but at the beginning and end of the regular working day there can often be delays caused by the congestion of too many users relative to the capacity. *Space crowding* can also

---

Box 6.5

... [the] process of predicting and minimizing the consequences of a single action has not adequately considered the accumulative nature of some effects, the nonlinear responses of some natural systems, nor the linkages between a single action and other related activities.

Source: Constant and Wiggins, 1991: 298.

occur, in combination with or separate from time crowding. Habitat fragmentation in forests or estuaries illustrates space crowding. *Compounding effects* occur when there are delayed consequences from continuous emissions, such as gaseous emissions into the atmosphere. At some point, the accumulation of emissions results in the air quality crossing a threshold from an acceptable level to one which is dangerous for living beings. *Time lags* can also occur, such as when small amounts of carcinogenic materials have no obvious impact until after the carcinogenic trigger has accumulated sufficiently, which may take years or decades.

All of the above pathways or triggers for cumulative effects represent major challenges for analysts and planners. It is difficult or impossible for us to isolate the impact of individual variables from others. When we would like to identify the cumulative effects of several variables, usually our knowledge is not adequate to predict all the various ways in which multiple variables might interact. From a planning point of view, if a time lag effect could be decades, it is difficult to persuade people to take action today if that means forgoing benefits in the short term. Yet time lag effects represent one dimension of *intergenerational equity* related to sustainable development, which was discussed in Chapter 2.

Compensation

Even with systematic and careful IA, not all negative impacts can be removed. These undesirable outcomes particularly occur with what are called *noxious facilities*, the type of facility we all require but no one wants close by. Thus, we collectively create a demand for sand and gravel for construction material for roads and foundations for houses. But few people are enthusiastic about having a working sand and gravel pit as a neighbour. The noise and pollution from heavy trucks coming and going from the pit, the danger to children walking along the road from increased levels of traffic, and the noise and dust from the operating pit itself can all be negative effects for nearby land owners. Even if a rehabilitation plan is developed and implemented for the site, if it were to operate for 15 or 20 years, that could be a major part of the adult lifetime of a nearby resident.

When society makes decisions to allow developments such as noxious facilities which serve general societal needs but cause inconvenience to a small number of people, equity suggests that the larger community should be prepared to compensate those who suffer negative effects. Compensation could vary from monthly or annual payments during the lifetime of the operation, to acquisition of the property or exchange of properties for a new location which would not be impacted by the activity, along with funds to relocate. As noted earlier in this chapter, however, compensation can become almost overwhelming for major projects such as the Three Gorges in which one million people have to be relocated. Generally, societies have not treated very adequately the minority who are negatively affected by development. There is scope for much work here, especially since the effects often have an intangible component, so that determining a fair compensation package is not always easy.

6.5 Techniques for impact assessment

At least four different techniques are used for identifying impacts. These are checklists, overlays, matrices and networks.

- **Checklists.** Checklists provide a list of specific considerations to be investigated. In this way, checklists serve as templates to remind the investigator about aspects that might be relevant. A checklist does not assume cause-and-effect links of the items on the checklist and project activities. The items are based on general experience in impact assessment, and the investigator has to determine which items are pertinent.

- **Overlays.** These are a set of maps which depict environmental and social characteristics of a project area. The maps are superimposed to generate a composite picture of the regional characteristics. A judgement is then made about which characteristic composites represent sensitive or valued attributes, and impacts are inferred.

- **Matrices.** These represent a more sophisticated version of a checklist, in that environmental and social characteristics are identified on one axis of the matrix and project activities are identified on the other axis. The purpose is to use the matrix to identify first-order cause-and-effect relationships between proposed activities and impacts.

- **Networks.** The starting point is identification of proposed activities, followed by consideration of cause-and-effect networks at various levels (direct, indirect). Networks explicitly recognize that a series of cascading impacts may be triggered by one action, and that it is necessary to follow through first-, second- and third-order effects.

The four techniques are listed with the simplest appearing first. Networks are conceptually the most sophisticated, but are also the most complex and time-demanding to use. Furthermore, the network approach is often difficult to use because there may not be sufficient information or understanding to trace the various levels of impacts. In contrast, checklists and overlays have often been used at initial or preliminary stages of impact assessment. Once key impacts have been identified by such techniques, follow-up work using matrices or overlays will often occur. It is also important to note that a fifth method is often used, which can best be described as *professional judgement*. This "technique" does not explicitly use any of the four techniques, but rather relies upon training and/ or experience to examine a project area and to identify which aspects are judged to have the most likely impacts. "Professional judgement" can be a misnomer, as a person with little formal education who has lived in an area for a lengthy period may be as capable of identifying impacts as a highly educated individual who has little or no experience of the area (see Chapter 9 on local knowledge systems).

Summarizing, impact assessment was introduced to ensure that environmental and then social considerations were given due attention relative to economic ones. In this manner, impact assessment is a useful tool for examining options that are consistent with sustainable development. Used in conjunction with benefit–cost analysis, impact assessment helps to integrate economic and environmental considerations.

6.6 Life cycle assessment

6.6.1 Definition and evolution

Life cycle assessment (LCA) was formalized during the early 1990s. It emerged from a conviction that it was important to conduct "cradle-to-grave" assessments of products, packages, processes and activities. The Ecobalance Study approach developed in Europe, emphasizing waste reduction to curtail water and air pollution, and Resource and Environmental Profile Analysis work in the United States during the 1980s, were the forerunners of LCA. However, it was at a workshop organized by the Society of Environmental Toxicology and Chemistry (SETAC) in the United States during the early 1990s that the basic approach for LCA was developed (SETAC, 1991, 1993, 1994).

6.6.2 Stages in life cycle analysis

As indicated in Figure 6.2, LCA can be divided into four stages or phases, Each is briefly considered below.

- Initiation. This stage is very similar to scoping in impact assessment. The main purposes are to establish the objectives for and detail of an assessment, to define the "system" to be assessed, and to identify types of data needed.
- Inventory. Primary attention is allocated to collecting data about raw materials

---

Box 6.6

Life cycle assessment
A concept and method to evaluate the environmental effects of a product or activity holistically, by analysing its entire life cycle. This includes identifying and quantifying energy and materials used and wastes released to the environment, assessing their environmental impact, and evaluating opportunities for improvement.

Life cycle stages
The set of major sequential stages that a product or service passes through over the course of its existence from cradle to grave. For all products, four generic stages apply: raw materials and energy acquisition, manufacturing (including materials manufacture, product fabrication, and filling/packaging/distribution steps), use/reuse/maintenance, and recycle waste management.

Source: Canadian Standards Association, 1994a: 6.

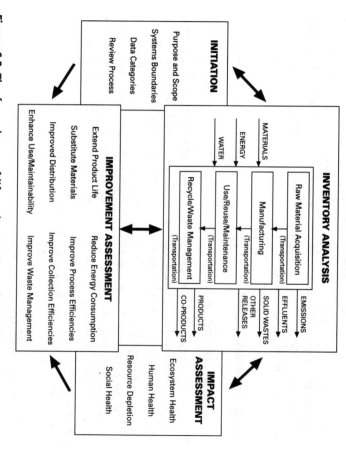

Figure 6.2 The four phases of life cycle assessment (with the permission of the Canadian Standards Association, 1994a: 13 material is reproduced from the CSA Standard: Z760-94 (Life Cycle Assessment), which is copyrighted by CSA, 178 Rexdale Blvd., Etobicoke, Ontario, M9W 1R3.)

needed for inputs, including energy and water, and about wastes produced as outputs during the process and at the end of the useful life of the product, process, package or related activity.

• **Impact.** This component is similar to the comparable phase in impact assessment. The focus here is upon identifying the effects, and reaching a judgement about the significance of such effects. Effects on the environment, economy, and health or well-being are usually included.

• **Improvement.** This can be characterized as the *normative* or *prescriptive* stage, in which attention is directed to possible actions to reduce or mitigate any negative impacts identified in the previous stage.

The four phases or components identified above and in Figure 6.2 are intended to assist resource and environmental managers to encourage better product design, more effective processes regarding raw material inputs or waste outputs, improved transportation methods, more careful consumer use, and better waste disposal practices. More specifically, in the context of resource and environmental management, LCA is intended to lead to decisions which result in greater conservation of resources and the environment, increased energy conservation and decreased waste generation, improved industrial processes related to providing resource-based products, and fewer problems in final disposal. Thus, regarding toxic wastes, for example, life cycle analysis would consider whether a toxic chemical needed to be used at all, and, if it were to be used, what should be done to ensure its proper production, transportation, storage, use and disposal.

Some key aspects of each of the four components are considered in more detail below.

Initiation

Defining the *system boundaries* for the life cycle assessment is a critical aspect during initiation. For example, the scope of an LCA for a box-making plant in Germany should not only include the raw materials and energy required at the plant to manufacture each box, and the wastes that must be disposed of. It should also examine the raw material and energy inputs for the other firms that provide component parts for the production of the boxes, even when those suppliers are located outside Germany. Furthermore, a decision must be taken as to whether the analysis focuses only on the primary manufacturers, or whether the assessment should include the forestry operations that provide the paperboard for the box, the natural gas industries that provide the resin and polyethylene, the aluminium industry that produces the aluminium foil, and so on. Figure 6.3 outlines in schematic form the various levels that could be involved in conducting a life cycle assessment of the process to produce laminated cartons. The choice of system boundaries is thus not always obvious or automatic. Furthermore, the definition of such boundaries can greatly complicate and extend the LCA, and add to the time and cost to complete it.

Decisions also have to be taken regarding who will complete the life cycle assessment. There are at least three choices. Employees of the firm could do the assessment. They probably are in the best position to be able to identify all of the inputs and outputs. However, the credibility of a self-evaluation can be low. The alternative is to have outside experts conduct the assessment. If such an external team does the work with reference to some generally accepted standards, then the credibility of the assessment is usually greater. The third option is to have a team involving both employees and outside experts conduct the task. For practical reasons, it is often some form of the third alternative which is used, since a firm often does not have all of the expertise to conduct an LCA, yet the outside experts need the input and advice of people within the firm.

Inventory

As Figure 6.2 indicates, inventory is required for raw material acquisition, manufacture, use/reuse/maintenance, and recycling/waste management. Partic- ular attention is given to the material, energy and water inputs, and to the emission, effluent, solid waste and other release outputs, as well as to products and co-products resulting from recycling or waste management. A thread common to many of the activities is transportation, as it is necessary to determine which inputs and outputs are needed to move material from one stage to another. As Box 6.7 indicates, inventory involves four major activities.

Assessing alternatives

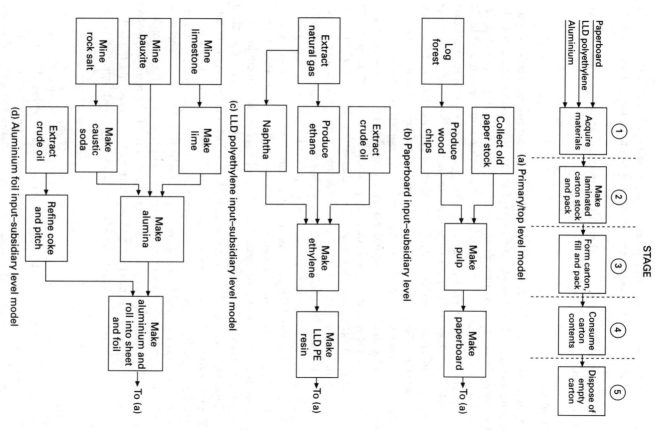

STAGE

Paperboard
LLD polyethylene
Aluminium

① Acquire materials

② Make laminated carton stock and pack

③ Form carton, fill and pack

④ Consume carton contents

⑤ Dispose of empty carton

(a) Primary/top level model

Log forest → Produce wood chips

Collect old paper stock

Produce wood chips + Collect old paper stock → Make pulp → Make paperboard → To (a)

(b) Paperboard input–subsidiary level

Extract natural gas → Naphtha

Produce ethane

Extract crude oil

Naphtha + Produce ethane + Extract crude oil → Make ethylene → Make LLD PE resin → To (a)

(c) LLD polyethylene input–subsidiary level model

Mine rock salt → Make caustic soda

Mine bauxite

Mine limestone → Make lime

Make caustic soda + Mine bauxite + Make lime → Make alumina

Extract crude oil → Refine coke and pitch

Make alumina + Refine coke and pitch → Make aluminium and roll into sheet and foil → To (a)

(d) Aluminium foil input–subsidiary level model

Figure 6.3 Life cycle assessment for production of laminated cartons (with the permission of the Canadian Standards Association, 1994b: 7, 8 material is reproduced from the CSA Publication: PLUS 1107 (User's Guide to the Life Cycle Assessment: Conceptual LCA in Practise, copyrighted by CSA, 178 Rexdale Blvd., Etobicoke, Ontario, M9W 1R3).

Box 6.7 Inventory: four key components

1. **Raw materials acquisition.** All activities necessary to collect a raw material or energy source from the Earth. This includes transportation of the raw material to the place of material manufacture.

2. **Manufacturing.** (a) *Materials manufacture.* This includes the activities needed to process raw material into a form useful for fabricating a product or package. The production of many intermediate materials or chemicals is often included in this subcomponent. Transport of intermediate materials is also included. (b) *Product fabrication.* This includes the activities which use raw or manufactured materials to fabricate a product to the point where it can be filled or packaged. The output here could be a product that may be distributed for retail sale, or that could be distributed for use by other industries. (c) *Filling/packaging/distribution.* Preparation of the final products for shipment to users, as well as transportation of products to the retail or other recipient.

3. **Use/reuse/maintenance.** This starts following the distribution of products or materials for use, and includes any activity which reconditions, maintains or services the product or package.

4. **Recycle/waste management.** This begins after the product, material or package has served its intended function, and either enters a new system through recycling or enters the environment through a waste management process.

Source: after Canadian Standards Association, 1994a: 14.

Impact assessment

The activities here are similar to what was described in the previous section dealing with environmental impact assessment. Particular concern usually focuses upon the implications of resource consumption associated with the creation of the product, material or packaging, and the releases into the environment during each of the life cycle phases. Ideally, the information here is in the form of *impact indicators*, which indicate whether critical thresholds have been passed. The challenge, of course, is that for many outputs we do not yet know what the critical thresholds are, and this aspect becomes even more problematic when the synergistic effects of two or more waste outputs are involved. One of the criticisms of LCA is that it is a very detailed, and potentially very expensive, procedure, but at the conclusion of the impact assessment stage there are still not enough environmental standards that are generally agreed upon to allow effective use of all the information which has been collected.

Improvement

The improvement component is often done in parallel with the impact component. An overriding purpose is to identify opportunities to reduce raw material inputs and waste outputs. Other benefits could be to streamline the production process so as to reduce costs to the firm and therefore make it more profitable. The alternatives normally considered include changes in product design to extend its life, to allow material or other input substitutions, to improve production, process or collection effectiveness, to improve distribution or transportation systems, to enhance consumer use or maintenance procedures, and to improve waste management.

6.6.3 Motivation for doing life cycle assessment

What would motivate a firm to conduct LCAs? Several incentives could provide the motivation. First, a firm may believe that with growing environmental awareness in many countries, completing a LCA may give it a marketing advantage by being able to promote its products as "clean". Second, with the introduction of *environmental labelling*, firms may decide that LCAs will help them become eligible to have their products certified as "green" or "environmentally friendly", and again provide a marketing advantage over competitors (Canadian Standards Association, 1993). Third, the International Standards Organization (ISO) guidelines, such as the ISO 14000 series, will be used to certify firms that have met environmental management and other requirements (see photograph in Figure 6.4). While such standards are currently voluntary for industries, it is not inconceivable that in the near future countries such as those in the European Union may prohibit the import of products or materials unless they are certified as having been manufactured by ISO-designated firms. Such an initiative would provide a "level playing field" for environmental standards among countries, and would definitely provide a major incentive for firms to have their products so identified.

6.6.4 Availability of LCA studies

There is not yet an extensive literature on LCA which is readily accessible. Most assessments have been completed by companies, or by consulting firms for clients. In either case, the reports have become the property of the company for which the LCA was completed. For competitive reasons, many companies are hesitant to make such reports generally available, since in most cases the assessment was completed to help them become more competitive in the market place. Nevertheless, LCA can be anticipated to be a "growth" industry for those interested in resource and environmental management, and people hoping to work in this broad field should be familiar with LCA.

Figure 6.4 ISO 9000 certification (Mitchell). ISO certification is used by companies to promote themselves and their products. The picture (taken in February 1996) of the sign on the property fence of Clemmer Industries, manufacturers of a variety of underground storage tanks, highlights its expected certification in May 1996. The ISO 14000 certification, which will succeed the 9000 certification, will explicitly recognize that a firm has an approved environmental management system incorporated into its activities.

6.7 Implications

Three methods or techniques – benefit–cost analysis, impact assessment, life cycle assessment – have been examined in this chapter. Each provides an entry point for the task of assessing alternatives. Benefit–cost analysis has been the one used for the longest period. It emphasizes economic considerations, especially economic efficiency. Environmental impact assessment appeared in the early 1970s in response to concern that benefit–cost analysis was not giving sufficient attention to environmental matters. In turn, environmental impact assessment became criticized for focusing unduly upon biophysical issues, and by the end of the 1980s procedures to deal with social impacts had appeared. In the 1990s, life cycle assessment has emerged, reflecting concern about the importance of tracking inputs and outputs in production processes "from cradle to grave". Such LCAs are receiving impetus from the development of the ISO guidelines, which certify firms as following "good" management practices. While ISO initially has been a voluntary procedure, it can be anticipated that national governments will in the near future require companies to conform to them, suggesting that LCA will become a growth industry in its own right.

However, it is important to emphasize that none of the three methods helps resource and environmental managers to know which vision, goals or objectives

Box 6.8 Environmental management system (EMS) principles specified in ISO 14004

Principle 1: Commitment and policy. An organization should define its environmental policy and ensure commitment to its environmental management system. Key elements to achieve this are (1) top management commitment and leadership, (2) initial environmental review, and (3) establishment of environmental policy.

Principle 2: Planning. An organization should formulate a plan to fulfil its environmental policy. Key elements are (1) identification of environmental aspects and evaluation of associated environmental impacts, (2) identification of legal requirements, (3) development and adoption of internal performance criteria, (4) specification of environmental objectives and targets, and (5) establishment of environmental management plans and programs.

Principle 3: Implementation. (a) *Ensure capability.* To implement the EMS, an organization should develop the capabilities and support mechanisms needed to achieve its environmental policy, objectives and targets; key elements are (1) dedicated human, financial and physical resources, (2) aligning and integrating EMS with other management systems, (3) establishing accountability and responsibility, (4) developing environmental awareness and motivation, and (5) improving knowledge, skills and training. (b) *Support action.* Develop the capabilities and support mechanisms needed to achieve environmental policies, objectives and targets; key elements are (1) communication and reporting, (2) creation of EMS documentation, (3) operational controls, and (4) emergency preparedness and response capacity.

Principle 4: Measurement and evaluation. An organization should measure, monitor and evaluate its environmental performance. Key elements are (1) measuring and monitoring of ongoing performance, (2) ensuring corrective and preventive action, (3) establishing EMS records and information management procedures, and (4) providing for audits of EMS (see Chapter 13).

Principle 5: Review and improvement. An organization should review and continually improve its EMS, with the objective of improving its overall environmental performance. Key elements are (1) reviews at regular intervals, and (2) continual improvement by identifying opportunities.

Source: based on Auditor General of Canada in cooperation with the Federal Committee on Environmental Management Systems, no date; and Auditor General of Canada, 1995.

are the most desirable. These methods most usually have been designed, and applied, to determine the best *means* to achieve *ends* which already have been chosen. The one exception is the relatively limited application of impact assessment to policies and programs, as opposed only to projects. Nevertheless, resource and environmental planners ideally should have a vision or direction established before they begin to make choices about which method(s) they will use to compare alternative means. Once that vision is in place, planners and managers should be encouraged to use a combination of these methods to make choices. Any one method by itself probably has too many weaknesses to be relied upon in isolation.

References and further reading

Abruzze W S 1995 The social and ecological consequences of early cattle ranching in the Little Colorado River basin. *Human Ecology* 23(1): 75–98

Auditor General of Canada 1995 *Environmental management systems: a principle-based approach.* Ottawa, Minister of Supply and Services Canada

Auditor General of Canada, with the Federal Committee on Environmental Management Systems (no date) *EMS self-assessment guide.* Ottawa, Minister of Supply and Services Canada

Barbier E B, A Markandya and D W Pearce 1990 Environmental sustainability and cost-benefit analysis. *Environment and Planning A* 22(9): 1259–66

Boustead I 1992 *Eco-balance methodology for commodity thermoplastics.* Brussels, European Centre for Plastics in the Environment (RMWI)

Butler R W and J G Nelson 1994 Evaluating environmental planning and management: the case of the Shetland Islands. *Geoforum* 25(1): 57–72

Cada G F and C T Hunsaker 1990 Cumulative impacts of hydropower developments. *Environmental Professional* 12(1): 2–9

Canadian Standards Association 1993 *Guideline on environmental labelling.* Publication Z761-93, Rexdale (Toronto), Canadian Standards Association

Canadian Standards Association 1994a *Life cycle assessment.* Publication Z760-94, Rexdale (Toronto), Canadian Standards Association

Canadian Standards Association 1994b *User's guide to life cycle assessment: conceptual LCA in practice.* Publication PLUS 1107, Rexdale (Toronto), Canadian Standards Association

Cocklin C, S Parker and J Hay 1992 Notes on cumulative environmental change I: concepts and issues. *Journal of Environmental Management* 35(1): 31–49

Conacher A 1988 Resource development and environmental stress: environmental impact assessment and beyond in Australia and Canada. *Geoforum* 19(3): 339–52

Constant C K and L L Wiggins 1991 Defining and analyzing cumulative environmental impacts. *Environmental Impact Assessment Review* 11(4): 297–309

Dirschl H J, N S Novakowski and M H Sadar 1993 Evolution of environmental assessment as applied to watershed modification projects in Canada. *Environmental Management* 17(4): 545–55

Dixon J and B E Montz 1995 From concept to practice: implementing cumulative impact assessment in New Zealand. *Environmental Management* 19(3): 445–56

Duinker P N and G L Baskerville 1986 A systematic approach to forecasting in environmental impact assessment. *Journal of Environmental Management* 23(3): 271–90

Gagnon C, P Hirsch and R Howitt 1993 Can DIS empower communities? *Environmental Impact Assessment Review* 13(4): 229–53

Gallagher T J and W S Jacobson 1993 The typography of environmental impact statements: criteria, evaluation, and public participation. *Environmental Management* 17(1): 99–109

Gibson R B 1993 Environmental assessment design: lessons from the Canadian experience. *Environmental Professional* 15(1): 12–24

Glasson J 1995 Regional planning and the environment: time for a SEA change. *Urban Studies* 32(4–5): 713–31

Goodenough R A and S J Page 1994 Evaluating the environmental impact of a major transport infrastructure project: the Channel Tunnel high-speed rail link. *Applied Geography* 14(1): 26–50

Greeno J L, G S Hedstrom and M DiBerto 1985 *Environmental auditing fundamentals and techniques.* Toronto, John Wiley and Sons

Heijungs R and J B Guinée 1995 On the usefulness of life cycle assessment of packaging. *Environmental Management* 19(5): 665–8

Hollick M 1993 *An introduction to project evaluation.* Melbourne, Longman Cheshire

Huang G H, W P Anderson and B Baetz 1994 Environmental input–output analysis and its application to regional solid waste management planning. *Journal of Environmental Management* 42(1): 63–79

Hunt R G, J D Sellars and W E Franklin 1992 Resource and environmental profile analysis: a life cycle environmental assessment for products and procedures. *Environmental Impact Assessment Review* 12(1/2): 245–69

Jolliet O, K Cotting, C Drexler and S Farago 1994 Life-cycle analysis of biodegradable packing materials compared with polystyrene chips: the case of popcorn. *Agriculture, Ecosystems and Environment* 49(3): 253–66

Jones T 1993 The role of environmental impact assessment in coal production and utilization. *Natural Resources Forum* 17(3): 170–9

Keoleian G A and D Menerey 1993 *Life cycle design guidance manual: environmental requirements and the product system.* Ann Arbor, University of Michigan, National Pollution Prevention Center, prepared for the United States Environmental Protection Agency

Little A D 1990 *Life cycle assessment of disposable versus cloth diaper systems.* Report commissioned and sponsored by Procter and Gamble, San Diego, California

McCold L and J Holman 1995 Cumulative impacts in environmental assessments: how well are they considered? *Environmental Professional* 17(1): 2–8

Miner R A and A A Lucier 1994 Considerations in performing life-cycle assessments on forest products. *Environmental Toxicology and Chemistry* 13(8): 1375–80

Mitchell B 1989 *Geography and resource analysis.* Harlow, Longman, second edition

Odum W E 1982 Environmental degradation and the tyranny of small decisions. *Bioscience* 32(9): 728–9

Orians G H 1995 Thought for the morrow: cumulative threats to the environment. *Environment* 6–14, 33–6

Pearce D W 1971 *Cost–benefit analysis.* London, Macmillan

Russell S O D 1994 Insights from the Three Gorges Study. *Canadian Journal of Civil Engineering* 21(4): 541–6

SETAC 1991 *A technical framework for life-cycle assessment.* Washington, DC, United States Society of Environmental Toxicology and Chemistry, and the SETAC Foundation for Environmental Education, Inc.

SETAC 1993 *A conceptual framework for life-cycle assessment.* Washington, DC, United States Society of Environmental Toxicology and Chemistry, and the SETAC Foundation for Environmental Education, Inc.

SETAC 1994 *Guidelines for life-cycle assessment: a code of practice.* Washington, DC, United

States Society of Environmental Toxicology and Chemistry

Sewell W R D, J Davis, A D Scott and D W Ross 1965 *Guide to benefit–cost analysis*. Ottawa, Queen's Printer

Shapcott C 1989 Environmental impact assessment and resource management, a Haida case study: implications for native people of the North. *Canadian Journal of Native Studies* 9(1): 55–83

Shoemaker D J 1994 *Cumulative environmental assessment*. Department of Geography Publication Series Number 42, Waterloo, Ontario, University of Waterloo

Smith L G 1993 *Impact assessment and sustainable resource management*. Harlow, Longman Scientific and Technical

Spaling H and B Smit 1993 Cumulative environmental change. *Environmental Management* 17(5): 587–600

Spaling H and B Smit 1995 A conceptual model of cumulative environmental effects of agricultural land drainage. *Agriculture, Ecosystems, and Environment* 53(2): 99–108

Street P and B Barker 1995 Promoting good environmental management: lessons from BS 5750. *Journal of Environmental Planning and Management* 38(4): 484–503

Taylor C N, C Goodrich and C H Bryan 1995 Issues-oriented approach to social assessment and project appraisal. *Project Appraisal* 10(3): 142–54

Therivel R 1993 Systems of strategic environmental assessment. *Environmental Impact Assessment Review* 13(3): 145–68

United States Environmental Protection Agency 1992 *Life-cycle assessment: inventory guidelines and principles*, EPA/600/R-92/036, Washington, DC, Office of Research and Development, Risk Reduction Engineering Laboratory

Wood C 1995 *Environmental impact assessment: a comparative review*. Harlow, Longman Scientific and Technical

Yarnal B 1995 Bulgaria at a crossroads: environmental impacts of socioeconomic change. *Environment* 37(10): 6–15, 29–33

Chapter 7

Adaptive Environmental Management

7.1 Introduction

As outlined in Chapter 4, complexity and uncertainty present challenges for environmental and resource analysts and decision makers. In this chapter, one response to deal with complexity and uncertainty is examined: adaptive environmental management. In the next section, the rationale for the concept is considered, as well as some of the basic ideas associated with it. Section 7.3 examines the strengths and weaknesses presented by *adaptive* and *programmed* strategies for implementing environmental policies and programs. Section 7.4 provides examples of adaptive environmental management, one from developing countries and one from developed countries. Finally, Section 7.5 highlights the main conclusions about adaptive environmental management, as well as the implications of this concept.

7.2 Adaptive environmental management

Holling (1978) has been a major contributor to developing the concept of adaptive environmental management. He edited a book entitled *Adaptive Environmental Assessment and Management*, whose purpose was to develop an alternative approach to environmental impact assessment and management for policy makers and managers who were dissatisfied with traditional principles and methods. The central message in the book was that a new process was needed to deal with a fundamental challenge "to cope with the uncertain and the unexpected. How, in short, to plan in the face of the unknown" (Holling, 1978: 7). The following comments summarize some of the main arguments presented by Holling and his colleagues in support of an adaptive approach to environmental management.

Holling concluded that people have always lived in an unknown world, and yet generally have prospered. The traditional way of dealing with the unknown has been through *trial-and-error methods*. What is known becomes the departure point for a trial. Errors provide new information and understanding, and become the basis from which new experiments are designed. "Failures" are accepted as necessary to gain understanding about previously unknown conditions, and to improve our capability to deal with them. With experience, new understanding is achieved, and progress is realized.

Box 7.1 Rationale for an adaptive approach

... But however intensively and extensively data are collected, however much we know of how the system functions, the domain of our knowledge of specific ecological and social systems is small when compared to that of our ignorance.

Thus, one key issue for design and evaluation of policies is how to cope with the uncertain, the unexpected, and the unknown.

Source: Holling, 1978: 7.

However, three minimum conditions must be met if the trial-and-error method is to work. First, the experiment cannot destroy the experimenter. Or, at least someone has to be able to learn from the experience. Second, the experiment also should not create irreversible changes in the environment. If that did occur, then it would be difficult, perhaps impossible, for the experimenter to gain from the new knowledge. Third, the experimenter must be willing to start again, having learned from failures. Holling concluded that for resource and environmental management it was increasingly difficult to meet these three minimum conditions. "Trials", such as release of greenhouse gases into the atmosphere, were becoming capable of producing "mistakes" with greater costs than societies could bear.

Other concerns existed. Errors might theoretically be reversible, but the commitment of resources and prestige could make it extremely unlikely that decisions would be reversed. Humans seem to have great difficulty in acknowledging failure or mistakes. Egos may be bruised, reputations tarnished, or face lost. As a result, rather than admitting mistakes, cutting losses and starting anew, it is more common for people to try to eliminate or "fix" problems. The outcome is usually further investment of resources and reputation, growing costs associated with maintenance and repair, and eventual loss of options. In addition, in some instances, such as the construction of a major dam and reservoir, the scale and implications of trying to modify decisions make them effectively irreversible.

Notwithstanding the many real difficulties and challenges, Holling argued that the need for innovative solutions required trial-and-error approaches, and that it was not sensible to try to *eliminate* the uncertain and the unknown. The proper direction, in his view, was to design approaches that allowed trial-and-error procedures to work. While we should strive to *reduce* uncertainty, Holling (1978: 9) also believed the following:

But if not accompanied by an equal effort to design for uncertainty and to obtain benefits from the unexpected, the best of predictive methods will only lead to larger problems arising more quickly and more often. This view is the heart of adaptive environmental management — an interactive process using techniques that not only reduce uncertainty but also benefit from it. The goal is to develop more resilient policies.

By *resilience*, Holling meant the ability of a system, natural or human-made, to absorb and use (ideally even to benefit from) change.

The concept of adaptive management has been addressed by others, two of whose ideas are considered here. Lee (1993) considered adaptive environmental management relative to achieving an environmentally sustainable economy. He argued that as part of earning a living, we use the resources of the world, even if we do not understand natural systems enough to know how to stay within environmental limits or thresholds. Adaptive managers explicitly consider uncertainty and lack of understanding, by treating human intervention in natural systems as *experimental probes*. More specifically, adaptive managers take particular care about information. In particular, regarding information, adaptive managers:

- are explicit about their objectives and what they expect as outcomes, so that they can design methods and techniques to monitor and measure what happens;
- collect and assess information so that outcomes and impacts can be compared with expectations; and
- take their new understanding and learn from it by correcting errors, and changing both plans and actions.

Given the above, what is the core or essence of adaptive environmental management? According to Lee, an adaptive approach is designed from the outset to test clearly expressed ideas or hypotheses about the behaviour of an ecosystem being changed through human use. The ideas or hypotheses usually represent predictions regarding how one or more components of the ecosystem will respond or behave as a result of implementation of a policy. When the policy is successful, the hypothesis is validated. However, when the policy fails, the adaptive approach is designed so that learning occurs, adjustments can be made, and future initiatives can be based on the new understanding. As Lee explained, experiments often produce surprises, but if resource and environmental management is accepted to have inherent uncertainty, then surprises become viewed as opportunities to learn from, rather than as failures to predict or avoid.

An adaptive approach is most appropriate when uncertainty is high. Nevertheless, it is not free from problems. The costs of collecting the necessary information from which to learn can be very high. In addition, the political risks of clearly documenting failures can also be very high. Furthermore, such an approach

Box 7.2 Adaptive management

Adaptive management is an approach to natural resource policy that embodies a simple imperative; policies are experiments; *learn from them*. . . . Linking science and human purpose, adaptive management serves as a compass for us to use in searching for a sustainable future.

Source: Lee, 1993: 9.

assumes there is capability and willingness to learn from errors. Organizations can vary markedly in their capacity for learning, and hence this aspect can represent a significant obstacle for effective application of an adaptive approach.

Challenges also exist in our ability to understand or analyse large ecosystems. Lee suggested that the following three obstacles create serious difficulties for analysts:

- **Sparse data.** Measurements of the natural and human world are inexact and imperfect. Time series data are often necessary, but it can take many years to assemble a credible data set. For example, data on the number of spawning fish in a run can only be determined once each year.

- **Limited theory.** Poor understanding makes it difficult to extrapolate very far from our experience (the rationale for the *incrementalist* approach described in Chapter 4). Human impacts on natural systems can also be both so large and so unprecedented that it is difficult to determine which of several alternative theories is most relevant.

- **Unexceptional surprises.** Predictions are frequently incorrect, and expectations are not fulfilled. Uncertainty ensures that errors and surprises will be inevitable.

To manage adaptively, Lee therefore argued that several aspects needed careful attention. These include the following three key points:

- The focus of adaptive management is *ecosystematic* rather than jurisdictional. In other words, the adaptive approach uses ecosystem rather than political or administrative boundaries. One outcome is that almost inevitably the adaptive approach ends up using a spatial unit which spills over or straddles one or more human-made boundaries and management functions.

- The focus of adaptive management is upon a *population* or *ecosystem*, not individual organisms or projects. Failures at the individual level have to be accepted or tolerated in order to gain understanding about the population or ecosystem. Risk taking relative to individuals is accepted in order to enhance the population.

- The time scale of adaptive management is a *biological generation* rather than the business cycle, electoral term of office or budget period.

Consideration of the above three points could lead to the conclusion that an adaptive approach would be ponderous and slow. However, as Lee (1993: 63) commented, "Just the opposite should be true. The adaptive approach favors action, since experience is the key to learning." And, consistent with Holling, Lee (1993: 63) argued that

... the adaptive approach does not aim for a fixed end point. ... The goal, instead, is resilience in the face of surprise. Surprise can be counted on. Resilience comes from the constant testing, that is, from change and stress, from survival of the fittest in a turbulent environment.

Table 7.1 highlights those contextual conditions that favour the successful application of adaptive environmental management. In Subsection 7.4.2, we will consider in more detail the role of these aspects in the application of the adaptive approach in the Columbia River basin in the United States.

Rondinelli (1993a, 1993b) shares Holling's and Lee's enthusiasm about an adaptive approach. He remarked that there has been a growing agreement among organizations in the public and private sectors that they operate in increasingly complex environments, as well as under conditions of rapid change, fewer resources and greater uncertainty. These aspects have to be addressed if organizations are to be effective and efficient in realizing goals and objectives (Rondinelli, 1993a: 1).

Rondinelli's interest is particularly with development issues in Third World countries. He noted that in the 1970s and 1980s, donor agencies emphasized what he called *blueprint approaches*, in which systems analysis techniques were used to maintain control and to minimize variation from specified objectives. Such an approach continues to be used for development projects for which it is relatively straightforward to define objectives and purposes, and for which general agreement exists about methods. Thus, this approach is usually well suited for projects emphasizing physical infrastructure and construction of

Table 7.1 Contextual conditions affecting adaptive management (Lee, 1993: 85, Table 3.5)

There is a mandate to take action in the face of uncertainty. *But experimentation and learning are at most secondary objectives in large ecosystems. Experimentation that conflicts with primary objectives will often be pushed aside or not proposed.*

Decision makers are aware that they are experimenting anyway. *But experimentation is an open admission that there may be no positive return. More generally, specifying hypotheses to be tested raises the risk of perceived failure.*

Decision makers care about improving outcomes over biological time scales. *But the costs of monitoring, controls, and replication are substantial, and they will appear especially high at the outset when compared with the costs of unmonitored trial and error. Individual decision makers rarely stay in office over times of biological significance.*

Preservation of pristine environments is no longer an option, and human intervention cannot produce desired outcomes predictably. *And remedial action crosses jurisdictional boundaries and requires coordinated implementation over long periods.*

Resources are sufficient to measure ecosystem-scale behaviour. *But data collection is vulnerable to external disruptions, such as budget cutbacks, changes in policy, and controversy. After changes in the leadership, decision makers may not be familiar with the purposes and value of an experimental approach.*

Theory, models, and field methods are available to estimate and infer ecosystem-scale behaviour. *But interim results may create panic or a realization that the experimental design was faulty. More generally, experimental findings will suggest changes in policy; controversial changes have the potential to disrupt the experimental program.*

Hypotheses can be formulated. *And accumulating knowledge may shift perceptions of what is worth examining via large-scale experimentation. For this reason, both policy actors and experimenters must adjust the trade-offs among experimental and other policy objectives during the implementation process.*

Organizational culture encourages learning from experience. *But the advocates of adaptive management are likely to be staff who have professional incentives to appreciate a complex process and a career situation in which long-term learning can be beneficial. Where there is tension between staff and policy leadership, experimentation can become the focus of an internal struggle for control.*

There is sufficient stability to measure long-term outcomes; institutional patience is essential. *But stability is usually dependent on factors outside the control of experimenters and managers.*

facilities (roads, sewage treatment plants).

However, as donor agencies and recipient countries moved away from emphasis on infrastructure and construction, and towards social and human development projects (rural development, poverty alleviation, health, education), they soon realized that conventional blueprint approaches were less appropriate. Political, economic and social conditions were also evolving in Third World countries, creating further difficulties in being able to predict what would be most appropriate. As a result, Rondinelli (1993a: 3) commented that due to "high levels of uncertainty, complexity, and risk in development activities, and the diminishing control . . . over factors affecting their success," various new challenges were emerging, such as the following.

- Precise goals and objectives were more difficult to state as a result of development problems being less easy to understand or define, solutions not always being obvious or transferable from country to country, impacts from activities being less easily predictable, and expectations and objectives of many participants being inconsistent, and often in conflict.

- Difficulties in estimating the feasibility of possible interventions, due to inadequate knowledge about the nature of the problem and the most appropriate interventions.

- Problems in being able to pre-design projects in detail. Technical experts were no longer accepted as being the only experts, and local participants increasingly expected to be involved in definition of the problem and in formulation of solutions.

- Difficulties in separating the design and implementation of projects, since activities needed to be capable of modification based on experience during implementation.

- Challenges in using standard criteria to judge the effectiveness or success of projects.

Given the above, Rondinelli (1993a: 4) concluded that:

The complexity, uncertainty, lack of control, inability to predict behavior, inability to predetermine outcomes, and inadequate knowledge about the most appropriate ways of promoting economic and social development, in reality, made all development projects and programs "experiments".

The obvious implication, in his view, was an extension of the last word in the above quotation. Development initiatives had to be considered as experiments in problem solving. Management strategies needed to encourage and reward experimentation, innovation and adaptation. As a result, he concluded that "the lessons of experience from more than 40 years of development assistance have led many observers to call for a more 'adaptive' approach to planning and management that is more strategic, iterative and responsive" (Rondinelli, 1993a: 4). He then offered Table 7.2 as a tool to determine when an adaptive approach would be most appropriate, and when a blueprint approach would be most effective. The information in Table 7.2 reflects the differences between *incremental* (right-hand column) and *synoptic* or *comprehensive rational schools* of planning. In Section 7.4, we will examine some examples of adaptive

Table 7.2 Management strategies (Rondinelli, 1993a: 5a)

Characteristics	Management strategy	
	Mechanistic	Adaptive
Environment	Certain	Uncertain
Tasks	Routine	Innovative
Management processes		
Planning	Comprehensive	Incremental
Decision-making	Centralized	Decentralized
Authority	Hierarchical	Collegial
Leadership style	Command	Participatory
Communications	Vertical, formal	Interactive, formal and informal
Coordination	Control	Facilitation
Monitoring	Conformance to plan	Adjust strategy and plan
Controls	Ex-ante	Ex-post
Use of formal rules and regulations	High	Low
Basis of staffing	Functions	Objectives
Structures	Hierarchical	Organic
Staff values	Low tolerance for ambiguity	High tolerance for ambiguity

approaches, and consider the insight which the ideas of Holling, Lee and Rondinelli provide.

7.3 Adaptive versus programmed approaches

In Chapter 12, attention will focus upon challenges in implementing resource and environmental policies and programs. Here, particular attention is given to the relative merits and weaknesses of using an *adaptive implementation strategy*, in contrast to a *programmed implementation strategy*.

Berman (1980) has explained that two schools of thought have arisen regarding the best way to achieve implementation. One school, called programmed implementation, reflects the view that implementation problems can be overcome by systematic and explicit pre-programming of procedures for implementation. The other school, adaptive implementation, reflects a conclusion that implementation will be facilitated through an approach that allows adjustments to changing circumstances, events and decisions. Thus, the proponents of these two schools have diagnosed the problems of implementation to come from different sources, and offer quite different solutions. Such perspectives are not new, as it is possible to recognize elements of synoptic or comprehensive rational planning in the programmed approach, and aspects of incrementalism in the adaptive approach (Chapter 4). And, as Berman's comment in Box 7.3 reminds us, often it is not helpful to think in either/or

---

Box 7.3 Approaches to implementation

There is no universally best way to implement policy. Either programmed or adaptive implementation can be effective if applied to the appropriate policy situation, but a mismatch between approach and situation aggravates the very implementation problems these approaches seek to overcome.

Source: Berman, 1980: 206.

---

terms. It may be that both approaches have merit, and that the challenge for analysts and planners is to determine which approach will be most useful in given situations.

7.3.1 Programmed implementation

The school associated with programmed implementation believes that implementation difficulties arise from several sources.

Source 1. Ambiguity or vagueness in policy goals, caused by or leading to misunderstandings, confusion or conflicts of values. Such ambiguity is thought to leave implementers without sufficient direction or guidance. The solution is for officials to provide specific, detailed and consistent objectives to be followed by those given the task of implementation.

Source 2. Involvement of too many participants with overlapping or conflicting responsibilities. The outcome is that no one person or agency is willing or able to take final authority or responsibility. The consequences are that implementers are able to do what they wish, with discretionary decisions thwarting realization of stated goals and objectives. The solution is to establish clear lines of authority, to minimize the number of participants, and to limit the scope for discretion.

Source 3. Resistance, ineffectiveness or inefficiency from those charged with doing the implementation. It is believed that lower-level implementers are more comfortable with a well-established routine, and that any policy initiatives that modify such routines will usually be met with resistance, inefficiency and ineffectiveness. The solution is to constrain the amount of discretion by providing explicit guidelines for operating procedures, monitoring behaviour so that implementers can be held accountable for what is (or is not) done, and providing incentives (salary bonuses, status awards) for desired actions.

Thus, the characteristics of a programmed approach include a well-specified plan with clearly defined objectives, unambiguous lines of responsibility, limited participation and minimal discretion.

7.3.2 Adaptive implementation

Both a different diagnosis and a different solution are offered by the adaptive approach. From this perspective, implementation difficulties occur because of over-specification and rigidity of goals, failure to involve a wide enough mix of people in decision making, and undue control over implementers. The solution is to create processes which allow a policy to be adjusted and revised (that is, adapted) as a result of changing circumstances. Outcomes are not assumed to be automatic or guaranteed. The issues are related to a number of sources.

Source 1. Over-specification and rigidity of goals. The solution is to use general and even vague goals. Or, if goals cannot be agreed upon, then agreement on means is acceptable (as with the incrementalists in Chapter 4, or as shown by Figures 1.5 and 1.6 in Chapter 1). Vagueness or ambiguity provides scope to custom-design implementation arrangements to suit differing conditions prevailing within a jurisdiction. The disadvantage is that some people will complain when they see people in other areas being treated differently from them, especially if they feel that those people are getting what is viewed to be preferential treatment.

Source 2. Not enough groups or interests are involved. The adaptive approach seeks active participation of relevant participants. This is done in the belief that more participants will bring more information and perspectives to help define issues and develop solutions. Another reason for this approach is the conviction that if people are involved in creation of a policy or a solution, then they will be more likely to be motivated to make it succeed.

Source 3. Not enough discretion. It is believed that too much direction and control stifle creativity and enthusiasm, and also lead to standardized approaches that may not fit local conditions. The solution is to give local implementers discretion to make modifications relative to local needs and conditions. It is also thought that this approach will allow people to "learn by doing", rather than mechanically following a set of guidelines which may not make a lot of sense for their situation. Monitoring has a different role. For programmed implementation, monitoring is used to determine whether objectives are being realized, and if expected outcomes and impacts are occurring. In adaptive implementation, monitoring is used to determine if there is a need to make modifications to objectives or processes in the light of experience accumulated with implementation.

Berman (1980) concluded that different policy situations exist. The trick in selecting the most appropriate implementation strategy (adaptive or programmed) is to be able to read a situation and determine which conditions are dominant. Table 7.3 shows different characteristics of policy situations. If a situation were to be characterized by all the attributes in the "Structured" column, a programmed approach would probably be most appropriate. An adaptive approach would probably be the best choice if the situation had the attributes shown in the "Unstructured" column.

Table 7.3 Policy situations (Berman, 1980: 214)

Characteristics	Situation type	
	Structured	Unstructured
Scope of change	Incremental	Major
Certainty of technology or theory	Certain within risk	Uncertain
Conflict over policy's goals and means	Low conflict	High conflict
Structure of institutional setting	Tightly coupled	Loosely coupled
Stability of environment	Stable	Unstable

The main message from the discussion of programmed and adaptive implementation strategies is that different policy situations do exist, and that each strategy offers advantages. Traditionally, the programmed approach has been favoured, but such an approach assumes need for only moderate changes, considerable certainty about means to be used, low conflict regarding goals, agencies that work collaboratively, and relative stability. However, we are aware from Chapter 4 that complexity, uncertainty and turbulence are often encountered, and in such situations an adaptive approach will probably be more effective. It is also possible that over the lifetime of a policy or program characteristics of both structured and unstructured conditions will occur. Thus, it could be that aspects of both approaches may be useful at different times. It should not be assumed, however, that it is always and inevitably a structured situation which will occur, and that a programmed approach should automatically be used.

7.4 Experiences with adaptive management

In this section, two examples are considered, one from Kenya in Africa, and the other from the Pacific Northwest in the United States. In different ways, they reflect many of the ideas contained in Box 7.4.

7.4.1 Pastoral societies

Drought and famine in sub-Saharan Africa have attracted considerable attention in the popular and scientific literature. However, they are not recent phenomena, and people in Africa have developed coping mechanisms over centuries to reduce vulnerability to them. Among those who have adapted the most are pastoralists, since they inhabit the most drought-prone regions. In this subsection, adaptive measures developed by the nomadic Ngisonyoka people in Kenya are examined regarding how they coped with a serious drought in the 1980s. As McCabe (1987: 371–2) remarked relative to this experience, "it is important from both a scientific and a development perspective to define how traditional systems are affected by drought and how they respond to drought

Box 7.4 Uncertainty and the adaptive approach

When policies are defined, management begins and the same process of design and analysis occurs, but now in an environment where action has to be taken, however uncertain the outcome. That is where active adaptive management can play a central role, because its premise is that knowledge of the system we deal with is always incomplete. Not only is the science incomplete, the system itself is a moving target, evolving because of the impacts of management and the progressive expansion of the scale of human influences on the planet. Hence, the actions needed by management must be ones that achieve ever-changing understanding as well as the social goals desired. That is the heart of active experimentation at the scales appropriate to the questions. Otherwise, the pathologies of management are inevitable – increasingly fragile systems, myopic management, and social dependencies leading to crises.

Source: Walters and Holling, 1990: 2067.

stress. We need to understand traditional management systems before we suggest changes to these systems." The role of traditional systems and local knowledge will be examined further in Chapter 9.

The Turkana district

The semi-arid and arid region of northwestern Kenya is home for the Turkana people (Figure 7.1). Bounded on the east by Lake Turkana, on the north by the borders with Sudan and Ethiopia, and on the west by the Ugandan escarpment, the region is one of the most arid in East Africa. It receives an annual average of 150 to 250 mm of rainfall at the district capital of Lodwar. The landscape includes low plains at an elevation between 600 and 650 metres, as well as mountain massifs with elevations ranging from 1,800 to 3,100 metres. Trees and dwarf shrubs are the dominant vegetation on the plains, while herbaceous species are found in the higher areas.

Some 200,000 Turkana are divided into well-established groups. Subsistence pastoralists, they raise five types of livestock: camels, cattle, sheep, goats and donkeys. As McCabe noted, *mobility* is a key adaptive feature of Turkana pastoralists. The Turkana often move, and separate their animals into milking and non-milking herds during the dry seasons. Homesteads may be moved as often as 15 times in a year. The movements are relatively short (about 8 to 12 km) and reflect adaption to changing environmental and social conditions. The life of the Turkana is not an easy one, but it has allowed them to adapt successfully to a harsh and unpredictable environment. Indeed, their adaptation strategies remind us that hazards such as droughts and famine should not be viewed as extremely unusual situations which always catch people unaware and by surprise. As Hewitt (1995: 322) has commented, for many people "emergency situations . . . might well describe the times in which we live."

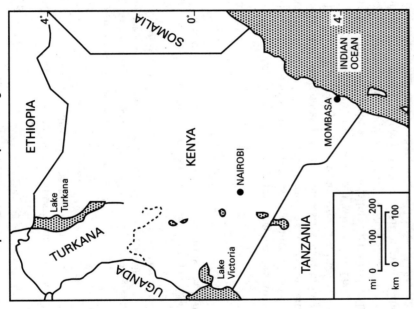

Figure 7.1 Turkana district in northwestern Kenya (McCabe, 1987: 373)

One of the earliest effects of the drought during the 1980s was a failure of annual grasses to germinate. The herbaceous vegetation was available for only a couple of months in higher and wetter areas. Large trees growing in floodplains, able to tap into ground water, remained in foliage for most of the drought period. The impact on animals was significant and diverse. Sheep and cattle depend upon herbaceous vegetation, while camels and goats rely on the leafy vegetation from dwarf shrubs and trees.

For the balance of this discussion, consideration is given to the area inhabited by the Ngisonyoka people, located about 50 km southwest of Lake Turkana. As with the rest of the region, this area is hot and dry, with a high variability in annual precipitation. While there are wet and dry seasons, "it is impossible to predict when the rains will begin, how long they will last, or how much rain will fall" (McCabe, 1987: 375). The period of interest here extended for 21 months, when only 149 mm of rainfall was recorded.

Responses to drought

Based on detailed documentation of the adjustments by four Ngisonyoka families, McCabe discovered that the people responded to the drought conditions by:

- moving more often than in non-drought years;
- dividing the human population into the smallest possible viable groups;
- separating the livestock into as many small herds as was feasible;
- moving into areas viewed as "dangerous" due to their nearness to tribal enemies; and
- reducing the number of people who had to be fed by requiring non-essential household members to seek food elsewhere, which normally meant migrating to towns to work as unskilled labourers.

Impacts of drought

These adaptive measures allowed the Ngisonyoka families to survive the drought period with no human deaths directly attributed to the drought, and no famine relief was needed. However, the period was one of extreme hardship for the families, with their suffering nutritional stress and losing significant numbers of livestock. For example, prior to the drought, the four families had 390 cattle. After the drought, they were left with 245. The impacts also continued after the drought. In the wet season following the end of the drought, the cattle population increased only slightly. The very small increase was due to a much lower than normal calving rate – a result of most of the pregnant cattle aborting their calves due to the nutritional stress during the drought. Another cause of the small increase was that in the year following the drought, a larger than usual number of cattle were slaughtered for food. Camels were more resilient than the cattle, but still suffered. Furthermore, some camels also had to be slaughtered to provide supplemental food. However, during the year after the drought ended, enough camel calves were born to offset the losses to the herd during the drought.

Implications

From the analysis of the experience of the Ngisonyoka families, McCabe drew a number of conclusions. First, the strategy for adapting to drought involved three phases: (1) significant reduction in herd size, including increasing death rates the longer the drought continues, (2) stabilization, during which there are low calving rates but also low mortality, and (3) a recovery period in which livestock numbers increase to pre-drought levels. In the "two-year" drought that was examined, the period of time to move through the three phases of the cycle was three years.

McCabe also noted another significant component of the adaptive strategy of the Ngisonyoka people, one that has led to their being criticized by animal husbandry "experts". Since these pastoral people have managed to devise ways to cope with droughts, the serious impact on them and on their animals is usually not understood or appreciated. They survive, and do not seek or need food relief. Underestimating the consequences of drought on their animals has supported critics' arguments that pastoralists graze too many animals, often viewed as the main cause of overgrazing and environmental degradation. However, it has been established that the livestock stocking rates by the Ngisonyoka are actually well below the carrying capacity of their range land. This is a result of maintaining a relatively large number of animals in relatively "wet" periods, to provide a buffer for the expected "dry" years.

Thus, for the Ngisonyoka people, droughts are not surprises or unexpected events. They anticipate their occurrence, and manage their livestock with a view to reducing their vulnerability to such events. In that regard, Hewitt's comments about extraordinary times describe the normal conditions for these people. They have responded by developing adaptive strategies which allow them to deal with changing and turbulent conditions, even though those conditions are not uncertain or surprises to them.

7.4.2 Columbia River basin

Holling (1989/90: 81) has stated that one of the best examples of the application of an adaptive approach has been the experiment with sustainable development in the Columbia River basin in the United States. It is is this experience that we will now consider.

Background

The Columbia River is the fourth largest river in North America. Flowing over 1,930 km, the river's basin drains parts of two Canadian provinces and seven US states (Figure 7.2). The Columbia River was once a major salmon spawning river, and provided an important source of food for Native Americans. Then, in the early nineteenth century, people from Europe began to arrive. The Native Americans were decimated by diseases brought by the newcomers, and logging, mining and farming significantly altered the landscape. The new economic activities had an impact on the capacity of the river to support spawning of salmon. No activity had a more dramatic impact than the construction of a series of dams and reservoirs under the strong influence of the Bonneville Power

---

Box 7.5 Adaptive management in the Columbia River basin

It is an explicit effort to apply the principles of adaptive management in a region the size of France, with different political jurisdictions, conflicting agencies, and the full range of resource and environmental conflicts. It is a mix of science, negotiation, planning and politics, from which remarkable lessons are emerging.

Source: Holling, 1989/90: 81.

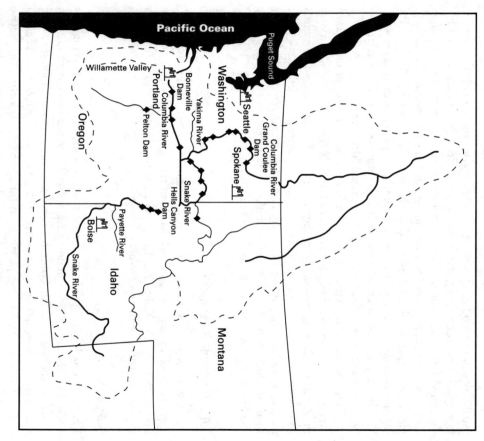

Figure 7.2 The Columbia River basin (Lee, 1993: 18)

Administration, a federal organization with a mandate to market electricity from the federal dams.

Beginning in the 1930s, 19 major dams were constructed; in combination with more than 60 smaller hydro projects, this became the world's largest system for hydroelectricity generation. Low-priced electricity became a magnet for industry, attracting companies which were large consumers of energy. As a result of the development of the hydroelectricity capacity of the Columbia River, by the late 1970s the annual salmon runs had fallen to 2.5 million, in comparison with runs ranging from 10 to 16 million prior to industrialization. Furthermore, the priorities for use of the river had been established as: (1) power, (2) urban and industrial use, (3) agriculture, (4) flood control, (5) navigation, (6) recreation, and (7) fish and wildlife. The operating guidelines for the dams emphasized maximizing electricity generation, even when that adversely affected fish and wildlife.

Northwest Power Act 1980

Until 1970, electric power capacity had been steadily expanded in the Columbia River basin. With demand growing, the utilities pressed for approval to construct even more new facilities. However, Indian people and recreationists began to lobby for greater emphasis upon energy conservation, arguing that such an approach made sense both economically and environmentally. The outcome was that Congress tried to accommodate both the hydro-power and fish interests through the Northwest Power Act. From the perspective of adaptive management, the interesting aspect is that the Northwest Power Planning Council, formed in 1981 under the legislation, created a Fish and Wildlife Program whose purpose was to elevate the position of fish and wildlife, especially salmon and steelhead, among the multiple uses of the Columbia River. As Lee and Lawrence (1986: 433) explained, the Fish and Wildlife Program became "the most ambitious and costly effort at biological restoration on the planet." When initiated, the estimated input costs were about $100 million annually, an amount which included forgoing 1% ($54 to $74 million) each year in federal wholesale power revenues. From the outset, the Fish and Wildlife Program explicitly used an adaptive approach.

Adaptive management in the Columbia River basin was based on five principles. These are summarized as follows.

1. Protection and restoration of fish and wildlife is a common objective. Nevertheless, short-run interests often overshadow long-term needs of the natural system. The focus of the Program is the shared, long-term interest in protecting and restoring fish stocks.
2. Projects have to be considered as experiments. Given incomplete understanding of the fish and their habitat, the outcome of any initiative cannot

---

Box 7.6 Fish and Wildlife Program

Adaptive management is learning by doing: by treating measures in the Fish and Wildlife Program as experiments, the implementation of the program becomes a set of opportunities to test and improve the scientific basis for action. Those opportunities, in turn, structure a systemwide planning regime that makes uses of information produced by implementation of the program.

... Adaptive management should be distinguished, however, from incremental policymaking generally. The emphasis in adaptive management on clear specification of outcomes *before* action is undertaken contrasts sharply to the incrementalist assumption that programs must be adjusted in light of political reaction. Although "disjointed incrementalism" does rely upon action to stimulate information, there is no expectation that the information will improve understanding of the system being affected by government action.

Source: Lee and Lawrence, 1986: 442.

be known in advance. Some will do better than anticipated; others will fail.

3. Action is overdue and required. Action cannot be deferred until "enough" knowledge is gained. New knowledge is best obtained if we seek it by expecting to encounter surprises.

4. Information offers value in two ways: as a basis for action, and as a result of action. To obtain such value, it is essential to pose questions that address management needs, and to use experimental designs that will provide answers to such questions. The adaptive approach seeks information not just from conducting an experiment, but to guide action.

5. Enhancement initiatives may be constrained to a specific time period. However, management is ongoing and for ever. In that manner, it is possible to learn from and benefit from both successes and mistakes. One purpose of adaptive management is to ensure that managers in the future will have a better understanding on which to base their decisions.

Adaptive and consensus approaches

Lee and Lawrence (1986) explained that the experience in the Columbia River basin provides insight as to how adaptive management is different from a *consensus approach* (Table 7.4). If a problem has the characteristics identified in the "Consensus" column of Table 7.4 then a consensus approach is likely to be appropriate. Attention focuses upon achieving agreement about the best solution for a specific problem. In contrast, the adaptive approach (Table 7.4) emphasizes exploring a mix of solutions, each of which has different strengths and weaknesses. A choice can then be made as to which alternative is likely to be most resilient and robust in the context of the many uncertainties that will prevail.

The consensus approach can be effective if agreement exists about goals and

Table 7.4 Consensus and adaptive management (Lee and Lawrence, 1986: 448–9)

Characteristics	Consensus management	Adaptive management
Process	Answer oriented	Question oriented
Design strategy	Optimal solution to problem at hand	Multiple solutions (resilient mix)
Burden of proof	Bias towards study (e.g. acid rain)	Bias towards action plus monitoring (e.g. water budget)
Purpose of monitoring	Compliance and crediting	Learning and adjusting
	Problem curable	Continuing management
Range of utility	Project not repeatable	Project repeatable
	Experiments too risky (e.g. to individuals)	Experiments acceptable (e.g. populations more important than individuals)

objectives. However, when there is disagreement about them, as was the case regarding fisheries in the Columbia River basin, the consensus approach quickly hits a major problem: "consensus management is vulnerable to value differences clothed as scientific dispute" (Lee and Lawrence, 1986: 450). No consensus among experts can end in inaction – exactly the situation that the *precautionary principle*, discussed in Chapter 4, was designed to overcome. A basic belief in consensus management is that inaction is better than taking action on a matter for which disagreement exists. In contrast, the adaptive approach does not expect consensus about the most appropriate short-term answer. Instead, it seeks to identify key questions to facilitate choices between options that provide for flexibility.

Notwithstanding the advantages of an adaptive approach, Lee and Lawrence (1986) also noted that it is not always appropriate. Specifically, they commented that four aspects can create problems for its application. These occur in the following circumstances.

- *The problem is curable rather than chronic.* The need to manage over an extended period of time makes learning from an adaptive approach more valuable than if a one-time remedy is feasible. Thus, restoration of fish and wildlife necessitates continuing management of living populations which can adjust to changing situations. Methods for ongoing restoration are thus different from those needed to clean up a polluted landfill site, a one-time solution.

- *The remedy is unique to the issue.* If lessons are not transferable, then the lessons from the adaptive approach may be less useful. In the Columbia River basin, five dams in the middle stretch of the river are uniquely different in design, meaning that lessons from improving fish passage at any one of them would probably not be transferable to the other four. Other dams were more similar, indicating that for them the time and cost of using an adaptive approach could be worthwhile.

- *Experiments are too risky.* In some situations, the benefits to the population may not justify the risk to individuals. This requires a *harm–benefit* calculation, one of the standard concepts associated with ethical matters in research (Mitchell and Draper, 1982: 5–7).

- *Project failure is a reasonable basis for holding managers accountable.* If uncertainty is low, management should be blamed for negative results. However, when uncertainty is high, failures in a project may contain valuable lessons that can help the entire system. Failure is not always from bad luck and lack of skill. Both success and failure can be instructive, if there is willingness to learn from them.

Redefining success

A final note needs to be made about adaptive management, based on the Columbia River experience. As Lee and Lawrence (1986: 431) remarked, "perhaps the most difficult part of adaptive management is the need to redefine success." Adaptive management stipulates that failure should be expected and anticipated, so that evaluation procedures can be designed to determine why expectations were not met. However, planning for, or accepting, failure can be

Box 7.7 Failure or success?

In the long run, the greatest hurdle may turn out to be the problem of adverse results. ... Adaptive management requires clear specification, in advance, of anticipated outcomes. Given biological uncertainty, one must expect even perfectly implemented measures to fail sometimes, either because of natural fluctuations or because the underlying concept is flawed. Thus, adaptive management increases the likelihood of both visible success and visible failure. Resource managers whose professional reputations hang in the balance will regard this prospect with mixed feelings.

Source: Lee and Lawrence, 1986: 457.

---

politically hazardous for decision makers. Even conceding the existence of uncertainty can be interpreted as a sign of weakness in an adversarial environment in which different interests are in conflict. Furthermore, sponsoring or funding agencies are more interested in supporting initiatives that they believe will succeed, even if the measures of success are short-term ones.

Thus, the concept that some failures are inevitable, and indeed that learning from them can help to achieve longer-term successes, may not be accepted enthusiastically in a turbulent setting in which interests and values are in conflict. It is for these reasons that the Columbia River initiative is even more important, and deserves close attention in the years to come. Further information about adaptive management in the Columbia River can be found in the following references: Lee (1993), Lee and Lawrence (1986), McGinnis (1995) and Volkman and McConnaha (1993).

7.5 Implications

The concept of adaptive environmental management seems to match well the conditions outlined in Chapter 4 (complexity, uncertainty, turbulence). The appropriate management strategy related to an adaptive approach would often challenge the conventional wisdom associated with the comprehensive rational planning model, also outlined in Chapter 4. The comprehensive rational planning model implies that by careful problem definition and diligent research it is possible to gain understanding of resource and environmental systems, and then to control or manage them. In contrast, the adaptive approach explicitly accepts that resource and environmental systems will contain surprises, and that often even the most carefully crafted policies and actions will turn out to be inappropriate. When that occurs, whether we have followed hedging or flexing strategies, change and adjustment will be necessary.

The adaptive approach encourages planners and managers to approach their work and make their decisions with the expectation that they may well be wrong, but that the experience and lessons gained from mistakes (more positively referred to as "lesser successes") can allow them to benefit and improve policies and practices.

One of the largest obstacles to more widespread adoption of an adaptive approach is for planners and managers to be able to acknowledge mistakes, and to make appropriate adjustments. We noted that the Ngisonyoka people in the Turkana district in northwestern Kenya have built-in adaptive mechanisms to deal with stressful environmental conditions, which they do not view as surprises, but rather as uncertain but almost inevitable expectations. Their outlook and approach highlight the fact that Western managers have much to learn from traditional or indigenous resource management systems, considered further in Chapter 9. Perhaps the lessons and implications from northwestern Kenya and the Pacific Northwest in the United States are not a "world apart", if we stop to consider how in each place effort is being made to incorporate adaptive strategies to deal with change, or to effect change.

References and further reading

Alexander D 1993 *Natural disasters*. New York, Chapman and Hall

Bennett J W 1969 *Northern plainsmen: adaptive strategies and agrarian life*. Chicago, Aldine

Berman P 1980 Thinking about programmed and adaptive implementation: matching strategies to situations. In H M Ingram and D E Mann (eds) *Why policies succeed or fail*. Beverly Hills, California, Sage: 205–27

Blaikie P, T Cannon, I Davis and B Wisner 1994 *At risk: natural hazards, people's vulnerability, and disasters*. London, Routledge

Brinkerhoff D W and M D Ingle 1989 Integrating blueprint and process: a structured flexibility approach to development management. *Public Administration and Development* 9(5): 487–503

Fratkin E 1986 Stability and resilience in East African pastoralism: the Rendille and the Ariaal of northern Kenya. *Human Ecology* 14(3): 269–86

Grayson R B, J M Doolan and T Blake 1994 Application of AEAM (Adaptive Environmental Assessment and Management) to water quality in the Latrobe River catchment. *Journal of Environmental Management* 41(3): 245–58

Gunderson L H, C S Holling and S L Light (eds) 1995 *Barriers and bridges to the renewal of ecosystems and institutions*. New York, Columbia University Press

Hewitt K (ed.) 1983 *Interpretations of calamity: from the viewpoint of human ecology*. London, Allen and Unwin

Hewitt K 1995 Excluded perspectives in the social construction of disaster. *International Journal of Mass Emergencies and Disasters* 13(3): 317–39

Hewitt K 1997 *Regions of risk*. Harlow, Longman Scientific and Technical

Hilborn R and J Sibert 1988 Adaptive management of developing fisheries. *Marine Policy* 12(2): 112–22

Holling C S (ed.) 1978 *Adaptive environmental assessment and management*. Chichester, John Wiley and Sons

Holling C S 1989/90 Integrating science for sustainable development. *Journal of Business Administration* 19(1&2): 73–83

Imperial M T 1993 The evolution of adaptive management for estuarine ecosystems: the

National Estuary Program and its precursors. *Ocean and Coastal Management* 20(2): 147–80

Kromm D E and S E White 1984 Adjustment preferences to groundwater depletion in the American High Plains. *Geoforum* 15(2): 271–84

Lee K N 1993 *Compass and gyroscope: integrating science and politics for the environment.* Washington, DC, Island Press

Lee K N and J Lawrence 1986 Restoration under the Northwest Power Act: adaptive management: learning from the Columbia River Basin Fish and Wildlife Program. *Environmental Law* 16(3): 431–60

Ludwig D, R Hilborn and C Walters 1993 Uncertainty, resource exploitation, and conservation: lessons from history. *Science* 260 (2 April): 17, 36

McAllister M K and R M Peterman 1992 Experimental design in the management of fisheries. *North American Journal of Fisheries Management* 12(1): 1–18

McCabe J T 1987 Drought and recovery: livestock dynamics among the Ngisonyoka Turkana of Kenya. *Human Ecology* 15(4): 371–89

McGinnis M V 1995 On the verge of collapse: the Columbia River system, wild salmon and the Northwest Power Planning Council. *Natural Resources Journal* 35(1): 63–92

Mitchell B and D Draper 1982 *Relevance and ethics in geography.* Harlow, Longman

Mulvihill P R and R F Keith 1989 Institutional requirements for adaptive EIA: the Kativik Environmental Quality Commission. *Environmental Impact Assessment Review* 9(4): 399–412

Palm R 1990 *Natural hazards: an interactive framework for research and planning.* Baltimore, Johns Hopkins University Press

Perevolotsky A, A Perevolotsky and I Noy-Meir 1989 Environmental adaptation and economic change in a pastoral mountain society: the case of the Jabaliyah Bedouin of the Mt. Sinai region. *Mountain Research and Development* 9(2): 153–64

Rondinelli D A 1993a *Strategic and results-based management: reflections on the process.* Ottawa, Canadian International Development Agency, June

Rondinelli D A 1993b *Development projects as policy experiments: an adaptive approach to development administration.* London, Routledge

Schmieglelow F K A and S J Hannon 1993 Adaptive management, adaptive science and the effects of forest fragmentation on boreal birds in northern Alberta. *Transactions of the 58th North American Wildlife and Natural Resource Conference*, 584–98

Smit B (ed.) 1993 *Adaptation to climatic variability and change.* Department of Geography Occasional Paper No. 19, Guelph, Ontario, University of Guelph

Smith K 1996 *Environmental hazards: assessing risk and reducing disaster.* London, Routledge, second edition

Stromgaard P 1989 Adaptive strategies in the breakdown of shifting cultivation: the case of Manbwe, Lamba, and Lala of northern Zambia. *Human Ecology* 17(4): 427–44

Volkman J M and W E McConnaha 1993 Through a glass, darkly: Columbia River salmon, the Endangered Species Act, and adaptive management. *Environmental Law* 23: 1249–72

Walters C J 1986 *Adaptive management of renewable resources.* New York, McGraw-Hill

Walters C J and C S Holling 1990 Large-scale management experiments and learning by doing. *Ecology* 71(6): 2060–8

Chapter 8

Partnerships and Participation

8.1 Introduction

Key aspects of sustainable development include empowerment of local people, self-reliance and social justice. One means to achieve these aspects is to move away from traditional forms of environmental and resource management, which are dominated by professional experts in the government and private sector, and towards approaches which combine the experience, knowledge and understanding of various groups and people. The words *partnerships* and *stakeholders* are often used to characterize an approach that includes both organized interest groups and the general public in resource and environmental planning.

In this chapter, discussion focuses initially upon outlining some characteristics of public participation. Attention then turns to examining some experiences with partnerships.

8.2 Fundamental aspects of participation and partnerships

8.2.1 Rationale for participation

Many reasons can be given for involving the public in resource and environmental management. By consulting with people living in a region who will be

---

Box 8.1

Natural resource managers have traditionally addressed biological and technical problems effectively. They have generally been less successful, however, in dealing with sociopolitical aspects of resource management. This failure may be due to the personality types attracted to resource management and the culture of natural resource management agencies. Most natural resource professionals entered their chosen fields out of love for the outdoors and an affinity for science. Often their interests lie 180 degrees from social and political matters. Many resource managers still cling to the concept of professional management, feeling they should make management decisions and that the public should trust their judgment implicitly.

Source: McMullin and Nielsen, 1991: 553.

Box 8.2

The changes in human attitudes that we call for depend on a vast campaign of education, debate, and public participation.

... environmental and economic problems are linked to many social and political factors.... It could be argued that the distribution of power and influence within society lies at the heart of most environment and development challenges. Hence new approaches must involve ... local participation in decision making.

Source: World Commission on Environment and Development, 1987: 23, 38.

affected by a policy, program or project, it is possible to (1) define the problems more effectively, (2) access information and understanding that fall outside the scientific realm, (3) identify alternative solutions that will be socially acceptable, and (4) create a sense of ownership for the plan or solution, which facilitates implementation. While a participatory approach may extend the time needed during the initial stages of analysis and planning, such an investment is normally "returned" later in the process by avoiding or minimizing conflict. While some elected and technical officials may feel challenged or threatened by a participatory approach, believing that it is their job to define the problem and develop solutions, in democratic countries most now appreciate that the complexity of problems means that it is sensible to draw on all possible sources of knowledge and understanding.

Given the above considerations, partnerships can be helpful for both idealistic and pragmatic reasons. With growing complexity, interdependence and uncertainty of issues, and the rapid rate at which conditions change, drawing upon many people and groups should help to achieve a balanced perspective relative to an issue. Furthermore, there is growing public expectation and demand for greater involvement, and less willingness to accept that "experts" necessarily know what is best. Members of the public are also increasingly willing to accept responsibilities and risks which accompany reallocation of power or authority to them when they become partners with government agencies which have legal mandates and responsibilities. And when economic conditions become difficult, and less public funding is available for resource and environmental initiatives, partners outside government can often

Box 8.3 Partnership

A partnership is a mutually agreed arrangement between two or more public, private or non-governmental organizations to achieve a jointly determined goal or objective, or to implement a jointly determined activity, for the benefit of the environment and society.

Box 8.4 Creating volunteer partnerships

Tens of thousands of volunteers across the country are increasingly becoming involved in activities – such as planting trees, hauling mulch, and assisting with public outreach – that contribute to the health of the urban forest. Enhancing and developing partnerships with volunteers can further strengthen the growing field of urban forestry. But urban forestry volunteer programs are not without controversy. Professional urban foresters may feel that volunteers aren't capable of highly skilled work, that they can't consistently count on volunteers, or that volunteers may challenge their professional authority and judgment.

Source: Westphal and Childs, 1994: 28.

---

contribute, in money or in kind, to expedite activity which otherwise would be difficult to support. In this manner, partnerships can help to maintain or to improve service.

8.2.2 Kinds of partners and partnerships

Partnerships are applicable to many management functions. They can be useful in policy development, data collection, research, analysis and planning, program development, design and delivery, evaluation, monitoring, enforcement, administration, and fund raising. Depending upon the situation, partnerships can be developed with client groups, volunteer associations, community groups, non-governmental organizations, educational institutions, business or industry, aboriginal people, and other levels of government.

Partnerships can be of many different kinds. They can range from the personal or informal through to voluntary or legally binding arrangements. They may be short-term and project specific, or long-term and broad in scope. They may involve sharing of work or financial costs, or the sharing only of information.

8.2.3 Key elements for successful participation and partnerships

Many elements for successful participation and partnerships are the same as for effective conflict resolution (Chapter 11). However, some key elements are as follows.

- *Compatibility* between participants. Such compatibility is often based on *respect* and *trust*, even when legitimately different expectations or needs exist. With respect and trust, differences can often be overcome, and indeed can be used to help each participant to broaden his or her outlook.
- *Benefits* to all partners. If there are not real benefits to all the participants, and if they are not perceived to be shared fairly, then a sustained partnership will be difficult to achieve.
- *Equitable representation and power* for participants need to be agreed upon and

Box 8.5 Effective participation

Often, the effectiveness of a public participation exercise is judged on the basis of how many people show up at a public meeting. However, more than attendance is involved in an effective public participation process. Trust, communication, opportunity and flexibility are the crucial elements that ultimately determine the effectiveness of a public participation program.

Source: Law and Hartig, 1993: 32.

- established. Even though some partners may have fewer resources or capacity than others, means must be found to ensure that all partners are involved.

- *Communication* mechanisms. There is a need to facilitate both communication internally between the partners, and communication with groups external to the partnership.

- *Adaptability*, especially given the uncertainty and changing circumstances that are often encountered in resource and environmental issues. A willingness to be flexible and to learn from experience, as outlined in Chapter 7, is usually a strong advantage.

- *Integrity, patience and perseverance* by partners. Often obstacles will be encountered, frustration will occur, progress will be slow or slowed down, and signs of progress may not appear for some time. These elements, combined with trust and respect, allow partners to get through the difficult times which inevitably occur.

The above elements are not essential for successful partnerships, but the more that are present the greater is the likelihood that a partnership will endure and be effective.

Box 8.6 Basis for effective partnerships

Planning and management agencies should aggressively move to strengthen and/or establish partnerships with relevant publics. But this partnering must be based on an understanding that the missions, legislative mandates, and administrative policies among partners may be very different. It requires that differences in view be identified and accepted, and that commonalities in interest be sought as the building blocks for consensus. The goal should be to ensure that there are no real losers, that all receive some spoils in pursuing a common target. Partners must recognize that tradeoffs must be made to improve the collective whole. A necessary condition for establishing mutual trust is that partnering arrangements be open, frank and honest. Unless that condition is met, there will be little incentive for meaningful cooperation.

Source: Viessman, 1993: 14.

8.2.4 Degree of involvement through partnerships

The degree or amount of public involvement which is desirable and feasible must be determined. As Arnstein (1969) observed, a participatory approach can represent a redistribution of power from managers to the public. On that basis, she argued that different degrees of involvement could be identified, ranging from non-participation, to tokenism, to actual sharing of power (Table 8.1). Traditional managers are often hesitant to go beyond the categories of non-participation or tokenism, in the belief that the general public is usually ignorant or apathetic, that the time required is disproportionate to the benefits, that the managers have a responsibility to exert professional judgement, and that public agencies have legally based obligations which cannot be transferred to another party. In contrast, citizens are increasingly expecting what they consider to be "meaningful" participation, which in their view usually means sharing some of the power. The sharing or reallocating of power raises the issue of *accountability*, in the sense of to whom a group given power can be held accountable regarding decisions taken.

Various degrees of participation are illustrated by the four types of *strategic alliances* which the Ontario Ministry of Natural Resources (1995) has identified regarding its involvement with potential partners (Table 8.2). These are described in the following paragraphs.

Contributory partnerships involve an arrangement in which a public or private organization has agreed to provide sponsorship or support, normally through actual funding, for some activities in which it will have little or no direct operational participation. While the financial contribution is often essential for the success of the activity, this type of arrangement is a weak type of partnership

Table 8.1   Arnstein's eight rungs on the ladder of citizen participation (Arnstein, 1969)

Rungs on the ladder of citizen participation	Nature of involvement	Degree of power sharing
1. Manipulation	Rubberstamp committees	Non-participation
2. Therapy	Power holders educate or cure citizens	
3. Informing	Citizens' rights and options are identified	Degrees of tokenism
4. Consultation	Citizens are heard but not necessarily heeded	
5. Placation	Advice is received from citizens but not acted upon	
6. Partnership	Trade-offs are negotiated	Degrees of citizen power
7. Delegated power	Citizens are given management power for selected or all parts of programs	
8. Citizen control		

since not all partners are actively involved in decision making.

Operational partnerships have partners sharing work rather than decision-making power. The emphasis here is upon reaching agreement on mutually desirable or compatible goals, and then working jointly to achieve them. Collaboration may be very high, in that the partners share non-financial resources to a considerable extent. Power is retained primarily or exclusively by the partner which provides the financial resources, and this is usually the public sector partner.

Consultative partnerships are those in which the resource management agency actively seeks advice from individuals, groups and other organizations outside government. The mechanism is usually a committee or council, which is primarily designed to provide advice to the public agency about a specified policy field or issue. Control is clearly retained by the public agency, which has the discretion to decide the extent to which it will respond to the advice received. However, the partners can exert significant influence on decisions, because the public agency recognizes the political costs of ignoring advice that it has actively sought. Out-of-pocket expenses or daily payments are often made to members of the advisory group, based on an agreement reached at the beginning of the process.

Table 8.2   Strategic alliances identified by the Ontario Ministry of Natural Resources (1995)

Type of strategic alliance	Purpose	Extent of power sharing
(1) Contributory	*Support sharing*: to leverage new resources or funds for program/service delivery	Government retains control, but contributors may propose or agree to the objectives of the strategic alliance
(2) Operational	*Working sharing*: to permit participants to share resources and work, and exchange information for program/service delivery	Government retains control. Participants can influence decision making through their practical involvement
(3) Consultative	*Advisory*: to obtain relevant input for developing policies and strategies, and for program/service design, delivery, evaluation and adjustment	Government retains control, ownership and risk, but is open to input from clients and stakeholders: the latter may also play a role in legitimizing government decisions
(4) Collaborative	*Decision making*: to encourage joint decision taking with regard to policy development, strategic planning, and program/service design, delivery evaluation and adjustment	Power, ownership and risk are shared

Real decision-making power is shared in *collaborative partnerships*. The intent is to achieve mutually compatible objectives, and the resources to be shared may involve information, labour or money. This is the only one of the four partnerships in which each partner explicitly gives up some autonomy. More specifically, in this arrangement, a public agency turns over some of its power to groups or organizations outside the government. Normally, such reallocation does not include any responsibilities for which the public agency is legally accountable. In the best form of collaborative partnership, decisions are reached through consensus. Such consensus building is usually most effective when the issue or problem is one that no partner can resolve unilaterally. Financially, there may be a mutual sharing, and indeed a two-way flow, of expenses and revenues.

The main implication of this discussion is that there is no one best "model" for partnerships. Many choices exist. The kind of partnership, and the nature of participation, have to be determined by the various people or groups involved.

8.2.5 Stakeholders

In designing partnerships, an issue can arise as to who are genuine stakeholders. In that regard, a distinction should be made between what is often called the *active* and the *inactive* publics. The active public involves those people who are organized into interest groups, such as Friends of the Earth, Sierra Club, Pollution Probe and Greenpeace. The largest of these groups are well organized and articulate, and often have financial resources and full-time staff to monitor activities, conduct research and make submissions to government. In contrast, the inactive public, or the silent majority, are those people who do not usually become actively involved in social or environmental issues, being more focused on coping with issues at work and at home. The reality is that many of the organized groups which form the core of the active public make it their business to become involved in environmental and resource issues, whether or not they are invited to become members in a partnership. Their voices are normally heard, and the public managers do not have to make special efforts to hear from them as they view part of their function as commenting upon and participating in planning.

The challenge for managers is to determine if a cross-section of active public interest groups reflects a reasonable cross-section of the stakeholders to be affected or impacted by decisions. There has often been concern that the members of the active public do not in fact fairly represent all of the stakeholders. As a result, resource and environmental managers often have made substantive effort to interact with members of the inactive public, even if that may be viewed by some as falling into Arnstein's categories of non-participation or tokenism, shown in Table 8.1. However, in fairness to environmental and resource agencies, it should be said that many people do not want to become actively involved. Their lives are full and complicated enough with day-to-day matters, and they are often content to rely on professionals to do what they were hired to do – plan and manage.

Box 8.7 Who is a stakeholder?

The currently popular colloquialism "stakeholder" is being tossed around the offices and boardrooms of the nation. It is turning up with increasing frequency in written form, occasionally in formal documents. The problem is that the context in which it is currently being used is inconsistent with the definition by which it found its way into the language in the first place. In fact it is being used in exactly the opposite sense to that for which it was intended.

. . . What is a stakeholder? Depending on the spelling, it could be a person waiting to put a particular cut of beef on a barbeque. Or it could describe someone carrying the requisite tool which will, according to legend, put an end to a vampire. Any reputable dictionary defines a stakeholder as just what is implied, someone who holds the stakes during the course of a wager; the person selected by the opponents in a wager, deemed by both of the betting parties to possess the required honesty and impartiality to be trusted to hold the money or valuables being wagered until the uncertainty is resolved. Therefore, quite contrary to the intended current application, a stakeholder is someone who has no stake in the particular issue in question.

Since a stakeholder is, in fact, a disinterested third party, as opposed to someone who has a vested interest, continued use of the term in current context shows a flagrant disdain for the integrity of the language. Most definitely, it should not be used in professional presentations, written or oral.

Source: Wiens, 1995: 3, 7.

8.2.6 Timing for public input

Partnerships may be established at varying times during analysis and planning. Smith (1982: 561–563) suggested that planning occurs at three levels: *normative*, in which decisions are taken to determine what ought to be done; *strategic*, in which decisions are made to determine what can be done; and *operational*, in which decisions are made to determine what will be done. He concluded that many public participation programs are used in the operational stage. However, Smith and others have argued that partnerships need to be established earlier in the planning process, so that members of the public can become involved at the normative and strategic stages. Otherwise, the public may conclude that their participation is little more than cosmetic, or tokenism in Arnstein's language, because many of the key decisions are taken before the operational phase is reached.

To illustrate, for energy planning a number of issues must be addressed. At an early phase, consideration should be given to what is the appropriate mix of strategies involving new sources of energy (conventional thermal, nuclear, hydroelectric, solar, wind) and changing patterns of energy use, through conservation and other initiatives to reduce demand. Having decided upon the supply sources, decisions must then be made regarding where the new sources will be located. Often it is at this stage that the public is invited to become involved to help identify acceptable sites. However, the public may wish to reopen questions related to whether or not there is a need for new sources of energy supply, if actions were taken to reduce demand. If people arrive at a public hearing or meeting with different expectations as to whether the issues being discussed are *normative* (mix of supply and demand management strategies) or *operational* (sites for new power sources), a high level of frustration can be created.

Critics of partnerships or public participation may charge that people came wanting to discuss issues that were already resolved, and therefore conclude that a participatory approach simply generates excessive costs and delays. In contrast, advocates of a participatory approach may conclude that the participation is superficial or tokenistic, with the most important decisions already made before the public is invited to become involved. The implication is that it is important to recognize the different stages or phases of planning, and to ensure that partners or public participation exercises are focused so that those involved understand the stages and agree on the purpose of the partnership exercise.

8.2.7 Components of partnership programs

As noted earlier, there are many ways in which partners can be drawn into a management process. How ever the partnerships are organized, there are normally three key functions which should be included. First, information must be shared with those whose views are being sought so that they can consider the nature of the problem being addressed, and appreciate the goals, mandates and legal obligations of the public resource and environmental agencies. Following the dissemination of information (the "information-out" phase), opportunity must be provided for the partners or the general public to provide their perspectives, whether related to the nature of the problem, the range of possible solutions, or their role in implementation and monitoring of results. This is often referred to as the "information-in" component. This is an important component, since it signals that the public agencies do not have all the information or understanding, and are explicitly seeking input from others. Since a number of iterations are usually required, such as to define the problem, to develop alternative solutions, and to design an implementation strategy, provision should also be made for continuous exchange or interaction between the representatives of the resource and environmental management agencies and the other partners.

8.2.8 Mechanisms for participation

Having agreed upon the functions to be included in the partnership program, it is then important to determine the mix of mechanisms to be used. As Table 8.3 indicates, many mechanisms exist. The challenge is to custom-design from the alternatives to meet conditions and needs of a particular situation. Lobbying is often not recognized as a form of participation, but it is definitely one method

Table 8.3 Public participation mechanisms (from Mitchell, 1989: 119)

	Representativeness	Information in	Information out	Continuous exchange	Ability to make decisions
Public meetings	Poor	Poor	Good	Poor	Poor-Fair
Task force	Poor	Good	Good	Good	Fair-Good
Advisory groups	Poor-Good	Poor-Good	Poor-Good	Good	Fair-Good
Social surveys	Good	Poor	Fair	Poor	Poor
Individual/group submissions	Poor	Good	Poor	Poor	Poor
Litigation	Poor-Fair	Good	Good	Poor	Good
Arbitration	Poor-Fair	Good	Good	Poor	Good
Environmental mediation	Poor-Fair	Good	Good	Fair	Good
Lobbying	Poor-Fair	Good	Fair	Good	Fair

used by interest groups to represent their views to decision makers. Advisory bodies may take many forms, but usually involve a group established to investigate a problem. Mediation and negotiation are methods which have emerged relatively recently to identify different interests and to find mutually satisfactory solutions. They will be considered in more detail in Chapter 11.

8.2.9 Balancing fairness and efficiency

Sustainable development emphasizes the ideas of equity and social empowerment. Creation of partnerships is usually justified on the basis that they provide for a more open and transparent management process, and therefore for greater equity. Furthermore, by being involved in defining the problem and identifying solutions, the partners are more likely to accept or "buy into" proposed recommendations. There is no doubt that, in the short term, a participatory approach often extends the time required for analysis and planning. If adequate time is to be allowed for "information out" and "information in" over a number of iterations, the process will be longer than if technical resource and environmental managers worked on their own. However, it is commonly accepted that in the long run a participatory approach is often also efficient in that it results in less challenging of findings and solutions towards the end of the planning process. In that regard, time "lost" in the early part of the analysis and planning is usually recaptured by the time of the implementation phase. Furthermore, if the investment of time in a participatory approach leads to less argument and opposition to recommendations, then it often seems to be the case during the overall life of an issue or problem that a participatory approach is both more efficient and equitable compared with an approach that does not incorporate participation.

8.2.10 Monitoring effectiveness of partnerships

If experience from partnerships and public participation is to be helpful in improving future initiatives, it is important that we build in the capacity to monitor effectiveness. In that manner, lessons from past and ongoing experience can become part of the *social learning* approach advocated in adaptive environmental management, as discussed in Chapter 7.

Smith (1983) has suggested that monitoring and evaluation could usefully focus upon three aspects: *context*, *process* and *outcome* (Table 8.4). Today, many people would split his third category into two separate categories: *outputs* and *outcomes*. The *context* category reminds us that any partnership or public

Table 8.4 Monitoring and evaluating public participation (from Mitchell, 1989: 121)

Context
1. Historical background
2. Institutional arrangements
   – political structure and processes
   – legislation and regulations
   – administrative structures
3. Agency features
   – status
   – function
   – terms of reference
   – financial arrangements

Process
1. Goals and objectives for participation
   – mandate given participation by agency
   – objectives of participants
2. Number and nature of public(s) involved
   – who are they?
   – how representative are they?
   – how organized are they?
3. Methodology employed
   – techniques
   – information access
   – resources

Outcome
1. Results of participatory exercise
2. Effectiveness
   – focus on issues
   – representativeness of participants
   – appropriateness of process
   – degree of awareness achieved
   – impact and influence of participation
   – time and cost

participation exercise occurs with reference to previous events and decisions, historical relationships between partners, changing interests, objectives and expectations, and shifting ideological, economic and political circumstances. If the effectiveness of a partnership initiative is to be determined, there must be awareness of such contextual aspects.

The *process* associated with a partnership arrangement is often crucial for its success, and indeed it is this aspect which has attracted the most attention in evaluation. As noted in previous subsections, there are many choices in designing a process, and it is important to be aware of what the range of choice is, before judging the adequacy of the choices actually made. Emphasis here usually concentrates upon the goals and objectives for participation, the number and type of stakeholders involved, and the methods used.

The final aspects are the coupled elements of *outputs* and *outcomes*. Outputs are normally measurable aspects, such as number of options considered, number of interests accommodated in the selected solution, and satisfaction of participants. Outcomes relate to the significance of the outputs, in the short, medium and long term. Here, interest is not just in the number of interests accommodated in the solution, but also in the capacity for them to be implemented, and in their ability to meet the ongoing needs and expectations of the participants. In that regard, the concept of outcomes is reflected in the points headed "Effectiveness" in Table 8.4.

8.2.11 Overview

Many aspects require attention in designing a partnership arrangement or a public participation program. As illustrated in the above subsections, consideration should be give to the following: (1) rationale, (2) kinds of partners and partnerships, (3) elements for success, (4) degrees of involvement, (5) types of stakeholders, (6) timing, (7) program components, (8) mechanisms, (9) balancing fairness and efficiency, and (10) monitoring and evaluation. With these in mind, we turn now to examples of partnerships and participation which illustrate some of these aspects.

8.3 Evolving patterns of participation and partnerships

Experience from Montana in the USA illustrates the manner in which public participation programs can evolve as a result of resource and environmental managers adjusting on the basis of earlier experiences. This example is based on a report by McMullin and Nielsen (1991).

8.3.1 Example of the Missouri River, Montana

South of Great Falls, the Missouri River is a high-quality and heavily fished trout stream. The Montana Department of Fish, Wildlife and Parks (MDFWP) had been monitoring the brown trout population in the stream, and became concerned about the low numbers, which it believed were due to heavy fishing pressure. The MDFWP proposed that the daily limit of five brown trout of any size be dropped to one brown trout longer than 56 cm, along with a continuing limit of up to five of the more abundant rainbow trout. The proposal also stated that fishing gear would be restricted to flies and lures. Baited hooks would be disallowed, based on evidence that the mortality of trout released after being caught with a baited hook was much higher than when released from flies and lures. Other than the opportunity to keep a trophy-sized fish (over 56 cm), the brown trout fishery would become a catch-and-release activity.

Several public meetings were held to obtain public input during development of the modified catch regulations. Those attending had the opportunity to provide comments and to complete a questionnaire. The conclusion of the managers from this input was that the majority of respondents supported the proposal. However, the fishers were polarized. Fly fishers were strongly in agreement. Bait fishers were opposed, believing that the brown trout could be protected without a restriction on bait.

During the formal open meeting at which the Montana Fish and Game Commission was expected to adopt the proposal, emotions were high. Bait anglers protested strongly and bitterly, and argued effectively that not all options to protect the brown trout population had been examined systematically. Fly and lure fishers spoke equally fervently in support of the proposal. The Commission members became uneasy about the sharp polarization, and about a proposal which was of a "take-it-or-leave-it" kind. They indicated that they wanted to have more than one option to consider, and rejected the proposed change of catch regulations. The outcome was dissatisfaction by all participants. The MDFWP believed that a special interest group had derailed its proposal to protect the fishery. Fly fishers were unhappy that the Commission had apparently chosen to ignore the majority of views, which favoured the proposal, from the public. Bait anglers felt that the MDFWP was favouring the fly fishers. And Commission members concluded that the MDFWP had not adequately addressed the polarized positions prior to the Commission's public hearing. However, the one thing that everyone agreed upon was that the image and credibility of the MDFWP, and the perceived value of "public participation", had been damaged. The next example provides a contrast, and indicates how the MDFWP adjusted its approach to public participation based on the experience with the proposed changes to catch regulations on the Missouri River.

8.3.2 Example of the Bighorn River, Montana

The Bighorn River is close to Billings, the largest city in Montana, and is also within a one-day drive of Denver. Construction of a dam in 1967 changed a warm and silty river into a cool and clear water trout stream. The Bighorn River soon gained a reputation for having a world-class trout fishery, and angling pressure grew. Furthermore, the river fishery was closed in the mid 1970s as a result of a legal challenge from the Crow Tribe native people, who claimed that only tribe members could fish. In 1981, the US Supreme Court ruled that the state of Montana had authority for management, and the river was reopened for recreation fishing. Sport fishing then grew quickly, and an associated guide and outfitter industry developed.

Concern peaked in 1986, when angling that summer doubled from 1985. Fishers complained that the fish population was being damaged, and that crowding by fishers was ruining the experience for many. Guides and outfitters were particularly outspoken, and called for the MDFWP to introduce rigorous restrictions. However, studies of the Bighorn River by the MDFWP indicated that angler pressure was much less a stress on the fish than were habitat problems. The managers believed that water releases from the dam were inadequate for the needs of the large brown trout so prized by fishers, that quality of the water from the dam was detrimental to the fish, and that the food supply for the brown trout was inadequate. Thus, in their view, the priority need was to improve the habitat, not change fishing regulations. Despite these findings from the MDFWP, the fishers focused on the merits and problems of regulations, and became polarized in the same way as had occurred at the Missouri River.

The MDFWP realized that it needed to modify its approach to participation and partnerships. Not only public participation was required, but also capacity for *conflict resolution*. Indeed, public participation and involvement of partners was deemed essential for resolution of the conflict, a general issue to be considered further in Chapter 11. Based on the experience with the Missouri River, the MDFWP developed the following five-stage management process.

(1) *Involving concerned citizens to establish management goals for the fishery*. Public meetings were held both in Billings, where many of the fishers came from, and in Fort Smith, a small community along the Bighorn River in which many of the guides and outfitters were based. Because of the controversy, the local media had provided detailed coverage of the issue and the upcoming meetings, which led to a large number of people attending. The management goal should be to manage the river for a high-quality, wild trout fishing experience with emphasis upon catching large, trophy-sized trout. Attendance rates were well above what would normally be expected for such events. After the MDFWP had outlined its understanding of the fishery and the habitat, a *facilitator* chaired the discussions and kept the focus on management goals. As a result, the meetings concentrated on *ends* (management goals) rather than on *means* (specific regulations). The meetings at Billings and Fort Smith generated the same conclusions. The management goal should be to manage the river for a high-quality, wild trout fishing experience with emphasis upon catching large, trophy-sized trout.

(2) *Preparing and distributing a draft management plan*. The draft plan accomplished several purposes. First, it provided a means to organize the concerns which had emerged during the goal-setting meetings. In addition to the concerns, the draft plan included measurable objectives which would allow achievement of the agreed goal. Second, the draft plan presented data in lay terms, which helped to inform people about the status of the fish populations and the variables affecting them. The draft plan was distributed widely and

included people who had contacted the MDFWP with concerns about the fisheries, as well as guides and outfitters, sports club officers and elected officials. Speaking engagements were arranged by the MDFWP at a number of fishing clubs and civic clubs over a three-month period.

(3) *Obtaining feedback to the draft plan through a brief, self-addressed survey.* People were given the opportunity to express agreement or disagreement to the draft plan through a survey form. The draft plan had accomplished its information and education functions, as 93% of respondents indicated that it had improved their understanding of both the river and the fishery. Agreement regarding the recommended objectives and strategies varied from 69% to 83%. For the MDFWP, a striking result from the survey was that 50% of respondents indicated that they had changed their views about how the fishery should be managed after they had read the plan. A number of people stated that they had initially believed that regulations were the best approach, but after reading the plan agreed that priority should be given to habitat issues.

(4) *Submitting the final plan to the Montana Fish and Wildlife Commission.* Following modifications to the plan based on the survey responses, the MDFWP made a formal presentation of the plan to the Commission, in which the implications for Commission action were highlighted. The Commission accepted the plan.

(5) *Following up with the public.* The MDFWP committed itself to report to the public when major milestones of the plan were met, or when conditions changed sufficiently for modifications to or departures from the plan to be required. The MDFWP staff prepared news releases, which were used by the local media, and staff members accepted speaking invitations both to give updates and to respond to questions.

Lessons

McMullin and Nielsen (1991) indicated that the revised management process did not eliminate all conflict and controversy. However, it did allow the MDFWP managers to address and resolve most of the difficulties during the 90-day period designated for review of the draft proposal. This more systematic and reflective approach to receiving input regarding a plan was viewed as much more useful by both the MDFWP and the Commission, compared with one pressure-packed Commission meeting in which short notice and limited options were involved. The effectiveness of the revised process was striking, particularly since the decision for the Bighorn River followed immediately after the disapproval by the Commission of the Missouri River proposal. A state-wide conservation group did present an option for a restrictive regulation for the brown trout fishery on the Bighorn River, but this was not accepted, because that option (and others) had already been systematically assessed during the planning process. The overall implications of this experience are presented in Box 8.8.

Box 8.8 Lessons from the Montana experience

Commonly cited problems of the public involvement process are: (a) a "representative" public is difficult to reach, (b) citizen participation may promote conflict rather than resolve it, (c) participatory democracy in resource allocation diminishes the role and stature of the professional manager, and (d) the public is often not sufficiently informed to make good resource allocation decisions.

The key to solving the first two problems is having reasonable goals for citizen participation programs and employing adequate techniques to achieve them.... Managers who seek consensus on controversial issues will invariably be disappointed because the public has real, deeply held differences in desires and outlooks. Instead of consensus, the goal should be informed consent.

The third problem is clearly an illusion. Montana managers found their professional credibility was enhanced rather than diminished by emphasizing their role in formulating management options and explaining the implications of each. When ecological conditions dictate that only one course of action is reasonable, resource managers should assert their authority. However, if multiple strategies will achieve an objective, resource clients should be equal partners in the decision making process. Moreover, many resource allocation decisions are based on incomplete ecological information or include significant, value-based elements. As stewards of publicly owned resources, resource managers have no more right to make these value-based decisions than any other member of the public.

In regard to the fourth problem, the Bighorn experience demonstrated that users can make informed decisions if data are presented to them in understandable form ... good communication between resource managers and resource users helps the public make an informed choice that benefits the resource even when it causes them economic hardship.

Resource managers must continue to evolve to be creators of management options, disseminators of information and facilitators in a publicly-oriented decision making process.

Source: McMullin and Nielsen, 1991: 557–8.

8.4 Stakeholders and the private sector

The experience in Montana reflects many of the issues encountered in a participatory approach designed by a public resource management agency. However, involvement of partners and stakeholders can also be initiated by the private sector. For example, Eckel *et al.* (1992) argued that involvement of stakeholders was critically important when designing a system of environmental performance measurement for a firm. They argued that a system for environmental performance measurement (SEPM) was desirable owing to the following realities in the business world:

- as well as having economic impacts, business activity also has environmental and social impacts;
- businesses are being held liable for environmental costs, as reflected by the increasing number of regulations, incentives and penalties; and
- incorporating environmental management into a firm is "good business" as it can result in direct cost reduction or indirect increases in goodwill.

The products of a good SEPM should include disclosure of (1) environmental obligations and contingencies, (2) environmental risks inherent in the operations of an organization, an item increasingly being expected by stakeholders, and (3) financial risk to the organization, as well as (4) separate disclosure of expenditures for environmental management, an item increasingly being asked for by regulators, investors and analysts.

One of the key tasks in preparing a corporate policy and objectives for environmental management is to identify environmental issues pertinent to the firm. Two methods are available to identify such issues: initial environmental audits, and consulting with stakeholders. Environmental audits will be discussed in Chapter 13 when considering monitoring and evaluation. Here, attention focuses on consultation with stakeholders. The gains from stakeholder consultation are identified in Box 8.10.

Eckel *et al.* (1992: 19) emphasized that "consulting with stakeholders should not be viewed as an act of altruism or public relations." In their view, stakeholder consultation should be viewed as an integral input into development of corporate policy, as it helps to develop direction and focus for a firm's

---

Box 8.9 Consulting with stakeholders

Consultation will clarify stakeholders' expectations about corporate environmental performance, information requirements, and preferred environmental solutions. It will help identify risk reduction projects that boost the firm's reputation with stakeholders. Stakeholders include: creditors, shareholders, regulators, employees, customers, suppliers, communities in which the company operates, and local, provincial and federal governments.

Source: Eckel *et al.*, 1992: 19.

Box 8.10 Benefits from stakeholder consultation

Essentially, consulting with stakeholders will enable the firm to avoid potential problems, identify and resolve potential conflicts, and develop strategies to maximize the benefits or minimize the costs of responding to future changes.

Source: Eckel *et al.*, 1992: 19.

short- and long-term environmental objectives and responsiveness. Stakeholders can help a firm to determine whether it will simply seek to "stay out of trouble" regarding environmental matters, or will strive to become a leader in developing "cutting-edge" practices and procedures regarding environmental monitoring and reporting standards. In that context, Eckel *et al.* argue that stakeholder consultation provides many benefits. Discussions with customers may identify unhappiness with a firm's environmental record that, without concerted attention, could result in decreasing demand for the firm's products or services. Discussions with government officers may assist the firm to become aware of impending regulatory changes. Perhaps more importantly, it may allow the firm to become a partner with the government in helping to design the nature and timing of such changes.

Thus, consulting with stakeholders can be as useful for the private sector as for the government sector. With increasing privatization and commercialization of resource and environmental management functions, more and more resource and environmental managers will be employed in the private sector. It will be important for them to remember that developing partnerships, and consulting with stakeholders, are as important in the private as in the public sector.

8.5 Stakeholder consultation in developing countries

Development of partnerships and involvement of stakeholders are increasingly occurring in the Third World. For example, in northwestern Botswana, Van der Sluis (1994) explained that a land use zoning plan developed for Planning Zone 6, or the Ngamiland Western Communal Remote Zone, used a participatory approach (Figure 8.1). Zone 6, a fragile area in the Kalahari Sandveld of Botswana, is primarily a hunter–gatherer region and a cattle post. Many conflicts have arisen among users. Crops and veld products have been damaged or destroyed by livestock. Ploughing is occasionally carried out in grazing areas, which reduces the fodder for livestock. Wild dogs and lions from the nearby Kaudom Game Reserve in Namibia kill livestock, and a growing tourism industry poses a threat to the integrity of national monuments.

Against the above background, a land use plan was created to try to minimize the conflicts between different uses and users. Van der Sluis (1994: 8) indicated that "to the extent possible, the residents of the area were involved in the planning process." Meetings were held in all the villages in the area to be covered by the plan. This created some major logistical challenges, as the population in the area is highly dispersed, with some of the remote cattle posts being more than a two-hour drive from a village. Since few of the local people had any means of transportation other than walking, they were collected and driven to village meeting places. Land use conflicts were identified and discussed, and alternative land use zoning arrangements were debated. Such meetings were not without controversy, as the BaMbukushu and Bushmen argued for their land to be zoned for grazing, ploughing, gathering of veld foods, and wildlife use. In contrast, the BaHerero had quite different interests because of their highly mobile pastoralist land use activities. Suggestions were

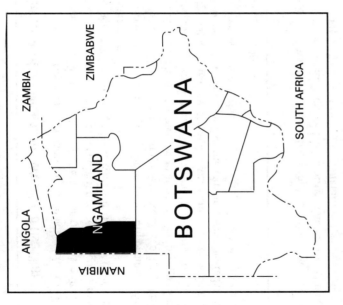

Figure 8.1 Ngamiland Western Communal Remote Zone, Botswana (Van der Sluis, 1994: 8)

sought as to how best to reconcile land degradation problems, and conflicting needs and activities. Records were kept for all of the meetings.

The outcome was a land use zoning system based on the suggestions of the land users, as well as on evaluation of both the capacity of the land and present land use. The land evaluation indicated that the present land use was "more or less optimal" for the area. All land use was marginal, with little gain to be achieved by modifying land use patterns other than the potential for improved dryland farming in valleys. The consultations revealed that land use conflicts could partially be avoided through zoning, but it would be almost impossible to remove cattle posts from areas used by hunter–gatherers and pastoralists. Van

---

Box 8.11 Consultation in Ngamiland West

Consultations with the people were considered crucial in the planning process, since experiences in other parts of the district showed that limited consultations can lead to serious delays in acceptance of the plans, both at the local and regional levels. Also, a zoning plan developed in cooperation with the people stands a better chance to be implemented and adhered to.

Source: Van der Sluis, 1994: 9.

Box 8.12 Outcome of the Ngamiland West Land Use Plan

Although the preparations and consultations took up to three years, the adoption and acceptance of the plan by the authorities was quick. The results have thus been quite satisfactory, especially when compared to the experience with some other land use zoning plans, which had yet to be accepted by the authorities after more than two years.

The socio-economic research has shown the importance of combining different activities in Zone 6, or the "multi-stranded" economy. From the land evaluation, it becomes clear why such large areas are "empty", without physical developments, cattle posts or settlements: the land users do not want to risk investing large sums in drilling boreholes, since the chances of finding water are very low. However, they do recognise the existing land degradation problems and welcome the assistance of the . . . zoning . . . to halt their deterioration.

Source: Van der Sluis, 1994: 10.

der Sluis (1994: 9) remarked that "the people's opinion was decisive in the planning: where no interest existed in zoning of land, the [Planning Team] zoned all land for 'mixed land use'." The Planning Team "did not attempt to change present land use or existing land rights, which would have been very difficult. . . . Instead, it prepared guidelines to assist the Land Board in future land allocations."

8.6 Implications

Participation and partnerships. These concepts are increasingly being incorporated into resource and environmental management initiatives. The rationale for using them is not only in order to be "politically correct". There is growing and persuasive evidence that public participation often leads to more effective resource and environmental management in the medium and long term, even if some extra time is required in the short term.

This chapter has shown that many kinds of partnerships and participation methods are possible. As a result, the resource and environmental manager has the opportunity to craft an approach that draws upon a mix of methods that best meet the conditions and needs in a given situation. Increasingly, managers are striving to involve partners and the public in *normative* and *strategic* stages of planning, rather than confining involvement only to the *operational* phase. Expectations by the public are growing for greater power sharing, which in some instances will cause a dilemma for resource and environmental agencies which are legally responsible for aspects of management. Nevertheless, there is a trend towards delegation of more power to local groups and people, as will be shown in Chapter 9 when discussing the concept of *co-management*.

The examples in this chapter, ranging from public sector initiatives in the United States and Botswana, and private sector strategies in North America, indicate that managers in many countries and cultures can anticipate encountering the same generic issues regarding partnerships and participation. As a result, resource and environmental managers need to develop a carefully thought out rationale for their use of partnerships and public participation, and also need to be aware of the range of methods and techniques that can be applied. It appears that in the future we can anticipate more pressure and demands for increased involvement of the public in resource and environmental management.

References and further reading

Arnstein, S 1969 A ladder of citizen participation. *Journal of the American Institute of Planners* 35(4): 216–24

Bartlett A G, M C Nurse, R B Chhetri and S Kharel 1993 Towards effective community forestry through forest user groups. *Journal of World Forest Resource Management* 7(1): 49–69

Bhatt C P 1990 The Chipko Andolan: forest conservation based on people's power. *Environment and Urbanization* 2(1): 7–18

British Columbia Commission on Resource and Environment 1995 *Public participation.* Volume 3, Victoria, Commission on Resources and Environment

Brown J M and E A Campbell 1991 Risk communication: some underlying principles. *International Journal of Environmental Studies, A* 37(4): 271–83

Cable S and M Benson 1993 Acting locally: environmental injustice and the emergence of grass-roots environmental organizations. *Social Problems* 49(4): 464–77

Chatterjee N 1995 Social forestry in environmentally degraded regions of India: case-study of the Mayurakshi Basin. *Environmental Conservation* 22(1): 20–30

Concepción C M 1993 Environment and industrialization in Puerto Rico: disen-franchising the people. *Journal of Environmental Planning and Management* 36(3): 269–82

Costello L N and K M Dunn 1994 Resident action groups in Sydney: people power or rat-bags? *Australian Geographer* 25(1): 61–76

Dale A P 1992 Aboriginal Councils and natural resource use planning: participation by bargaining and negotiation. *Australian Geographical Studies* 30(1): 9–26

Eckel L, K Fisher and G Russell 1992 Environmental performance measurement. *CMA Magazine* March: 16–23

Goh B L 1991 Urban environmental management: a new challenge to local authorities. *Malaysian Journal of Tropical Geography* 22(1): 9–17

Greene J 1988 Stakeholder participation and utilization in program evaluation. *Evaluation Review* 12(2): 91–116

Grimble R and M-K Chan 1995 Stakeholder analysis for natural resource management in developing countries. Some practical guidelines for making management more participatory and effective. *Natural Resources Forum* 19(2): 113–24

Hartig H N and N Law 1994 Institutional framework to direct development and implementation of Great Lakes Remedial Action Plan. *Environmental Management* 18(6): 855–64

Hartig J H and P D Hartig 1990 Remedial action plans: an opportunity to implement sustainable development at the grassroots level in the Great Lakes basin. *Alternatives* 17(3): 26–38

Hartup B K 1994 Community conservation in Belize: demography, resource use, and attitudes of participating landowners. *Biological Conservation* 69(3): 235–41

Hill K A 1991 Zimbabwe's wildlife conservation regime: rural farmers and the state. *Human Ecology* 19(1): 19–34

Jakes P and J Harms 1995 *Report on the Socioeconomic Roundtable convened by the Chequamegon and Nicolet National Forests*. St Paul, Minnesota, US Department of Agriculture, Forest Service, North Central Forest Experiment Station, General Technical Report NC-177

Kangas J 1994 An approach to public participation in strategic forest management planning. *Forest Ecology and Management* 70(1–3): 75–88

Kernaghan K 1994 Partnerships and public administration: conceptual and practical considerations. *Canadian Public Administration* 36(1): 57–76

King S, M Conley, B Latimer and D Ferrari 1989 *Co-design: a process of design participation*. New York, Van Nostrand Reinhold

Landre B K and B A Knuth 1993 Success of citizen advisory committees in consensus-based water resources planning in the Great Lakes basin. *Society and Natural Resources* 6(3): 229–57

Larritt C 1995 Taking part in Mutawintji: aboriginal involvement in Mootwingee National Park. *Australian Geographical Studies* 33(2): 242–56

Law N and J H Hartig 1993 Public participation in Great Lakes Remedial Action Plan. *Plan Canada* March: 31–5

Lerner S (ed.) 1993 *Environmental stewardship: studies in active earthkeeping*. Department of Geography Publication Series No. 39, Waterloo, Ontario, University of Waterloo

Lobster D J 1992 Using forest guards to protect a biological reserve in Costa Rica. *Journal of Environmental Planning and Management* 35(1): 17–41

MacLaren V W 1995 Assessing public participation in waste management planning in Toronto. *Environments* 23(1): 52–9

Makombe K (ed.) 1994 *Sharing the land: wildlife, people and development in Africa*. IUCN/ROSA Environmental Issues Series No. 1, Harare, Zimbabwe, International Union for the Conservation of Nature and Natural Resources (IUCN) Regional Office for Southern Africa, and Washington, DC, IUCN Sustainable Use of Wildlife Programme

Martin S 1995 Partnerships for local environmental action: observations on the first two years of Rural Action for the Environment. *Journal of Environmental Planning and Management* 38(2): 149–65

McMullin S L and L A Nielsen 1991 Resolution of natural resource allocation conflicts through effective public involvement. *Policy Studies Journal* 19(3–4): 553–9

Mercer D, M Keen and J Woodfall 1994 Defining the environmental problem: local conservation strategies in metropolitan Victoria. *Australian Geographical Studies* 32(1): 41–57

Miller A 1993 The role of citizen scientist in nature resource decision-making: lessons from the spruce budworm problem in Canada. *The Environmentalist* 13(1): 47–59

Mitchell B 1989 *Geography and resource analysis*. Harlow, Longman, second edition

Mitchell P and E Brown 1992 Local government: a social resource for environmental control. *Environmental and Planning Law Journal* 8(1): 41–68

Ontario Ministry of Natural Resources 1995 *Memorandum: MNR Guide to Resource Management Partnerships – Administrative Considerations*. Toronto, Ontario Ministry of Natural Resources, 25 July

Perera L A S R and A T M N Amin 1996 Accommodating the informal sector: a strategy for urban environmental management. *Journal of Environmental Management* 46(1): 3–15

Petts J 1995 Waste management strategy development: a case study of community involvement and consensus-building in Hampshire. *Journal of Environmental Planning and Management* 38(4): 519–36

Pinkerton E (ed.) 1989 *Co-operative management of local fisheries: new directions in improved management and community development.* Vancouver, University of British Columbia Press

Reed M G 1993 Governance of resources in the hinterland: the struggle for local autonomy and control. *Geoforum* 24(3): 243–62

Reed M G 1994 Locally responsive environmental planning in the Canadian hinterland: a case study in northern Ontario. *Environmental Impact Assessment Review* 14(4): 245–69

Reed M G 1995 Cooperative management of environmental resources: a case study from northern Ontario, Canada. *Economic Geography* 71(2): 132–49

Richards E M 1993 Lessons from participatory natural forest management in Latin America: case studies from Honduras, Mexico and Peru. *Journal of World Forest Resource Management* 7(1): 49–69

Selin S and D Chavez 1995 Developing a collaborative model for environmental planning and management. *Environmental Management* 19(2): 189–95

Smith L G 1982 Mechanisms for public participation at a normative planning level in Canada. *Canadian Public Policy* 8(4): 561–72

Smith L G 1983 The evaluation of public participation in water resources management: a Canadian perspective. In J W Frazier, B J Epstein, M Bardecki and H Jacobs (eds) *Papers and Proceedings of Applied Geography Conferences.* Vol. 6, Toronto, Ryerson Polytechnical Institute, Department of Geography, 235–44

Thompson J 1994 Kenya's catchment approach – lessons for the SADC region. *Splash* 10(1): 15–16

Van der Sluis T 1994 Community-based land use planning – Ngamiland West. *Splash* 10(1): 8–10

Viessman W 1993 The water management challenge. *Water Resources Update* 90 (Winter): 13–15

Vizayakumar K and P K J Mohapatra 1991 Coal mining impacts and their stakeholders: a SIAM approach. *International Journal of Environmental Studies, A* 37(4): 297–303

Westphal L and G Childs 1994 Overcoming obstacles: creating volunteer partnerships. *Journal of Forestry* 92(10): 28–32

Wiens L H 1995 Stakeholders misrepresented. *Water News*, Canadian Water Resources Association, 14(2) June: 3, 7

World Commission on Environment and Development 1987 *Our common future.* New York and Oxford, Oxford University Press

Chapter 9

Local Knowledge Systems

9.1 Introduction

In Chapter 8, attention focused upon the concepts of *partnerships* and *stakeholders*. The main implication of that chapter was the advantages from a participatory approach in resource and environmental management. Such an approach recognizes that professionally trained experts can usually learn and benefit from the experiential knowledge of people who live and work in an area. Such knowledge has been called *traditional*, *indigenous* or *local*, to differentiate it from knowledge based upon science or formal study. In this chapter, some of the characteristics of what will be called *local knowledge systems* are reviewed. Then, consideration is given to the method of *participatory local appraisal*, a method increasingly being used to analyse local understanding. The following section focuses on *co-management*, an approach that explicitly seeks to incorporate local

---

Box 9.1 Scientific and local knowledge

Modern scientific knowledge, with its accompanying world view of humans as being apart from and above the natural world has been extraordinarily successful in furthering human understanding and manipulation of simpler systems. However, neither this world view nor scientific knowledge have been particularly successful when confronted with complex ecological systems. These complex systems vary greatly on spatial and temporal scales rendering the generalizations that positivistic science has come up with of little value in furnishing practical prescriptions for sustainable resource use. Science-based societies have tended to overuse and simplify such complex ecological systems, resulting in a whole series of problems of resource exhaustion and environmental degradation.

It is in this context that the knowledge of indigenous societies accumulated over historical time, is of significance. The view of humans as a part of the natural world and a belief system stressing respect for the rest of the natural world is of value for evolving sustainable relations with the natural-resource base.

Source: Gadgil *et al.* 1993: 151.

and scientific understanding, and that often results in a reallocation of authority for management. Section 9.3 provides some examples of integration of local knowledge into resource and environmental management situations.

9.2 Local knowledge systems

The concept of local knowledge systems has its roots in the idea of indigenous or traditional knowledge and management systems. Indigenous or native or tribal peoples today are found on every continent and in many countries. Definitions of indigenous peoples vary. Nevertheless, common elements usually include the following: (1) descendants of original inhabitants of an area which has been occupied by more powerful outsiders, (2) distinctly different language, culture or religion compared with the dominant group, (3) often associated with some type of subsistence economy, (4) frequently descendants of hunter-gatherers, fishers, nomadic or seasonal herders, shifting farmers or cultivators; (5) social relations which emphasize kinship, group decision making by consensus, and collective sharing and management of natural resources (Durning, 1992: 8). Durning has suggested that if spoken language is used as a measure, the people of the world belong to 6,000 cultures, 4,000 to 5,000 of these being indigenous.

Because of their close ties to the environment and resources, indigenous people developed, by trial and error, understanding of the ecosystem in which they lived. Such people did not always live in harmony with their environment and resources, and did and could cause degradation. At the same time, since their survival depended on maintaining the integrity of the ecosystem from which they derived their food and shelter, any major mistakes were usually not repeated. Their accumulated understanding of their environment was often transmitted in oral rather than in written form, and often could not be explained in scientific terms.

In many instances, their practices mimicked the patterns and behaviours

---

Box 9.2 Emergence of indigenous knowledge and management

It thus appears plausible that over the course of human history, there have been human groups whose interests were strongly linked to the prudent use of their resource base, and that such groups did indeed evolve appropriate conservation practices. These practices were apparently based on some simple rules of thumb that tended to ensure the long term sustainability of the resource base. These rules were necessarily approximate. They would have been arrived at through a process of trial and error, with the continued acceptance of practices which appear to keep the resource base secure, coupled with the rejection of those practices which appear to destroy the resource base.

Source: Gadgil and Berkes, 1991: 136.

of natural systems. For example, the practice of mixed cropping as an element of shifting cultivation replicated much of the complexity and diversity of subtropical or tropical vegetation systems. Different foods such as maize, plantain, taro and groundnuts are often grown side-by-side on the same plots. To the Western-trained scientist, such an approach appears primitive and inefficient. However, the different rates of development of the crops ensure that the soil is kept under permanent cover. This reduces exposure to the sunlight and heating of the surface. Continuous cover also protects against soil erosion, especially during the wet season, when rainfall can be intense. The various root systems result in effective use of the soil volume. The mix of crops also minimizes the vulnerability of the plot to infestation by weeds or pests, as it is unlikely that any such infestations will harm the entire range of crops.

Western, science-based resource management has provided many useful concepts and methods for resource management and use. In many cases, "productivity" has been multiplied significantly, and higher population densities of people can be supported. However, as indicated in Box 9.3, the scientific approach has not always been able to avoid or restore degradation, or to sustain productivity.

The growing recognition that indigenous people who live in an area have understanding and insights about resources, environment and ecosystems as a result of observation over various seasons and many years has been extended to recognize that any people, indigenous or otherwise, living in an area may be aware of aspects that a scientist could miss. Such awareness has led to the acceptance of the participatory approach outlined in Chapter 8, and in growing interest in combining *local knowledge systems* with science-based knowledge. In the balance of this chapter, attention is given to ways of understanding such

---

Box 9.3 Limitations of science for resource management

To many, it is a paradox that with all its power, modern science seems unable to halt and reverse the depletion of resources and the degradation of the environment. Part of the reason for this paradox may be that scientific resource management, and Western reductionist science in general, developed in the service of the utilitarian, exploitive, "dominion over nature" world view of colonialists and developers. It is best geared to the efficient utilization of resources as if they were boundless. . . .

Thus, modern resource management science is well suited, by design, for conventional exploitive development, but not for sustainable use. The task then is to re-think and re-construct a new resource management science that is better adapted to serve the needs of ecological sustainability and the people who use these resources.

Source: Gadgil and Berkes, 1991: 138.

local knowledge systems, how they may be used in co-management arrangements, and some experiences related to local knowledge.

9.3 Participatory local appraisal

Participatory local appraisal is used here to describe a method of studying local or indigenous knowledge systems. It has emerged from what have become known as *rapid rural appraisal* and *participatory rural appraisal*. Each is described below.

9.3.1 Rapid rural appraisal

Rapid rural appraisal (RRA) has been defined as "a systematic, but semi-structured, activity carried out in the field by a multidisciplinary team and designed to acquire quickly new information on, and new hypotheses about, rural life" (Conway and McCracken, 1990: 223). Conway and McCracken (1990) concluded that two central characteristics of RRA have been as follows.

- **Pursuit of "optimal ignorance"**. When collecting information about rural systems in a limited time frame, costs should be minimized. Thus, any approach should facilitate rapid collection of information by focusing on selected key variables.

- **Use of "triangulation"**. Triangulation emphasizes a diversity of sources and means of gathering data, and analytical methods. Accuracy and completeness will be greater if each aspect of a problem is investigated using various means. Understanding is sought by using a diversity of information, rather than through statistical replication. There can be tension between completing the data collection rapidly, and wanting to use a wide variety of sources and methods, but at a minimum it is important not to over-rely on a single source or method.

Given the above two characteristics, they concluded that effective RRAs have five notable features, shown in Box 9.4. It should be clear from those features that RRA is intended to facilitate collection of data as quickly as possible, but to do so by interacting informally with local people in their own environments. The emphasis is qualitative rather than quantitative.

The five key features shown in the box emerged in response to what have been viewed as three aspects of much development work in Third World countries (Chambers, 1994: 956–957). These include the following.

(1) *Anti-poverty bias*. Much research in developing countries is conducted by urban-based professionals. Often, the work of such people has numerous biases: (1) *spatial*, with visits usually focusing on areas near cities or other easily accessible areas, to the neglect of peripheral areas; (2) *temporal*, with visits normally in the dry and cool seasons, whereas most problems are exacerbated in the wet and hot seasons; (3) *people*, with attention frequently on officials or elites rather than the poor, and on men rather than women; (4) *project*, with emphasis on officially supported activities, rather than on local, informal initiatives; and (5) *diplomatic*, with outside experts avoiding issues or questions considered to be offensive or sensitive to officials of the host country.

Box 9.4 Five features of RRAs

Iterative. The goals and process of the study are not rigidly set at the outset; they can be and often are modified as the investigators learn what is and is not relevant.

Innovative. No standardized methodology exists. Techniques are custom chosen for specific situations, and depend significantly upon available knowledge and skills.

Interactive. Normally, RRAs are conducted by a team. The team members are selected to encourage a diversity of interdisciplinary insights, and to foster synergy.

Informal. In contrast to the formality of many "scientific" methods, emphasis is upon informal interviews and discussions, and partly structured interviews.

In the field. Learning occurs in the field, often by helping or working with local people. Learning occurs "as you go". Field work often is followed by a workshop to share and discuss findings. Reports are written quickly after the field work.

Source: after Conway and McCracken, 1990: 224.

---

(2) *Over-reliance on questionnaire surveys* Too often questionnaire surveys have been designed by people with inadequate understanding of local cultures and languages. As a result, ideas are raised that are difficult or impossible for local people to understand, and the meaning of answers often becomes distorted or changed during translation.

(3) *Emergence of better alternatives* Unlike the other two aspects, this one was positive. It reflected a growing awareness about more cost-effective methods. A core idea was recognition by professionals that local people were often very knowledgeable about matters which affected their lives, including the behaviour and patterns of local ecosystems. This led to interest in what was termed *indigenous technical knowledge* or *indigenous ecological knowledge*, and acceptance that it had much practical value for problem solving. As Matowanyika (1991: 89)

Box 9.5 Problems with questionnaire surveys

Again and again, over many years and in many places, the experience had been that large-scale surveys with long questionnaires tended to be drawn-out, tedious, a headache to administer, a nightmare to process and write up, inaccurate and unreliable in data obtained, leading to reports, if any, which were long, late, boring, misleading, difficult to use, and anyway ignored.

Source: Chambers, 1994: 956.

explained, such indigenous knowledge systems were based on the following characteristics related to resource use: (1) primarily rural; (2) relying on primary production based on a local physical environment; (3) integration of economic, social and cultural values and institutions, with kinship being a central unifying characteristic and the household being the base for the division of labour; (4) distributive systems that encourage mutual support and reciprocity; (5) a wide variety of resource ownership systems, but always including major communal ownership; and (6) relying mainly on local knowledge, information and experience.

Agroecosystem analysis, discussed briefly in Chapter 3, has been applied in several countries in Southeast Asia, and helped to create credibility for RRA. By the mid 1980s, work at the University of Khon Kaen in Thailand was viewed by many as the global leader in developing and applying RRA, and in providing training for RRA. In 1985 an international conference on RRA was hosted at Khon Kaen, and the proceedings from that conference became the standard reference (University of Khon Kaen, 1987). The outcome was different types of RRA, as shown in Box 9.6, each designed for different purposes but often able to be used in combination or in sequence.

With RRA well established, people began to consider how it could be strengthened. RRA had been designed to facilitate the rapid collection of data about rural systems, or ecosystems. The intent was also to be sensitive to the local context, especially the culture, traditions and languages. However, RRA was viewed by some as too "extractive" in that the process remained one-sided, similar to the questionnaire survey it had been designed to replace. Considerable time of the respondents was still taken up by an outsider. Little or nothing was returned to the respondents, as the outsiders had controlled the information which had been assembled. Thus, in the mid 1980s, two new words began to be used: *participation* and *participatory*. This led to RRA being renamed *participatory rural appraisal*.

9.3.2 Transition to participatory rural appraisal

During the Khon Kaen conference in 1985, different types of RRA were identified, one of which was labelled "participatory". As noted in Box 9.6, the orientation of a participatory rural appraisal was to facilitate or stimulate community awareness and capability regarding a problem or issue. Particular attention was given to enabling local people to conduct their own analyses of problems, and to share their findings. The role of the outsider became one of catalyst, rather than one of expert. Stimulation of community awareness and capability was also intended to reduce the extractive nature of RRA, and to help local people to empower themselves. In that regard, what became known as participatory rural appraisal (PRA) is consistent with some of the basic aspects of sustainable development (local empowerment, equity, social justice).

RRA and PRA have some common elements, but the main distinction has been that RRA was designed to allow outsiders to quickly and efficiently collect

Box 9.6 Kinds of RRA

Exploratory. Obtain initial information about a problem or ecosystem. The goal is to identify preliminary key questions or hypotheses.

Topical. Investigate a particular topic, often emerging from one or more questions or hypotheses identified during the exploratory RRA. The product is a detailed proposition to be used as the basis for management decisions, or for further research.

Participatory. Include local resource users and officials in decisions about new initiatives based on the findings from exploratory or topical RRAs. The output becomes locally managed experiments or activities in which local people have central roles.

Monitoring. Track progress of the experiments, and the implementation of the activities. The output is a revised hypothesis, along with changes in the experiments or activities.

Source: after Conway and McCracken, 1990: 225.

---

data about a problem or ecosystem using a mix of informal methods and a variety of sources. PRA was focused more on enabling local people to undertake their own investigations, to develop solutions, and to implement action. Tables 9.1 and 9.2 highlight the similarities and differences between these two approaches. It is suggested here that PRA should more properly be called *participatory local appraisal* (PLA), to indicate that it can be applied in either rural or urban settings, incorporates the participatory ideas discussed in Chapter 8, and focuses upon appraisal that leads to action. An important concern continues to be the relatively rapid and systematic collection of information related to key questions and variables, rather than a comprehensive analysis. In this manner, PLA is consistent with the ideas expressed in Chapter 3 regarding *integrated resource management*.

9.3.3 Methods for participatory local appraisal

Chambers (1994) and Conway and McCracken (1990) have identified the range of methods that are often used in different combinations for PLA. Some of the more important are summarized below.

(1) *Secondary sources* This source includes more than books and journal articles. It includes reports, maps, aerial photographs, satellite imagery, files, memoranda, annual reports, survey results, computerized data records, census information, project documents and newspaper stories. Scanning as many secondary sources as possible will help to avoid unnecessary duplication of work already completed, will help to identify important issues and potential data sources, and may help to identify key people to contact.

Table 9.1   A comparison of RRA and PRA (after Chambers, 1994: 958)

	RRA	PRA
Period of major development	Late 1970s, 1980s	Late 1980s, 1990s
Major innovators based in	Universities	NGOs
Main users at first	Aid agencies, universities	NGOs, government field organizations
Key resource earlier undervalued	Local people's knowledge	Local people's analytical capabilities
Main innovations	Methods, team management	Behaviour, experiential training
Predominant mode	Elicitive, extractive	Facilitating, participatory
Ideal objectives	Learning by outsiders	Empowerment of local people
Longer-term outcomes	Plans, project publications	Sustainable local action and institutions

(2) *Semi-structured interviews* These have been viewed as a central method for PLA. These can be completed with individuals or groups, and can cover resource users (farmers, hunters and gatherers), officials (government officers) or local elites (school teachers, village leaders). Interviews are always conducted in an informal manner, preferably in the usual surroundings of the informant. A written questionnaire is not used, but notes are taken of key ideas and information. The interview is usually based on some key questions, but is deliberately left open-ended, and there is willingness, even anticipation, to explore unexpected topics or issues. Any semi-structured interview normally would not last more than one hour, but there might be more than one interview with a respondent over a period of time.

(3) *Direct observation* Direct observation occurs while the outsider is conducting other work, and can involve the systematic observation of events, processes, relationships or patterns. This type of data collection is similar to what social

Table 9.2   RRA and PRA as a continuum (Chambers, 1994: 959)

Nature of process	RRA . . . . PRA		
Mode	Extractive . . . Elicitive . . . Sharing . . . . Empowering		
Outsiders' role	Investigator . . . . Facilitator		
Information owned, analysed and used by	Outsiders . . . . Local people		
Methods used	Mainly RRA plus sometimes PRA . . . . Mainly PRA plus sometimes RRA		

scientists refer to as *participant observation*. Direct observation is often used to verify the insights obtained from secondary sources and from semi-structured interviews. The danger, of course, is that there can be a *reactive effect*. That is, normal processes and relationships may not be seen, as the presence of an outside observer may change "normal" behaviour. The longer the analyst is able to observe people or an ecosystem, the greater are the chances that what is seen will be patterns not influenced by a reactive effect.

In PLA, useful methods can involve asking to be, and being, taught by local resource users, and helping them with their tasks. In that way, barriers between the outsider and local people will be gradually broken down. The outsider will also gain a new appreciation for tasks which, on the basis of superficial examination, may appear to be rudimentary or simple but turn out to require considerable skill.

(4) *Visual models* These are increasingly being used, particularly in cross-cultural situations or ones in which formal education of respondents is minimal. Visual models refer to the use of diagrams such as sketch maps (on paper or on the ground), transects, seasonal calendars, bar diagrams, time trends, Venn diagrams and decision trees. It is not just the researcher or outsider who uses these methods. Local people can complete transects, sketch maps, seasonal calendars and time trends. The following methods are frequently used in PLA.

- *Participatory modelling*. Local people use the ground, floor or paper to construct social, demographic or natural resource maps, showing existing patterns of use, capacity for different uses, ownership, shared uses, etc.

- *Transect walks*. The outsider or local people walk through an area, systematically making observations about problems, solutions and opportunities. Transects are often done along a slope, or involve "combing" or "looping". While walking with others, it is possible to observe, ask questions and discuss.

- *Seasonal calendars*. Changes and/or activities by month, season or other meaningful time period can be recorded. These can include patterns of resource use, distribution of rain, and prices for ecosystem products.

- *Time lines and trend/change analysis*. A chronology of events with approximate dates can be created. Attention can be directed to how things have changed; ecosystem histories can be created; changes in customs, practices and activities can be recorded; changes in resource use patterns can be noted. These records can be established by groups, and often become a source of considerable interest, particularly when it almost inevitably emerges that people have different perceptions about the timing or significance of changes.

- *Institutional Venn diagrams*. Individuals and organizations, important to the community, can be identified, and their relationships can be depicted diagrammatically.

(5) *Workshops* Workshops may occur throughout the period of data collection, but most usually are used towards the end of the data collection period. The outsiders meet with local people with whom they have been working to examine the information collected, share analysis and interpretations, consider opportunities and possible actions, and search for preferred initiatives. The

number of participants can be small or large, but if the latter then it is usually helpful to combine full group sessions with other sessions involving smaller discussion groups. The workshops may be short (less than half a day) or may extend over several days.

Many of the methods outlined above will be familiar to the social scientist; some will not. As indicated earlier, there is no formula, menu or recipe to determine which is the right mix of methods to use. The choice will be governed by judgements about needs and circumstances related to the system being studied, and by the creativity of the analyst. In Section 9.5, in which experience with local knowledge systems is considered, there will be opportunity to consider how PLA methods could be used to understand what has been and is happening.

9.4 Co-management

Co-management arrangements reflect one means of achieving the partnership approach reviewed in Chapter 8. However, it is included here because co-management has often been explicitly designed to recognize and incorporate local knowledge systems from resource users.

Co-management is an approach which incorporates local- and state-level management systems. The state-level responsibilities are conducted by a government agency with a legal mandate. The management style is often characterized as centralized and hierarchical, with a headquarters determining overall policy, and regional offices implementing the policy. Its approach is normally based on "science" or "scientific data", and on calculations or estimates

---

Box 9.7 Co-management defined

Co-management arrangements in general involve genuine power sharing between community-based managers and government agencies, so that each can check the potential excesses of the other.

Source: Pinkerton, 1993: 37.

There is no widely accepted definition of co-management. The term broadly refers to various levels of integration of local- and state-level management systems. Co-management [is defined here] to mean the sharing of power and responsibility between the government and local resource users. A more precise definition is probably inappropriate because there is a continuum of co-management arrangements from those that merely involve, for example, some local participation in government research being carried out, to those in which the local community holds all the management power and responsibility.

Source: Berkes *et al.*, 1991: 12.

based on such knowledge or data. Enforcement is based on the authority provided through legislation and regulations. Local-level management systems, in contrast, are based on experiential knowledge, cultural traditions, customary practices and self-regulation. The approach is highly decentralized. Decisions are based on development of consensus, and enforcement occurs through social sanctions.

Given the striking differences between the two approaches, there is often lack of understanding and respect by followers of one system for the other. In addition, problems can occur because they often represent fundamentally different ideas about the concept of *rights* to resource use. State-level management systems are normally based on the idea that there is ownership of the resource, or that rights to use of the resource are allocated by the government, which owns the resource on behalf of the society. For local-level systems, the concept of ownership is often a foreign one. No one "owns" the resource, but people have the right of access to the resource, as determined by customary practices and arrangements. The challenge, therefore, is to determine how to incorporate each system's strengths, many of which are complementary.

As noted above, one key issue is to determine the extent to which control of, or power over, the resources or environment will be shared. Berkes *et al.* (1991: 12–13) suggested that a parallel can be made between co-management arrangements and Arnstein's "Ladder of Citizen Participation", discussed in the previous chapter. Their view is that different types of co-management can be represented as rungs on a ladder, each reflecting different degrees of power sharing between citizens and the government. To illustrate, for situations in which resources can be managed locally, such as beaver, nearly all the management power can be delegated to the local people. With full community control, given credibility by the state government, local people can make decisions about allocations and patterns of use. On the other hand, situations exist in which resources cannot readily be managed locally, such as for migratory species like birds or mammals. In these situations, local people can participate as partners, and can share their local knowledge about the behaviour of the species in their region. However, the state government also has an important role to play since the species move across a number of regions, each of which contains local users.

Co-management agreements most frequently have been developed with reference to renewable resources, especially fish, birds and forests. Box 9.8 outlines some of the rationale for, and benefits from, a co-management agreement between a government and fishers. It is usually agreed that co-management agreements contribute to encouraging community-based development, decentralizing regulatory power, and reducing conflict through consensus building and participatory principles.

9.4.1 Aspects which contribute to effective co-management

Pinkerton (1989) reviewed both more and less successful co-management arrangements, and developed a check list of "preconditions" which seem to

Box 9.8 Co-management for fisheries

Co-management agreements between government and fishing interests have arisen out of crises caused by rumoured or real stock depletion or from political pressure resulting from claims that the government's ability to manage is insufficient to handle specific problems. Co-management agreements are a creative way to break the impasse in government/fishermen conflicts over the most effective solutions to such crises. Typically in such cases, fishermen demand a real voice in decision-making because they have lost faith in government's ability to solve management problems: they point to government's lack of adequate data and to its role in making the problems worse. Government officials, who may equally distrust fishermen, whom they see as unrelenting predators who will eliminate the fish unless more strictly regulated, become willing to surrender some power in exchange for fishermen's co-operation and assistance in management. A balance of power is struck so that fishermen do not believe they have been simply co-opted into government's convenience. For its part, government can act as a check to any local violations which do not conserve fish stocks or fairly share the benefits of fish production.

Co-management regimes work by altering the relationships among the actors in the fishery – primarily between fishermen and government, but also those among individual fishermen and among fishermen's groups. Basically, by instituting shared decision-making among these actors, co-management systems set up a game in which the pay-offs are greater for co-operation than for opposition and/or competition, a game in which the actors can learn to optimize their mutual good and plan co-operatively with long-term time horizons.

Source: Pinkerton, 1989: 4–5

support successful agreements for co-management related to fisheries. The following points, taken from her checklist, have been modified so as to apply to most resources.

(1) *Most favourable preconditions* (1) The presence of a real or imagined crisis in the depletion or degradation of the resource, such as the crash of a fish species; (2) willingness of local resource users to contribute financially or in kind, or to obtain other sources of support, for the rehabilitation of the resource or to contribute to management tasks; and (3) opportunity for negotiation and/or introduction of a co-management experiment focused on a specific management task or function, which subsequently could be expanded to other tasks.

(2) *Most favourable mechanisms and conditions* (1) Agreements are reached which are formalized, legal, and multiple-year; (2) a mechanism exists to return back into local communities some of the wealth produced by co-management; (3) a mechanism exists which both conserves and enhances the resource and the

integrity of the local cultural system; and (4) external support (such as from universities, NGOs) can be recruited, and external forums for discussion (technical advisory committees) which include more than the immediately affected stakeholders can be created.

(3) *Best spatial scale* (1) A relatively small area, meaning an area such as a watershed, in which benefits can be readily identified and appreciated by participants; (2) the number of participants and local communities is relatively small so that effective communication can occur; and (3) the government bureaucracy is relatively small, and its mandate can be related specifically to the local or regional scale.

(4) *Groups most predisposed towards co-management* (1) The existing group(s) already has a cohesive social system, often based on kinship, ethnicity, or similar method of resource use; and (2) the group(s) can effectively define its boundaries, leading to clear identification of membership in the group and ease of allocating access to the resource and applying sanctions.

(5) *The human factor* While preconditions, conditions, mechanisms and spatial scale are all important, successful co-management agreements ultimately depend upon the relationships between people. Co-management is therefore most likely to be successful when a dedicated person or core group creates ongoing and consistent pressure to move forward the provisions in the agreement. Furthermore, co-management is more likely to be successful if new and sustainable relationships are created between the people, and this occurs when (1) cooperation is fostered among individuals and groups in the local community of resource users; (2) commitment is generated among local people to share both the benefits and the costs of their efforts to enhance and conserve the resource; (3) allocation decisions generate an approach to conflict resolution which motivates people to negotiate shared and equitable access to the resource; (4) a negotiating relationship is established which includes people who are directly and indirectly affected by the resource allocation decisions (e.g., regarding a fishery, other water users are included); (5) a willingness exists or is created to share data about the resource; and (6) trust and respect grow between resource users and government officials, leading government to turn over more power to local people.

Box 9.9 Importance of people

... the motivations and attitudes of key individuals can make or break co-management, no matter how much legal backing or supportive arrangements an agreement has.

Source: Pinkerton, 1989: 29.

Box 9.10 Distinguishing between co-management in name and in practice

... the procedures adopted by the committee were not consistent with the premises of co-management. The Township Council, with members of the Business Association, acted to avoid local division by influencing initial membership of the committee toward local business interests. Once the committee was operating, it exerted close control over information provided to the public and restricted opportunities for the broader community to become involved in its deliberations. Committee members maintained close control over aspects such as access to information, rules for participation, mechanisms used, timing of participation, and feedback to the public. Thus, the co-management committee ... simply replaced the paternalistic approach previously associated with the MNR [Ministry of Natural Resources] with paternalism initiated by the local committee.

Source: Reed, 1995: 145.

In an ideal form, co-management arrangements reflect many aspects of sustainable development. However, it is important not to over-idealize the co-management approach. As Reed (1995) has observed, based on her study of a co-management initiative in northern Ontario, Canada, the preconditions and conditions are not always met. In the Ontario example, which involved a local community in partnership with a provincial government agency, she found that some local people coalesced to skew participation towards those who shared their economic values. Key participants maintained close control of the participation process within the local community, and they also became a conduit to promote particular values and views to the provincial government. In Reed's view, the outcome was a set of proposals for modest change which lacked an overall vision, or a commitment for implementation. Unequal access to power, both within the local community and between the local community and the provincial government, resulted in the co-management initiative being more in name than in deed. Reed's analysis is a helpful caution not to become uncritically enthusiastic about co-management agreements.

9.5 Local knowledge for resource and environmental management

9.5.1 Cod fisheries in Atlantic Canada

In July 1992, the government of Canada announced a two-year fishing moratorium for northern cod in the waters off Atlantic Canada because of depleted stocks. It was anticipated that up to 20,000 fishers and fish process workers, many of whom lived in small coastal communities with few alternative job opportunities would lose their jobs. In subsequent decisions up to December 1993, other fisheries were closed, the outcome being a total loss of jobs for 40,000 to 50,000 people. Many reasons were offered for the depletion of the fisheries, including domestic and foreign fleet overfishing, changing environmental conditions and predation by seals. Others suggested that fishery managers needed to share some of the blame, as apparently they had badly miscalculated the extent of the fish stocks.

How could the fishery scientists and managers have been so wrong? Many reasons can be offered. First, their data about the fishery were poor, due to the challenges of sampling a migratory resource whose habitat extends over a vast area. Second, the scientists' models contained many assumptions, based on theory of fish behaviour. The scientists used their models, and data taken from research vessels, but rarely had experience of fishing or talking to fishers, who were seeing patterns that did not always show up in their data. It is the latter point that is of interest here.

What insights did the local fishers have and, if they had been heeded, how might that have helped the scientists? Could the local knowledge of fishers have provided an early warning which the "scientific" data and computer models did not capture? One expert who was appointed to conduct an inquiry into the status of the fishery expressed doubt about the adequacy of the scientific understanding of the fishery, as highlighted by his comments in Box 9.12. Given all the problems in studying fish stocks and behaviour, it is difficult to understand why any potentially valuable source of information would be overlooked or discounted.

Neis (1992) examined the ecological knowledge of local fishermen in Newfoundland. She provided some insights regarding their understanding, and why scientists have been slow or reluctant to consider their knowledge. Based on a study of fishers in one area (Petry Harbour), she found that they were among the first groups to argue that the scientific assessments regarding the health of the northern cod stocks were incorrect. Their questioning of the assessments was based on their experience of catching smaller fish, requiring longer fishing days, and needing a longer fishing season to maintain catches of previous years. During 1986, they subsequently took a leading role in creating the Newfoundland Inshore Fisheries Association a group which consistently

---

Box 9.11 Scientists ignore early warnings from fishers

Newfoundland's inshore fishery continued to fail. To the inshore fishermen, the reason was clear: fish were scarce, and offshore draggers were catching them before they came closer to shore.

Maybe not, said the scientists. Maybe the fish were staying offshore. Maybe fewer crews were actually fishing. Maybe it was the water temperature, or food cycles, or . . .

No, said the fishermen. There are not enough fish. And they were right.

Source: Cameron, 1990: 31–3.

Box 9.12 Ignorance about the fishery

The state of our ignorance is appalling. We know almost nothing of value with respect to the behaviour of fish. We don't even know if there's one northern cod stock, or many, or how they might be distinguished. We don't know anything about migration patterns or their causes, of feeding habits, or relationships in the food chain. I could go on listing what we don't know.

Source: Dr Leslie Harris, as quoted in Cameron, 1990: 35.

questioned the accuracy and validity of the scientific assessments of the cod stocks. At the same time, however, Neis (1992: 156) noted that "the scope and nature of the ecological knowledge of Newfoundland inshore fishers has never been the direct focus of either scientific or social science research."

Franklin (1990: 40) has observed that "it should be the experience that leads to a modification of knowledge, rather than abstract knowledge forcing people to perceive their experience as being unreal or wrong." That is, if the facts do not match the theory, analysts have two choices. One is to assume that the theory or model is correct and the data are flawed, and therefore to renew efforts to obtain better data. During the 1980s, this was the approach of many fishery scientists regarding their computerized models of fish behaviour in the

Box 9.13 A scientist's view about local knowledge

. . . to separate out testable elements of this [scientific] view of the fishery system from the fishermen's point of view is really difficult. I imagine there is probably integration of all kinds of variables going on simultaneously in any particular fisheries situation on any given day, and also over the years, as people modify the traditional lore. You can't really do a controlled experiment under these situations to say, "we falsified the null hypothesis so now we can move on to the next step in the method." That reductionist approach would seem to me to be different from what you would consider to be traditional lore that integrates a lot of different observations and people's intuitions and gut feelings and is kind of tested but you don't know what kind of testing it's undergone from generation to generation. Have the conditions remained constant over time, or have they been changing? If they have, then how do you know what you are seeing is really the result of the causal mechanism that is attributed to it? So it's basically at odds with scientific method because traditional knowledge has so much more information in it that is unspoken or already subsumed and the scientific method says reduce it and test it at each point and control for all of the other co-current variables. It is hard to integrate those two views of the system.

Source: as quoted in Neis, 1992: 166.

northwest Atlantic waters. The other choice is to conclude that the model is flawed, and return to the drawing board to determine what changes should be made to the model or theory. The local fishers were arguing that the model was flawed, not their experiential evidence. However, as the comments in Box 9.13 from one scientist reveal, there are often different values and mindsets held by scientists and local resource users, resulting in hesitation by scientists to place much weight on "evidence" provided by local people. This situation is changing, as local knowledge systems are increasingly being accepted. However, the experience with the Atlantic fisheries of Canada confirms the observation of Reed that we must not take a romanticized view of local knowledge and co-management agreements, and assume that there will always be trust, respect and cooperation from the outset.

Thus, a major challenge for local indigenous knowledge can be scepticism from scientists that such knowledge is "only" anecdotal. Such vernacular knowledge is often not given much weight or respect by scientists. The irony is often that "scientific" data can be viewed as equally anecdotal. Scientific information can be badly flawed, and often isolated from a broader context which is critical if it is to be interpreted sensibly. For example, the expert who conducted the investigation about the decline of the northern cod stocks indicated little confidence in sampling methods to assess the stock, as shown by his comments in Box 9.14. As Neis concluded, only after many crises related to fishery stocks have scientists began to recognize the neglect in their computer models of ecological relationships, such as those among species, between stocks and oceanographic conditions, and between catch levels and human and marine ecology. In her view, such relationships are the ones that provide the framework for traditional ecological knowledge.

The experience with the Atlantic Canada fisheries is not unique. Other examples demonstrate that governments have often developed policies or practices which have turned out to be very much less than perfect, as a partial result of either ignoring or misunderstanding local knowledge or management systems. Thus, Dove (1986) convincingly showed that the Indonesian government pursued poorly conceived agricultural policies in South Kalimantan due to misunderstanding of swidden agricultural practices. Even when confronted

---

Box 9.14 Questionable data

… to say we are going to do our survey in the first three weeks of October every year and that creates a constant for us is not correct because it's not constant. It's constant in terms of time, our calendar, but that's meaningless to fish who don't use our calendar. They use another calendar entirely, which is based on temperature, food availability, and salinity and a number of other environmental circumstances.

Source: Dr Leslie Harris, as quoted in Neis, 1992: 169.

with evidence showing that their policies and practices were based on misunderstanding, the government was unwilling to make any changes. Thus, it may still be some time before local knowledge systems and participatory approaches are widely accepted and endorsed. Nevertheless, it appears that both of them should become mainstream elements in resource and environmental management.

9.6 Implications

The existence of local knowledge systems reinforces the importance of incorporating partnerships and participatory approaches more systematically into resource and environmental management. As the example of the northern cod fishery in the northwest Atlantic Ocean emphasized, scientists and their models can often be incorrect. In many situations, local knowledge systems can provide the "ground truthing," to help verify basic assumptions or building blocks in analysts' and managers' models. The track record of scientific understanding and predictions regarding resource and environmental matters is not so good that scientists can dismiss local knowledge as "only" vernacular or anecdotal.

If local knowledge is to be understood by those with scientific backgrounds, many of the traditional social science methods of collecting information, especially the use of questionnaire surveys, need careful review and assessment. Concern about the problems with questionnaires and social surveys has led to the emergence of what has been called here participatory local appraisal. The intent is to obtain data that will be useful to planners and managers, but to do so in a less extractive or exploitive way. Indeed, participatory local appraisal has a central goal to help empower local people, and to assist them to help define, understand and resolve their own problems. The techniques associated with participatory local appraisal should not be considered to be applicable only in developing countries; they offer considerable potential for work in developed countries as well.

Perhaps one of the most impressive examples of incorporating local knowledge systems into resource and environmental management has occurred through co-management initiatives. When co-management exercises have worked well, they have explicitly accepted the value of local knowledge and have incorporated it into management strategies. Furthermore, such initiatives have also been most successful when some genuine power or authority has been allocated to the local users or managers. Co-management offers one of the exciting opportunities for creating effective partnerships for resource and environmental management in the future.

References and further reading

Adams W M, T Potkanski and J E G Sutton 1994 Indigenous farmer-managed irrigation in Sonjo, Tanzania. *Geographical Journal* 160(1): 17–32

Agrawal A 1995 Dismantling the divide between indigenous and scientific knowledge. *Development and Change* 26(3): 413–39

Amanor K 1994 Ecological knowledge and the regional economy: environmental management in the Aseesewa District of Ghana. *Development and Change* 25(1): 41–67

Berkes F (ed.) 1989 *Common property resources: ecology and community-based sustainable development*. London, Belhaven

Berkes F, P George and R J Preston 1991 Co-management: the evolution in theory and practice of the joint administration of living resources. *Alternatives* 18(2): 12–18

Berkes M F and R J Wolfe 1992 Commercialization of fisheries and the subsistence economies of the Alaska Tlingit. *Society and Natural Resources* 5(3): 277–95

Brokensha D W, D M Warren and O Werner 1980 *Indigenous knowledge systems and development*. Lanham, Maryland, University Press of America

Brondizio E, E F Moran, P Mausel and Y Wu 1994 Land use change in the Amazon estuary: patterns of Caboclo settlement and landscape management. *Human Ecology* 22(4): 249–78

Brouwe R 1995 *Baldíos* and common property resource management in Portugal. *Unasylva* 46(1): 37–43

Cameron S D 1990 Net losses: the sorry state of our Atlantic fishery. *Canadian Geographic* 110(2): 28–37

Castro A P 1991 Indigenous Kikuyu agroforestry: a case study of Kirinyaga, Kenya. *Human Ecology* 19(1): 1–18

Chambers R 1994 The origins and practice of participatory rural appraisal. *World Development* 22(7): 953–69

Chandler P 1994 Adaptive ecology of traditionally derived agroforestry in China. *Human Ecology* 22(4): 415–42

Cizek P 1993 Guardians of Manomin: aboriginal self-management of wild rice harvesting. *Alternatives* 19(3): 29–32

Cleveland D A, D Soleri and S E Smith 1994 Do folk crop varieties have a role in sustainable agriculture? *BioScience* 44(11): 740–51

Colchester M 1994 Sustaining the forests: the community-based approach in South and South-East Asia. *Development and Change* 25(1): 69–100

Collier G A, D C Mountjoy and R B Nigh 1994 Peasant agriculture and global change. *BioScience* 44(6): 398–407

Conway G R and J A McCracken 1990 Rapid rural appraisal and agroecosystem analysis. In M A Altieri and S B Hect (eds) *Agroecology and small farm development*. Boca Raton, Florida, CRC Press, 221–35

Critchley W R S, C Reij and T J Willcocks 1994 Indigenous soil and water conservation: a review of the state of knowledge and prospects for building on traditions. *Land Degradation and Rehabilitation* 5(4): 293–314

Dove M R 1986 Peasant versus government perception and use of the environment: a case-study of Banjarese ecology and river basin development in South Kalimantan. *Journal of Southeast Asian Studies* 17(1): 113–36

Durning A T 1992 *Guardian of the land: indigenous peoples and the health of the earth*. Worldwatch Paper 112, Washington, DC, Worldwatch Institute

Franklin U 1990 *The real world of technology*. Toronto, CBC Enterprises

Gadgil M and F Berkes 1991 Traditional resource management systems. *Resource Management and Optimization* 8(3/4): 127–41

Gadgil M, F Berkes and C Folke 1993 Indigenous knowledge for biodiversity conservation. *Ambio* 22(2–3): 151–6

Gill N 1994 The cultural politics of resource management: the case of bushfires in a conservation reserve. *Australian Geographical Studies* 32(2): 224–40

Harris G R 1992 A practical and theoretical assessment of sustainable development – a case study. *International Journal of Environmental Studies, A* 39(4): 313–23

Hawkes S 1996 The Gwaii Haanas agreement: from conflict to consensus. *Environments* 23(2): 87–100

Hitchcock R K and J D Holm 1993 Bureaucratic domination of human-gatherer societies: a study of the San in Botswana. *Development and Change* 24(2): 305–38

Hviding E and G B K Baines 1994 Community-based fisheries management, tradition and the challenges of development in Marovo, Solomon Islands. *Development and Change* 25(1): 13–39

Martin P and S Lockie 1993 Environmental information for total catchment management: incorporating local knowledge. *Australian Geography* 24(1): 75–85

Matowanyika J Z Z 1991 In pursuit of proper contexts for sustainability in rural Africa. *The Environmentalist* 11(2): 85–94

McGregor J 1994 Woodland pattern and structures in a peasant farming area of Zimbabwe: ecological determinants and present and past use. *Forest Ecology and Management* 63(2–3): 97–133

McKean M A 1992 Success on the commons: a comparative examination of institutions for common property resource management. *Journal of Theoretical Politics* 4(3): 247–81

Morin-Labatur G and S Akhatoar 1992 Traditional environmental knowledge: a resource to manage and share. *Development* 4: 24–30

Mosse D 1994 Authority, gender and knowledge: theoretical reflections on the practice of participatory rural appraisal. *Development and Change* 25(3): 497–526

Neis B 1992 Fishers' ecological knowledge and stock assessment in Newfoundland. *Newfoundland Studies* 8(2): 155–78

Notzke C 1995 A new perspective in aboriginal natural resource management: co-management. *Geoforum* 26(2): 187–209

Ostrom E 1987 Institutional arrangements for resolving the commons dilemma. In B J McKay and J M Acheson (eds) *The question of the commons: the culture and ecology of communal resources.* Tucson, University of Arizona Press: 250–65

Ostrom E 1990 *Governing the commons: the evolution of institutions for collective action.* Cambridge, Cambridge University Press

Ostrom E 1992 The rudiments of a theory of the origins, survival and performance of common-property institutions. In D W Bromley (ed.) *Making the commons work: theory, practice and policy.* San Francisco, Institute for Contemporary Studies: 293–312

Ostrom E, J Walker and R Gardner 1993 Covenants with and without a sword: self-governance is possible. In T L Anderson and R T Simmons (eds) *The political economy of customs and culture: informal solutions to the commons problem.* Lanham, Maryland, Rowman and Littlefield Publishers: 127–56

Ostrom E, R Gardner and J Walker 1994 *Rules, games, and common-pool resources.* Ann Arbor, University of Michigan Press

Osunade M A A 1994a Community environmental knowledge and land resource surveys in Swaziland. *Singapore Journal of Tropical Geography* 15(2): 157–70

Osunade M A A 1994b Indigenous climate knowledge and agricultural practice in southwestern Nigeria. *Malaysian Journal of Tropical Geography* 25(1): 21–8

Pinkerton E 1989 Attaining better fisheries management through co-management prospects, problem and propositions. In E Pinkerton (ed.) *Co-operative management of local fisheries: new direction in improved management and community development.* Vancouver, University of British Columbia Press, 3–33

Pinkerton E 1993 Co-management efforts as social movements: the Tin Wis Coalition and the drive for forest practices legislation in British Columbia. *Alternatives* 19(3): 33–8

Pinkerton E 1996 The contribution of watershed-based multi-party co-management agreements to dispute resolution: the Skeena Watershed Committee. *Environments* 23(2): 51–68

Prins H H T 1992 The pastoral road to extinction: competition between wildlife and traditional pastoralism in East Africa. *Environmental Conservation* 19(2): 117–23

Quiggin J 1993 Common property, equality and development. *World Development* 21(7): 1123–38

Rai S C, E Sharma and R C Sundriyal 1994 Conservation in the Sikkim Himalaya: traditional knowledge and land-use of the Mamlay watershed. *Environmental Conservation* 21(1): 30–4, 56

Reed M G 1995 Cooperative management of environmental resources: a case study from Northern Ontario, Canada. *Economic Geography* 71(2): 132–49

Singleton S and M Taylor 1992 Common property, collective action and community. *Journal of Theoretical Politics* 4(3): 309–24

Stevens J E 1994 Science and religion at work. *BioScience* 44(2): 60–5

Thomson J T and C Coulibaly 1995 Common property forest management systems in Mali: resistance and vitality under pressure. *Unasylva* 46(1): 16–22

Ulluwishewa R 1995 Traditional practices of inland fishery resources management in the dry zone of Sri Lanka: implications for sustainability. *Environmental Conservation* 22(2): 127–32

University of Khon Kaen 1987 *Proceedings of the 1985 International Conference on Rapid Rural Appraisal*. Rural Systems Research and Farming Systems Research Projects, Khon Kaen, Thailand, University of Khon Kaen

Unruh J D 1995 The relationship between indigenous pastoralist resource tenure and state tenure in Somalia. *GeoJournal* 36(1): 19–26

Usher P J 1987 Indigenous management systems and the conservation of wildlife in the Canadian north. *Alternatives* 14(1): 3–9

Vadya A P 1983 Progressive contextualization: methods for research in human ecology. *Human Ecology* 11(3): 265–81

Zimmerer K S 1994 Local soil knowledge: answering basic questions in highland Bolivia. *Journal of Soil and Water Conservation* 49(1): 29–34

Zurick D N 1990 Traditional knowledge and conservation as a basis for development in a West Nepal village. *Mountain Research and Development* 10(1): 23–33

Chapter 10

Gender and Development

10.1 Introduction

The important role of women in economic and social development in both their communities and their countries is increasingly being recognized. Numerous formal "events" have helped to enhance recognition of this role. For example, the United Nations Decade for Women from 1975 to 1985 drew global attention to women, especially the trying conditions under which many of the poorest live. The United Nations Conference on Environment and Development (UNCED) in Rio de Janeiro during 1992, which was discussed in Chapter 2, presented a global action plan to institutionalize the role of women in environment and development. Some of the key objectives and actions related to women and environment in *Agenda 21*, one of the main documents to emerge from UNCED, are shown in Boxes 10.2 and 10.3.

The United Nations Fourth World Conference on Women, held in Beijing, China, during September 1995, further highlighted important issues if the gap between men and women is to be narrowed. This conference followed earlier major meetings in Mexico City (1975), Copenhagen (1980) and Nairobi (1985). The Beijing Conference was attended by representatives from 189 countries, and involved an official conference held in Beijing as well as a parallel conference for non-governmental organizations in nearby Huariou. Together the two

---

Box 10.1

Studies show that because of their responsibilities for securing food, fuel, and water – and the labor burdens imposed on them when the resources needed to produce these goods become scarce – women tend to have a greater interest in preserving and conserving croplands, forests and other natural resources for perpetual use, whereas men are more often concerned with converting these resources into cash. Development programs that vest control over natural resources solely within the hands of men, or profit-making enterprises in general, are in effect explicitly supporting short term consumption at the expense of long term sustainability.

Source: Jacobson, 1992: 13.

Box 10.2

Selected objectives proposed for national governments in Chapter 24 (Global Action for Women Towards Sustainable and Equitable Development) in Agenda 21

1. To implement the Nairobi Forward-looking Strategies for the Advancement of Women [1985], particularly with regard to women's participation in national ecosystem management and control of environmental degradation.

2. To increase the proportion of women decision makers, planners, technical advisers, managers and extension workers in environment and development fields.

3. To consider developing and issuing by the year 2000 a strategy of changes necessary to eliminate constitutional, legal, administrative, cultural, behavioural, social and economic obstacles to women's full participation in sustainable development and in public life.

4. To establish by the year 1995 mechanisms at the national, regional and international levels to assess the implementation and impact of development and environment policies and programmes on women and to ensure their contributions and benefits.

Source: United Nations Conference on Environment and Development 1992, Agenda 21, New York, United Nations. Taken from diskette provided by the Rectors of the Costa Rican Public Universities, with agreement of United Nations, to facilitate distribution of Earth Summit documents; also distributed via BITNET and INTER-NET.

---

conferences attracted some 50,000 people.

The spate of conferences, formal declarations and intentions over the past 15 years suggest that the role of women is changing, and its importance is receiving growing recognition. Yet deeds do not always match words, nor does action necessarily follow from good intentions. Furthermore, many people are arguing that the issue is not one that can be simplified into a question of women versus men. Instead, they argue that the more fundamental issue is that of *gender*. In this chapter, attention will be given to the differences between women's and gender issues, their implications for resource and environmental management, and some experiences in which attempts have been made to institute gender-focused change.

10.2 Multiple roles for women

For gender planning, one of the greatest challenges to be overcome is the frequent assumption about gender-based divisions of work within and outside the household. Especially in Third World countries, women's work usually involves three components. *Reproductive* work relates to child bearing and raising, as well as nurturing all family members to ensure their health and

Box 10.3

Areas requiring urgent action, as stipulated in Chapter 24 of Agenda 21
Countries should take urgent measures to avert the ongoing rapid environmental and economic degradation in developing countries that generally affects the lives of women and children in rural areas suffering drought, desertification and deforestation, armed hostilities, natural disasters, toxic waste and the aftermath of the use of unsuitable agro-chemical products.

In order to reach these goals, women should be fully involved in decision-making and in the implementation of sustainable development activities.

Research, data collection and dissemination as stipulated in Chapter 24 of Agenda 21
Countries should develop gender-sensitive databases, information systems and participatory action-oriented research and policy analyses with the collaboration of academic institutions and local women researchers on the following:

(1) knowledge and experience on the part of women of the management and conservation of natural resources for incorporation in the databases and information systems for sustainable development;

(2) the impact on women of environmental degradation, particularly drought, desertification, toxic chemicals and armed hostilities; and

(3) the integration of the value of unpaid work, including work currently designated "domestic", in resource accounting mechanisms in order to better represent the true value of the contribution of women to the economy . . . ;

(4) measures to develop and include environmental, social and gender impact analyses as an essential step in the development and monitoring of programmes and policies.

Source: United Nations Conference on Environment and Development 1992, Agenda 21, New York, United Nations. Taken from diskette provided by the Rectors of the Costa Rican Public Universities, with agreement of United Nations, to facilitate distribution of Earth Summit documents; also distributed via BITNET and INTERNET.

---

well-being. Such reproductive work extends beyond biological reproduction to include those domestic tasks necessary to maintain and reproduce the labour force for a society. While child *bearing* is obviously a biological function unique to women, there is no particular reason or logic as to why child *rearing*, and nurturing and caring for the family, should be women's work.

Productive work involves activity outside the home by both women and men, for payment in cash or in kind. Such work can be "market-based production", which results in earning of money. Or it can be subsistence or home production, which generates an in-kind rather than a monetary value. Much of the productive work of women, especially in rural areas, generates in-kind returns which are essential for the well-being of their families. However, because there is no exchange value, such activity is normally invisible in the regional or national economy, and therefore does not get the same recognition as market-based activity. In many societies, men dominate market-based economic activity, whereas women are often more frequently active in non-market-based activity. As with most aspects of reproductive work, there is no reason why there should be such a gender division of labour. However, those involved in market-based activity tend to have more power because of their income-earning capacity.

Community managing involves time allocated to participating in activities within the local community to help further the welfare of its members. In many ways, this kind of activity is an extension of the reproductive role. The focus here is normally to ensure both provision and maintenance of facilities for collective needs, such as water, health care and education. The community managing work is usually voluntary and is done in "free time" after reproductive and productive tasks have been attended to. In contrast, men tend to allocate their time to *community politics*, where that involves participation at the formal political level. Their community work is often paid, either directly or indirectly, by earning wages or by achieving enhanced status and power. There is no good reason why women should concentrate upon community managing and men upon community politics, but traditional gender divisions of labour often result in this split.

The implications of the multiple roles of women are significant regarding issues of empowerment, social justice and equity. First, the triple role for women in many Third World countries means that they are the first to begin working during the day, and often the last to finish their work. As a result, there is little time for self-improvement, or to pursue interests of their own. Second, much of their productive and community managing activities are invisible in any economic accounting, so their contribution to the household, community and country is often undervalued by family members and political leaders. Third, the lesser opportunity for monetary income contributes to reduced overall status and power in the household and community. Fourth, the lack of involvement in community politics reinforces a gender bias in many decisions, and helps contribute to maintenance of a status quo in which the role of and opportunities for women are significantly less than for male counterparts. All of these implications have fundamental ramifications for resource and environmental management, as will be illustrated later in Sections 10.4 and 10.5, which consider initiatives about forestry and water.

10.3 From "women in development" to "gender and development"

10.3.1 Women in development

Moser (1993) has explained that the concept of "women in development" appeared during the early 1970s in the United States by a Women's Committee of the Washington DC chapter of the Society for International Development.

Box 10.4 Difference between biological sex and gender

Gender differs from biological sex in important ways. Our biological sex is given; we are born either male or female. But the way in which we become masculine or feminine is a combination of these basic biological building blocks and the interpretation of our biology by our culture. Every society has different "scripts" for its members to follow as they learn to act out their feminine or masculine role, much as every society has its own language. . . .

Gender is a set of roles which, like costumes or masks in the theatre, communicate to other people that we are feminine or masculine. This set of particular behaviours – which embrace our appearance, dress, attitudes, personalities, work both within and outside the household, sexuality, family, commitments and so on – together make up our "gender roles".

Source: Mosse, 1993: 2.

The term was then adopted by the United States Agency for International Development (USAID) in its development activities. Women in Development, or WID, was based on the belief that women were an untapped and under-used resource who could contribute directly to economic development.

As Mosse (1993: 158) noted, however, WID focused upon initiatives such as development or transfer of better (and, hopefully, locally appropriate) technologies that could reduce workloads for women. In that manner, WID emphasized the productive role of women in the economy, particularly their capacity for generating income, but neglected their reproductive and community managing roles. Nevertheless, WID was a first step in sensitizing people about a need to alter their thinking about the role of women.

10.3.2 Gender and development

The shift in attention from women to gender occurred as a result of unhappiness that the difficulties of women were being interpreted with reference to their *sex*, or biological differences from men, rather than with regard to their *gender*, or their social relationships with men. It was the gender relationship through which women systematically had been subordinated. A Gender and Development (GAD) perspective emphasized that while sex is biologically determined, gender is a socially or culturally determined concept. As a result, while a person's sex is difficult to change, gender roles can be altered if societal values can be modified. Thus, gender roles need not be static. They can vary between cultures at any given time, and can vary with a culture over time. The different emphases between WID and GAD are outlined in Box 10.5.

GAD is also preferred over WID because it does not treat women as a homogeneous group. The notion that women have a "position" in a society implies the presence of some universal slot for women. However, it is not sensible to consider women as a group with common values and interests. Rich

Box 10.5 Differences between WID and GAD

The WID approach, despite its change in focus from one of equity to one of efficiency, is based on the underlying rationale that development processes would proceed much better if women were fully incorporated into them (instead of being left to use their time "unproductively"). It focuses mainly on women in isolation, promoting measures such as access to credit and employment as the means by which women can be better integrated into the development process. In contrast, the GAD approach maintains that to focus on women in isolation is to ignore the real problem, which remains their subordinate status to men. In insisting that women cannot be viewed in isolation, it emphasizes a focus on gender relations, when designing measures to "help" women in the development process.

Source: Moser, 1993: 3.

and poor women may have less in common than poor women and poor men. In white-dominated societies, a black woman may believe she has more in common with black men than with white women. In addition to gender, therefore, the status of and opportunities for women will also be influenced by their financial, ethnic, class and other situations.

Gender is, therefore, very much focused on empowering women in their relationships with men. It emphasizes a bottom-up rather than a top-down approach to management. It seeks to facilitate women becoming more self-reliant, through changing and transforming practices and structures – such as labour codes, civil codes, religious and cultural customs and property rights – that have been disadvantageous to them. Not surprisingly, some government, religious and cultural leaders have been unsettled by GAD since it often challenges basic values and traditional customs of a society. For example, at the UN Fourth World Conference on Women in Beijing during 1995, representatives from the Vatican and from some conservative Islamic nations opposed recommendations regarding various sexual rights and freedoms for women.

In the following sections, some specific experiences related to resource and environmental management are examined. The examples are taken from forestry and water.

10.4 Women and forestry

10.4.1 Chipko movement, India

"Perhaps the most famous example [of a women's grassroots movement] of this resistance is the Chipko – or tree-hugging – movement of the Indian Himalayas" (Jacobson, 1992: 14). During the 1970s, the Chipko movement emerged when local women demonstrated to protect stands of forests from commercial harvesting which had been endorsed by the government of India.

Forest ecosystems play many roles. They serve to stabilize soil conditions by retarding runoff, thereby sharply reducing soil erosion. Wetlands also act as sinks to collect runoff after snowmelt or rainfall, and then release the water more slowly than would occur if they or other vegetation were not there to slow down the runoff. Forests also provide fuelwood, and fodder for animals, as well as traditional medicines. On the other hand, forests also offer commercial products such as timber and resin.

The deforestation of the Himalayas, primarily driven by the interests of governments and commercial forestry companies interested in the marketable products from forest ecosystems, had been a major contributor to landslides and flooding, and associated erosion of soil. Growing recognition of this problem led to a popular protest led by women who were concerned about the over-emphasis on the commercial uses of forests, increasing environmental degradation, and the loss of non-commercial functions (sources of domestic fuelwood, fodder, traditional herbal medicines, berries and other food).

The literal interpretation of the word "chipko" is "to embrace", and this was the tactic used by the women, first throughout villages in the Garhwal Himalaya in the north during the 1970s, and later in states such as Karnataka in the extreme south of India. The women successfully stopped the cutting down of trees in the forests by using their own bodies to block the loggers. Once the cutting was stopped, the women organized themselves to protect the forests on an ongoing basis. This usually involved a group of women taking turns to watch a forest during the day, and even at night, to stop goats or cattle from grazing, and people from cutting firewood or collecting fodder. Once the forests began to recover, traditional uses were restarted. As Jacobson (1992: 14) remarked, Chipko evolved into a full-fledged ecological movement and became an outstanding example of female empowerment. The Chipko movement has often been used to point out what women in the Third World can accomplish when they organize and challenge traditional gender-defined patterns of resource use. However, such initiatives are not always so successful, as shown in the next subsection.

Box 10.6 Gender differences illustrated by the Chipko movement

In some of the conflicts . . . , the different gender issues of women and men were painfully highlighted, when women embraced the trees that were to be cut down by their own husbands, employed by the forest contractors. The demands of the women, for a supply of fuel, fodder and water, conflicted absolutely with the demands of the men for a cash income.

Source: Mosse, 1993: 147.

Gender and development

10.4.2 Community forestry management, India

Sarin (1995) has suggested that decentralized and "participatory" forest management has long been considered an appropriate long-term solution to deforestation and environmental degradation in India. There are numerous ways to achieve decentralization and participation, but since the late 1970s there has been emphasis on the following two approaches at the local level. Each has had implications for the role of women.

- Joint Forest Management (JFM). Several state forestry departments in India have introduced what are called Joint Forest Management initiatives as ways to involve local people, especially women and tribal people who live in villages dependent on forests. JFM arrangements involve a negotiated partnership between local institutions (LIs) of forest users, and the state departments responsible for forests. The basic principle is sharing of the duties for protecting the forests, and of the income from forest products. The largest and most well-established JFM program is in the state of West Bengal, with more than 2,500 forest protection committees (FPCs) involved in regenerating 300,000 hectares of forest land.

- Village initiatives. In areas in which the state forestry department has not taken the initiative, thousands of villages have organized themselves to regenerate adjacent forests in the states of Orissa, Bihar, Madhya Pradesh, Andhra Pradesh, Rajasthan, Gujarat and Himachal Pradesh. The villagers have developed rules and ways to enforce them, have allocated responsibilities among their groups, and have stopped outsiders from using forests. The latter task has often required men to go into the forest during the night to confront outside cutters. Such confrontations have sometimes resulted in physical violence.

Implications for women

Women are often more dependent on the forests for subsistence needs (fuel, fodder, food), and hence are often affected more than men when degradation occurs. However, Sarin (1995) has suggested that frequently the women's needs have received no more consideration under community-oriented initiatives than under the unilateral programs of forestry departments.

Much of the marginalization of women can be related to traditional gender roles with regard to forest responsibilities and uses. Men are normally responsible for cutting wood for timber to be used in house construction and for agricultural implements. Such needs occur relatively infrequently for a household. In contrast, women normally have responsibility for collecting daily fuelwood, fodder and water. While these roles are not fixed absolutely, and certainly vary depending upon caste, tribe and village, such role differentiation is fairly common, and is especially the norm in the villages most dependent on forests. The joint programs and locally initiated programs have been dominated by men, who tend to be dominant in local politics, and hence the programs usually emphasize extraction of timber for house and implement building. As Sarin (1995: 28) noted, "women continue to lack a voice in community decision-making for a because of the unquestioned assumption that their household men will automatically take care of their interests." Unfortunately, this assumption is not often reflected in what

---

Box 10.7 Role of women in community-based forestry

Women remain as marginalised at the community level as in national policies because of their disadvantaged position defined by patriarchal gender relations, which traditionally exclude women from the arena of political participation, even at the community level.

Source: Sarin, 1995: 27.

---

happens, with negative consequences for the women.

To illustrate, in a number of tribal villages in the state of Gujarat, Sarin (1995) explained that the male leaders organized the men to protect some seriously degraded forests. Rigorous rules were established, which were more restrictive than a state forestry department would have considered. They were also enforced. Entry into designated forests with any tools was completely banned, and people were appointed as watchmen to ensure compliance. Each village household contributed a portion of its grain harvest to pay the watchmen for their time. In the early years, even grazing was disallowed. No women were present when the objectives and rules were established.

The purpose of these restrictions was to allow the regeneration of a teak forest from which timber could be cut for house construction and agricultural implements. No consideration was given to the implications for the women's tasks of collecting firewood or green fodder. Women from higher-income families were able to purchase alternatives for firewood and fodder, usually by buying agricultural residuals from landless or marginal households. Poorer households experienced humiliation when their female members were stopped from collecting wood and fodder in the restricted forests by the village watchmen. Arguments often ensued, and the confrontations between the men and women became so unpleasant that some men began to refuse to serve as watchmen. The resolution involved the women making the greatest concessions, by agreeing to obtain substitutes, either by using poorer-quality cooking fuels (such as dung or weeds) or by going to more distant but still open forests to collect wood (see Box 10.8).

This experience illustrates how preoccupation with men's *productive* roles dominated decisions, and generated more effort for women in their *reproductive* and *community managing* roles. The implications are several, and include the necessity to recognize (1) the different needs of women and men when developing resource use policies and practices, (2) the desirability of including both men and women in decision making about resource allocation, and (3) the heterogeneity of women in a community. As Sarin (1995: 29) remarked, "the 'community' is not a homogeneous, faceless entity but encompasses a diversity of needs and interests with gender differences being a major variable."

Box 10.8 Women's workload increases

For the women this meant an increase in the labour and time required for fetching cooking fuel as well as a worsening of their quality of life due to switching to poorer quality, smokier fuels. In terms of the sustainability of the forest protection efforts, the new arrangement meant shifting the pressure of unsustainable extraction of firewood to other, more distant, areas so that those closer by could be regenerated as timber reserves.

Source: Sarin, 1995: 28.

10.5 Women and water

Lynch (1991: 37) has observed that gender roles in Peru have changed significantly since the early 1980s. At a national level, women's issues have captured attention, and women's groups have often been in the vanguard of grassroots movements for decentralization and deconcentration of power. In resource and environmental management, however, Lynch concluded that women's role in water management had received relatively little attention either from women's groups or from government agencies. Given the importance of water in the highlands of Peru, and the growing role of women in irrigation, this lack of attention initially appears puzzling. However, a closer examination of gender roles indicates that this lack of attention is not so surprising. Some significant societal changes will have to occur before women become more prominent in water management.

Experience with two government-supported irrigation systems, San Marcos and Santa Rita, in the department of Cajamarca, illustrates the issues. Cajamarca, in northern Peru, is populated by Spanish-speaking and *mestizo* people. The two project areas are adjacent to district and departmental capitals, and have reasonable road connections to the coast. As with many areas in the Sierra Andes, these areas had been experiencing a transition to an open, cash economy, replacement of indigenous irrigation systems by ones introduced and managed to a considerable extent by government irrigation agencies, and an increase in women's participation in irrigation-based tasks because of out-migration and/or different work patterns by men. With regard to the last point, both rural men and women work outside the agricultural sector, but women are more likely to remain in agriculture and the men more likely to migrate for seasonal occupations. As a result, women are left both to be heads of households and to perform the irrigation tasks normally handled by the household head.

According to Lynch, other research in the Central Sierra had found that irrigation tasks were normally allocated to men, as part of a patriarchal society in which a gender division of labour gave men control over critical resources (land, water, transportation, cash) which bestowed relatively more power to them. In Lynch's (1991: 39) words, "women are prevented from performing key tasks so that they depend on men for resource allocation. Thus, to the extent that women are structurally excluded from key institutions, their power is limited."

What has been the practice regarding irrigation agriculture in the Peruvian Andes? Lynch suggested that delivery of water from the farm gate to the crop, or the on-farm management, was traditionally men's work. Women usually became involved in irrigation only if they were members of small households (fewer than five people) or if the men left the farm to obtain more remunerative work. This pattern became more pronounced in poorer families, which usually had smaller land holdings, so that the man was pushed to work full time for wages away from the farm. With the exception of small land holdings in which women basically took on what was traditionally men's work, women would not normally be hired to perform on-farm irrigation work for others as labourers or share croppers.

Women did not normally participate in the construction and maintenance of irrigation systems. Indigenous irrigation systems are based on unpaid community labour for construction and maintenance. Women's roles normally involved preparing food for male workers, unless the irrigation system was very small and then women might contribute labour. If a full day's work was required, women would send a *peon* or pay some money as their contribution. Similar arrangements prevailed for maintenance. However, over time and as more men migrated to look for work in the market economy, women had become more involved in work crews for both construction and maintenance. Thus, with regard to construction and maintenance work, gender divisions of labour had become less distinct.

However, when water management is interpreted to involve the organization of labour, cash and materials to build, repair and maintain irrigation infrastructure, and to make decisions about the acquisition, allocation and distribution of water, women have been mainly absent. Several reasons account for this. First, at the community or local level, a group of irrigators sharing a common system elect a board of directors to be responsible for management decisions. The directors almost inevitably are men of high status, which includes wealthier landowners who often hold other community positions, and people with experience outside the local community. Women rarely have either of these characteristics. When Lynch did her work, the San Marcos project had no women members, and Santa Rita had one. Second, the state agency responsible for irrigation is dominated by men. According to Lynch (1991: 47), women employed in the state irrigation bureaucracy most often are extension specialists or sociologists who work primarily with women's groups and on women's issues. "Rarely, if ever, do they play central roles in system design, construction, or water allocation."

A number of characteristics of societal and government traditions thus impede a fuller role for women, as noted in the comments in Box 10.9. These patterns are reinforced by the fact that men are more likely than women to have experience in the market or cash economy, in interacting with government officials, and outside their communities. The experience of the Andean peasant women is usually restricted to the household and the community, emphasizing

Box 10.9 Barriers to greater women's involvement in irrigation

First, societal norms in the highlands that define water management as men's work, as well as sexist stereotypes present in the larger society, make women seem invisible to government officials. Because irrigation institutions at all levels are male-dominated, irrigation is not a sector where the state has encouraged movement of women into a political sphere beyond the community. Nor has the state tried to use irrigation projects to mobilize peasant women.

Source: Lynch, 1991: 47.

their *reproductive* and *community managing* roles, while the men's roles emphasize *productive* work. The outcome is that while the government bureaucracy does provide some role for women in irrigation and water management, the irrigation agencies mostly seek to co-opt women rather than to encourage them to have a central role in management. Where there has been a significant change in their roles within the local community, that has often been as a result of men leaving the local area to seek wage employment elsewhere, leaving the women to take on traditional men's work by default, as well as continuing traditional women's work.

10.6 Women and agriculture

The examination by Jarosz (1991) of the role of women as rice share croppers in Madagascar provides further insights into the *reproductive*, *productive* and *community managing* roles that women have in natural resource use. Share cropping is a long-standing tradition in agriculture in the developing world. It can involve sharing of a crop, or of agricultural tasks. In many societies, such as Madagascar, share cropping is a well-established way of organizing rural

Box 10.10 Opportunity for women must be expanded

Despite women's critical role in agriculture, their access to education and their representation in research, extension, and other support services is woefully inadequate. Women should be given the same educational opportunities as men. There should be more female extension workers, and women should participate in field visits. Women should be given more power to take decisions regarding agricultural and forestry programmes.

... In many countries women do not have direct land rights; titles go to men only. In the interests of food security, land reforms should recognize women's role in growing food. Women, especially those heading households, should be given direct land rights.

Source: World Commission on Environment and Development, 1987: 140, 141.

labour and agricultural production. Share cropping provides young people with access to land and capital, and it also gives elderly peasant farmers access to labour. As a result, a fairly negotiated share cropping agreement can be advantageous for both young and older people, and can contribute to intergenerational equity. The disadvantage can be unfair agreements which increase the productivity and benefits for some, and lead to dispossession or economic stagnation for others. Jarosz was interested in the roles of class and gender in share cropping arrangements in Madagascar as farmers used this system to gain access to resources.

Madagascar is an island country of 586,560 km^2, has a population of slightly over 11 million people with about 75% living in rural areas, and is one of the 12 poorest nations in the world. Agricultural exports, especially coffee, vanilla and cloves, are the main source of foreign exchange. Sharply fluctuating prices for coffee, and increasing use of synthetic vanilla, have had major negative impacts on the national economy. The basis of the Malagasy diet is rice, which is grown as both a subsistence and a cash crop.

Analysis was completed in the Alaotra region, a fertile basin at an elevation of about 800 metres in the north–central part of the island. Some 90,000 hectares of irrigated rice were under cultivation at the time of Jarosz's study. One-third of that area was devoted to an intensive irrigation project started in 1960, and was seeded with the high-yield rice varieties introduced during the Green Revolution. Dryland farming in the area also produces rice, along with maize, manioc, peanuts and vegetables. Share cropping has been used in the Alaotra since the nineteenth century. When Madagascar achieved independence from France in 1960, data indicated that about half the people in this region were landless share croppers involved in many types of agreements with landholders. The normal arrangement is for the rice crop to be divided in half between the landowners and share croppers.

Regarding gender roles in share cropping, Jarosz discovered that marital status and class were key variables influencing the kind of share cropping in which women participated. Female heads of households almost invariably participate in share cropping if they have one or more hectares of irrigated rice. In addition, women who inherited land near their ancestral homes but subsequently moved away to live closer to their husbands' lands also share crop, normally in agreement with family members who live in the ancestral village. If a married couple divorce, the husband is allocated two-thirds, and the wife one-third, of all the property acquired during their marriage. Middle-class women normally share crop their land to obtain the needed male labour, and if necessary also the capital needed for production. These differences highlight the fact that women are not a homogeneous group, but that there are differences depending upon their marital and class situation.

Field work tasks, including clearing, ploughing and harrowing, are considered to be men's work. Ploughing particularly requires considerable physical strength, and teamwork. One person guides the plough, and the other controls a team of either two or four zebu cattle. The latter task can be dangerous, because the zebu cattle are temperamental and unpredictable. Men have been badly gored by the zebu while pulling ploughs, and women are rarely seen ploughing. Other field work can be done by men or women, although transplanting and weeding are normally viewed as women's jobs. This characterization of tasks as customarily men's or women's work illustrates that a partial gender division of labour exists.

Not surprisingly, Jarosz found that landless female-headed households were the most marginal and vulnerable in the Alaotra agricultural community. Such women found work on an irregular basis as seasonal labourers or laundresses. Incomes were usually inadequate to meet the basic needs of their families, and such families often lived from day to day. The poorest of these poor people are usually homeless.

In Madagascar, Jarosz's findings indicated that the workloads for women had increased across all classes over the previous 20 to 30 years. In order to meet their *reproductive* responsibilities related to feeding their families, during the preharvest season (normally a relatively idle period for men) women would sell horticultural products, chicken, geese, fish, mats and baskets. The income from such subsidiary activities was not as great as from irrigated rice cultivation, but was still needed to provide for the needs of families. As farm people, the women have also been increasingly marginalized within the irrigated rice production system. Part of the cause for that has been the Green Revolution style of agriculture, with emphasis on high-yielding rice varieties, more technology-based irrigation, and growing reliance on agrochemicals. All these aspects of agricultural production are more men's than women's work. A particularly challenging time for the poorest female-headed households is the November to March period. Except for several weeks of transplanting work in the last two months of the year, very few income-earning tasks are available until April. As a result, the women and their children do not have enough to eat during this time. Furthermore, this period overlaps with the malaria season, a time when there is little money that can be used for anti-malarial medicine.

The experience in Madagascar led Jarosz (1991: 61–62) to conclude that not everyone gained from share cropping. Her findings indicated that wealthy and middle-class people did well both socially and economically as a result of share

---

Box 10.11 Vulnerability of poor rural women

One young women [sic] and her two tiny children live in a neighbor's tool shed. She has no direct access to a cooking fire, and she and her children are ill and malnourished. Single, landless men can earn $66 per year as permanent farm workers who can room and board on the farm of their employers. Landless women without children can earn $40 per year as domestic workers who room and board with their employers. Landless men can sharecrop dryland or marshland, options that are unavailable to landless female-headed households.

Source: Jarosz, 1991: 58.

cropping arrangements. However, "the young and landless, poor, female-headed households, and descendants of former slaves are at the greatest disadvantage and subject to the most severe exploitation." As a result, while gender by itself did not define the most vulnerable segment of the population, it was central, along with class and kinship variables, in influencing "who gains and who loses in cropping rice on shares in Madagascar." The poorest people, both men and women, were the most vulnerable and marginalized. However, the poor women were more vulnerable than the poor men. Their situation will not be improved until there is a shift in societal values regarding *reproductive, productive and community managing* needs, tasks and roles.

10.7 Integrating gender and environment

In some of the previous sections, attention focused on initiatives at the local or village level to increase the role of women in resource and environmental management, and thereby to soften or remove gender-based divisions. A common thread in the various experiences (forestry, water, agriculture) is the difficulty in getting women's issues recognized by the formal state agencies responsible for resource and environmental management. Changes in attitudes and values of senior managers will have to occur if women's issues are to be addressed systematically and on a sustained basis.

However, a structural or organizational issue must also be addressed. Levy (1992) has argued that both "environment" and "gender" have encountered the same dilemma regarding the best way to incorporate them into government bureaucracies. There have been at least two choices. On one hand, custom-built women's or environmental agencies were created. Certainly for the environment, following the Stockholm Conference in 1972 (see Chapter 2), a proliferation of environmental ministries, departments and agencies was created in many countries. This approach made the "environment" more visible within government, but it also allowed traditional line or sectoral agencies to ignore or neglect many resource and environmental matters since they could argue that such a concern was the responsibility of the environmental ministry or department. On the other hand, women's or environmental considerations can be integrated into existing organizations and agencies. This option does not make gender or environmental issues as visible within a governmental structure, but it does require each agency to consider the implications of its objectives and activities for them.

The choice between custom-built agencies and integration within existing agencies is a generic issue for managers, as indicated in the comments in Box 10.12 from the Brundtland Commission about alternative ways to incorporate environmental issues into management.

Levy (1992) indicated that, regarding women's issues, the choice has usually been to create special women's bureaus, ministries or departments, particularly in Asia, Africa and Latin America. Levy expressed concern that the focus of such special-purpose women's organizations was primarily at the project level, resulting in a very narrow and limited role. The outcome has been that the

Box 10.12 Incorporating environmental issues into management

The mandates of central economic and sectoral ministries are also often too narrow, too concerned with quantities of production or growth. The mandates of ministries of industry include production targets, while the accompanying pollution is left to ministries of environment. Electricity boards produce power, while the acid pollution they also produce is left to other bodies to clean up. The present challenge is to give the central economic and sectoral ministries the responsibility for the quality of those parts of the human environment affected by their decisions, and to give the environmental agencies more power to cope with the effects of unsustainable development.

Source: World Commission on Environment and Development, 1987: 10.

Box 10.13 Problems of not focusing on gender

A focus on women is recognized as legitimate in its own right and the basis of one of the most important political movements of the century. However, when translated into professional practice over the last 15 years, it has resulted in a sector which is marginalized from mainstream development policies, programmes and projects, with little impact on overall development processes and economic, social and political relations in many countries.

Source: Levy, 1992: 136.

women's "sector" has often been a very weak one. In Levy's (1992: 136) words, the women's sector is usually "characterized by a lack of any real political influence, and is therefore under-funded and under-staffed, both in numbers and qualifications. A key factor underlying these characteristics is the conceptualization of both the problems and the strategies of this sector in terms of women, not gender." Levy's analysis highlights the fact that, as in most situations, there are choices between imperfect options. Which alternative do you believe is most likely to result in the most effective treatment of gender issues?

10.8 Implications

The Earth Summit in Rio de Janeiro (1992) and the Fourth World Conference on Women in Beijing (1995) have helped to draw attention to the issues of *women* and *gender* in resource and environmental management. It is concluded here that gender is a more appropriate focus, since it is often social relationships and customary practices that need to be shifted if women are to have the same opportunities as men.

In seeking to improve opportunities for women, it is important to recognize various roles – reproductive, productive, community managing – which women often hold in their households, communities and regions. Too often, initiatives to improve the conditions of women have concentrated only upon the productive role. A gender approach reminds us that all three roles deserve attention and action. A gender approach also reminds us that women are not a homogeneous group, and that therefore gender should not be considered in isolation from other variables such as financial and social status.

Experiences over the past one or two decades are both encouraging and discouraging. The well-known Chipko movement in India illustrates how women can change gender relationships related to resource use practices by directly challenging conventional attitudes and practices. Yet in the same country some of the joint forest management and village initiatives continue to marginalize women. Experiences with irrigation agriculture in Peru and share cropping in Madagascar illustrate that often there need to be profound changes in societal attitudes and values towards women if customary gender roles are to be changed.

The examples in this chapter have focused on experiences in developing countries, as situations there are usually more stark in gender relations. However, gender-defined roles also exist in developed countries, and there are often gender differences in approaches and attitudes to environmental issues. As the comment in Box 10.14 indicates, however, existing studies offer conflicting

Box 10.14 Gender and environmental concern in developed countries

The results from … empirical studies, which related gender to environmental concern and activism, are contradictory. Studies have consistently shown that women are more concerned than men about *local* environmental issues that constitute a potential hazard to the community. In contrast, gender difference in concern for *gender* environmental issues is unclear; measured differences have tended to be modest, and whether it is men or women who are found to be more concerned varies from study to study.

The translation of concern for the environment into action is critical to achieving change. In general, on both an individual and professional level, there appear to be significant differences in the way women and men respond to increased environmental awareness and concern. Several studies have found that women participate in more environmentally friendly behaviours than men; the differences noted "are particularly pronounced in their shopping behavior." For example, women are more likely to seek out environmentally friendly products, such as baking soda for cleaning, rather than a cleaner that produces toxic residues. Women's greater participation seems to be due in large part to traditional gender roles and task divisions that are still prevalent in society.… However … the limited evidence indicates that women are less politically active in environmental issues than men.

Source: Nesmith and Wright, 1995: 83–4.

findings and interpretations, suggesting that much more work remains to be done in this field.

References and further reading

Ahmed M R 1992 Unseen workers: a sociocultural profile of women in Bangladesh agriculture. *Society and Natural Resources* 5(4): 375–90

Awumbila M and J H Momsen 1995 Gender and the environment: women's time use as a measure of environmental change. *Global Environmental Change* 5(4): 337–46

Blocker T J and D L Eckberg 1989 Environmental issues as women's issues: general concerns and local hazards. *Social Science Quarterly* 70(3): 586–93

Chen L C, W M Fitzgerald and L Bates 1995 Women, politics, and global management. *Environment* 37(1): 4–9, 31–3

Cuomo C J 1992 Unravelling the problems in ecofeminism. *Environmental Ethics* 14(4): 351–63

Cutter S L 1995 The forgotten casualties: women, children and environmental change. *Global Environmental Change* 5(3): 181–94

Dankelman I and J Davidson 1988 *Women and environment in the Third World: alliance for the future*. London, Earthscan Publications with IUCN

Davis D L and J Nadel-Klein 1992 Gender, culture, and the sea: contemporary theoretical approaches. *Society and Natural Resources* 5(2): 135–47

Fratkin E and K Smith 1995 Women's changing economic roles with pastoral sedentarization: varying strategies in alternate Rendille communities. *Human Ecology* 23(4): 433–54

Gray L 1993 The effect of drought and economic decline on rural women in Western Sudan. *Geoforum* 24(1): 89–98

Greed C H 1994 *Women and planning: creating gendered realities*. London, Routledge

Jacobson J L 1992 *Gender bias: roadblock to sustainable development*. Worldwatch Paper 110, Washington, DC, Worldwatch Institute

Jarosz L 1991 Women as rice sharecroppers in Madagascar. *Society and Natural Resources* 4(1): 53–63

King R J H 1991 Caring about nature: feminist ethics and the environment. *Hypatia* 6(1): 75–89

Kinnaird V and D Hall (eds) 1994 *Tourism: a gender analysis*. Chichester, John Wiley

Levy C 1992 Gender and environment: the challenge of cross-cutting issues in development policy and planning. *Environment and Urbanization* 4(1): 134–49

Levy D E and P B Lerch 1991 Tourism as a factor in development: implications for gender and work in Barbados. *Gender and Society* 5(1): 67–85

Little J 1994 *Gender, planning and the policy process*. Oxford, Pergamon

Lynch, B D 1991 Women and irrigation in highland Peru. *Society and Natural Resources* 4(1): 37–52

Mackenzie F 1990 Gender and land rights in Marang'a District, Kenya. *Journal of Peasant Studies* 17(4): 609–43

Mayoux L 1995 Beyond naivety: women, gender inequality and participatory development. *Development and Change* 26(2): 235–58

McStay J R and R E Dunlap 1983 Male–female differences in concern for environmental quality. *International Journal of Women's Studies* 6(4): 291–301

Merchant C 1989 *Ecological revolutions: nature, gender, and science in New England*. Chapel Hill, University of North Carolina Press

Merchant C 1995 *Earthcare: women and the environment*. London, Routledge

Mohai P 1992 Men, women and the environment: an examination of the gender gap in environmental concern and activism. *Society and Natural Resources* 5(1): 1–19

Moser C O N 1989 Gender planning in the Third World: meeting practical and strategic gender needs. *World Development* 17(11): 1799–825

Moser C O N 1993 *Gender planning and development: theory, practice and training*. London, Routledge

Mosse D 1994 Authority, gender and knowledge: theoretical reflections on the practice of participatory rural appraisal. *Development and Change* 25(3): 497–526

Mosse J C 1993 *Half the world, half a chance: an introduction to gender and development*. Oxford, Oxfam

Nesmith C and P Wright 1995 Gender, resources, and environmental management. In B. Mitchell (ed.) *Resource and environmental management in Canada: addressing conflict and uncertainty*. Toronto, Oxford University Press: 80–98

Ngwa N E 1995 The role of women in environmental management: an overview of the rural Cameroonian situation. *GeoJournal* 35(4): 515–20

Norr J L and K F Norr 1992 Women's status in peasant-level fishing. *Society and Natural Resources* 5(2): 149–63

Peluso N L (ed.) 1991 Special issue: women and natural resources in developing countries. *Society and Natural Resources* 4(1): 90 pp

Plumwood V 1994 *Feminism and the mastery of nature*. London, Routledge

Sarin M 1995 Community forestry management: where are the women? *The Hindu Survey of the Environment* 25: 27–9

Seager J 1993 *Earth follies: coming to feminist terms with the global environmental crisis*. London, Routledge.

Stern P C, T Dietz and L Kalof 1993 Value orientations, gender and environmental concern. *Environment and Behavior* 25(3): 322–48

Swain M 1995 Gender in tourism. *Annals of Tourism Research* 22(2): 247–66

Thomas-Slayter B 1995 *Gender, environment, and development in Kenya: a grassroots perspective*. Boulder, Colorado and London, Lynne Rienner Publishers

Thomas-Slayter B and N Bhatt 1994 Land, livestock and livelihoods: changing dynamics of gender, caste and ethnicity in a Nepalese village. *Human Ecology* 22(4): 467–94

Thomas-Slayter B, A L Esser and M D Shields (eds) 1993 *Tools for gender analysis: a guide to field methods for bringing gender into sustainable resource management*. ECOGEN Research Project, International Development Program, Worcester, Massachusetts, Clark University

Townsend J G 1995 *Women's voices from the rainforest*. London, Routledge

Warren K J (ed.) 1995 *Ecological feminism*. London, Routledge

White G F, D J Bradley and A U White 1972 *Drawers of water: domestic water use in East Africa*. Chicago, University of Chicago Press

World Commission on Environment and Development 1987 *Our common future*. Oxford, Oxford University Press

Chapter 11

Alternative Dispute Resolution

11.1 Introduction

"Conflict is a clash of interests, values, actions or directions, and has been a part of life since time began" (Johnson and Duinker, 1993: 17). Thus, conflicts are inescapable, but they can be positive as well as negative. Positive aspects occur when conflict helps to identify a process for resource and environmental management which is not working effectively, to highlight poorly developed ideas or inadequate or misleading information, and to draw attention to misunderstandings. Conflict can also be helpful when, by questioning the status quo, it leads to new creative approaches. In contrast, conflict can be negative if it is ignored or consciously set aside. "An unresolved conflict breeds mis-information, misunderstanding, mistrust and biases. A conflict is bad when it allows higher and stronger barriers to be built up between the involved parties" (Johnson and Duinker, 1993: 19).

In this chapter, alternative methods for resolving disputes are examined, with particular attention to what has become known as *alternative dispute resolution* (ADR). The following section describes the characteristics of different ways of dealing with conflicts, and the next one reviews different ADR

Box 11.1 Resolving conflicts

Conflict resolution, or alternative dispute resolution (ADR), techniques are intended to facilitate consensus decision making by disputing parties, thereby avoiding legal or administrative proceedings to resolve disputes. Some characteristics of this group of techniques include: (1) focusing on the underlying interests of the disputing parties, rather than on their bargaining positions; (2) using creative thinking to dovetail unlike interests, preferences, capabilities, and risk tolerances and change disputes from zero-sum games to situations with the potential for joint gains; (3) appealing to jointly-accepted objective standards for apportioning gains; and (4) requiring consensus among parties to a decision, rather than majority rule. An independent mediator is often used to direct the process of dispute resolution.

Source: Maguire and Boiney, 1994: 33.

Box 11.2 Conflict is common

Environmental assessment is often characterized by conflict and controversy. . . . This is an inevitable consequence of the differences in values and interests that exist in a pluralistic society with respect to the use and management of land, water and other natural resources. Dispute settlement is usually difficult to achieve for two inter-related reasons: first, the benefits and costs of development are unevenly distributed and include intangibles that are hard to evaluate and compare; and, second, many affected and interested parties with diverse views and interpretations are often involved.

Source: Sadler and Armour, 1987: 1.

methods. Then the discussion considers the conditions or factors necessary or desirable for effective use of ADR. That review is followed by some examples of the application of ADR approaches.

11.2 Different approaches to dispute resolution

When conflicts arise over resource allocation or different interests regarding the environment, at least four approaches can be used to deal with them: (1) political, (2) administrative, (3) judicial, and (4) alternative dispute resolution. These approaches are not necessarily mutually exclusive; some can be used together.

Political approaches involve elected decision makers considering the range of competing values and interests, and then making a decision. In this approach, the decision makers are not normally specialists in resource and environmental management, but they do receive advice from technical experts in the public service. In addition, through various participatory mechanisms they can seek to involve the public, and to hear directly from the public about needs, aspirations and preferences. In a democracy, the decision makers are accountable to all their constituents. However, not all constituents are equal, owing to different access to financial and other resources. As a result, some constituents may have a disproportionate influence on decision makers. Where corruption is prevalent, elected decision makers may not try to balance all interests, but instead focus on the interests of a select few. Furthermore, the decision makers are usually distant from the place and the people most affected by their decisions, and may not always be aware of, or sensitive to, specific local conditions. This latter point is of less concern, of course, when the decision makers are elected at a local level.

Administrative approaches are built into resource and environmental management organizations, and allow bureaucrats to take decisions regarding some kinds of disputes. Thus, a district or regional manager may be empowered to bring conflicting groups together, listen to their views, consider information provided by technical experts, and then reach a decision. In some situations, such as co-management discussed in Chapter 9, power can be shared with or delegated to people who will be affected by the decisions. Generally, however, administrative approaches are best suited to what might be called *routine* as opposed to *strategic* types of decisions. If the people affected by the decisions are unhappy with the outcome, there is often provision for an appeal to an administrator at a different level in the management system, or to elected officials. As with the political approaches, if corruption exists, then decisions will not necessarily reflect consideration of all interests in the system.

Judicial approaches involve litigation and the courts. This approach is well suited for situations in which parties in dispute are so entrenched in their positions, or so angry at other participants, that they will not voluntarily meet with the other parties to try to reach a resolution. The judicial approach has the power (through the police) to ensure that people participate at hearings, and once a decision is taken, has the power to impose and enforce sanctions (fines, prison sentences). The judicial approach is based on procedures and guidelines which have evolved over centuries. Emphasis is placed on *facts*, *precedents*, *procedures* and *argument*. Accountability is normally high, as provision exists for appeals to a higher court.

Notwithstanding the many advantages of the judicial approach, there are also some disadvantages. The main weaknesses are the *adversarial*, *time consuming* and *expensive* nature of the judicial approach. The adversarial nature means that opposing sides do not try to work with each other to solve a problem, but instead do everything in their power to present only information which supports their interests, and to discredit information or views supporting the interests of their opponents. The process can be time consuming and expensive, making it difficult for some parties to participate if they do not have funds to employ legal experts. Even if they can hire legal advisors, they may not be able to match the team of legal and other technical advisors that another group may be able to assemble.

For many people, another disadvantage of the judicial approach is that

---

Box 11.3 But what if conflicts appear irreconcilable?

Conflicting interests that are perceived to be mutually exclusive present a special problem. The wilderness versus industrial development issues ... are examples of this phenomenon. Wilderness advocates define wilderness in terms of a lack of industrial development: an area that is partly developed is not wilderness. From this perspective, the dispute becomes an all-or-nothing, win–lose contest. In other words, the integrity of the contested wilderness area, from the wilderness advocates' perspective, is a non-negotiable issue. Negotiation, from this perspective, will likely be perceived as offering nothing and may be perceived as exposing the wilderness advocate to mollification and manipulation.

Source: Wood, 1989: 45.

Box 11.4 Contrast between judicial and mediation approaches

The internal dynamics of environmental mediation are completely different than the courtroom context. Participants in mediation often develop bonds of trust, understanding, and even affection, toward their opponents. The climate of understanding and progress in working toward mutually satisfactory solutions creates subtle pressures to be reasonable and conciliatory. These dynamics may undermine the determination of unsophisticated parties to stand their ground on issues. . . . The typical low key atmosphere, and press exclusion, of the proceedings protects the parties from the scrutiny of their constituents, and shields them from the awareness that they might be sacrificing constituent concerns in the interests of achieving a settlement. The parties with less experience and sophistication may walk away with an agreement which favors their perspective much less than would have been possible in a more public, adversarial context.

The context of litigation is not conducive to intimacy and trust between contending parties. Adversarial relationships and the development of competing evidence heighten the differences between opponents. The use of expert witnesses leads to the development of elaborate information and contrasting interpretations of the same data to support different positions. The public nature of the courtroom spurs lawyers and experts to make their utmost efforts to enhance their reputations in light of future opportunities, and helps to attract the resources to involve highly skilled professionals. The public context assures widespread awareness of the proceedings, and protects litigants from the temptation to sacrifice the interests of their constituents in the desire to achieve a settlement. The dynamics of starkly competing perspectives, the context of legal precedent, and the emphasis upon proper procedure help to assure that each side ends up with the maximum benefit which is justified within the law. The internal dynamics of litigation protect the interests of weaker parties much better than environmental mediation.

Source: Blackburn, 1988: 569–70.

it usually results in *winners* and *losers*. That is, the outcome in a court decision is normally that one party wins and the other loses. The judicial system has enough sanctions (fines, imprisonment) to make sure that the decision in the court is upheld, but often the decision generates considerable ill-will and makes future cooperation unlikely. Thus, while it is important to appreciate that the judicial approach has many strengths and will always be required as a means for resolving disputes, like every approach it also has some distinct weaknesses.

Alternative dispute resolution (ADR) approaches have emerged in response to the perceived weaknesses of the judicial approach, and also in response to the growing expectations in many societies for more participation and local empowerment in resource and environmental management. Alternative dispute resolution approaches try to avoid the adversarial and winner–loser character-istics of the judicial approach. The dominant characteristics of ADR include (1) attention to interests and needs over positions and precedents, (2) persuasion rather than coercion, (3) commitment to joint agreement rather than imposed settlement, (4) constructive communication and improved understanding instead of negative criticism and preoccupation with justifying or defending interests, (5) achievement of settlements that will be long lasting because of shared commitment, (6) effective sharing and use of information, and (7) greater flexibility.

These characteristics of ADR represent ideals which cannot always be achieved, and sometimes require satisfaction of preconditions which cannot be met. For example, people with different and conflicting interests may not be prepared to meet to share information, and to try to reach a long-lasting settlement. As a result, ADR is not inevitably an improved approach to resolving conflicts relative to the judicial approach. In this chapter, the interest is in examining the strengths and weaknesses of ADR for dispute resolution, and to review some situations in which it has been applied. Before doing that, however, it is important to appreciate that ADR is not a single approach or mechanism. Different types of ADR exist and are considered below.

11.3 Types of alternative dispute resolution

Four types of ADR exist: (1) public consultation, (2) negotiation, (3) mediation and (4) arbitration.

11.3.1 Public consultation

In Chapter 8, various aspects of partnerships and participatory approaches were examined. Basic motivations for public consultation are to allow more sharing of experience and information, to ensure that many perspectives are considered, to open up management processes so that they can be seen to be both efficient and fair, and thereby to ensure that more people will be satisfied with decisions and plans. If all these characteristics are achieved through public participation, then many issues which might trigger conflicts can be dealt with before they emerge as full-scale disputes.

As described in the above paragraph, public consultation is a means to resolve conflict, and is an alternative to the judicial, administrative and political approaches. However, public consultation could also readily become a compo-nent of administrative and political approaches, when appointed or elected decision makers seek to consult with the public before decisions are taken, or to allow some decisions to be made by the public. Because public consultation concepts and mechanisms were discussed in detail in Chapter 8, they will not be examined further here.

11.3.2 Negotiation

Negotiation is one of three approaches normally considered to comprise ADR. Negotiation involves situations in which two or more groups meet voluntarily in order to explore jointly an issue which is causing conflict between them. The purpose is to reach a mutually acceptable agreement by *consensus*. There is no external person or group providing assistance, and the parties in dispute have to be willing to meet with the other side to examine the issue.

11.3.3 Mediation

Mediation has all the characteristics of negotiation, plus the involvement of a neutral third party (a mediator). The third party has no power to develop or impose an agreement, but functions as both facilitator and fact finder, in order to help the parties in conflict reach an agreement. A mediator may be used when the parties in conflict are prepared to meet to discuss their problem, but also when feelings may be so strong that it is unlikely that face-to-face meetings would be constructive. In such a situation, the mediator might separate the groups, help them to identify the main points of contention, and then serve as a messenger to facilitate dialogue between the parties.

11.3.4 Arbitration

When arbitration is chosen, a third party is involved. Unlike mediation, however, the person serving as the arbitrator has power to make a decision, which may or may not be binding. If it is binding, then the parties in dispute have agreed before the arbitration process begins to abide by the settlement developed by the arbitrator. The option of binding arbitration in many cases is sufficient to make parties work diligently, in order to avoid a situation in which a third party imposes an agreement upon them. Usually the participants in the dispute are directly involved in the selection of the arbitrator, which is one of the key differences between arbitration and judicial approaches. Normally, in a judicial situation the disputing sides have no role in determining which judge or magistrate will preside over their case.

Box 11.5 Role of a mediator

... as a guardian of the process, a mediator can intervene to correct miscommunications, to clarify ambiguous messages, and to challenge deceptive communications. Also, a mediator can point out when differences in inter-pretations have arisen....

Source: Ozawa and Susskind, 1985: 35.

11.3.5 Summary

The four ADR mechanisms represent a continuum from public consultation to arbitration, in which the process becomes increasingly more structured and the participants relinquish more and more control of the process. Which specific mechanism is appropriate depends upon the history of the relationships between the groups in conflict, and particularly upon their willingness to come together voluntarily to try to reach a solution which will be long lasting and beneficial for all interests.

11.4 Conditions for effective alternative dispute resolution

ADR is not a guaranteed recipe for effective resolution of conflicts. Experience shows that a number of conditions ideally should be met before a decision is taken to use ADR. All these conditions reflect beliefs that (1) the individuals or parties in a dispute may be in the best position to identify and settle the issues causing the conflict, (2) direct face-to-face discussions can be productive, (3) voluntary commitment exists for joint problem solving, and (4) a genuine desire is present to work towards consensus and reach a mutually agreeable settlement. If these beliefs are not realistic, then ADR is unlikely to be effective. If these beliefs are valid, however, then attention must turn to some other considerations.

11.4.1 Acknowledgement of a dispute

It may seem too obvious to mention, but a key aspect is that all parties recognize the existence of a dispute, and are able to agree upon the components or dimensions of the problem. Situations can occur, however, in which one group feels its interests are being damaged by the activities of another party. However, if the latter does not recognize or acknowledge the problem which is bothering the first party, the prospects for mutual problem solving are slim to non-existent.

11.4.2 Motivation to find a joint solution through ADR

For ADR to be effective, all parties must conclude that meeting together to search for a mutually acceptable solution is preferable to any other option they could pursue. For example, if one party to a dispute decides to "play hard ball", and to ignore the concerns of others being affected by its decisions or activities, there is little benefit for the others who feel their interests are being damaged to come together in some form of ADR mechanism. The motivation or incentive to use ADR is normally to avoid the time, expense and adversarial nature of a judicial approach. Thus, there can be some very compelling reasons for parties to want to work together. However, if any party concludes that it has a better alternative (ignore the concerns of others; go to court), then ADR will not be effective.

Box 11.6 Incentive to use ADR

A key element that determines whether a dispute may be mediated is whether or not there are sufficient incentives for the conflicting parties to enter into negotiations. Initially, however, each party must decide whether or not to recognise various groups and their interests. Mediation, and negotiations as a whole, are processes revolving around a desire, to varying degrees, to accommodate the opposing party. Implicit within this process is the recognition of the legitimacy of the opposition's demand and the opposition's right to represent those interests. The decision to mediate a dispute must be based upon a shared perception that it will provide the least-costly method of resolution and will provide the highest joint benefit. This type of cost benefit analysis is extremely difficult to gauge, given the unpredictability of negotiations and the potential for the variation of goals and objectives during negotiations.

Source: Rankin, 1989: 14.

11.4.3 Representation of interests

If a long-lasting, mutually agreeable solution is to be found, then it is important that all significant interests are represented in the ADR process. Achieving such representation can be challenging for various reasons. Governments can usually send representatives, since for the public servants such involvement is part of their job. Large corporations can also normally provide representatives, as they have staff whose jobs include such activity. But representatives from small businesses, labour groups and many small non-governmental organizations often find it difficult to send representatives for a sustained period because time spent at the ADR meetings is time taken away from jobs and involves loss of income. Thus, *financial* considerations can constrain an appropriate mix of representation.

The *scope* of an issue can also create problems for representation. In a conflict between the proposed development of a remote area for mining or timber extraction, or for its use as a national park or protected area, the interests to be represented regarding the heritage aspects could be those of citizens who live far away from the area. Or if the site is judged to be of global significance, then the question becomes how to ensure that representatives relative to its global value are incorporated into the process.

Another challenge is to achieve *intergenerational* representation. In Chapter 2, it was noted that intergenerational equity is a basic component of sustainable development. How to achieve representatives of "future generations" is clearly problematical, other than encouraging or expecting participants to take a temporal perspective that is longer than their own generation.

11.4.4 Involvement in design of the ADR process

A well-accepted tenet of ADR is that the process to be used needs to be agreed upon before the substantive aspects of the dispute are addressed. Normally, the various parties in the dispute would participate in the development of the process. A number of matters require attention.

Since ADR usually strives to reach agreements on the basis of consensus, it is important that there be a common interpretation about what consensus means. Consensus normally implies a "general agreement" as opposed to an agreement based on majority voting rules or a unilateral decision made by an individual in a position of authority. More than any other basis for reaching decisions, consensus requires the greatest amount of trust, goodwill and positive attitude. Consensus also treats everyone as equals, since no one need fear that he or she will be overwhelmed by a majority vote if they hold a minority opinion. In order to reach consensus, people are usually less concerned about the number of votes that will be given to a particular option than they are to identify aspects for accommodation and innovative resolution.

There is no single definition of what constitutes a "consensus" – the key concern is that the parties in a dispute agree in advance what the criteria should be to identify a consensual agreement. For example, 100% agreement or unanimity may represent an ideal, but another interpretation could be lack of dissent (with silence meaning acceptance) or agreement by a "vast majority" (only a few parties dissenting). Provision usually should also be made for a "fallback" position, such as agreeing to focus initially on aspects for which near-unanimous agreement can be reached, and then moving on to more difficult matters.

Other procedural issues need to be resolved. These include arrangements for different parties to communicate with their constituents, understanding about whether or not there is to be confidentiality of discussions, arrangements about the sharing of information, and creation of deadlines or targets. The key is that such matters should be sorted out before discussions begin on the substance of the conflict.

Box 11.7 A search for consensus can be problematical

The ideal of harmony, so prevalent in the West today . . . can be used to suppress criticism. It locks out those who continue to protest and discourages disagreement among those who have accepted a seat at the negotiation table. Confrontations can destroy the trust and assumption of shared goals which negotiation requires, jeopardizing the whole process of conflict resolution. Aiming for consensus, the process reinforces the status quo; radical change is unlikely to emerge when any change has to be agreed to by all parties.

Source: Beder, 1994: 236.

11.4.5 Acceptance of need for challenging constructively

The notion of "challenging constructively" could be included as a component of the process (Subsection 11.4.4 above), but is significant enough to deserve separate discussion. If trust and goodwill are to be built up, it is important that participants seek to be constructive in their dialogues, rather than engage in the type of destructive challenging that often occurs in an adversarial approach. Some key considerations in this regard include striving to avoid a negative and combative manner, seeking to bring people to the table who have relevant experience and interests, trying to gain a joint understanding of issues through systematic consideration of assumptions, data and logic, and viewing the group as "problem solvers" rather than as "argument destroyers".

11.4.6 Scope for compromise

"Compromise" often has a negative connotation, in that it can imply giving up or sacrificing important values or principles. If ADR is to work, however, there has to be a willingness to accept the validity of another party to hold a different perspective, to try to understand if not always agree with those other perspectives, and to search for solutions that will accommodate diverse interests. If a party comes to an ADR meeting with the view that it will not be flexible,

---

Box 11.8 Should be willingness to compromise: coastal erosion example

The erosion of coastal barrier islands presents a classic environmental policy problem characterized by both uncertainty and conflict.

Stakeholders with an interest in shoreline property cling to the conventional characterization of the problem. Owners of shoreline property view erosion as a threat to their economic interests. They insist on the right to protect their property and strongly support government programs that subsidize protective measures such as flood insurance and publicly funded erosion control projects. Real estate and development business, along with local governments that rely on oceanfront property for a substantial portion of their tax revenues, have similar interests and concerns.

Environmentalists, scientists, and people with an interest in the public value of the beach and its environment challenge the right to protect private property at the expense of the natural system. Shoreline protection structures such as groins and seawalls are criticized for intruding visually and physically onto the public trust beach and for interfering with natural geologic and ecologic processes. Publicly-funded beach protection and restoration projects, and emergency response initiatives following major storms, are viewed as inequitable subsidies for the elite who own beachfront property.

Source: Deyle, 1994: 461.

and will only accept solutions that satisfy its interests, then the likelihood of ADR being effective is very low.

On the other hand, it is understandable that at some point a party may indicate that an item associated with the dispute involves a matter of such principle that compromise is not possible. It is also possible that a solution could have such a heavy and onerous impact on one or more parties that they are unwilling to accept the decision, even if most of the other parties would benefit significantly. If a participant can clearly demonstrate that a decision is problematical because of a principle or an unreasonably negative impact for her or his group, and therefore is unable to compromise, then "it becomes incumbent upon the rest of the group to make an explicit effort to address those concerns. In many instances, simply identifying the point of dissension and having it accepted by the rest of the group is half the battle in resolving impediments to a general agreement" (British Columbia Round Table on the Environment and the Economy, 1991a: 5).

11.4.7 Acceptance of a "principled approach"

Fisher and Ury (1981) developed a "principled approach" for dispute resolution, which they contrasted with a "positional approach". In the positional approach, parties arrive for negotiations having already decided on a desirable solution, and attempt to persuade or coerce others to accept their terms and solution. Thus, they arrive with a "position", and their goal is to achieve it. Such an approach tends to constrain flexibility, and a willingness to be open-minded about alternative solutions. A positional approach also tends to create a win/lose situation, as some parties attain their positions and others do not achieve theirs.

In contrast, a principled position emphasizes avoiding the acceptance of a position from the outset, but instead stresses working with other parties to develop a creative solution which will meet most people's needs. The attributes of the principled approach are shown in Box 11.9 and discussed in the following paragraphs.

Box 11.9 Characteristics of a principled approach

(1) *Separate the people from the problem* Fisher and Ury argue that it is important to be "soft" on the people but "hard" on the problem. In other words, the goal should be to look beyond the idiosyncrasies of the people involved, and instead

(1) Separate the people from the problem.
(2) Focus on interests, not positions.
(3) Invent options for mutual gain.
(4) Insist on explicit, "objective" criteria to guide decisions.

Source: after Fisher and Ury, 1981.

concentrate on the problems of common concern. Clearly, there are times when the people are part of the problem, especially if they are being bloody-minded, vindictive or Machiavellian. However, other than in such obvious instances in which the people are indeed part of the problem, the idea is that people should overlook differences in personality and style, and focus on the substantive problems. This approach does not require parties to view one another as friends, but the argument is that they should view themselves as joint problem solvers, rather than as adversaries or argument destroyers.

(2) *Focus on interests rather than positions* In their work on dispute resolution, Fisher and Ury have found that groups with different, publicly declared, *positions* often have similar or shared *interests*. Thus, for example, two opposing parties may find that they share a common interest in avoiding the pollution of an estuary. However, one may have a public position that a new factory is essential for providing jobs in an area with a high unemployment rate, and the other may have a public position opposing the factory. More productive discussions would occur if they focused on their common interest in protecting the water quality in the estuary, and then explored alternative ways of accommodating the needs of the factory and the quality of the estuary.

(3) *Invent options for mutual gain* Rather than each party considering only those solutions that provide benefits to itself, the belief is that it is more constructive to search for solutions that will generate benefits for all parties. This view does not reflect a belief that every party will always get everything that it wants. However, it does reflect a belief that if some groups get most or all of what they want, and others get little or nothing of what they want, any decision is likely to face a long period of challenges in the courts.

(4) *Insist on explicit, "objective" criteria* If options for mutual gain are to be developed, then it is important that the parties in a conflict agree at the outset of their negotiations regarding the criteria or basis on which possible solutions will be assessed. If it can be established at the outset which criteria will be used, then the expectation is that options for mutual gain will more likely be considered on the basis of "principled" rather than "positional" criteria. The use of such criteria should allow the parties in the conflict both to use reason and to be open to reason concerning identification and evaluation of options. The intent then would become to identify one or more solutions that provided the greatest benefits relative to the agreed criteria, rather than the positions of any one group.

The use of these four elements of a "principled" approach does not guarantee that a mutually acceptable solution will be generated and that conflicts will be resolved. However, they do provide a systematic structure or framework to help guide groups who agree to use some form of ADR to address their dispute.

11.4.8 Capacity for implementation

Unlike the judicial approach, which has the power of the courts and law enforcement systems to uphold decisions, the voluntary, mutual-agreement approach of ADR does not have a built-in mechanism for implementing agreements. As a result, it is usually important to specify what arrangements will be made to implement decisions resulting from ADR. Furthermore, to provide credibility for the process, it is also useful to design some form of *monitoring* and *reporting* so that accountability is provided. Without such accountability, the legitimation or credibility of the ADR agreement may be called into doubt if people do not have evidence of action following the agreements.

11.5 Applications of alternative dispute resolution

Kartez and Bowman's (1993) analysis of the experience with resource developments in Colorado and Texas illustrates effectively the factors which help and hinder ADR methods for resolving conflicts. Their basic message is that "quick deals" are often no better than "no deal" in environmentally based conflicts, if a long-term resolution is desired.

11.5.1 Colorado and Homestake Mining

In 1980, the Homestake Mining Company negotiated an agreement with a number of Colorado environmental groups and affected residents regarding an open-pit uranium mine. This experience is often cited as one of the earliest examples of successful use of voluntary dispute resolution procedures as an alternative to what could have been lengthy and costly litigation. Prior to the use of voluntary dispute resolution, Homestake had experienced four years of conflict regarding obtaining permits for the mine, and anticipated up to five more years of costly legal processes. In eighteen months of mediated direct negotiation, an agreement was reached which led to the permits being granted.

The conflict

The proposed open-pit uranium mine was to be sited in the high country of a national forest, triggering vocal protests from a coalition involving local and statewide conservation groups, as well as from local residents concerned about environmental degradation and safety. Other concerns reflected ideological views about the appropriateness, or otherwise, of nuclear power. The mining company had completed a required environmental impact statement (EIS) as part of the permitting process, but the conservation groups immediately criticized the EIS and threatened litigation owing to what they considered to be inadequacies in the statement. As Kartez and Bowman (1993: 321) remarked, "Although the opponents 'got the company's attention,' they realized they would be unable to 'get the assurances they really wanted' on mine reclamation, backfilling, long-term water quality maintenance, and revegetation. Litigation over procedural issues is notoriously inept at solving complex environmental management problems that really require creative solutions."

For its part, while Homestake believed that the adequacy of the EIS and reclamation plan would be verified, it wanted assurance that it could indeed resolve the environmental problems, rather than simply winning on legal or technical grounds. The counsel for Homestake noted that his client wanted to avoid a situation in which opponents would demand that every possible technical issue, how ever remote, had to be answered definitively before the mine was approved. He noted that reliance on administrative appeals and litigation almost guaranteed such a tactic would be used by opponents. Thus, all sides (the mining company, the conservation groups, the local residents) had reached a stage in which alternatives to a "win–lose" adversarial process became appealing. In the jargon of ADR, the issue had become *ripe*. The parties had arrived at a point where they recognized the presence of a conflict, and when voluntary searching for a mutually agreeable solution appeared to be more attractive than any other method to resolve the dispute.

The ADR process

Kartez and Bowman commented on four problems that the parties had to overcome if ADR were to be used. The first issue was whether there was scope for compromise through negotiations. The *position* of the opponents that the mine project should be halted appeared to leave little scope for consideration of alternatives. However, informal discussions prior to the actual mediation discussions revealed that the basic *interests* of the parties in dispute were more similar than their publicly declared positions: both sides shared an interest that the mine property should be reclaimed properly. As a result, discussion shifted from whether or not the mine site should be reclaimed, to how it might be reclaimed. This change reflected the similarities in interest. The conservation groups' position that the mine operation should be disallowed had been its way of trying to avoid degradation and safety problems. Those groups were willing to consider other solutions that would meet their concerns. As a result, "the significance of this step was that the players defined a problem that might be solved, based on a common interest" (Kartez and Bowman, 1993: 321).

The second issue involved *representation* of interests for the mediation discussions. An "anti-nuke" group refused to negotiate with Homestake on any basis. As a result, the mining company, the conservation groups and the residents agreed to search for a voluntary settlement through mediation, recognizing that any agreement would be susceptible to attack from the "anti-nuke" group, which would not be at the table.

The third problem to be resolved was *data, access to data*, and the *role of experts*. The parties in the dispute agreed that technical experts would not be the main negotiators, but would serve as resource people. Furthermore, the mining company agreed to provide answers to a detailed set of technical questions. The outcome was that rather than information being used strategically by each side to bolster its position and interests, information became a shared resource to

Box 11.10 Consensus and compromise

Rarely do negotiation and consensus processes result in "all win" solutions. This approach searches for a middle ground and areas of accommodation or compromise. For many, however, the term "compromise" conjures up visions of sacrificing "good" solutions for expediency, and long-term solutions for "quick fixes".

In every dispute, there may be interests that cannot and should not be compromised: for example, those that define the fundamental identity of an individual or organization. It is important that all parties in negotiations understand where those essential interests lie. In addition, compromise does not mean sacrificing principles or fundamental values. Consensus-building can recognize fundamental values and still reach accommodations on such things as "how" rather than "whether" these values will be satisfied.

Source: British Columbia Round Table on the Environment and the Economy, 1991a: 7.

help in identifying new solutions. This decision moved the discussions away from the common challenge and counter-challenge regarding assumptions and facts, and focused attention upon solving shared concerns.

The fourth issue involved the relationship between the negotiating parties and the government regulatory agencies. The people selected as mediators emphasized that it was important for the parties involved in the negotiations to communicate early and continuously with the regulatory agencies. The advantage of this approach was that the regulatory agencies would be aware of the issues and possible solutions being considered, and could provide advice about their legal, administrative and political feasibility. In this manner, time was not spent on options which were "non-starters", and in addition the regulatory agencies did not have to worry that their roles and statutory authority were being undermined by the voluntary negotiation process.

Implications

The dispute over the open-pit uranium mining operation met many of the conditions which support the effective use of ADR. The parties in dispute believed that ADR was likely to be more helpful than a judicial approach, and there was willingness by each party to recognize the needs and concerns of the other parties in the conflict. There was willingness to ensure full representation of interests, to the extent that was practical, to share information and expert understanding, and to work with the regulatory agencies.

The outcome was a resolution containing three key elements. A *statement of understanding* specified the mining company's commitment to manage water quality, restore the mine pit, and monitor erosion and revegetation. These provisions were also to be included in the permits required from the regulatory

Box 11.11 The settlement

For the opponents, the settlements led Homestake to accept higher standards for managing mine reclamation and environmental impacts and for ongoing rather than one-shot mitigation. Homestake received assurance that the uncertainty of legal tactics-of-delay would be avoided.

Source: Kartez and Bowman, 1993: 323.

agencies. A *mediation agreement* stipulated that the company would make specified data about the reclamation work available to the conservation groups, and also that it would fund research related to high-altitude revegetation. Finally, a *covenant not to sue* was signed by each member of the environmental coalition, committing them to refrain from legal action as long as Homestake abided by its commitments outlined in the other two documents.

11.5.2 Texas, Mitsubishi Metals Corporation and Texas Copper Company

During early 1989, the Mitsubishi Metals Corporation (MMC) announced that it intended to construct a quarter-billion-dollar smelter in Texas City, which would be operated by a subsidiary, Texas Copper Company (TCC). By the end of the year, the proposal was under vigorous criticism from environmental groups concerned about the possible impact from the discharge of heavy metals into Galveston Bay. In 1991, MMC signed an agreement with some of its critics, hoping to avoid protracted legal proceedings. However, as the comments in Box 11.12 show, the outcome was not as satisfactory as the experience in Colorado.

The conflict

The conflict divided groups into those who saw the smelter as an important addition to the local economy, and those who viewed it as a threat to Galveston Bay. After reviewing an initial environmental impact statement, the US

Box 11.12 The Texas Copper conflict

Although an agreement was signed in one evening, there was continued acrimony and threats of legal action by other opponents of the facility, new requirements by the state regulatory agency after a change of administration (requirements which the project proponents rejected), eventual withdrawal of the proposed project by the company, and charges of bad faith from most quarters.

Source: Kartez and Bowman, 1993: 320.

Environmental Protection Agency and the Corps of Engineers agreed that there was no significant threat of pollution from the proposed smelter, which meant a full impact statement was not required. However, during the early part of 1990, critics appeared before the Texas Water Commission to express concern about possible pollution in the bay. The critics included representatives of several conservation groups, an upper-class community sited on a bay island, and a broadly based coalition opposing the smelter due to concern about its impact on health of nearby residents. The protest quickly became highly visible, as the critics initiated petitions, released press statements and began public demonstrations. The critics also complained that Texas Copper "was with-holding key information, being deceptive, and letting a Japanese corporation exploit Galveston Bay" (Kartez and Bowman, 1993:323). The critics demanded a full environmental impact assessment, and also that Texas Copper should be required to use state-of-the-art waste water technology if the smelter were to be built.

In June 1990, the Texas Water Commission did grant a discharge permit to Texas Copper, but its own legal department challenged that decision. When the decision to grant the permit was upheld, opponents filed for a hearing, and late in the year the Water Commission reopened hearings which were to focus on technical aspects which were in dispute. By the spring of 1991, the company had been given a three-year permit with specific directions regarding how to handle discharges. Opponents of the smelter immediately filed for another hearing.

A dispute settlement process

By the middle of 1991, the positions of the opposing parties had hardened and had moved further apart. Concern of the opponents about technical issues had become less significant than their lack of trust in the president of Texas Copper. As a result, substantive issues became subsidiary to issues related to personal-ities and previous decisions. Thus, the parties in dispute were increasingly focusing on people rather than the problem, and on positions rather than on interests. They also had not established mutually acceptable criteria for evaluating options, and were not searching for a solution with benefits for all parties. The dispute was becoming increasingly adversarial.

Against this background, the Japanese chief operating officer contacted the lawyer for the Galveston Bay Foundation, one of the opponents, and arranged to meet over dinner. The result of the dinner meeting was an agreement between Texas Copper, the Galveston Bay Foundation, and the Galveston Bay Conservation and Preservation Association. The agreement was very similar to that in Colorado with Homestake Mining. The two opponents agreed not to pursue legal action regarding the water permit. The company agreed to install additional waste water treatment capacity, which would be subject to approval by the two groups, as well as by the regulatory agencies. The director of the Galveston Bay Foundation indicated that her group had never been opposed to the smelter *per se*, but to unnecessary contamination of the bay.

Thus, they were pleased to have reached a mutually developed solution to a shared concern – how to avoid pollution of Galveston Bay.

Thus, the parties at the dinner meeting concentrated upon substantive problems rather than the people, upon interests rather than positions, and on finding a mutually beneficial solution. However, the effectiveness of such an agreement is "also influenced by who is or is not involved, and the conditions under which settlement occurs" (Kartez and Bowman, 1993: 325). The agreement reached in a single evening had excluded participation of the two most vociferous opponents: the bay island community, and the grassroots group concerned about health impacts.

The bay island community and the grassroots group were shocked at the agreement, and felt left out and betrayed by the Galveston Bay Foundation and the Galveston Bay Conservation and Preservation Association. They announced that their opposition would continue, and that they would pursue their concerns through the courts. Furthermore, the agreement about appropriate technology was not approved by the chair of the regulatory agency, who simply said that Texas Copper would have to meet a zero discharge target within one year of operation. This decision meant that a cooperative and joint evaluation of the treatment technologies was unlikely to be feasible. Within a few months of the dinner agreement, the Japanese parent corporation reduced the staff at Texas Copper and announced cancellation of the smelter project, referring to unreasonable local opposition and environmental standards.

Implications

The dispute in Texas generated by the proposed smelter and associated concerns about pollution of Galveston Bay had many of the same characteristics of the Colorado experience with the open-pit uranium operation. Both situations involved concerns about what were acceptable environmental impacts. Each included a mix of opponents with differing interests. Both involved concern about technical options, cumulative impacts, and capacity for mitigation measures. Both included the need to obtain multiple permits. All these common characteristics normally provide a strong incentive for use of ADR, to avoid what could be prolonged and potentially intractable battles.

The main reason that ADR was successful in Colorado and was not successful in Texas can be linked to a key consideration essential for ADR: "appropriate representation and willing participation" (Kartez and Bowman, 1993: 326). These two aspects were not incorporated into the design of the dispute settlement process used by Texas Copper and its opponents. As a result, a quickly developed solution could not be implemented.

11.6 Implications

It has been stated before in this book that often we do not manage resources and the environment, but we manage *human interaction* with resources and the environment. When that is indeed the situation, then very often planners and

Box 11.13 Key elements for successful ADR

... deciding the boundaries of who should be included as legitimate parties is one of the most important elements of effective pre-negotiation protocols or preparations.... A large part of the durability of outcomes from voluntary negotiations is "procedural satisfaction." That is the parties' belief that they have been better served by using a voluntary process than by fighting on, and that they would use such a process again.

... No competent mediator would have failed to tell the Texas Copper combatants that their exclusion of parties, rushing of negotiations, and avoidance of coordination with regulators was a recipe for useless negotiations.

... One clear lesson is that environmental issues by their nature require an open process. The minute the process is closed for tactical reasons, any opponent often has a case to dispute the outcome by indicting the process, including the technical adequacy of any scientific analysis which by its nature requires open argument.

Source: Kartez and Bowman, 1993: 327.

managers have to decide how best to address and resolve conflicts. The impacts of resource development or use of the environment normally generate benefits and costs which have different implications for the interests of various groups. Almost inevitably, one or more groups will feel disadvantaged, and will protest against a proposed policy or development related to use of resources or the environment. As a result, an important skill is conflict or dispute resolution.

This chapter has noted that societies have developed various ways to address conflicts. The judicial approach is the most frequently used method. The use of courts and their well-established processes and procedures is often the most appropriate way to deal with a dispute. However, increasing concerns about the time, costs and adversarial nature of the judicial approach have led to increasing attention being given to alternative dispute resolution (ADR) methods. It has never been argued that ADR should totally replace the judicial approach, but that some disputes, handled through ADR, might be resolved at less cost and reduced time.

There are different types of ADR, such as negotiation, mediation and arbitration. However, each shares core ideas that voluntary searches for solutions which represent mutual gain for parties in a dispute can be feasible. For ADR to be used, however, it is critical to recognize that some preconditions must be satisfied. Some of the most critical include general recognition of the presence of a dispute, motivation to consider ADR for joint problem solving, willingness to compromise, preparedness to use a "principled approach", and determination to facilitate implementation of an agreement. If these preconditions cannot be satisfied, ADR is unlikely to be effective.

It can be anticipated that ADR will be used increasingly in the future, especially in countries with a tradition of democratic governance. Even if

ADR is not directly applicable, awareness of and sensitivity to some of the key ideas associated with that approach are likely to make planners and managers more effective in resolving disputes related to resource and environmental issues.

References and further reading

Allor D J 1993 Alternative forums for citizen participation: formal mediation of urban land use disputes. *International Journal of Conflict Management* 4(2): 167–80

Amy D 1987 *The politics of environmental mediation.* New York, Columbia University Press

Armour A 1992 The cooperative process: facility siting the democratic way. *Plan Canada* March, 29–34

Bacow L S and M Wheeler 1984 *Environmental dispute resolution.* New York, Plenum

Beder S 1994 Consensus or conflict? *Ecologist* 24(6): 236–7

Bingham G 1986 *Resolving environmental disputes: a decade of experience.* Washington, DC, The Conservation Foundation

Blackburn J W 1988 Environmental mediation as an alternative to mitigation. *Policy Studies Journal* 16(3): 562–74

British Columbia Round Table on the Environment and the Economy. Dispute Resolution Core Group 1991a *Consensus processes in British Columbia* Volume 1, Victoria, British Columbia Round Table on the Environment and the Economy

British Columbia Round Table on the Environment and the Economy. Dispute Resolution Core Group 1991b *Implementing consensus processes in British Columbia* Volume 2, Victoria, British Columbia Round Table on the Environment and the Economy

Brown S, H E Schreier, W A Thompson and I Vertinsky 1994 Linking multiple accounts with GIS as decision support system to resolve forestry/wildlife conflicts. *Journal of Environmental Management* 42(4): 349–64

Buckle L G and S Thomas-Buckle 1986 Placing environmental mediation in context: lessons from failed mediations. *Environmental Impact Assessment Review* 6(1): 55–70

Carlisle T J and L G Smith 1989 Examining the potential for a negotiated approach to water management in Ontario. *Canadian Water Resources Journal* 14(4): 16–34

Carpenter S L and W J D Kennedy 1988 *Managing public disputes: a practical guide to handling conflict and reaching agreements.* San Francisco, Jossey-Bass

Cormick G W 1980 The "theory" and practice of environmental mediation. *Environmental Professional* 2(1): 24–33

Cormick G W 1989 Strategic issues in structuring multi-party public policy negotiations. *Negotiation Journal* 5(2): 125–32

Coughlan B A K, N Burkardt and D Fulton 1993 Assessing the "need to negotiate" in FERC licensing consultations: a study of two hydropower projects. *Environmental Impact Assessment Review* 13(6): 331–51

Deyle R E 1994 Conflict, uncertainty, and the role of planning and analysis in public policy innovation. *Policy Studies Journal* 22(3): 457–73

Dorcey A H J 1986 *Bargaining in the governance of Pacific coastal resources: research and reform,* Vancouver, BC, University of British Columbia, Westwater Research Centre

Dorcey A H J and C L Riek 1987 Negotiation-based approaches to the settlement of environmental disputes in Canada. In *The place of negotiation in environmental assessment*. Ottawa, Canadian Environmental Assessment Research Council, 7–36

Emel J 1990 Resource instrumentalism, privatization, and commodification. *Urban Geography* 11(6): 527–47

Fisher R and W Ury 1981 *Getting to yes: negotiating without giving in*. Boston, Houghton Mifflin

Gadgil M and R Guhn 1994 Ecological conflicts and the environmental movement in India. *Development and Change* 25(1): 101–36

Grandy M 1995 Political conflict over waste-to-energy schemes: the case of incineration in New York. *Land Use Policy* 12(1): 29–36

Gunton T and S Flynn 1992 Resolving environmental conflict: the role of mediation and negotiation. *Environments* 21(3): 12–16

Harashina S 1995 Environmental dispute resolution: process and information exchange. *Environmental Impact Assessment Review* 15(1): 69–80

Hollander G M 1995 Agroenvironmental conflict and world food system theory: sugarcane in the Everglades Agricultural Area. *Journal of Rural Studies* 11(3): 309–18

Hurwitz D 1995 Fishing for compromises through NAFTA and environmental dispute-settlement: the tuna–dolphin controversy. *Natural Resources Journal* 35(3): 501–40

Johnson P J and P N Duinker 1993 *Beyond dispute: collaborative approaches to resolving natural resource and environmental conflicts*. Thunder Bay, Ontario, Lakehead University, School of Forestry

Karez J D and P Bowman 1993 Quick deals and raw deals: a perspective on abuses of public ADR principles in Texas resource conflicts. *Environmental Impact Assessment Review* 13(5): 319–30

Klior N 1993 *Water resources and conflict in the Middle East*. London, Routledge

Maguire L A and L G Boiney 1994 Resolving environmental disputes: a framework incorporating decision analysis and dispute resolution techniques. *Journal of Environmental Management* 42(1): 31–48

Margairo A V, S Laska, J Mason and C Forsyth 1993 Captives of conflict: the TEDS case. *Society and Natural Resources* 6(3): 273–90

Mercer, D 1987 Patterns of protest: native land rights and claims in Australia. *Political Geography Quarterly* 6(2): 171–94

Nepal S K and K E Weber 1995 The quandary of local people–park relations in Nepal's Royal Chitwan National Park. *Environmental Management* 19(6): 853–66

Osborne P L 1995 Biological and cultural diversity in Papua New Guinea: conservation, conflicts, constraints and compromise. *Ambio* 24(4): 231–7

Ozawa C P and L Susskind 1985 Mediating science-intensive policy disputes. *Journal of Policy Analysis and Management* 5(1): 23–39

Rankin M 1989 The Wilderness Advisory Committee of British Columbia: new directions in environmental dispute resolution? *Environmental and Planning Law Journal* March: 5–17

Rogers P 1993 The value of cooperation in resolving international river basin disputes. *Natural Resources Forum* 17(2): 117–32

Sadler B and A Armour 1987 Common ground: on the relationship of environmental assessment and negotiation. In *The place of negotiation in environmental assessment*. Ottawa, Canadian Environmental Assessment Research Council, 1–6

Shafroe D (ed.) 1993 *Responding to changing times: environmental mediation in Canada*. Waterloo, Ontario, Conrad Grebel College, The Network: Interaction for Conflict Resolution

Stern A J 1991 Using environmental impacts for dispute resolution. *Environmental Impact Assessment Review* 11(1): 81–7

Susskind L E and J Cruikshank 1987 *Breaking the impasse: consensual approaches to resolving public disputes*. New York, Basic Books

Susskind L E and S McCreary 1985 Techniques for resolving coastal resource management disputes through negotiation. *Journal of the American Planning Association* 51(3): 365–74

Talbot A R 1983 *Settling things: six case studies in environmental mediation*. Washington, DC, The Conservation Foundation

Walker G 1995 Social mobilization in the city's countryside: rural Toronto fights waste dump. *Journal of Rural Studies* 11(3): 243–54

Weed T J 1994 Central America's "peace parks" and regional conflict resolution. *International Environmental Affairs* 6(2): 175–90

West L 1987 Mediated settlement of environmental disputes: Grassy Narrows and White Dog revisited. *Environmental Law* 18: 131–50

Wood P M 1989 Resolving wilderness land-use conflicts by using principled negotiation. *Forest Planning Canada* 8(3): 42–7

Chapter 12

Implementation

12.1 Introduction

Implementation is usually interpreted to mean taking action, or taking something such as a promise or statement of intent and translating it into specific activity. In resource and environmental management, a challenge is often to move from *normative* planning (what should be done) to *operational* planning (what will be done) (also discussed in Chapter 8). An often heard criticism is that the world is littered with good intentions, policies and plans, but little follow-up action. As the statement in the box below indicates, expressions of intent without associated activity normally have little value.

In this chapter, attention focuses upon some of the obstacles which hinder effective implementation of policies and programs. Ideas to improve our capacity for implementation are explored, and experiences with implementation are reviewed.

Box 12.1

Policies, by themselves, have very little value. Without the development of implementation strategies and the will to carry those policies into actual practice, all that is left are hollow words.

Broad statements of policy create expectations which must be met. A failure to meet expectations creates significant credibility gaps which, at a minimum, hamper further action. Moreover, a failure to implement good policy is also a failure to address significant problems in a meaningful way.

... policy makers must be held accountable not only to enunciate policy, but also to insure that the means exist to carry that policy out. We cannot be satisfied with the creation of policy alone. We must force the policy makers to address what is necessary to bridge the policy–practice gap. ... The key ... is to understand that most policy is not self-implementing and requires a conscious effort toward implementation before it will be actually realized in practice.

Source: Somach, 1993: 19, 20, 22.

Box 12.2 What is "implementation"?

Implementation, to us, means just what Webster and Roget say it does: to carry out, accomplish, fulfill, produce, complete. But what is it that is being implemented? A policy, naturally. There must be something out there prior to implementation; otherwise there would be nothing to move toward in the process of implementation.

Source: Pressman and Wildavsky, 1973: xiii.

12.2 Implementation issues

Weale (1992: 43) remarked that "implementation failure is like original sin: it is everywhere and it seems ineradicable." If we are to eradicate, or at least reduce, such failure, it is important to have a clear understanding about what implementation implies, what some of the most important obstacles are, and what type of an implementation framework might help to structure our approach. Each is considered below, with the discussion based on the following references: Pressman and Wildavsky (1973), Sabatier and Mazmanian (1981), Smith (1985) and Weale (1992).

12.2.1 Dimensions of implementation

Weale (1992) suggested that attention needs to be given to two matters regarding implementation failure:

- policy outcomes not complying with policy objectives or expectations; and
- government or other organizations failing to recognize a problem or to take decisions about it. In other words, there is a lack of policy, or the intentions are not sufficient relative to the need.

Table 12.1 shows the relationship between a focus on policy or problems, with regard to both *outputs* (laws, regulations and agencies created to deal with a policy problem) and *outcomes* (changes in environmental degradation or resource use). Each of the four cells in this table draws attention to different issues and questions, as follows.

Table 12.1 Classification of implementation problems; for description of cells (1)–(4) see text (after Weale, 1992: 45)

Orientation to problem	Focus of analysis	
	Output	Outcomes
Orientation to policy intentions	(1)	(2)
Orientation to problem	(3)	(4)

Cell 1 Attention here is concerned with the extent to which governments or any other organizations have been able to take their declared intentions and change them into tangible outputs. Interpretation of the significance of outputs is not always straightforward, however. For example, some environmental legislation may have been created, so an output has been generated. However, if the government is slow or reluctant to use and enforce the act, the outcome may be negligible.

Cell 2 Here the interest is not just on the creation of an output, but also on the extent to which environmental degradation has been stopped or reversed, or resource patterns have become more efficient or equitable. The major challenge here is to determine the influence of the implemented policy on the outcome, given that there could well be other variables contributing to it. Thus, air pollution may improve as a result of a Clean Air Act, but other contributing factors could include changes in relative prices of fuel contributing to greater use of a less polluting fuel, or development of more efficient heating units for homes, leading to reduced fuel consumption and therefore reduced emissions.

Cells 3 and 4 While the interest in Cells 1 and 2 is upon the matching of outputs or outcomes with intent, in Cells 3 and 4 attention focuses upon whether the outputs and outcomes are the most appropriate relative to a problem. An analogy can be made with the focus of a book review. The approach indicated by Cells 1 and 2 would be to review the book relative to the objectives stated by the author. The approach in Cell 3 would be to review the book relative to some other objectives or criteria deemed to be more pertinent or significant. The key here is to determine the range of options considered in developing what was to be implemented, and then to judge whether the chosen alternative was the most appropriate. From the perspective of Cell 4, the interest would be to judge whether the impact (outcome) would have been more significant if some other measure had been implemented. The viewpoint taken in Cells 3 and 4 diverges from that reflected in the comments by Pressman and Wildavsky in Box 12.2. They consider that judgements about implementation should only consider actions which follow policy. In other words, they position their view of implementation in Cells 1 and 2.

The value of Table 12.1 is not so much to determine into which cell or category implementation initiatives fit, or whether they fit neatly into one or another cell. More significant is the idea that we should differentiate between outputs and outcomes when considering the (in)effectiveness of implementation. Furthermore, attention to policy intention and problem orientation broadens our outlook, and should encourage us to start any review of implementation by considering the "bigger picture".

12.2.2 Important obstacles for implementation

From the research dealing with implementation, it is possible to identify several major factors which can affect implementation. These include: (1) tractability of the problem, (2) lack of clarity of goals, (3) commitment of those responsible for implementation, (4) resources (means) available to achieve goals (ends), (5) inadequate access to information, (6) inappropriate assumptions about cause–effect relationships, (7) the dynamics of enforcement, (8) conditions specific to developing countries, and (9) different styles due to cultural variations.

(1) Tractability

As already noted in Chapter 4, some problems are more complex than others, leading to their being characterized as "messes" or as "wicked". Thus, the effectiveness of implementation will be influenced by the tractability, or resolvability, of the problem to which the action is addressed. It may be relatively easy to implement a "Greenways" trail system in a community in a developed country. It may be more difficult to reverse soil erosion and other environmental degradation in a developing country as a result of people who, below a subsistence level, are over-harvesting a resource. The latter problem is a symptom of structural poverty and inequity in a society, and increased extension services and information programs focused on land use practices will not by themselves remove the fundamental causes of the environmental degradation.

Tractability is also influenced by the diversity of behaviour to be modified. The greater the diversity, the more difficult it will be to develop responses applicable to all situations, and therefore the less likely that objectives will be realized. For example, water pollution regulations ideally have to match with the circumstances of the thousands of point sources (industrial factories,

---

Box 12.3 Considerations which increase intractability

During the period since the heady days of the 1960s many of the poorer LDCs [less developed countries] have been subject to intense pressure from the world system: commodity prices fell, energy prices rose astronomically, interest payments on debts became a drain on capital resources and the perpetual balance of payments crises, reschedulings and conditionalities focused attention in two areas. The first of these was running faster to stand still (the "White Queen" phenomenon) and the other was the inability to look much beyond tomorrow. Neither of these is conducive to the longer-term perspective of environmental management. In a situation of cutback the conservation budget is often the first to go in an LDC, simply because it does not give a rapid and visible return to the balance of payments.

Source: Baker, 1989: 33–4.

municipal sewage treatment plants) and non-point sources (farms, road surfaces). The same dilemma is encountered for air pollution, when both point sources (factory and household emissions) and non-point sources (automobiles, trucks, trains, airplanes, ships) exist. Variation among the kinds, magnitudes, timing, duration and significance of so many sources "makes the writing of precise overall regulations essentially impossible" (Sabatier and Mazmanian, 1981: 8).

Other factors contribute to increased intractability. The larger the proportion of the population for which behavioural change is needed, or the greater the extent of behavioural change required, the more intractable will be the problem. All of these "tractability factors" contribute to an uneven playing field when comparisons are made regarding the effectiveness of different implementation initiatives. Some problems are fairly straightforward and resolvable. Others are more like a Gordian knot, and may defy all but extraordinary or ingenious solutions.

(2) Lack of clarity of goals

It is much easier to determine implementation "success" if a well-established vision and clearly defined objectives exist. As we saw in Chapter 7, some people believe that sharply defined objectives are most likely to lead to their realization because discretionary interpretation is less likely to distort what was intended. This perspective was called a *programmed approach* in Chapter 7. However, having well-defined goals is not sufficient for successful implementation. It is also important for the priority of objectives regarding resource and environmental management to be established relative to objectives of other policies. Such priority setting is often difficult, since at any given time societies normally pursue multiple objectives (protect biodiversity; create jobs; increase exports). Some of these will conflict with each other, and often there is expectation that some objectives will always prevail over others.

However, we also saw in Chapter 7 that not everyone agrees with the merits of having clear and unambiguous objectives. Those who support an *adaptive approach* argue that some deliberate vagueness and ambiguity are highly desirable, as they allow resource and environmental managers discretion to ensure that policies are implemented with regard to local conditions and needs. Nevertheless, if there is no consensus about what the goals and objectives are, such an approach makes it more difficult to track or monitor the success in implementing policies or programs. This problem will be considered further in Chapter 13.

(3) Lack of commitment

Highly committed and enthusiastic resource and environmental managers are often capable of implementing even poorly crafted or designed policies so that they will provide benefits. In contrast, unmotivated or incompetent people may be unable to implement the most sophisticated and carefully designed policy. Sustained commitment and interest are critical for effective implementation.

Box 12.4 Commitment and leadership

... the variable most directly affecting the policy outputs of implementing agencies, namely, the commitment of agency officials to the realization of statutory objectives.

Source: Sabatier and Mazmanian, 1981: 20–1.

Box 12.5 Sustaining commitment

In general, the commitment of agency officials to statutory objectives, and the consequent probability of their successful implementation, will be highest in a new agency with high visibility that was created after an intense political campaign. After the initial period, however, the degree of commitment will probably decline over time as the most committed people become burned out and disillusioned with bureaucratic routine, to be replaced by officials much more interested in security than in taking risks to attain policy goals.

Source: Sabatier and Mazmanian, 1981: 20.

However, as Weale (1992) indicated, there can be many reasons for an implementing agency to move forward in a reluctant or tentative manner. For example, the governments in both the United States and Britain revealed great reluctance to curtail the contribution from their countries to acid precipitation. One of the main reasons for such reluctance was that the costs of curtailment would be borne in their own countries, while many of the benefits to the environment would accrue to neighbouring countries (Canada in the case of the United States; the Scandinavian countries in the case of Britain). Another reason for hesitation can be conflict with other, higher priorities. A government may be sincerely concerned about environmental degradation, but it could have a greater concern about economic development which could contribute to creation of jobs, regional stability or national security. Or, again, it could be genuinely concerned about the environment, but give higher priority to reducing a national debt or deficit, and therefore be unprepared to allocate the necessary funds to reduce waste emissions, and to begin to rehabilitate degraded areas.

(4) Lack of means

Even if a strong commitment exists to deal with environmental problems, governments often find that they do not have the necessary means or tools to implement the most desirable package of activities. Inadequate means can involve much more than shortages of money. For example, constitutional constraints may limit what can be implemented. In many countries, responsibility for resources and the environment is shared between central and state governments. The result is that joint initiatives are often required. However, if the other level of government with a shared responsibility does not give the same priority to an environmental initiative, it is likely that unilateral implementation will be only partially effective at best. Thus, for example, the German central government has concurrent power for air pollution with the *Wassergenossenschaften* and the *Länder* levels of government, but not the same shared power for water pollution because of unwillingness of the latter levels to give up traditional authority. As a result, more progress has been achieved regarding air pollution than for water pollution.

Political constraints can also be limiting, in that both governments and their public servants have to be sensitive to public expectations and values. Thus, Weale (1992) explained that in Britain the Director-General of the Health and Safety Executive noted that his organization has allocated more resources to regulating the nuclear power industry than the mining and construction industries – notwithstanding the fact that fatality rates are much higher for the latter two industries. However, the public has a higher level of concern about nuclear power, and it would be politically unwise for the Health and Safety Executive not to be seen to allocate substantial resources to the nuclear industry.

Another constraint can be the administrative or institutional structure for implementation. As already discussed in Chapter 3, the design of government agencies only occasionally reflects or matches the holistic character of ecosystems. As in most organizations, government departments are divided and subdivided into parts with specialized functions. This is done to provide focus and to achieve efficiency. However, this division and subdivision of organizations and management functions makes it difficult to maintain a holistic approach. To illustrate, Weale (1992) explained that in the Netherlands, nature

---

Box 12.6 Consequences of administrative fragmentation

… governments can find that one arm of government is unaware of what another arm of government is doing. Just at the time that the UK's environment department was grasping the importance of fossil fuel combustion and global environmental change, the transport department was publishing plans that proposed greatly to expand the motorway system with only the most cursory acknowledgement of their damaging environmental potential. Just at the time that the Dutch environment ministry … was beginning to warn of the adverse environmental implications of increased NO_x emissions from increases in vehicle mileages, so the transport ministry raised the speed limit on motorways.

Source: Weale, 1992: 52.

conservation matters were handled in the ministry responsible for agriculture, while pollution control was allocated to the environmental ministry. One consequence was a difficulty in generating strategic thinking which crossed over nature conservation and pollution issues. As another example, in most countries the regulation of automobiles and other vehicles is done by a transportation agency. While road traffic is a primary non-point source of pollution, however, pollution is not usually the concern of a transportation agency. The outcome of such administrative arrangements can be difficulty in coordination and communication, considerable duplication, and overall loss of efficiency – all of which can be obstacles to implementation.

(5) Access to information

A major problem can occur when different participants do not have access to information. This dilemma often occurs with regard to environmental policy. Officials in regulatory agencies usually do not know the full implications of adopting various pollution-reducing technologies for a specific industry or firm, nor do they always understand the implications of new costs to firms as a result of changed environmental standards. Industries or individual firms often know much more about their waste streams and costs than does the regulator. And the general public usually does not know what type of lobbying occurs behind closed doors between industry and government. As a result, there is not an even playing field for information. Some participants have greater access than others to information, and to the extent that "knowledge is power" may be able to facilitate or frustrate implementation activities. This takes on more significance in the context of Weale's (1992: 55) comment that "implementation is always a process of interpretation in which new information is added or required."

(6) Assumptions about cause–effect relationships

If a policy or program is to have its anticipated impact, there should be understanding of the causal linkages between stated objectives and activities. In many situations, our understanding of biophysical and human systems is inadequate for us to be confident that we understand such cause-and-effect relationships, and therefore to be confident that interventions will produce anticipated effects.

However, even if our understanding of ecological and social systems is good, there is still scope for the outputs or outcomes of implementation to be different from what is expected. One explanation is the concept of *perverse effects*. A good example of this is the effort to implement a coastal protection policy in California. Weale (1992: 56) explained that the policy was effective in protecting visual amenities, but was very inadequate in ensuring access to the resource. The faulty assumption was that planning controls by themselves would be adequate to ensure public access to coastal areas. However, as the comment in Box 12.7 shows, if an adaptive approach is used and we learn from such an error, then gradually management can be improved.

Despite the attractiveness of an ideal of learning from mistakes, such self-

Box 12.7 Learning from mistakes

... opportunities are needed within a policy system to learn from mistakes and to correct policy in the light of experience. In the absence of these opportunities, implementation failures remain unremedied.

Source: Weale, 1992: 57.

correction is not always easy to incorporate. First, there needs to be the willingness within an organization to test assumptions, which requires an approach that encourages self-evaluation and accepts external criticisms. Such conditions are difficult to establish, since most organizations are hesitant to expose themselves to ongoing evaluation by their own officers, their clients, or the public at large.

(7) Dynamics of enforcement

Despite all the concepts and theories that can be brought to bear regarding implementation, most implementation is done by people working at the field level. Such officials can rarely implement policies or procedures in a mechanical way, but instead have to make interpretations and exert judgement. For example, "when dischargers are in breach of limits the inspector has to make a series of judgements as to culpability, intentionality, likelihood of recurrence and so on" (Weale, 1992: 57).

Another complication is that field officers or inspectors are often more oriented towards negotiating to achieve compliance with environmental regulations, rather than only with enforcing rules. It is usual for some latitude to be given to an offender, in the expectation that such consideration will result in future compliance with regulations. An inspector has to decide whether strict enforcement will lead to improved environmental conditions, or may so antagonize business and industry that in the long run it will be more difficult to achieve environmental improvements. Thus, once again, judgement and discretion are involved, so outcomes from implementation may be uneven across a jurisdiction. This situation also indicates that we need to judge the effectiveness of implementation efforts in both the short and the long term. Something which may appear to be ineffective in the short term could well be effective if a longer time perspective is taken. The opposite is also possible. That is, implementation that appears to be very effective in the short term may not turn out to be sustainable.

(8) Factors in developing countries

The seven factors identified above address implementation issues primarily in the context of developed nations. As Smith (1985: 135) has commented, however, while Third World countries have many impressive policies and objectives, there is "immense slippage" in translating the policies into programs and projects. In his words, "many policies remain only symbolic statements by political leaders or laws on statute books, while others that are implemented achieve little of what was originally intended."

Third World countries encounter all the implementation obstacles of their developed country counterparts. In certain respects, however, they also deal with some other, more formidable challenges. By almost any standards of measurement, the problems to be addressed, whether meeting basic needs, alleviating poverty or reversing environmental degradation, are usually of a magnitude and intensity well beyond those of developed countries. As a result, the *tractability* of many problems is almost overwhelming. Using the language of Chapter 4, the problems are wicked, or messes.

Beyond the tractability discussed by Sabatier and Mazmanian, Smith (1985) noted the following problems regarding implementation in developing countries: (1) government bureaucracies which are ineffective, inefficient and not task oriented, (2) managerial leadership skills which are poor, and (3) corruption which is well entrenched. While Smith (1985: 135) recognized that all governments have policies and laws to stop corruption, nevertheless "corruption in some form exists in all political and administrative systems." Numerous reasons can be identified for the presence of corruption, ranging from low salaries for public officials, who are almost forced to seek bribes in order to support their families, to some well-connected senior officials who have opportunities to earn significant incomes through payoffs. These comments do not imply that corruption does not and cannot occur in developed countries. However, the pressures or incentives for corruption often appear to be greater in less developed countries. The outcome is that some initiatives may not get implemented, or will do so only in a token manner, if no supporters provide payoffs to the public officials responsible for their implementation.

(9) Cultural differences

This factor becomes particularly critical in situations involving multilateral approaches to resource and environmental management, in which two or more countries must work together. As Rayner (1991) has commented, capitalist-oriented Kenya and socialist Tanzania may have difficulty in agreeing on measures to implement joint land use controls to protect biodiversity in cross-boundary regions. Implementation may founder or suffer because the two countries have different approaches to resource and environmental management, each of which reflects distinct cultural traditions and practices, or differing ideologies.

Rayner (1991: 96–97) argued that there are three managerial or institutional cultures: market, hierarchical, and collective. Which one dominates in a country will to a large extent reflect cultural norms. To illustrate, he suggested that market-oriented cultures will "favor implementation policies that maximize the discretion of individual decision makers and firms. We may therefore suppose that they will favor carrots rather than sticks." In contrast, societies that emphasize the collective welfare are more likely to emphasize sticks over carrots.

Box 12.8 Expectations can vary

It may make sense to choose a convention or agreement that can be most fully and flexibly implemented, rather than a more stringent agreement that, because it is essentially unenforceable, remains of symbolic rather than instrumental importance. In other circumstances, however, it may be perfectly appropriate to conclude symbolic agreements that cannot be implemented by states, with the intention of encouraging action by nongovernmental institutions (such as industry or voluntary organizations).

Source: Rayner, 1991: 99.

They are likely to prefer "command and control" approaches to implementation procedures, which result in the uniform application of policy with minimal scope for discretion by individual managers of firms because such discretion in principle violates principles of equity. Rayner recognized that cultural preference by itself "will not determine which implementation instrument will be selected." Nevertheless, culturally based preferences may have a strong influence in choice of ends and means, which can cause major difficulties when several countries have to reach agreement on ends and then develop compatible means for implementation.

Summary

The nine obstacles noted above help us to understand why implementation of policies and programs often does not go smoothly, and why unexpected outputs and outcomes occur. Beyond these considerations, it is also necessary to appreciate that judgements will be made about what should and can be accomplished, and policies and implementation procedures may be crafted accordingly, as indicated in the comments in Box 12.8.

12.3 Implementation: waste management in Sweden and France

The strikingly different approaches to high-level nuclear wastes in Sweden and France emphasize that there is no single, correct model for policy development or implementation. It is usually necessary to custom-design policy and practice to fit the needs, conditions and norms of a society. That Sweden and France should have developed different approaches is unlikely to be a surprise. A variety of means or methods can be used to achieve a common end.

Cook, Emel and Kasperson examined the approaches in Sweden and France, and their findings provide the basis for this section. By the early 1990s, Sweden had 12 operating nuclear power plants, which provided 45% of the electricity for the country. In contrast, France had 51 operating nuclear power plants, producing more than 70% of its electricity.

Box 12.9 High-level nuclear waste treatment in Sweden and France

Sweden and France are in many respects in the vanguard of HLW disposal efforts. They have both successfully sited and licensed low-level waste disposal sites. . . . France and Sweden also offer the sharpest contrast in basic waste-management strategies and underlying philosophies regarding nuclear power, research and development, and repository site investigation and selection.

Source: Cook *et al.*, 1991/92: 103.

12.3.1 Sweden

The Ministry of Environment and Energy is responsible for regulating the nuclear power industry, which involves both public and private utilities. Regulations for nuclear power are guided by a statute created in 1977 and a national referendum in 1980. The act specifies that before any new nuclear reactor can be loaded with fuel, there has to be an approved plan for reprocessing spent fuel and for safely storing high-level waste, or a plan for safe storage of unreprocessed spent fuel. The national referendum results confirmed that Swedes wanted to have the existing nuclear reactors dismantled at the end of their useful lifetime. The Swedish parliament, or *Riksdag*, interpreted those results to mean that by 2010 all the nuclear power plants in the country would be decommissioned.

Regarding high-level nuclear wastes, a plan was developed to store spent fuel in water-filled pools for 40 years. The fuel would be placed in copper containers, and then would be buried and covered in a mixture of sand and clay. The target is to have a final repository site opened in 2020 to take unreprocessed spent fuel and reactor core elements. The repository will be located in crystalline bedrock some 500 metres below the surface.

Key elements in the storage plan are disposal at great depth, and containment by long-life engineered barriers. Two principles underlie the storage plan: (1) the onus for final storage should not be on future generations, but future generations should have an opportunity to take such responsibility if they wish; and (2) the design of the repository should make surveillance and maintenance unnecessary, but there should be flexibility to make changes if new knowledge indicates that the design is flawed.

The waste disposal plans have been reviewed by experts and technical organizations both inside and outside Sweden. In the view of Cook *et al.* (1991/92: 105), the result has been that "Sweden's nuclear waste research and development program and its long-range waste disposal plans are perhaps the most advanced, and certainly the most extensively reviewed, of any nation with a nuclear power industry." Sweden also provided for significant input from a broad mix of interest groups, including anti-nuclear groups. This input occurred through what is called a *remiss procedure*, under which any government organization proposing policy changes must allow almost any group to comment. The intent is to ensure that the maximum experience and information are made available and shared. The philosophy behind this approach is that controversies are not best treated as if they occur from misinformation, and that sustained two-way communication between the regulatory agencies and the public must occur. Thus, the regulatory agencies do not view their task as being only to inform the public. The agencies must also listen to the public. This approach reflects some of the basic ideas for dispute resolution which were discussed in Chapter 11.

Such openness and transparency, and willingness to treat non-government groups as real partners, has facilitated acceptance of the high-level waste storage policies in Sweden. The process has not been without controversy, strong views and feelings, and heated argument. However, progress is occurring in what could have been viewed by many as an intractable problem.

12.3.2 France

Following the energy crisis of 1973, France made a conscious policy decision to replace oil with uranium for electricity generating plants, and by the early 1990s over 70% of its power came from nuclear plants. All aspects of the nuclear power industry are overseen by an Atomic Energy Commission which reports to a minister of the French government. France has also become a world leader in the development of facilities for reprocessing spent fuel, and in related waste treatment capability. By emphasizing reprocessing of spent fuel, France has been able to reduce the need for waste disposal facilities. However, it has an active program in which deep geological disposal areas are being investigated.

Cook *et al.* (1991/92) concluded that the underlying philosophy in France is that the safety of high-level radioactive waste disposal is a technical issue, best handled by experts. At the same time, however, the officials accept that citizens have the right to know what is being considered and done about waste management and selection of waste disposal sites, and that citizens should have a significant role in the management of a site after it has been chosen. The differences in the approaches of France and Sweden are identified in Box 12.10.

Cook *et al.* indicated that, at the time of their study, the approaches of Sweden and France to high-level nuclear waste management had not been fully tested. Neither had chosen a geological repository site for deep-level storage, although Sweden had located and built facilities for low- and intermediate-level wastes. However, the purpose of using the example of these two countries is to highlight the fact that both policies and implementation strategies can vary between nations. As a result, there is little point in searching for a universal "implementation model". None exists. The specific needs and characteristics of a society and a place must be considered when determining how best to address the nine obstacles to implementation identified in Section 12.2.2.

Box 12.10 Approaches of Sweden and France to nuclear power

Sweden has a strong tradition of local autonomy in the *kommunes* despite its unitary form of government. The Swedish bureaucracy is omnipresent, but tightly controlled politically. Interest groups have an institutionalized procedure for voicing opposition to government policy decisions through the remiss process, and local governments have a constitutionally protected veto over local land uses that can only be overridden by the *Riksdag*.

France's feudal, Napoleonic, and liberal democratic traditions have combined to produce a powerful, centralized government system. The French bureaucracy is a pervasive influence in France with a strong tradition of social engineering anchored in the *grand corps*, the organizations of technical and administrative experts representing fraternal societies. Local governments and the courts, moreover, are essentially appendages of the civil administration ... interest groups remain quite weak ... and have no effective veto over policy decisions.... The French waste-management strategy is thus in the hands of technocrats and firmly oriented toward "the problem of techniques".

The core difference in nuclear waste-management strategies between the two countries, then, is that scientific, technical and cost considerations have forged the French waste-management strategy and have guided decisions about how to face the social and political implications of nuclear waste disposal. Quite the reverse is evident in Sweden, where the fears and concerns of the citizenry about nuclear power and the need to shape social consensuses are paramount, and the social and political responses to them have guided the scientific and technical decisions at the core of the Swedish waste-management strategy.

Source: from Cook *et al.*, 1991/92: 110–11.

12.4 Implementation: forest management in the United States

Brown and Harris (1992) conducted a study of the United States Forest Service regarding its evolution during the 1980s. A special interest was the capacity for *policy implementation*, or those activities which followed policy directives. In their view, implementation issues required more attention because "well-intentioned policy formulation by no means ensures realization of desired policy outcomes" (Brown and Harris, 1992: 459).

Among other matters, they considered how the values and attitudes of field officers influenced the achievement of the Forest Service goals. Values and attitudes were chosen because they believed that policy makers and implementers often search for, and select, data which reflect their own values, and facilitate implementation of activities consistent with their values. Also, where implementers are given discretion to make choices, or have to make choices because of contradictory directives, it is likely that decisions will reflect basic values and attitudes. Brown and Harris believed that it was normal rather than unusual for policy implementers to have to deal with a "smorgasbord" of goals,

Box 12.11 Implementing the National Forest Management Act

But the official goals established by the NFMA were multiple, conflicting, difficult to put into operation, and difficult to achieve. As a result, the Forest Service has to choose which NFMA goals to implement and pursue, which goals to satisfy, and which goals to displace or substantially ignore; these decisions are reflected in activities that actually get carried out on the ground.

Source: Brown and Harris, 1992: 459.

a situation in which they had to interpret directives, assign priorities and resolve conflicts.

The introduction of the National Forest Management Act in the mid 1970s was greeted as a landmark statute that would help to resolve many conflicts which were being encountered in forest management. However, the act also illustrates a directive which contained multiple and inconsistent signals, forcing implementers to exercise discretion, judgement and choice.

The comments of Brown and Harris highlight the challenges faced by those given responsibility for implementation of the act. Furthermore, if their conclusion that the most controversial and pressing national forest management policy outcomes will be determined by choices made during the implementation process, and that those choices are made by field managers using their discretion, then the values and attitudes of the forest managers become very significant.

During the 1980s, they found that the values of the field forest managers were increasingly challenging the traditionally dominant principle of *timber primary* in the Forest Service. While timber management remained a central and important goal for the Forest Service, more managers were accepting the legitimacy of other goals and interests. More interest was being given to maintenance of healthy ecosystems, and to non-consumptive uses of forests. While this increasingly diverse set of values and mindsets of forestry professionals bodes well for a more balanced approach to management, it also will enhance the conflicts among some of the basic choices that foresters have to make. In the short term, such conflicts may make the implementation process less smooth. In the longer term, however, it should result in the goals, objectives and activities being implemented to reflect the overall mix of interest in late twentieth century society.

12.5 Implementation: integrated catchment management in Australia

During the mid 1980s, the state government of New South Wales introduced the concept of *total catchment management*, which quickly became known as "TCM". The intent was to manage soil, land, water, vegetation and other environmental components together in order to achieve sustainable use and production. Particular emphasis was to be placed on coordination of the

Box 12.12 Total catchment management, New South Wales, Australia, mid 1980s

Total Catchment Management involves the co-ordinated use and management of land, water, vegetation and other physical resources and activities within a catchment, to ensure minimal degradation and erosion of soils and minimal impact on water yield and quality and on other features of the environment.

Specifically, Total Catchment Management aims to –

• encourage effective co-ordination of policies and activities of relevant departments, authorities, companies and individuals which impinge on the conservation, sustainable use and management of the State's catchments, including soil, water and vegetation;

• ensure the continuing stability and productivity of the soils, a satisfactory yield of water of high quality and the maintenance of an appropriate protective and productive vegetative cover; and

• ensure that land within the State's catchment is used within its capability in a manner which retains as far as possible, options for future use.

Source: Cunningham, 1986: 4.

interests, activities and uses of all land users to avoid degradation and/or to facilitate rehabilitation of degraded landscapes. TCM was consistent with an ecosystem approach, as outlined in Chapter 3. A more detailed outline of TCM is given in Box 12.12.

In May 1988, the Australian Water Resources Council co-sponsored a National Workshop on Integrated Catchment Management. Representatives from all the states and territorial governments went to this workshop with proposed policies and strategies for *integrated catchment management*, or ICM, which had become the favoured term for what earlier had been called TCM in New South Wales. At the conclusion of the workshop, delegates voted to indicate which state or territory had developed the best approach. They were unanimous that the team from Western Australia had developed the best proposal for ICM. However, their ideas still had to be implemented. In the remainder of this section, the experience in making the transition from concept to implementation in Western Australia is considered (Mitchell and Hollick, 1993).

The government of Western Australia made some key decisions regarding implementation of ICM. First, implementation would occur through coordination of the policies and activities of existing agencies. Second, a small secretariat would be created to facilitate the desired coordination. Third, priorities would be established.

Thus, no new legislation or new agencies would be created, based on the belief that institutional arrangements in Western Australia were not unduly complex, and that using existing capacity was preferable to creating more bureaucracy. The coordinating mechanism became the Integrated Catchment Management Coordinating Group. This group later was served by a small secretariat called the Office of Catchment Management (OCM). The OCM had very few staff and a modest budget. Finally, Community Catchment Groups were also established to allow local people to become involved in identifying problems and developing solutions. Technical Advisory Groups, consisting of individuals with technical expertise, were established to work in parallel with the Community Catchment Groups.

A review of the experience with implementation was conducted using the six-part framework shown in Figure 12.1 (Mitchell, 1990). The parts of the framework include:

- **Context.** Attention focuses upon historical, cultural, economic and institutional dimensions, as well as the state of the biophysical environment.
- **Legitimation or credibility.** If a policy or program is to be implemented, it receives legitimation through political commitment, statute, financial support or administrative support. Legitimation is strengthened when more than one of these elements is present.
- **Functions.** Decisions must be taken regarding which management functions are to be integrated. Functions can be *generic* (policy development, data collection, planning, development, regulation, enforcement) or *substantive* (water supply,

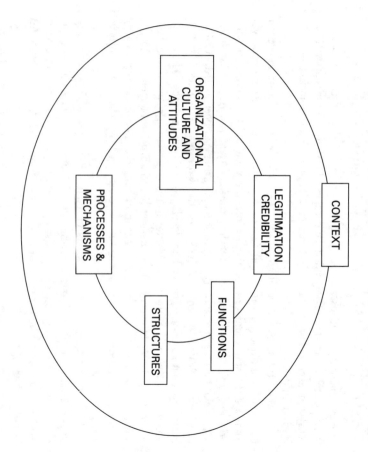

Figure 12.1 Framework for integrated resource management (from Mitchell's work)

ORGANIZATIONAL CULTURE AND ATTITUDES

LEGITIMATION CREDIBILITY

CONTEXT

FUNCTIONS

STRUCTURES

PROCESSES & MECHANISMS

pollution control, flood plain management, wetland management). It is not automatic that all functions should be integrated, and indeed there can be good arguments to separate some of them, such as development and enforcement.

- **Structures.** These involve the number and type of organizations responsible for management functions. They can be few in number and centralized, or more in number and decentralized. How ever they are crafted, there always will be *edge* or *boundary* problems between agencies, which involve areas of overlapping interest and responsibility.

- **Processes and mechanisms.** No matter how well functions and structures are designed, there will be mismatches, or areas of overlap and underlap. Thus, there is a need for processes and mechanisms, such as interdepartmental working groups or public participation, to address edge or boundary issues.

- **Organizational culture and attitudes.** The effectiveness of implementation will usually be strongly influenced by the people who have the responsibility for it, as well as by the *culture* of an organization (does it promote competition or cooperation?) and the *attitudes* of participants (do they strive to share and cooperate?).

These points were used to consider the effectiveness of implementation of ICM in Western Australia.

Regarding *legitimation*, ICM was supported by a state policy, and by creation of an inter-agency coordinating group and a small secretariat (Office of Catchment Management) to support that group. Also, modest resources were provided to help form Community Catchment Groups. However, as with most jurisdictions, the mandates of different line agencies (agriculture, forestry, wildlife, water) often conflicted, and neither the Office of Catchment Management nor the coordinating group had any real power to force competing agencies to resolve their differences. This meant that the OCM and the coordinating group had to rely on persuasion and exhortation, which in many instances fell on inattentive ears.

The *functions* to be integrated were never clearly identified. As a result, while the coordinating group served as a forum to coordinate policies and activities, and had some notable successes, there was no systematic consideration at a state level regarding which functions needed to be integrated, or how that would be done. *Structures* also served as an impediment, as there were well-established line agencies with readily identifiable constituencies (agriculture, water) which seemed more comfortable in protecting long-standing mandates and activities than in actively sharing through joint programs. And, as already noted, because of no strong political commitment, enabling legislation or significant financial support, a good strategy for those opposed to ICM was simply to go slowly and outwait it. This approach, used by some line agencies, was effective as in late 1995 the OCM was terminated, and its responsibilities were assigned to various other agencies.

The inter-agency working group was the principal *mechanism* used to search for coordination and cooperation. A critical ingredient for the success of such committees is that senior representatives of participating agencies attend the meetings on a regular basis. A good way to undermine or undercut such a working group is to send junior or intermediate people who do not have the

Box 12.13 Need for human cooperation

Too often the emphasis is on "amalgamating and restructuring agencies in an attempt to foster cooperation. Not surprisingly, this does not work. The crucial thing is to get people at all levels working together, and you cannot make this happen simply by amalgamating agencies — you still have to do the hard work of fostering cooperation and a team spirit."

Source: Robinson, 1992:4.

---

authority to make commitments on behalf of their organizations, and continuously have to take matters back to their agencies for consultation. When this happens, or when people do not regularly attend meetings, the time taken to make decisions becomes much longer. And, because decisions are not being taken and action is not occurring, this situation can and will be used by participating agencies to suggest that the working group is not effective, and can become sufficient justification for sending even more junior people. Thus, once this pattern starts, it can become self-perpetuating and self-fulfilling.

As important as any of the variables were the *organizational cultures* and *attitudes*. Some senior officers in line agencies were sceptical or antagonistic to the concept of ICM, or to the individuals appointed to the OCM. As a result, where cooperation might have been forthcoming, in many instances it was not. In addition, the agriculture ministry had established Land Care Community Groups in many parts of the state, and was more inclined to devote resources to them than to the Community Catchment Groups. Thus, considerable efforts at developing functions, structures and processes are unlikely to be effective unless there is enthusiasm and willingness to make an integrated approach work.

The experience in Western Australia reflects many of the challenges for implementation identified earlier in this chapter. In addition, it illustrates some of the dilemmas which must be addressed when trying to implement an ecosystem or holistic approach. The task of implementation is not easy, and many difficulties can be encountered.

12.6 Implications

In Chapter 2, it was argued that effective planning and management requires a *vision* (an appreciation of which ends are wanted), a *process* (agreement of means to use in reaching the ends) and a *product* (a strategy or plan to guide the use of means). However, this chapter has emphasized that a fourth essential component is the capacity for *implementation*. If there is not the will and ability to implement, then all the visions, processes and plans are unlikely to achieve desired changes.

Many obstacles can thwart implementation. Indeed, the examples from

Sweden, France, the United States and Australia indicate the challenges which can be encountered during implementation of policies or programs. If implementation failure is not to be like "original sin" (occurring everywhere and being ineradicable), then resource and environmental managers need to be thinking about implementation in parallel with thinking about visions and other matters. Too often it seems to be assumed that implementation will logically follow a well-crafted policy or plan. However, many people and societies are resistant to change, and new policies or policy changes usually imply an intent to change the status quo. If existing interests and institutional inertia are to be overcome, then considerable thought and time must be devoted to the implementation component of resource and environmental management. If such effort is not made, then the likelihood of implementation failure is likely to be very high.

References and further reading

Baker R 1989 Institutional innovation, development and environmental management: an 'administrative trap' revisited, Part I. *Public Administration and Development* 9(1): 29–47

Boehmer-Christiansen S 1994 Policy and environmental management. *Journal of Environmental Planning and Management* 37(1): 69–85

Brekke J 1987 The model-guided method for monitoring program implementation. *Evaluation Review* 11(3): 281–99

Brown G and C C Harris 1992 The United States Forest Service: changing of the guard. *Natural Resources Journal* 32(3): 449–66

Cook B J, J L Emel and R E Kasperson 1991/92 A problem of politics or technique? Insights from waste-management strategies in Sweden and France. *Policy Studies Review* 10(4): 103–13

Courtner H J 1976 A case analysis of policy implementation: the National Environmental Policy Act of 1969. *Natural Resources Journal* 16(2): 323–30

Cunningham G M 1986 Total catchment management – resource management for the future. *Journal of Soil Conservation, New South Wales* 42(1): 4–5

Gardner A 1990 Legislative implementation of integrated catchment management in Western Australia. *Environmental and Planning Law* 7(3): 199–208

Gow D D and E R Morss 1988 The notorious nine: critical problems in project implementation. *World Development* 16(12): 1399–418

Harvey L D D 1995 Creating a global warming implementation regime. *Global Environmental Change* 5(5): 415–32

Hull A 1995 New models for implementation theory: striking a consensus on windfarms. *Journal of Environmental Planning and Management* 38(3): 285–306

Leu W-S, W P Williams and A W Bark 1995 An evaluation of the implementation of environmental assessment by UK local authorities. *Project Appraisal* 10(2): 90–102

Loske R and S Oberthur 1994 Joint implementation under the Climate Change Convention. *International Environmental Affairs* 6(1): 45–58

Mazmanian D A and P A Sabatier (eds) 1981 *Effective policy implementation*. Lexington, D C Heath and Co.

Mitchell B 1990 Integrated water management. In B Mitchell (ed.) *Integrated water management: international experiences and perspectives*. London, Belhaven: 1–21

Implementation

Mitchell B and M Hollick 1993 Integrated catchment management in Western Australia: transition from concept to implementation. *Environmental Management* 17(6): 735–43

Morgan R K 1995 Progress with implementing the environmental assessment requirements of the Resource Management Act in New Zealand. *Journal of Environmental Planning and Management* 38(3): 333–48

Noble J H, J S Banta and J S Rosenburg (eds) 1977 *Groping through the maze*. Washington, DC, The Conservation Foundation

Padgitt S and P Lasley 1993 Implementing conservation compliance: perspectives from Iowa farmers. *Journal of Soil and Water Conservation* 48(5): 393–400

Parikh J K 1995 "Joint" implementation and North–South cooperation for climate change. *International Environmental Affairs* 7(1): 22–41

Pressman J L and A B Wildavsky 1973 *Implementation: how great expectations in Washington are dashed in Oakland*. Berkeley, University of California Press

Rayner S 1991 A cultural perspective on the structure and implementation of global environmental agreements. *Evaluation Review* 15(1): 75–102

Robinson S 1992 Horses for courses are galloping along in WA. *Catchment Matters* 5, September: 4–6

Sabatier P A and D A Mazmanian 1981 The implementation of public policy: a framework of analysis. In D A Mazmanian and P A Sabatier (eds) *Effective policy implementation*. Lexington, D C Heath: 3–36

Sheirer M and E Rezmovic 1983 Measuring the degree of program implementation: a methodological review. *Evaluation Review* 7(5): 599–633

Silva E 1994 Thinking politically about sustainable development in the tropical forests of Latin America. *Development and Change* 25(4): 697–721

Smith T B 1985 Evaluating development policies and programmes in the Third World. *Public Administration and Development* 5(2): 129–44

Somach S L 1993 Closing the policy-practice gap in water resources planning. *Water Resources Update* 90, Winter: 19–22

Wallis R L and S J Robinson 1991 Integrated catchment management: the Western Australian experience. *Environment* 33(10): 231–40

Weale A 1992 Implementation failure: a suitable case for review? In E Lykke (ed.) *Achieving environmental goals: the concept and practice of environmental performance review*. London, Belhaven: 43–63

Wood A 1993 The multilateral fund for the implementation of the Montreal Protocol. *International Environmental Affairs* 5(4): 335–54

Wynne B 1993 Implementation of greenhouse gas reductions in the European Community: institutional and cultural factors. *Global Environmental Change* 3(1): 101–28

Chapter 13

Monitoring and Evaluation

13.1 Introduction

Monitoring can be done in many ways, by members of non-governmental organizations observing and recording changing conditions in their local area, to government-based monitoring programs, to remotely sensed images generated from orbiting satellites. How ever monitoring is conducted, it is usually done for one or more of the following reasons: (1) to assess general environmental conditions, (2) to establish environmental baselines, trends and cumulative effects, (3) to document environmental loading, sources and sinks, (4) to test environmental models and verify research, (5) to determine effectiveness of environmental regulations, (6) to educate the public about environmental conditions, and (7) to provide information for decision making.

Monitoring often focuses upon *describing* changing conditions and *explaining* cause–effect relationships. When assessments of the effectiveness, efficiency or equity of public and private sector initiatives related to changing conditions are included, then an *evaluative* component is added. Evaluation is not always included, as elected and senior government managers are often hesitant to subject themselves to such scrutiny and evaluation.

In the remainder of this chapter, attention focuses on monitoring and evaluation, with regard to *state of the environment reporting and environmental auditing*.

13.2 State of the environment reports

State of the environment reporting emerged during the late 1980s, following recognition that monitoring or tracking of progress was needed if sustainable development was to be achieved. In other words, without monitoring it would be difficult to know whether policies or actions were moving a society towards or away from characteristics consistent with sustainability. As a result, national, provincial or state, and municipal governments began to initiate state of the environment reporting, often as a follow-up to the preparation of a conservation or sustainable development strategy (Nelson, 1995).

State of the environment (SOE) reporting was usually introduced for one or more of the following reasons: (1) to provide early warning signals to decision makers about changing environmental conditions to facilitate policy or institutional changes, (2) to encourage, and ensure, accountability of public

Box 13.1 Monitoring can be done in novel ways: Skywatch surveillance by the Ninety-Nines

Since 1978 in Ontario, Canada, a group of women pilots have donated their time to fly surveillance missions to document violation of environmental court orders by practices which were prohibited but which are continuing. The photographs from the air reveal shapes or patterns that from the ground would be difficult to notice, such as a buried tanker truck which is slowly leaking toxic materials, or illegal dumping pits which have been covered. Air pollution plumes also can be identified.

The women are members of the "Ninety-Nines", a worldwide organization for women pilots formed in 1929 with Amelia Earhart as the founding president. About twenty members of the Toronto chapter fly in the Skywatch surveillance program.

The provincial government rents a Cessna air plane for the pilots, and a surveillance officer from its Ministry of Environment acts as navigator and photographer on the Ninety-Nine flights. On average, a Skywatch team is in the air somewhere over Ontario during half the working days in summer and a quarter of the working days in winter.

The results of this monitoring have been significant. In a court case, the introduction of photographs taken from the air is usually more effective than a verbal description of alleged polluting activity. The outcome has been more successful prosecutions and higher fines. The highest fine to the end of 1995 was $320,000.

Source: based on a report by Cameron Smith, 1996: D6.

Box 13.2 State of the environment reporting defined

The purpose of SOE reporting is to provide timely, accurate and accessible information on ecosystem conditions and trends, their significance and societal responses, emphasizing the use of indicators. This information should increase public understanding and education, and inform priority setting and decision-making about matters related to the environment by providing objective and scientifically valid information. The information should also establish linkages between environmental conditions and socio-economic factors, reflecting the holistic and integrative nature of the relationship that should exist between humans and the environment.

Source: Dovetail Consulting, 1995: 8.

agencies for their decisions and initiatives, (3) to identify inadequate knowledge, and therefore assist in prioritizing research needs, and (4) to sensitize the public about the implications of decisions and actions.

13.2.1 Types of questions addressed in state of the environment reporting

SOE reporting usually includes some mix of four questions, and occasionally will include another three questions (Dovetail Consulting, 1995: 5, 9). Each is considered below.

1. What is happening in the environment?
2. Why is it happening?
3. Why is it significant?
4. What is being done about it?

The third question requires consideration of threats to integrity of ecosystems, human health, and human values and cultures. At this stage, the relationships between environmental, economic and social systems are usually addressed. The fourth question necessitates understanding of ongoing resource and environmental policies, practices and initiatives, and about the information that decision makers require and can use. It is implicit that, when dealing with this question, social and economic considerations are also considered.

5. What has happened since the previous SOE report?
6. What further action should be taken?
7. What conclusions can be reached about the performance of resource and environmental organizations?

The fifth question seeks to identify changes as a result of ongoing degradation, as well as from remediation and rehabilitation efforts. The intent is to document patterns or trends which have resulted from (in)action by planners and managers. In the sixth question, the intent is *normative or prescriptive*, in that the thrust is to recommend interventions to stop or reverse undesirable change, or to enhance desirable change. Consideration of the connections between the state of the environment, and social and economic aspects, is essential here. The sixth question, leading to possible recommendations, begins to take SOE reporting into the "political" realm. As a result, government-generated SOE reports do not usually address this question. Nevertheless, they may strive to provide enough information for individuals or members of non-government organizations to use the SOE material to reach their own conclusions about what needs to be done.

The seventh question is even more "political" than the sixth, and it is only relatively recently that it has begun to be, or been advocated to be, included in SOE reports. For example, the International Union for the Conservation of Nature and Natural Resources (1991: 75) argued that governments should monitor "performance of policy, laws and other institutional arrangements." According to Dovetail Consulting (1995: 6), by the mid 1990s only the Netherlands had included explicit evaluation of government policies and programs in SOE reporting. When it has been included, evaluation is often presented in the form of a "report card", an example of which will be considered in Section 13.2.4.

A final comment about orientation of SOE is that in some countries the practice has evolved from SOE (state of the environment) to SOS (state of sustainability) reporting. This shift partially reflects the agreement at the Earth Summit during 1992 that all countries endorsing *Agenda 21* were obliged to provide regular reports regarding progress in achieving sustainable development. SOE reporting emphasizes the natural environment, and considers social and economic systems only to the extent that they have direct implications for the environment. In contrast, SOS reporting allocates equal attention to social, economic and environmental systems, and to the relationships between them.

13.2.2 Types, spatial focus and target audiences of SOE reports

The *type* of SOE reporting can vary, with at least four different types being produced. They include SOE reports which are (1) comprehensive (national, state, city), (2) sectoral (forests, agriculture, water, fisheries), (3) issue-based (global change, wastes) and (4) indicator-based (air quality, water quality). The most common SOE reports have a sectoral or issue orientation. The comprehensive type has been the least often produced, probably because of the many challenges of integrating all the components that need to be included. Another way of characterizing SOE reporting is by the type of analytical model used. A *stress–response* model is often used. This model directs attention to indicators of either human or environmental stress, and the way in which people and societies respond to such stresses (or to opportunities).

The *spatial focus* can also vary. SOE reports can be based on either a political or an administrative region, or on a natural area or bioregion. The appeal of using political or administrative regions is that if the SOE reporting is to provide information for decision making, such decisions are normally taken by elected people who are accountable to constituents who live in politically or administratively defined areas. On the other hand, many resource and environmental issues do not respect human-made boundaries, and in such instances use of other spatial units may be more sensible, as long as there is decision-making capacity which relates to such natural units. There appears to be increasing use of an ecosystem approach in SOE reporting, as that often facilitates consideration of environmental processes, patterns and relationships.

The choice of *target audience* is an important decision, since that should influence the type of information assembled and the manner in which it is reported. So far, most SOE reports have been aimed at what might be called the "informed public" and "decision makers". However, many SOE reports are designed with a more general educational purpose in mind, and then decisions have to be taken regarding what age group and educational level is the primary target.

13.2.3 Indicators

Developing a set of environmental indicators for a region, a sector or an issue ideally requires a partnership approach in which the experience and knowledge

Box 13.3 SOE indicators

State of the Environment (SOE) reporting provides continuous assessments of environmental conditions and trends. . . . Because the environment is a complex system of interrelated components, there is no easy way to assess or measure the state of the environment. There are currently thousands of environmental data parameters, captured as part of baseline inventory and survey programs by environmental, natural resource and socioeconomic agencies. Consequently, it is difficult to assimilate and interpret the masses of environmental data available. **SOE indicators are key measures** that must represent the state of the environment and that collectively provide a comprehensive profile of environmental quality, natural resource assets, and agents of environmental change.

Source: Gélinas, 1990: 3 (emphasis in the original).

of the public and private sectors, and the local people, can be combined. Many believe that the success of state of the environment reporting is determined to a considerable extent by the choice of indicators. Indicators must be both meaningful and understandable. Sophisticated indicators which cannot be understood or interpreted by users are unlikely to result in effective monitoring of environmental conditions and trends.

Using a modification of the ideas of Gélinas (1990: 3), a set of indicators should be able to:

- translate and synthesize complex scientific or experiential data into understandable information that can be communicated effectively to users;
- enhance appreciation and understanding of how and why an environment is changing;
- influence decisions taken by elected officials, technical experts, the media and the public;
- provide a measure of quality of life for an area or people, and serve as a measure of progress towards sustainable development or other objectives; and
- become a departure point to evaluate the effectiveness of policies, programs, projects or other activities and initiatives.

13.2.4 Examples of state of the environment reporting

Forestry

The Canadian Council of Forest Ministers has developed six criteria and related indicators to help achieve sustainable forest management (see Box 13.4 for details of sustainable forest management principles). The six criteria are: (1) conservation of biological diversity, (2) maintenance and enhancement of forest ecosystem condition and productivity, (3) conservation of soil and water resources, (4) forest ecosystem contributions to global ecological cycles, (5)

Box 13.4 Principles for sustainable forest management in Canada

(1) Managing forests as ecosystems;
(2) Integrating environmental, socioeconomic and cultural benefits and values, and institutional arrangements to formulate and implement appropriate policies and programs and to monitor their effectiveness;
(3) minimizing impairment and avoiding unacceptable disturbance to forest ecosystems as a result of human activity within forests (e.g., inappropriate harvesting practices) and outside forests (e.g., airborne pollutants; and
(4) involving Canadians in determining how their forests are used.

Source: Environment Canada, 1995a: 2.

multiple benefits to society, and (6) accepting society's responsibilities regarding sustainable development.

One set of indicators relates to timber harvesting in general, as a result of growing concern about the impacts of harvesting on forest ecosystems, and its capacity to generate the broader mix of benefits and values that society desires. The indicators were designed to provide insight about human activities, environmental conditions, ecological and socio-economic effects, and societal response regarding the magnitude of the harvest, socio-economic implications, and changes to the ecosystem (Figure 13.1). More specifically, the indicators help managers to answer the following types of questions: Are forests being managed to provide a long-term supply of timber? Is the capacity of the forest ecosystem for renewal being impaired by timber harvesting practices? Will the forests be able to provide the wide mix of benefits over the long term that society increasingly expects? Figure 13.2 provides examples of two of the indicators: (a) natural disturbance trends, and (b) regeneration after harvesting.

The Fraser River basin in British Columbia, Canada, covers about one-quarter of the province, and contains about two-thirds of its population (Figure 13.3, page 270). Rapid population growth, a changing economy and degradation of the resource and environmental base led the federal, provincial and municipal governments, in conjunction with First Nations people, non-government organizations and the private sector, to develop a sustainability strategy for the basin.

One of the components of the strategy was an assessment of the "State of the Fraser Basin" (Fraser Basin Management Program, 1995b). A state of the basin report was intended to help provide information that could answer the question as to whether practices and activities in the basin were becoming more sustainable. The report addressed a mix of issues, ranging from population change and the economy and forests, water, fisheries, aboriginal people, planning processes and decision making. Thus, it fits into the category of a *comprehensive* state of sustainability report. Each issue was considered with regard to four aspects: (1) significance, (2) baseline information and trends, (3) issue

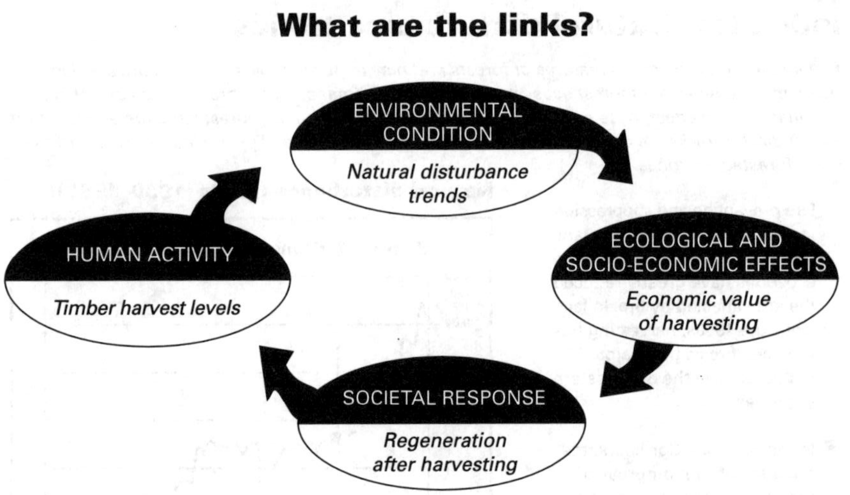

What are the links?

Figure 13.1 Framework for sustainable forestry indicators in Canada (Environment Canada, 1995b: 1)

definition and responses, and (4) signs of progress, and areas in which further work is required. The 114-page report, with considerable data and technical comments, appears oriented to an audience of managers and decision makers.

To disseminate the findings to a broader audience, the Fraser Basin Management Program (1995a) also released what it called a *Board Report Card*, in which progress towards sustainability in the basin was presented. For each of the major issues addressed in the technical report, the report card provides a definition of the issue, an outline of responses, highlights of positive and bad news, and recommendations for further initiatives. Most summaries for each issue received a letter grade of A, B, C, D or F (two examples are shown in Figure 13.4, pages 272–3). High grades were allocated for situations in which measurable results of positive progress were available. Middle grades indicated situations in which procedures had been developed to address the issues, but no results had emerged. Low grades were given when little or no progress towards sustainability had been achieved, and where introduction of new initiatives (e.g. policies, laws) appeared to be a low priority. Each grade reflected the *overall* performance in the entire basin, therefore sometimes masking exceptional progress or the lack of progress in a particular part of the basin.

Implications

The two examples related to indicators for forestry and water management illustrate different ways in which monitoring can be used. The forestry indicators are oriented to a more technical or professional audience. In the Fraser River basin, a technical report presented detailed information for specialists, but also provided a report card to popularize the results. The Fraser River basin SOS report also illustrates a comprehensive kind of monitoring, whereas the

Indicator: Natural disturbance trends

Fire and insects are natural features of forests and play important roles in the health, species diversity, and renewal of forest ecosystems. Thus, forest management practices to control fire and insects may affect these natural ecosystem processes, changing forest structure and function. This indicator tracks the change in total forestland area affected by fire and insects in four of the main forested ecozones.

▼ Fire prevention and suppression in the Pacific Maritime, Montane Cordillera, and Atlantic Maritime ecozones have greatly reduced the area affected by fire. In fact, since the 1950s, harvesting has replaced fire as the major disturbance in the two western ecozones.

▼ In the Montane Cordillera, the most significant outbreak of mountain pine beetle, an insect that targets lodgepole pine, started during the early 1970s and increased rapidly in the early 1980s. Chemical controls and salvage cutting were used to minimize the spread of the beetle.

Natural disturbance trends (1930–1992)

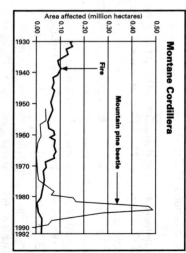

(a)

Figure 13.2 Indicators for timber harvesting: (a) natural disturbance trends; (b) regeneration after harvest (Reproduced from Environment Canada, State of the Environment Reporting Program, National Environmental Indicators Series. SOE Bulletin No. 95–4, Summer 1995, 1995b)

13.3 Environmental auditing

In order to prepare a vision and a policy for an organization, public or private, it is important to identify relevant environmental issues. Eckel, Fisher and Russell (1992: 18) suggested that two principal methods can be used for

forestry information is an example of a sectoral report. The Fraser Basin report covered all seven of the questions identified earlier, whereas the forestry indicators focused on the first four. These different characteristics indicate that there is not one correct model for monitoring or state of the environment reporting. There are choices, and resource and environmental managers have to decide which mix is most appropriate for their needs and situation.

Indicator: Regeneration after harvest

The public is concerned that forests are disappearing because trees are not being replaced as rapidly as they are being cut. This indicator shows the relative success of replacing commercial timber after harvesting. Delays in regenerating harvested areas to commercial species can reduce the long-term timber supply.

▶ The total area successfully regenerated increased 10-fold between 1975 and 1992, while the area not successfully regenerated peaked at 2.9 million hectares in 1991.

▶ An intensive planting effort in the 1980s concentrated on reforesting the backlog of areas that had not regenerated, and probably accounts for the increase in area successfully regenerated in 1992 (see inset).

▶ Today, foresters generally rely on two-thirds of the harvested area to regenerate naturally.

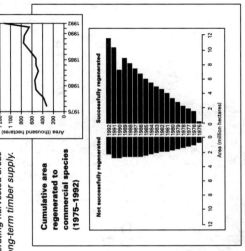

Cumulative area regenerated to commercial species (1975–1992)

Annual area successfully regenerated to commercial species (1976–1992)

Note: Data on regeneration represent Crown land only.

Source
Natural Resources Canada, Canadian Forest Service, Ottawa, Ontario, Canada.

(b)

Figure 13.2 (continued)

identifying such issues: consulting with stakeholders, and environmental auditing. Stakeholder consultation was addressed in Chapter 8; environmental auditing is examined here.

Environmental auditing emerged during the 1980s, and is increasingly being done as public agencies and private firms strive to be more efficient and cost-effective. Another motivation has been to demonstrate that *due diligence* has been practised. In other words, organizations need to be able to establish that they have systematically examined the environmental implications of their activities, and have taken what would be considered to be reasonable measures to avoid negative impacts. As Dunn (1995: 1–2) has indicated, environmental audits can be conducted to achieve one or more of the following purposes: (1) assess regulatory compliance, (2) assess environmental risks, (3) assist facility managers to improve performance, (4) identify waste reduction opportunities, (5) identify cost saving potentials, (6) demonstrate due diligence, and (7) improve public image.

Eckel *et al.* (1992) noted that environmental auditing requires a team which includes more people than those with accounting expertise. The actual mix will vary depending upon the situation, but could easily include some combination of engineers, lawyers, natural scientists and social scientists. The audit can be

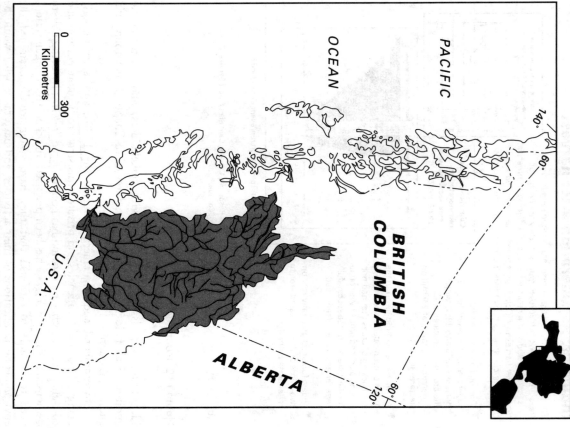

Figure 13.3 Fraser River basin, British Columbia, Canada (Dorcey and Griggs, 1991: 3)

completed by a team internal to the organization, or by external consultants. Normally, a mix of internal and external people is required to ensure a balance of people who understand the activities of the organization, and also have the necessary auditing expertise. Finally, the time horizon is usually very short, as noted in the comment in Box 13.7. In the following subsections, some strategic aspects of environmental audits are considered, and then an example of an audit will be given.

Box 13.5 Report card for the Fraser River basin

Schools have been using report cards for decades to track students' progress. The Fraser Basin Management Board is adopting this useful tool to evaluate progress towards sustainability in the Fraser Basin. Our report card assigns a grade to certain issues, pointing out where we've done well and where we need to do better.

Ian Waddell, Chair, Fraser Basin Management Board

Source: Fraser Basin Management Program, 1995a: 2.

13.3.1 Establishing scope and objectives

One of the first tasks is to determine the scope and objectives for the audit. Regarding the scope, decisions have to be taken about several dimensions, including: (1) spatial scale (building, factory site, region, country), (2) operating unit (group, department, division, entire firm), (3) environmental considerations (water quality, air quality, solid and hazardous wastes), (4) land and vegetation, (5) environmental management systems, and (6) worker health and safety. The mix of considerations will have implications for the kind of expertise and time required to complete the audit.

For objectives, two general aspects require attention. First, the purpose of the audit needs to be established. That is, whether a site is to be developed for residential or heavy industry use will have implications for the standards that should be considered. However, even if the use is clearly specified, further decisions may be required. For example, if a site with contaminated soils is to be used for heavy industry, the nature of the audit could be different depending upon whether the intent is to leave the soil in its present state, or to surface the area with asphalt or concrete. If the latter choice is made, and it has been determined that the contaminants in the soil are unlikely to move off the site, then the questions to be asked and information to be collected during the audit will be different than if it is thought that the soil should be excavated or "cleaned up".

Once decisions have been made about the purpose of the audit, then it is possible to decide which criteria will be used to guide the audit. Normally, more than one set of criteria might apply. As Dunn (1995: 5) indicated, the audit criteria could include one or more of the following: (1) government regulations, (2) permits and approvals, (3) municipal or regional bylaws, (4) government guidelines, (5) internal policies and procedures, (6) institutional guidelines (e.g. World Bank, commercial bank), (7) industry standards (e.g. ISO standards), (8) industry guidelines, or (9) generally accepted good environmental practices. The final point needs some elaboration. Many firms seek to operate well above minimum thresholds or guidelines established by government regulations, as they do not want to risk being closed down owing to a low-probability but high-impact event. Thus, a judgement is involved regarding

Monitoring and evaluation

Water Resources – Non-Point Source Pollution

The Issue:

- Non-point source pollution is associated with a variety of land-based human activities such as agriculture, forestry, motor vehicle use, urban development and mining.
- Water quality objectives and criteria have not been met in some waterbodies close to agricultural activities (e.g., Williams Lake, Sumas River and Matsqui River).
- Pesticides use more than doubled in the Basin between 1970 and 1990.
- Many municipalities do not collect and treat storm water.

Responses:

- New iniatives such as the paint recovery program, code of Agricultural Practice, the Forest Practices Code and integrated pest management are addressing specific non-point source pollution.
- Federal and provisional government agencies have begun working together on a strategy to address non-point source pollution.
- The federal government's Fraser River Action Plan is in the final stages of implementing an Operational Plan for reducing combined sewer overflows (CSO) to Burrard Inlet. The $2 million plan will reduce annual CSO discharges to Burrard Inlet by an average of over 30%.
- The Greater Vancouver Regional District (GVRD) is in the final stages of funding studies on the environmental effects of urban and agricultural runoff in Basin tributaries (e.g., Brunette and Sumas Rivers).

Good News:

- Source-reduction programs have helped reduce non-point source pollutants (e.g., the magnitude of the problem is not well understood.
- Participation in integrated pest management is increasing and leading to less reliance on chemical pesticides.
- Codes of practice for agriculture and forestry should begin to reduce pollution from those activities.

Bad News:

- Because data on non-point source pollution is limited, the magnitude of the problem is not well understood.
- The dispersed nature of non-point source pollutants makes them difficult to regulate and manage.
- Urban runoff continues to increase as development and road-building increases.
- Many Basin residents are not aware that chemicals used on lawns and gardens, and waste anti-freeze and oil, are significant non-point source pollutants.

Progress towards addressing non-point source pollutants: **C–**

- Source-reduction programs have helped reduce non-point source pollutants (e.g., lead concentrations in the Fraser Estuary have decreased 60% from 1985 to 1992 as a result of restrictions on leaded gasoline).

Next Steps:

- Non-point source polluters to adopt codes or guidelines to reduce discharges
- Provincial and federal governments to produce a non-point source pollution strategy and action plan and carry out a public and stakeholder review of the strategy
- Provincial government to follow through on its commitment to update the inventory of pesticide use in 1995 and work towards achieving the goal of 25% reduction by 2001
- Public to reduce use of chemical pesticides and fertilizers on their lawns and gardens

Figure 13.4 Samples of report card grades for the Fraser River basin (Fraser Basin Management Program, 1995a: 6, 7)

Water Resources – Lower Mainland Municipal Sewage Wastes

Progress towards upgrading Annacis and Lulu Island Wastewater Treatment Plants

The Issue:

- Municipal sewage wastes constitute the largest volume of point-source liquid wastes entering the Basin: approximately one million cubic metres of treated effluent are discharged daily into the Fraser River and Georgia Strait.
- 93% of all municipal sewage wastes in the Basin originate in the lower Fraser where sewage receives only primary treatment. Upper and middle Fraser municipalities provide secondary treatment for sewage wastes.
- Effluents from Greater Vancouver Regional District (GVRD) wastewater treatment plants are frequently in non-compliance with provincial waste management permits for certain parameters and with regulations under the federal Fisheries Act.

Responses:

- The GVRD is committed to upgrading the Annacis Island and Lulu Island wastewater treatment plants to secondary treatment by 1999, subject to financing.
- Federal, provincial and local governments have provided $207 million for upgrading through the Canada/BC Infrastructure Program.
- The GVRD and the provincial government have committed an additional $70 million for upgrading the two wastewater treatment plants on a 50/50 basis.

Good News:

- The GVRD has made a commitment to upgrade wastewater treatment plants in the lower Fraser and some funds have been allocated.
- 90% of the design for secondary sewage treatment has been completed by the GVRD.

Bad News:

- While federal, provincial and GVRD governments debate who will pay for upgrading sewage treatment, salmon and other aquatic species are being subjected to sewage wastes that have received only primary treatment.

Next Steps:

- Federal, provincial and local governments to cooperate and develop a new cost-sharing agreement and a practical time schedule for upgrading both the Annacis Island and Lulu Island wastewater treatment plants
- GVRD and the provincial government to explore policies on reducing volumes of sewage
- GVRD to introduce education material designed to reduce generation of sewage

Figure 13.4 (continued)

what corporate practices will be followed with reference to external regulations or guidelines. The key point to recognize is that the audit criteria are not set in stone and are not absolute. They can vary from situation to situation, and usually involve judgement by planners and managers.

Box 13.6 What is environmental auditing?

A systematic process of objectively obtaining and evaluating evidence regarding a verifiable assertion about an environmental matter, to ascertain the degree of correspondence between the assertion and established standards and criteria, and then communicating the results to the client.

Source: Canadian Standards Association, 1994: 2.

13.3.2 Performance measures and indicators

After the scope and objectives have been established, decisions must be taken regarding what measures and indicators will be used to determine whether or not objectives are being achieved. In conjunction with such measures and indicators, there must also be capacity to monitor performance, to ensure evaluation of the results, and to modify either the objectives or the performance in the light of the monitoring and assessment.

Eckel *et al.* (1992: 20) argue that performance measures should have several characteristics. They should be able to (1) reflect cause-and-effect relationships by being based on well-accepted and verifiable theories regarding the links between actions and outcomes, (2) be as measurable and quantifiable as possible, to minimize ambiguity in interpretation of results or recommended corrective actions, and (3) reinforce one another. The recommended procedure is to use indicators which highlight both *inputs* and *outputs*. In this way, it is usually possible to determine whether difficulties in realizing objectives are due to the manner in which the recommendations are being implemented (see Chapter 12).

Input indicators

Many indicators for inputs are available, and include the following: (1) presence of an external member of the board of directors chosen because of environmental expertise, (2) approval of capital and operating expenditures for environmental concerns, (3) creation of an environmental affairs unit or department, (4) establishment of a community advisory committee, or community outreach programs related to environmental issues, (5) presence of recycling activities,

Box 13.7 Time frame

Because the audit assesses performance, it is impossible to look into the future, and it is impractical and irrelevant to look far into the past. Typically, the audit will examine performance over a time period of three years or less.

Source: Dunn, 1995: 5.

and (6) provision of employee education programs regarding environmental management.

Use of such indicators helps to establish the commitment of the organization to dealing with environmental problems, and thereby the degree to which legitimation or credibility has been given to environmental concerns. However, inputs by themselves do not ensure desired outputs or outcomes. The fact that a member of the board of directors is selected for environmental expertise will have little effect if that board member is not actively involved on the board, does not have influence or "clout" with other board members, or has not pushed for initiatives which actually affect environmental performance. Again, education programs by themselves do not ensure that the employees actually learn what is taught, or are given opportunity to apply their new environmental knowledge. It is for this reason that good audits use both input and output indicators.

Output indicators

As with inputs, there are many possible indicators for outputs. Some of these include: (1) volume and types of materials processed by internal and waste recycling programs, (2) volume and types of waste generated and treated, (3) measures of efficiency, energy conservation, and rates of spoilage for products and production processes, (4) air emission rates for contaminants, (5) water quality concentration measures, (6) volume of pesticides or other hazardous chemicals used, (7) monetary value of damages to the natural and social environments, (8) frequency with which applicable legal or regulatory requirements are exceeded, (9) number, kind and volume of hazardous or toxic spills, (10) number and type of environmentally related complaints received from stakeholders, and (11) number and kind of environmental liabilities, lawsuits or unethical business practices.

Implications

The indicators for outputs are selected to provide evidence of whether an organization's environmental policies and objectives are being realized, and whether they satisfy regulations. In this manner, when the answer is affirmative, an organization can claim that it is practising *due diligence* or *due care*, and is doing everything that could reasonably be expected. However, while some of the output indicators are relatively easy to define, others are much more difficult to put into practice. Furthermore, whether or not indicators are easy to define, obtaining information for some of them can be a major challenge. This situation, usually more common with output than with input indicators, is a main reason why audits often focus on inputs. As already noted, however, while it is often possible with input indicators to determine whether or not they are present, it is much more difficult to establish a cause-and-effect relationship with desired outcomes. For this reason, wherever possible it is good practice to use indicators for both inputs and outputs.

Box 13.8 Using indicators

Existing accounting and financial systems are particularly designed to focus on input measures, such as expenditures on environmental research and development, waste disposal, and site remediation, or disclosure of the extent of environmental liabilities and contingencies. While these systems may provide information on efficiency and productivity measures, they concentrate on financial performance rather than broader environmental performance issues.

Source: Eckel *et al.*, 1992: 21.

13.3.3 Environmental audit model for First Nations

In 1993, an environmental audit was completed for the First Nations or aboriginal people who live on Walpole Island, at the mouth of the St Clair River, where it enters Lake St Clair in Ontario. The total area of Walpole Island and several smaller islands is 350 square kilometres, and almost 7,000 hectares or 48% of the area is marshland, making it the largest and probably the most significant wetland in the entire Great Lakes system. Walpole Island is also downstream of the chemical companies near Sarnia, which have become known as "chemical valley". Long-term disposal of wastes, which have gradually been curtailed, and still occurring accidental spills (averaging one a week) into the river have degraded the environment and posed a threat to the well-being of people and other living species.

Based on the 1993 audit experience, the Walpole Island Heritage Centre and Chreod Ltd developed an environmental audit model that could be used by other First Nations people. That model is outlined below. It should be noted that in September 1995, the Walpole Island Heritage Centre was one of 50 organizations from around the world to receive an award from the Friends of the United Nations for its community-level work regarding sustainable development.

The Walpole Island Heritage Centre and Chreod Ltd (1995) suggested that most environmental audit reports should have three distinct sections: (1) setting and context, (2) analysis of individual environmental elements, and (3) synthesis and recommendations. The audit report should highlight distinctive features as

---

Box 13.9 What is an environmental audit?

The phrase "environmental audit" means different things to different people. Here it means a report on the relationship of a First Nation to its environment and resource base, that identifies current problems and needs, and that can be used as a basis for planning a sustainable future for the First Nation.

Source: Walpole Island Heritage Centre and Chreod Ltd, 1995: 1.

well as potential environmental or other conflicts, provide a bibliography or list of sources on which audit statements are based so that further information can be obtained, and identify gaps in knowledge and understanding that need to be filled if a sustainable relationship between people and their environment is to be achieved. Each of the three main sections is outlined in more detail below.

(1) Setting and context

Information should be provided on the *physical setting* of the area regarding its landscape, climate, vegetation and water, on its *population and society*, with particular regard to changes in numbers of people, age structures, settlement patterns, employment and health; and on its *history and political context*.

(2) Analysis of individual environmental elements

As with many impact assessments, the model provides a checklist for possible environmental elements to be considered. It is recommended that the audit should review the adequacy and significance of information which is available, noting where gaps are present. The checklist includes the following elements.

- *Solid and liquid wastes.* Solid waste collection and disposal systems; separation of hazardous, recyclable and residual wastes; type of landfill and other disposal sites; long-term adequacy of present systems; feasible alternatives; types of sewage systems, proportion of population serviced by different sewage systems, maintenance information and needs; implications for wildlife and human health; available public health data.

- *Water supply.* Systems in use (individual, collective); sources (surface or ground water); treatment; quality monitoring; sources of contaminants and prospects for improvement; long-term adequacy of present and alternative systems.

- *Air quality.* Air pollution from local and distant sources; types and adequacy of data; implications for public health and plant and animal life (including agriculture).

- *Toxic dumps and other contaminated sites.* Location and condition of known or suspected toxic sites (including earlier or currently uncontrolled dumps and landfills, underground storage tanks); sources external to the area under audit affecting air, surface waters or ground water; potential or known health hazards; plans or need for removal or remediation.

- *Natural hazards and other dangers.* Nature and frequency of the hazard (riverine or lake flooding, forest fires, tornadoes); risk of accidents or other dangers from human activity (release of toxic material from train derailment or traffic accident); potential for damage to humans and local environment; opportunity for hazard avoidance or risk reduction; adequacy of emergency planning.

- *Agriculture.* Kinds and character of activity (crops, owner-operated or rented, size of units); tillage practices; use of fertilizers and pesticides; known or potential impacts on soils, watercourses and adjacent areas; evidence of soil erosion; long-term sustainability.

- *Forests.* Extent, character and ownership; existence and implementation of long-term management plans; fire protection; liability from pests and diseases; value of forests for associated flora and fauna.

- *Fish and wildlife resources.* Character of and significance for economy and society;

recent and long-term trends (declining, recovering, sustainable); vulnerability to persistent and bioaccumulating contaminants; implications for human health; long-term plans and prospects.

- *Important habitats, species and sites.* Knowledge about or probability of rare or endangered species or habitats within the area; data or information about archaeological or historic sites; vulnerability of sites and species to natural erosion or development plans (roads, water and sewage systems); long-term plans and prospects.

- *Knowledge, education and systems for sustainability.* Knowledge and documentation, based on both traditional and scientific sources, about the environment and resource base; extent to which such knowledge is accessible; level of commitment by leaders to sustainability (measured by policy statements and actions, voluntary recycling); incorporation of sustainability and environmental protection in development planning; access to professional expertise.

This checklist of environmental elements provides a systematic way for an audit team to identify potentially significant matters for a First Nations area. A similar or modified checklist could be developed for any site, region or firm.

(3) Synthesis and recommendations

An audit for an area or region could involve collection of substantial information regarding input and output indicators. The final section of an environmental audit report, therefore, should systematically identify the key linkages between the environment and the people living there. Furthermore, it can usually be expected that numerous opportunities for improvement will be identified, and thus there may be many recommendations. However, it is not sufficient to provide a list of recommendations. If that is done, a likely result is that the recipients of the report will decide that they "can tackle only a few of the recommendations, with those selected being chosen more on the basis of simplicity or available funding than because of urgency or overall importance" (Walpole Island Heritage Centre and Chreod Ltd, 1995: 19). The most useful way to present recommendations is outlined in Box 13.10.

The above discussion illustrates how important monitoring, through state of the environment or state of sustainability reports, can be for environmental audits. Environmental audits require systematic data about inputs and outputs significant for environmental management, and SOE or SOS reports often contain such data. In many situations, however, an environmental audit team will draw upon SOE or SOS data but will have to collect other information to document the extent to which an organization is achieving its environmental policies, goals and objectives, and the extent to which it is complying with any external regulations or expectations.

13.4 Implications

In this chapter, attention has focused upon state of the environment reports and environmental audits. Other kinds of monitoring can be and have been done in

Box 13.10 Presentation of recommendations

The auditor . . . needs to offer recommendations with some indication of relative importance and priority, and the reasons for these priorities. One way is to offer a small number of formal "recommendations", covering the key needs and inadequacies, with less important matters offered as "suggestions". Of course, the First Nations may not agree with the priorities indicated by the auditor, but the main reason for conducting an environmental audit is to provide an overall view of a complex situation; the auditor's advice on what are the key elements of that situation is an essential part of the audit.

Source: Walpole Island Heritage Centre and Chreod Ltd, 1995: 19.

resource and environmental management. For example, a need exists to track the perceptions, attitudes and values of people and societies over time. Such tracking is not often done, and yet if there is to be an attempt to shift basic values it seems sensible that planners and managers should know current perspectives and how they are evolving. In addition, there is a need to monitor and evaluate resource and environmental policies and programs. There is a tradition of such research in resource and environmental management, and some of the references at the end of this chapter provide an entry point to examine this type of monitoring and evaluation.

State of the environment reporting and environmental auditing also highlight conceptual and methodological issues which must be addressed. The scope and objectives need to be clarified, as they have major implications for the kind of information that will be collected. Also, we have become aware that choices need to be taken between the mix of data regarding inputs and outputs. While ultimately we are most interested in outcomes, it is often the case that inputs are easier than outputs to measure. As a result, indicators of inputs tend to be used most frequently in monitoring or audits. An important research need is to develop more output indicators that are conceptually and operationally sound.

Monitoring and assessment considerations are similar to implementation. Too often, resource and environmental managers do not give them enough attention, preferring to focus on the specification of ends and means. However, if we are unable to implement or to track what is happening, then it is difficult to determine if we are on the desired path. In the future, an opportunity and challenge will be to determine how local citizens' groups and non-government organizations can become more involved in monitoring and assessment. Many governments are reducing their activities, and partnerships for monitoring and assessment offer opportunities to maintain capacity for tracking progress, even at a time of fewer financial resources.

References and further reading

Adams W M 1991 Large scale irrigation in northern Nigeria: performance and ideology. *Transactions of the Institute of British Geographers* New Series 16: 287–300

Adams W M 1993 Development's deaf ear: downstream users and water releases from the Bakolori dam, Nigeria. *World Development* 21(9): 1405–16

Barrett B F D 1995 From environmental auditing to integrated environmental management: local government experience in the United Kingdom and Japan. *Journal of Environmental Planning and Management* 38(3): 307–31

Benarie M 1988 Delphi and Delphi-like approaches with special regard to environmental standard setting. *Technological Forecasting and Social Change* 33(2): 149–58

Bromley R and M Coulson 1991 GIS in British Local Government: the benefits to resource management and planning. In L Worrall (ed.) *Spatial analysis and spatial policy using Geographic Information Systems*. London and New York, Belhaven Press: 38–61

Brown G and C C Harris 1992 The United States Forest Service: changing of the guard. *Natural Resources Journal* 32(3): 449–66

Cahill L B (ed.) 1984 *Environmental audits*. Third Edition, Rockville, MD: Government Institutes Ltd

Canadian Institute of Chartered Accountants 1992 *Environmental auditing and the role of the accounting profession*. Toronto, Canadian Institute of Chartered Accountants

Canadian Standards Association 1994 *Guidelines for environmental auditing: statement of principles and general practices*. Publication Z75194, Rexdale (Toronto), Canadian Standards Association

Canter L W 1993 The role of environmental monitoring in responsible project management. *Environmental Professional* 15(1): 76–87

Cheremisinoff P N and N P Cheremisinoff 1993 *Professional environmental auditor's guidebook*. Park Ridge, NJ, Noyes Publications

Chipeniuk R 1993 Vernacular bio-indicators and citizen monitoring of environmental change. In J G Nelson, R Butler and G Wall (eds) *Tourism and sustainable development: monitoring, planning, managing*. Department of Geography Publication Series No 37 and Heritage Resources Centre Joint Publication No 1, Waterloo, Ontario, University of Waterloo, 269–78

Culhane P J 1993 Post-EIS environmental auditing: a first step to making rational environmental assessment a reality. *Environmental Professional* 15(1): 66–75

Dickman M D 1993 Waterways walkabout: learning to see what's missing. In S Lerner (ed.) *Environmental stewardship: studies in active earthkeeping*, Department of Geography Publication Series No 39, Waterloo, Ontario, University of Waterloo, 367–73

Dorcey, A H J and J R Griggs (eds) 1991 *Water in sustainable development: exploring our common future in the Fraser River basin*. Vancouver, BC, University of British Columbia, Westwater Research Centre

Dovetail Consulting 1995 *A strategy for the harmonization of state of environment reporting across CCME member jurisdictions*. Prepared for the Canadian Council of Ministers of the Environment State of Environment Reporting Task Group, Winnipeg, Manitoba

Dunn K 1995 *Fundamentals of environmental auditing*. Toronto: 9th Annual Toronto Environmental Conference and Trade Show

Eckel L, K Fisher and G Russell 1992 Environmental performance measurement. *CMA Magazine* March: 16–23

Edwards F N (ed.) 1992 *Environmental auditing: the challenge of the 1990's*. Calgary:

University of Calgary Press, The Banff Centre for Management

Elkin T J 1990 State of the environment reports and national conservation strategies: the linkage. *Alternatives* 16(4): 52–61

Environment Canada 1991 *The state of Canada's environment*. Ottawa, Minister of Supply and Services Canada

Environment Canada 1995a *Sustaining Canada's forests: overview*. Overview SOE Bulletin No 95-4, Summer 1995, Ottawa, Environment Canada, 1–3

Environment Canada 1995b *Sustaining Canada's forests: timber harvesting*. SOE Bulletin No 95-4, Summer 1995, Ottawa, Environment Canada, 1–7

Environment Canada 1995c *Stratospheric ozone depletion*. SOE Bulletin No 95-5, Fall 1995 update, Ottawa, Environment Canada

Environment Canada 1995d *The state of Canada's climate: monitoring variability and change*. SOE Report No 95-1, Ottawa, Minister of Public Works and Government Services Canada

Fox J M 1991 Spatial information for resource management in Asia: a review of institutional issues. *International Journal of Geographical Information Systems* 5(1): 59–72

Fraser Basin Management Program 1995a *Board report card: assessing progress toward sustainability in the Fraser basin*. Vancouver, BC, Fraser Basin Management Program

Fraser Basin Management Program 1995b *State of the Fraser basin: assessing progress towards sustainability*. Vancouver, BC, Fraser Basin Management Program

Gélinas R 1990 Towards a set of SOE indicators. *State of the Environment Reporting*, No 5, Ottawa, Environment Canada: 3

Goodall B 1995 Environmental auditing: a tool for assessing the environmental performance of tourism firms. *Geographical Journal* 161(1): 29–37

Greeno J L, G S Hedstrom and M DiBerto 1985 *Environmental auditing fundamentals and techniques*. Toronto, John Wiley and Sons

Greer T, I Douglas, K Bidin, W Sinum and J Suhaimi 1995 Monitoring geomorphological disturbance and recovery in commercially logged tropical forest, Sabah, East Malaysia, and implications for management. *Singapore Journal of Tropical Geography* 16(1): 1–21

Hicks B B and T G Brydges 1994 A strategy for integrated monitoring. *Environmental Management* 18(1): 1–12

Howe G and T Zdan 1992 Monitoring sustainable development: an overview of concepts to link natural resource and economic accounting systems. *Canadian Water Resources Journal* 17(4): 373–82

International Union for the Conservation of Nature and Natural Resources, United Nations Environment Programme, and World Wildlife Fund 1991 *Caring for the earth: a strategy for sustainable living*. Gland, Switzerland, IUCN

Jacobs M 1992 Environmental auditing and management in local government. *Journal of the Institute for Water and Environmental Management* 6(5): 583–87

Jordan C, E Mihalyfalvy, M K Garret and RV Smith 1994 Modelling of nitrate leaching on a regional scale using a GIS. *Journal of Environmental Management* 42(3): 279–98

Judd G 1996 Environmental accounting and reporting practices. In B Ibbotson and J-D Phyper (eds) *Environmental management in Canada*. Toronto, McGraw-Hill Ryerson, 61–84

Kaiserman M and B Kelly (eds) 1994 *Guidelines for environmental auditing: statement of principles and general practices*. Toronto, Canadian Standards Association

Kreutzwiser R D and M J Slaats 1994 The utility of evaluation research to land use regulations: the case of the Ontario shoreline development. *Applied Geography* 14(2):169–81

Lange J H, G Kaisir and K W Thomulka 1994 Environmental site assessments and audits: building inspection requirements. *Environmental Management* 18(1): 151–60

MacDonald L H 1994 Developing a monitoring project. *Journal of Soil and Water Conservation* 49(3): 221–7

Martin V 1993 How field naturalists gear up for monitoring. In S Lerner (ed.) *Environmental stewardship: studies in active earthkeeping*, Department of Geography Publication Series No 39, Waterloo, Ontario, University of Waterloo, 375–81

Matsuro T and N Tanaka 1993 Data analysis of daily collection tonnage of residential solid waste in Japan. *Waste Management and Research* 93(11): 333–43

McLean R 1994 *International trends in environmental auditing*. Brussels, Arthur D. Little International Inc.

Nelson J G 1995 Sustainable development, conservation strategies, and heritage. In B Mitchell (ed.) *Resource and environmental management in Canada: addressing conflict and uncertainty*. Toronto, Oxford University Press: 384–405

Nerbas M 1992 An environmental audit of the Eastern Irrigation District, Brooks, Alberta, 1991. *Canadian Water Resources Journal* 17(4): 391–403

Organisation for Economic Co-operation and Development 1985 *OECD state of the environment report*. Paris, Organisation for Economic Co-operation and Development

Petts J and G Eduljee 1994 Integration of monitoring, auditing and environmental assessment: waste facility issues. *Project Appraisal* 9(4): 231–42

Phyper J-D and B Ibbotson 1996 Environmental audits. In B Ibbotson and J-D Phyper (eds) *Environmental management in Canada*, Toronto, McGraw-Hill Ryerson, 211–28

Pilgrim W and R N Hughes 1994 Lead, cadmium, arsenic and zinc in the ecosystem surrounding a lead smelter. *Environmental Monitoring and Assessment* 32(1): 1–20

Prochazkova D 1995 Theoretical background of environmental monitoring and its conception in the Czech Republic. *Environmental Monitoring and Assessment* 34(2): 105–13

Rasmussen K, H Skriver, J Tychsen, P Gudmandsen and M Olsen 1994 Environmental monitoring by remote sensing in Denmark. *Geografisk Tidsskrift* 94: 12–21

Richards L and I Biddick 1994 Sustainable economic development and environmental auditing: a local authority perspective. *Journal of Environmental Planning and Management* 37(4): 487–94

Sandén P and A Danielsson 1995 Spatial properties of nutrient concentrations in the Baltic Sea. *Environmental Monitoring and Assessment* 34(3): 289–307

Schaeffer D J, H W Kerster, J A Perry and D K Cox 1985 Environmental audit. I. Concepts. *Environmental Management* 9(3): 191–8

Schmidt M G, H E Schrier and B Shah Pravakar 1995 A GIS evaluation of land use dynamic and forest soil fertility in a watershed in Nepal. *International Journal of Geographic Information Systems* 9(3): 317–27

Slaats M J and R Kreutzwiser 1993 Shoreline development and regulations: do they work? *Journal of Soil and Water Conservation* 48(3): 158–65

Smith C 1996 Ontario's anti-pollution angels. *Toronto Star* 6 January 1996: D6

Sokolik S L and D J Schaeffer 1986 Environmental audit. III. Improving the management of environmental information for toxic substances. *Environmental Management* 19(3): 311–17

Soyez D 1995 Assessing energy projects in the Saarland, Federal Republic of Germany. *Environment* 23(1): 82–92

Stevens D L 1994 Implementation of a national monitoring program. *Journal of Environmental Management* 42(1): 1–29

Thompson D and M J Wilson 1994 Environmental auditing theory and applications. *Environmental Management* 18(4): 605–15

Tomlinson P and S R Atkinson 1987 Environmental audits: proposed terminology. *Environmental Monitoring and Assessment* 8(3): 187–98

Tusa W 1990 Developing an environmental auditing program. *Risk Management* August: 24–9

Walker G and D Bayliss 1995 Environmental monitoring in urban areas: political contexts and policy problems. *Journal of Environmental Planning and Management* 38(4): 469–82

Walpole Island Heritage Centre and Chreod Ltd 1995 *An environmental audit model for First Nations*. Wallaceburg, Ontario, Walpole Island Heritage Centre, and Ottawa, Chreod Ltd

Woodley S 1993 Tourism and sustainable development in parks and protected areas. In J G Nelson, R Butler and G Wall (eds) *Tourism and sustainable development: monitoring, planning, managing*. Department of Geography Publication Series No 37 and Heritage Resources Centre Joint Publication No 1, Waterloo, Ontario, University of Waterloo, 83–96

Zaleski J, R Serafin and T Palmowski 1995 Assessing planning in Poland's coastal region. *Environments* 23(1): 16–20

Zeide B 1994 Big projects, big problems. *Environmental Monitoring and Assessment* 33(2): 115–33

Chapter 14

Managing for Change, Complexity, Uncertainty and Conflict

14.1 Introduction

Change. Complexity. Uncertainty. Conflict. Each requires attention in resource and environmental management. The Montagnais, Innu, Naskapi and Inuit people, described in Chapter 1, who are contending with the impacts of military low-level flights over their traditional territory, certainly are encountering each of them. The Balinese in Indonesia, who seek to implement a sustainable development strategy which will balance economic, environmental and cultural considerations, are addressing them. The precautionary principle was created as a guideline to handling them. Hedging and flexing have been recognized as alternative approaches towards them. Adaptive environmental management and backcasting are being increasingly used to respond to them. Techniques such as life cycle analysis and environmental audits have been created to help managers address them. And increasing attention to implementation, and to monitoring and evaluation, explicitly acknowledge the need to be able to modify approaches as a result of them.

As mentioned throughout this book, it is often presumptuous to believe that humans "manage" environment and resources. More realistically, humans manage their interactions with environment and resources. For that reason, uncertainty (as a result of our imperfect understanding) and conflict (as a result of many different and legitimate interests) are common. Furthermore, the complexity of biophysical and socio-economic systems is great, and is exacerbated by ongoing change, some of which is influenced or caused by human activity. Thus, to develop policies or programs for resource and environmental management, or to be able to appraise the effectiveness of initiatives, it is important for us to recognize and deal with change, complexity, uncertainty and conflict.

In the rest of this chapter, discussion focuses on four matters deserving systematic attention: (1) developing a vision, (2) creating a process, (3) generating a product, and (4) ensuring implementation and monitoring.

14.2 Developing a vision

In Chapter 2, reference was made to a comment by Alice in Wonderland – if you do not know where you want to go, any road will get you there. In other words, if there is no sense of vision or direction regarding a desirable future, then almost any choice will do. In contrast, if we have a sense of where we would like to get to, then it should be possible to take actions or intervene to try to move in the desired direction.

Given the above comments, a key task for resource and environmental managers is to help develop a vision for a desired future. This task is never easy, since societies rarely if ever are homogeneous. Many interests exist, and conflicts frequently emerge. Thus, what may be a desirable future for one group or interest may be viewed as undesirable by another. However, by considering *desirable* futures, we should be able to move away from what too often is a preoccupation with *most probable* futures. If backcasting is to be used, we need a vision of where we want to get to, so that decisions can then be taken which take us in the prescribed direction.

Since many different interests normally coexist in a society, determining a vision is not a task only for professional resource and environmental managers. Consultation and interaction with people living in an area are important, in order to draw upon their knowledge and understanding of conditions and processes in that area, to address their needs, and to incorporate their expectations. For this reason, *partnerships* and *participatory approaches* should be important features of resource and environmental management, with particular need to draw upon *local knowledge systems*. Furthermore, in developing partnerships, greater attention needs to be given to achieving *gender balance*.

Since publication of *Our Common Future* in 1987, *sustainable development* has been viewed by many as the vision to be pursued. As explained in Chapter 2,

---

Box 14.1 A Jeremiah* parable

I imagine spaceship earth as a kind of fortunate Titanic. On the ship's prow in the middle of the night, Jeremiah Jones peers into the dimness. Faintly perceiving some ominous shapes ahead, he cries out lustily "icebergs ahead". Unsure if he is heard, he cries out again and again. On the ship's bridge, the captain, hearing Jeremiah only after some time, turns to the navigator and asks for a course correction to avoid a collision. Ten degrees to the starboard she says. The Captain, thinking "What luck that I have already started to turn because of the bad weather ahead" orders a five degree correction. The helmsman looks at his compass and suddenly realizes that he had been dozing for a few minutes and that the ship has actually been drifting, fortunately in the right direction. Without saying anything, he then corrects the course by two degrees. Up ahead, alone and in the cold, Jeremiah awaits a hard starboard course correction, maybe even a reversal of engines. Sensing none, he mutters to himself "they never listen to me" and prepares for the worst.

(*The prophet Jeremiah is the archetype of those who warn of future woes, hence the term *jeremiad* as a tale of woe)

Source: Kates, 1995: 635, 625.

Box 14.2

It is extremely important to approach sustainability as a learning process rather than as series of blueprints.

Source: Brooke and Rowan, 1996: 115.

the World Commission on Environment and Development did not present one blueprint for sustainable development, arguing instead that different countries and cultures have to custom-design an individual strategy reflecting their conditions and needs.

The outcome is that different interpretations have been given to sustainable development in various countries, particularly between developed and developing nations. Such differences or inconsistencies are not inherently bad. Indeed, Ralph Waldo Emerson wrote that foolish consistency is the hobgoblin of little minds. Various interpretations of sustainable development are appropriate if they reflect the different situations in countries or regions. Furthermore, within a country or region, the emphasis in a sustainable development strategy could reasonably be expected to evolve over the years as conditions change. Ongoing interest in sustainable development, as a vision, can be expected to continue because it provides a way to consider how to balance economic, environmental and cultural matters.

14.3 Creating a process

In the mid 1990s, the Ontario Ministry of Natural Resources undertook a review of its planning process. As the person responsible for the review explained, the process had to be modified so that it was not the main "issue" when resource allocation decisions were made. In other words, the official meant that too often the Ministry of Natural Resources was finding that people were not satisfied with decisions because of concerns about weaknesses in the planning process. Ministry of Natural Resources staff understood that it was not possible for every resource allocation decision to satisfy every interest, given the many conflicting interests to be considered. However, they did believe that an improved process should be able to result in those who did not get what they wanted from a decision being left satisfied that the planning process had been fair and reasonable.

The experience in Ontario emphasizes therefore that a vision for resource and environmental management requires an accompanying process to identify issues and problems, assemble necessary information and viewpoints, determine alternative solutions and select a course of action. Increasingly, lay people expect to be involved in such planning and management processes, highlighting the importance of partnerships and local knowledge systems. And, as mentioned in Section 14.2 on the development of a vision, much opportunity exists to ensure greater gender sensitivity in the construction of partnerships. One form of partnership that has attracted increasing attention is *co-management*, in which specific roles and powers are delegated to local people. Co-management has been particularly effective in incorporating local knowledge systems.

The complexity and uncertainty associated with natural and human systems have also encouraged the development of what has become known as an *adaptive environmental management* process, or AEM. AEM explicitly recognizes that planners and managers deal with turbulent conditions, and that they can expect to be surprised on a regular basis. As a result, in this approach, planning and management are designed to encourage learning from mistakes and to facilitate ongoing adjustments. ADM is realistic in its recognition of complexity and uncertainty, and of often rapidly changing conditions. However, many planners and managers still have difficulty acknowledging when they are mistaken or wrong. Furthermore, many clients or constituents are unlikely to be impressed by plans and management strategies which are continuously being changed, as that makes it difficult to know what investment decisions to make. Thus, while the concept of AEM is in many ways realistic, it also contains much idealism which will often be resisted in the "real world".

The presence of conflict has led to the emergence of *alternative dispute resolution* (ADR) processes. As indicated in Chapter 11, ADR is not a panacea for resolving all conflicts. Instead, it is an alternative to the longer established judicial or legal process. The judicial system can be unduly adversarial and expensive, and lead to winners and losers. In contrast, ADR seeks to create a process in which parties in conflict come together voluntarily for joint problem solving. When parties are prepared to address their conflicts on a voluntary and joint basis, ADR offers an attractive alternative. However, if the various sides in a dispute are too entrenched in their positions and not interested in looking for mutually beneficial solutions, then ADR is not likely to be helpful.

The process does not end with the development of a strategy or a plan. As noted in Chapters 12 and 13, it is also important to have created processes to facilitate implementation and monitoring. These will be considered in more detail in Section 14.5.

14.4 Generating a product

Careful thought in the crafting of a vision and a process is essential. However, planners and managers should never forget that the ultimate purpose is to resolve a problem. As a result, a vision and process should lead to an output, which could be a strategy or plan. As we became aware when examining adaptive environmental management, a strategy or plan should not be viewed as a static product. In other words, the preparation of a strategy or plan does not mean that the work of resource and environmental planners and managers is completed. Due to changing conditions, turbulence and surprises, it may become necessary to modify the product. Furthermore, as a result of new understanding and knowledge, planners and managers may become aware of opportunities for improvement. A key lesson is that the product should never be viewed as fixed and unchangeable.

The design of the strategy should incorporate some basic ideas. First, it should reflect the spirit of the precautionary principle. In other words, lack of knowledge or understanding should not be used as a reason for not taking action. Second, in situations characterized by high uncertainty, it is appropriate to base the approach on *flexing*. In other words, the approach should strive to achieve what is considered to be the option providing the most benefits, but also recognize that there may be a need to make adjustments as time unfolds.

In developing a product which can guide actions to resolve a problem or to create opportunities, planners and managers should draw upon a mix of techniques or tools. In this book, it has been argued that in the early stages we should use a combination of *forecasting* and *backcasting* to ensure that we consider the most probable, desirable and feasible futures. Having outlined some options, we then need to analyse them systematically. Such analysis should use various techniques. *Benefit–cost analysis* provides insight regarding the relative economic efficiency of options. *Environmental impact assessment* should draw attention to the environmental gains and losses of possible choices. And, if impact assessment is broadened to incorporate *social impact assessment*, then sociocultural issues should also be systematically considered. *Life cycle analysis* emphasizes that we should consider the implications of options "from cradle to grave". Finally, *environmental audits* provide another way to determine performance relative to some generally accepted standards or guidelines.

It is apparent that resource and environmental planners and managers have a broad suite of techniques from which to choose when analysing options along the way to developing a strategy or plan. As in all good analysis, it is important not to over-rely on any one method or technique, but to use a combination to ensure that the strengths of one offset the weaknesses of another. Judgement has to be exercised about the number of techniques to be used, since the addition of each extra technique implies that more time and resources will be needed to complete the task. At some point, diminishing returns will set in, and the advantages of conducting one more type of analysis become marginal. There is no recipe book which can identify what is the most appropriate mix of methods to use. Analysts will have to make choices, based on their judgement about conditions and needs.

A continuing theme in this book is that the resource and environmental management process never ends. Nothing highlights that more than the concepts of *implementation and monitoring*. Visions, processes and products are unlikely to have an impact if action does not occur, and there is the capacity to make adjustments. It is these two latter aspects which are considered in the next section.

14.5 Ensuring implementation and monitoring

In Chapter 11, it was noted that many obstacles can thwart effective implementation of policies, programs or plans. Indeed, it was commented that implementation failure seems to be similar to "original sin". Both appear to be unlikely to have an impact if action does seem to occur, and there is the capacity everywhere and to be ineradicable! And evidence would seem to support this conclusion, since there often seem to be more plans generated than action taken.

The discussion in Chapter 11 identified many obstacles which can hinder implementation. We also became aware in Chapter 7 that there are *programmed* and *adaptive* approaches to implementation. The conclusion in that chapter was not that one approach was correct and the other was wrong, but rather that each offers advantages in different conditions. As planners and managers, we should be aware of the strengths and weaknesses of programmed and adaptive approaches, and be able to determine which is most likely to be effective for a given situation. In Chapter 4, we also reviewed the merits of different *planning models* or *schools*. These make different assumptions about problem situations. Regarding implementation issues, it would seem that more use of *incremental* and *transactive* planning models might lead to improvements.

It has been said that it is a wise person who learns from his or her, or other people's, mistakes. To be able to learn from experience requires a willingness and capacity to track or monitor. Certainly, monitoring is one of the cornerstones of adaptive environmental management, which approaches problem-solving as a social learning experiment, and deliberately seeks information which will allow improvements to be made. In Chapter 13 we saw that many agencies and countries have introduced *state of the environment* or *state of sustainability reporting* as a way to monitor policies, programs and plans. *Environmental auditing* is also used, often at a site level, to measure performance relative to some predetermined standards. Much monitoring is still at a fairly basic level, with attention being given more to *inputs* than to *outputs*, mainly for the pragmatic reason that inputs are usually easier to measure and collect data on.

It is difficult to conceive how we can learn from experience or mistakes if we do not systematically monitor our initiatives and activities. Yet the reality is that there is often considerable resistance to monitoring. People who have invested professional reputations or egos in policies or plans are often not anxious to see them monitored, if there is significant likelihood that errors will then become public knowledge. This reluctance and inertia in many instances still has to be overcome, and this will not be a minor task.

14.6 Anticipating the future

Will we encounter the future like a Captain Ahab travelling on the *Pequod* in pursuit of Moby Dick, or like a Jeremiah Jones travelling on a "fortunate" *Titanic*? A main message from this book is that we do have choices; it is up to us to identify what those are and how we might act on them. The future may appear unclear and fuzzy, and conflicting signals may be seen regarding the most appropriate course of action to pursue. Nevertheless, as expressed so well in the Latin phrase, *tuum est* (it is yours), it is up to you.

While the "right" course of action may not be obvious, decisions must still be taken and commitments made since needs exist and problems emerge or persist. In that context, we should heed the words of Emil Salim (1988: v), the first Minister of Population and Environment for Indonesia and a member of the World Commission on Environment and Development. While he was speaking about his own country, his comments have much more general relevance:

As a developing country, Indonesia faces the necessity of having to start sailing while still building the ship. We don't have the time to wait until all concepts are well established; until the theories are completed. The problems cannot wait until we can think the problems through.

Tuum est.

References and further reading

Brooke J and L Rowan 1996 Professionalism, practice and possibilities. *Local Environment* 1(1): 113–18

Kates R W 1995 Labnotes from the Jeremiah experiment: hope for a sustainable transition. *Annals of the Association of American Geographers* 85(4): 623–40

Salim E 1988 Foreword. In M Soerjani (ed.) *Enhancing the role of Environmental Study Centres for sustainable development in Indonesia*. Jakarta, UNDP/World Bank/ Government of Indonesia, Development of Environmental Study Centres Project: v

Index

Index